Nuclear Waste Politics

T0320276

The question of what to do with radioactive waste has dogged political administrations of nuclear-powered electricity-producing nations since the inception of the technology in the 1950s. As the issue rises to the forefront of current energy and environmental policy debates, a critical policy analysis of radioactive waste management in the UK provides important insights for the future.

Nuclear Waste Politics sets out a detailed historical and social scientific analysis of radioactive waste management and disposal in the UK from the 1950s up to the present day; drawing international comparisons with Sweden, Finland, Canada and the US. A theoretical framework is presented for analysing nuclear politics: blending literatures on technology policy, environmental ethics and the geography and politics of scale. The book proffers a new theory of 'ethical incrementalism' and practical policy suggestions to facilitate a fair and efficient siting process for radioactive waste management facilities. The book argues that a move away from centralised, high capital investment national siting towards a regional approach using deep borehole disposal, could resolve many of the problems that the high stakes, inflexible 'megaproject' approach has caused across the world.

This book is an important resource for academics and researchers in the areas of environmental management, energy policy, and science and technology studies.

Matthew Cotton is a Lecturer in Human Geography at the University of York, UK.

Routledge Studies in Waste Management and Policy

Nuclear Waste Politics

An Incrementalist Perspective

Matthew Cotton

Routledge
Taylor & Francis Group

LONDON AND NEW YORK

First published 2017 by Routledge

2 Park Square, Milton Park, Abingdon, Oxfordshire OX14 4RN

52 Vanderbilt Avenue, New York, NY 10017

Routledge is an imprint of the Taylor & Francis Group, an informa business

First issued in paperback 2018

British Library Cataloguing in Publication Data
A catalogue record for this book is available from the British Library

Library of Congress Cataloging in Publication Data
Names: Cotton, Matthew, author.
Title: Nuclear waste politics : an incrementalist perspective /
Matthew Cotton.
Description: Abingdon, Oxon ; New York, NY : Routledge is an imprint
of the Taylor & Francis Group, an Informa Business, [2017] | Includes
bibliographical references.
Identifiers: LCCN 2017001796| ISBN 9781138785281 (hbk) |
ISBN 9781315767963 (ebk)
Subjects: LCSH: Radioactive wastes–Political aspects.
Classification: LCC TD898.14.S63 C68 2017 | DDC 363.72/8956–dc23
LC record available at https://lccn.loc.gov/2017001796

ISBN: 978-1-138-78528-1 (hbk)
ISBN: 978-0-367-17928-1 (pbk)

Typeset in Goudy
by Wearset Ltd, Boldon, Tyne and Wear

Contents

Illustrations

Figures

Tables

Abbreviations

AEA	Atomic Energy Authority
AGR	Advanced gas-cooled reactor
APM	Adaptive Phased Management
BAND	Billingham Against Nuclear Dumping
BGS	British Geological Survey
BNFL	British Nuclear Fuels
BPEO	Best Practicable Environmental Option
BVG	Borrowdale Volcanic Group
CBA	Cost benefit analysis
CEA	Cost effectiveness analysis
CEGB	Central Electricity Generating Board
COND	Campaign Opposing Nuclear Dumping
CORE	Cumbrians Opposed to a Radioactive Environment
CoRWM	Committee on Radioactive Waste Management
DDLP	De-fuel, De-equip and Lay-up Preparation
DECC	Department of Energy and Climate Change
DEFRA	Department for Environment, Food and Rural Affairs
DETR	Department for Environment, Transport and the Regions
DoE	Department of Energy
DTI	Department of Trade and Industry
DtP	Decision to Participate
EA	Environment Agency
EDF™	Électricité de France (subsidiary)
EIA	Environmental Impact Assessment
ENGO	Environmental non-governmental organisation
EoI	Expression of Interest
GDF	Geological disposal facility
GWe	Gigawatt (electricity)
HA	Holistic analysis
HoLSCST	House of Lords Select Committee on Science and Technology
IAEA	International Atomic Energy Agency
ICI	Imperial Chemical Industries
INES	International nuclear events scale

IRP	Independent review panel
ISOLUS	Interim Storage of Laid-Up Submarines
KBS-3	Kärnbränslesäkerhet, the Swedish waste disposal model
kWh	Kilowatt hour
LoC	Letter of Comfort/Letter of Compliance
MADA	Multi-attribute decision analysis
MAFF	Ministry of Agriculture, Food and Fisheries
Magnox	Magnesium Oxide (Fuel cladding). Also refers to a reactor type and a nuclear energy company.
MOD	Ministry of Defence
MWe	Megawatt (electricity)
NDA	Nuclear Decommissioning Authority
NDARWMD	Nuclear Decommissioning Authority Radioactive Waste Management Directorate
NEI	Nuclear Energy institute
NII	Nuclear Installations Inspectorate
Nirex	Nuclear Industry Radioactive Waste Executive
OECD	Organisation for Economic Co-operation and Development
OPEC	Organisation of the Petroleum Exporting Countries
PGRC	Phased Geological Repository Concept
PPFPE	Principle of Prima Facie Political Equality
PSE	Public and stakeholder engagement
pTA	Participatory technology assessment
PUS	Public understanding of science
RCEP	Royal Commission on Environmental Pollution
RCF	Rock Characterisation Facility
RWM	Radioactive Waste Management Limited
RWMAC	Radioactive Waste Management Advisory Committee
RWMO	Radioactive waste management organisation
SCRAM	Scottish Campaign to Resist the Atomic Menace
SDO	Special Development Order
SEPA	Scottish Environmental Protection Agency
SKB	Svensk Kärnbränslehantering Aktiebolag (Swedish Nuclear Fuel and Waste Management Co.)
THORP	Thermal Oxide Reprocessing Plant
TMI	Three Mile Island
ToR	Terms of Reference
TVO	Teollisuuden Voima Oyj (Finnish nuclear energy company)
TWF	The Way Forward consultation
UKAEA	United Kingdom Atomic Energy Authority
UN	United Nations
UNEP	United Nations Environment Programme
vCJD	Variant Creutzfeldt-Jakob disease
WCMRWSP	West Cumbria Managing Radioactive Waste Safety Partnership
WIPP	Waste Isolation Pilot Plant

1   The problem of radioactive wastes

Introduction

What should we do with nuclear waste? Or perhaps more accurately: where should we put it? It is this second question that has dogged the political admin-istrations of all nuclear-powered electricity-producing nations since the incep-tion of the technology in the 1950s and 1960s. In this book, I look specifically at the case of nuclear waste (though I use the alternative term 'radioactive waste') in the United Kingdom of Great Britain and Northern Ireland (UK). In the UK, alongside other advanced industrial economies with nuclear capabil-ities, the safe long-term management and eventual disposal of radioactive wastes has risen to the forefront of environmental and energy policy debates. The current consensus amongst scientific and technical communities, is that the safest way to dispose of radioactive wastes is underground, in what is referred to as a geological disposal facility (GDF). A GDF is (usually) an engineered under-ground repository, built roughly 500 m below the surface. In the UK, a GDF is a multi-barrier solution. It involves packaging up wastes, placing them within a built facility that prevents water intrusion within a mined repository, all within 'host' rock that is geologically stable over long time frames. Such a facility is designed to ensure that wastes remain sealed away for tens of thousands of years, until the radioactivity contained within has decayed to a point where it no longer poses a threat to human and non-human health. Though there is an apparent technical consensus that this can provide a safe solution, a political consensus on exactly where a GDF should be situated is not so easy to reach. The historical experience of GDF siting in countries such as the United States of America, Germany, Switzerland, Belgium and the United Kingdom makes it clear that social and ethical acceptability remain the cornerstone of site selec-tion. It is a prerequisite for radioactive waste policy-making in democratic soci-eties; and the inability to gain social and ethical acceptability has proven to be the Achilles' heel for most efforts to choose a GDF site for the last 50 years (Blowers & Sundqvist, 2010; Metlay, 2016).

To understand why social acceptability is so hard to come by, we need to understand a bit more about what radioactive waste is and why it is politically important. In technical terms, *radioactive waste* refers to a range of different materials. It covers both sources of radionuclides and the materials that they contaminate (so wastes can be potentially any materials that have come into direct contact with a radioactive medium). It is the radioactive nature of the material that is significant. In simple terms, radioactivity is a process by which unstable atomic nuclei release energy in the form of particles or waves. This is of concern from an environmental and public health perspective, because *ionising* radiation is potentially dangerous. Depending upon the amount of radiation exposure and its route into the body, ionising radiation can potentially damage the DNA of living organisms. In humans, genetic damage can lead (in acute cases) to potentially fatal radiation sickness, and over the longer term, to excess cancers and deaths across affected populations. Radioactive waste is, therefore, one potentially dangerous source of radiation in the natural environment (though it is by no means the only, or indeed the biggest source of ionising radiation for most people). The radioactive wastes produced by nuclear electricity production, by the decommissioning of nuclear facilities, by medical and manufacturing processes, and by government agencies concerned with nuclear weapons manufacturing and nuclear submarines, remain some of the most politically contentious subjects in environmental management. This is primarily due to the risks that they pose to human and animal life.

The overwhelming majority of wastes, both in terms of physical quantities and total radioactivity, are produced by the operations of the nuclear fuel cycle. A basic flow diagram overview of the nuclear fuel cycle is shown in Figure 1.1. It's important to note that wastes are produced at multiple stages of this fuel cycle, and are managed in very different ways.[1]

The most potent wastes are produced by nuclear fission within a reactor. This occurs when low-enriched or natural uranium undergoes a fission chain reaction, where the uranium atom is bombarded with neutrons, splitting it into smaller atoms. The total mass of the fission products is smaller than that of the original uranium atom, with the lost mass released at heat. In a commercial nuclear reactor, the heat from this reaction is used to produce steam, which drives turbines in the production of electricity. This latter aspect is essentially identical to that of fossil-fuelled electricity production, it is only the heat source that differs. This stage of the nuclear fuel cycle is significant because wastes are produced both during the commercial fission process and in the reprocessing of the spent (used) nuclear fuel components. When uranium is used in the processes of nuclear fission for power generation, what is produced at the other end is what are termed *fission products*,[2] *spent fuel* and *fuel debris*. Fission products are a category of materials that incorporate a variety of radioactive isotopes. In the fission of uranium in a civil nuclear reactor, these elements include plutonium: a highly radiotoxic product that could potentially be used in nuclear weapon manufacture, and hence poses a national security risk. Eventually, the concentration of chain-reacting isotopes drops to the point where the fuel is considered 'spent'. The spent fuel is both heat-producing and highly radioactive, but so too are the materials that clad the fuel assembly, the reactor components and other contaminated items. This latter material is termed *fuel debris*. It primarily

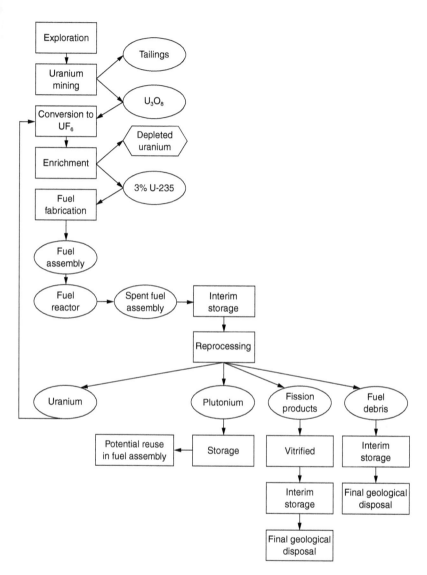

Figure 1.1 Nuclear fuel cycle.

Source: author.

consists of the radioactive contamination of non-radioactive materials in contact with the fuel rods (such as the metal cladding around them).[3] It is notable that under different political conditions these materials are classified either as waste or as a resource. Notable differences exist between the United Kingdom and United States for example: in the UK spent fuel has been reprocessed in the manufacturing facility called the Thermal Oxide Reprocessing

Plant (or THORP),[4] whereas in the United States or Sweden, spent fuel is treated as a waste product and therefore as an industry or taxpayer liability. Plutonium remains a problem material for the UK. The UK currently stores the largest 'separated' civil plutonium stockpile in the world. It is currently stored in powder form in steel and aluminium cans kept in reinforced concrete buildings above ground at the Sellafield nuclear site in the northwest of England. Plutonium could potentially be chemically immobilised (the two most likely materials are glass or ceramic; Donald, Metcalfe, & Taylor, 1997; Lee, Ojovan, Stennett, & Hyatt, 2013), and then stored in a GDF, either alongside spent fuel or other wastes (or indeed separately). Alternatively, it could be used in new nuclear reactors, either alone or in mixed-oxide (MOX) fuel assemblies. This has been the government's preferred strategy, though it has never been achieved in practice (see in particular Department of Energy and Climate Change, 2011). As such, plutonium exists in a sort of political limbo, neither classified as waste nor resource, and so remains a contentious and unresolved facet of nuclear policy.

Global nuclear power and radioactive wastes

When understanding the radioactive waste problem, it is important to establish the global nuclear industry context. In 2012, the generation of electricity from nuclear power constituted 10.9 per cent of global production (NEI, 2016a) across 450 reactors, producing a total of more than 390,000 Megawatts (MWe) of electricity (IAEA, 2016). Thirteen countries currently rely on at least a quarter of their electricity from nuclear sources, with the leader (by percentage of total generation) France operating at over 76 per cent (NEI, 2016a). As of the end of 2016, the largest producer by total capacity is the United States of America with 99 reactors and 99,868 MWe; and the smallest is Armenia, with one reactor and 375 MWe of total production (IAEA, 2016). The United Kingdom sits in the 'Top 10' by total generation, with 15 currently operating reactors and 8,918 MWe of current capacity, though its reactor fleet is ageing and its share of total electricity production from nuclear power has consistently dropped as reactors built in the 1970s are deactivated and decommissioned. The oldest currently operating reactors, Hinkley Point B1 and B2, became operational in 1976. The newest currently operating reactor is Torness 2 in Dunbar (NEI, 2016b), on the east coast of Scotland.

From this global industry, collectively, every year about $10,000 \, \text{m}^3$ (a total weight of roughly 12,000 tonnes) of higher activity (radioactive and heat producing) wastes is produced. In addition, the materials in contact with the spent fuel such as the fuel cladding are highly radioactive (considered intermediate level waste – ILW). Other contaminated materials form the bulk of the radioactive wastes (these include tailings, but also contaminated clothing and building materials, for example). Every year, nuclear powered electricity generation results in roughly $200,000 \, \text{m}^3$ of what are termed lower activity wastes (low- and intermediate-level radioactive wastes, LLW [low level waste] and ILW, respectively). We can compare the radioactive waste production volumes to other waste types to give a sense of comparison. For example, in the OECD there are some 300 million tonnes of toxic chemical wastes, compared with approximately 81,000 m^3 of conditioned radioactive wastes (WNA, 2016). When compared with municipal solid waste (MSW), the figures are closer to 1.3 billion tonnes per year, and are expected to nearly double to approximately 2.2 billion tonnes per year by 2025 (Hoornweg & Bhada-Tata, 2012). The significance of these comparative volumes of radioactive waste will be discussed throughout this book, as different actors use different comparisons to discursively 'scale up or scale down' the relative problems that radioactive wastes present to society.

What is clear is that we can, for the most part, construe the current generation of radioactive wastes as an industrial problem. Wastes arise from a range of activities including medical, industrial and defence-related uses of nuclear materials, though in the UK it is the electricity generating *nuclear industry* that is now by far the largest producer, both in terms of waste volume and total radioactivity. Though the industry is one of the most tightly regulated in the world, the radiotoxic legacy of wastes stretches back to the first nuclear power generation of the 1950s, 1960s and 1970s, and the construction of the infrastructure required to contain wastes over trans-generational time frames is a slow, protracted and also a deeply contested process. For many within the global nuclear industry, this problem is construed as a political rather than technical one: that radioactive waste disposal lacks political will and a socially acceptable solution, rather than a safe design for geological disposal. It is this political dimension to the waste problem that will be examined within this book, though I wish to emphasise at this point that the science and technology of waste management is not so neatly separated from the politics of site selection as it might first appear.

Deep geological disposal and its alternatives

For the highest activity wastes, the industry 'gold standard' is commonly understood to be, what is referred to as, deep geological disposal. As Feiveson, Mian, Ramana, and von Hippel (2011) argue: 'there is general agreement that placing spent nuclear fuel in repositories hundreds of meters below the surface would be safer than indefinite storage of spent fuel on the surface'. As mentioned in the introduction, geological disposal typically involves isolating radioactive wastes within a multi-barrier system. The first barrier is the waste form itself. For example, high-activity wastes can be vitrified (converted to a chemically stable glass form before storage and eventual disposal). The second barrier is the packaging of the waste – this might be steel drums or in some cases copper canisters that are potentially more resistant to corrosion over long periods of time. The third, is an engineered barrier (or buffer) which is commonly designed to be water resistant and protect the waste packages, and prevent further migration of radionuclides in the case of a package leak. The engineered feature of the facility is emplaced within a stable geological formation at a depth below 300 m, so the rock itself forms the fourth barrier between radionuclides and the biosphere on the surface.

The geophysical basis for deep geological disposal has its roots in what are termed 'natural analogues'. One specific example is the natural nuclear fission reactor, examples of which are found in Oklo in Gabon. A natural nuclear fission reactor is a uranium deposit, which has spontaneously undergone a chain reaction. In 1972 French physicist Francis Perrin discovered the conditions under which a natural nuclear reactor could exist. Oklo contains 16 sites at which self-sustaining nuclear fission reactions took place nearly 1.7 billion years ago. These nuclear reactions ran for a few hundred thousand years, but importantly, the radionuclides resulting from the fission reactions were contained within the host rock (Cowan, 1976). This example is important, because it demonstrated that under specific conditions radionuclides could be successfully contained from the biosphere over the periods of time necessary to ensure environmental protection.

The aim of a geological disposal facility is to provide long-term isolation and the containment of wastes in a way that doesn't require future maintenance. This includes trying to not only protect the integrity of the waste form, its packaging and the repository infrastructure from natural forces such as water intrusion, but also to try and prevent human intrusion either from intentional activity (such as trying to get hold of wastes for what we currently presume would be nefarious purposes such as the theft of plutonium for weapon-making purposes), or from accidental breach of waste containment from surface drilling for mineral resources or fossil fuels. It is important to understand that disposal of waste in engineered facilities must remain safe for tens of thousands to hundreds of thousands of years. This presents a significant challenge, however, which is both geophysical and political. In geological terms, a storage space for wastes hundreds of metres below the surface must be able to withstand the pressures of future glaciations (for example). Glaciation during an ice age involves thick sheets of ice resting on top of the surface, the weight of which may deform the rock below, creating internal strains upon the engineered repository. Others are more political. When thinking of tens of thousands of years, or indeed millions of years, we are trying to imagine a period of time that extends beyond any previous period of human history (Rosa, 1993). We can trace certain analogues between geological disposal of radioactive wastes, and other purportedly eternal forms of engineered barriers. What comes to mind is the Great Pyramids of Giza: tombs for ancient pharaohs that were supposed to be maintained as sealed sanctuaries in perpetuity, but have since been opened either by thieves or archaeologists 4500 years later.

The great pyramids raise another challenge. They were lined with spells and curses, warnings to communicate danger and scare away potential intruders. But their effectiveness requires the reader to first understand the warning and then second to heed it as genuine. Being able to communicate the biophysical danger associated with the radioactive contents of a repository across a broad time horizon faces these two challenges. Given inevitable language change, there are no new universal symbols which we can use to communicate with all future societies. Symbols that we recognise as representing danger, or to avoid entering a certain place, may not be understood in the future, as such symbols are cultur-ally specific rather than universally understood. This issue was explored in the film *Into Eternity* by director Michael Madsen, where the semantic difficulties in meaningfully marking the repository as dangerous for people in the distant future is discussed. There are also problems of ensuring that visual warnings on the surface are physically maintained, as well as concerns about long-term data storage and data integrity. A simple example might be the floppy disk: a techno-logy for data storage that existed only 30 years ago now requires relatively hard-to-find equipment and software to be read. Extrapolate that over many thousands of years and the likelihood of effective trans-generational communi-cation becomes ever more remote.

Geological disposal alternatives

It is important to note that although there is consensus amongst material and waste engineers that geological disposal is the most passively safe radioactive waste management option, there is not universal agreement. The Risk Working Group of the European Nuclear Energy Forum (ENEF) stated that:

> For final disposal of the types of wastes mentioned (HLW and other higher activity wastes), the only available option that does not place continuing burdens on future generations is the implementation of geological reposi-tories. This is a consensus opinion of the great majority of scientific and technical experts in the field and it is subscribed to by governments of most [European] Member States. It is nevertheless recognised that there are diverging views in some groups and that there are remaining concerns in the public about geological repositories.
>
> (ENEF, 2009)

Amongst the stakeholders that remain sceptical about geological disposal, it is 'the general public' that has been most vocal about this. From a political per-spective, it is important for proponents of geological disposal to understand that publics require several conditions to be met before they are likely to support such a technology. As we shall see in Chapter 5 so-called lay citizens commonly call for demonstrations of safe containment of wastes over a long period, but this is of course impossible to do empirically. Safety can be demonstrated statis-tically by modelling what is likely to happen to repositories over time, it can also be demonstrated empirically from the results of underground research labo-ratory investigations and boreholes (for example IAEA, 2001) or natural ana-logues. However, as Ewing notes, we can make comparisons to radioactive waste management and other engineered disasters such as the sinking of the Titanic. The Titanic sank in 1912, likely due to a combination of human errors and unforeseeable conditions across multiple spatial and temporal scales. These include the atomic-scale embrittlement of iron rivets to global-scale fluctuations in climate and ocean currents. This catastrophic failure, led, however, to improvements in both ship design and navigational practice. Nuclear waste management doesn't have this luxury. A geological disposal facility must operate over long time scales without being able to fail, so we never have the benefit of studying a failed system. This means that we rely instead upon statistical modelling of post-closure safety assessments, and a settled scientific consensus that geological disposal in a mined facility is safest. Ewing cautions, however, that the consensus on geological disposal may in fact lead to complacency and compromise, 'both of which are harbingers of disaster' (Ewing, 2014).

It is also important to note that concepts of risk, uncertainty and safety are not understood by non-specialist citizens in purely statistical terms; so relying upon risk assessments to communicate safety is a flawed premise. Technical and scientific authorities, particularly those within RWMOs, must be aware that the uncertainties associated with the deep future create anxieties for those potentially affected by radioactive wastes in their locality. It is this uncertainty that has fuelled the political conflicts associated with radioactive waste facility siting when it comes down to choosing specific places for the facilities to be built. These fears are not easily mollified by better maths.

Also of significance are the governments that reject geological disposal as the final endpoint for domestically produced radioactive wastes. Notable in this regard is Scotland. The issue of radioactive waste management in the United Kingdom is a devolved issue, with the Scottish Government policy differing quite substantially from that in Westminster. Scottish Government policy is that long-term management of higher activity radioactive wastes should be in near surface facilities rather than in deep geological facilities. On 20 January 2011, the Scottish Government published Scotland's Higher Activity Radioactive Waste Policy of 2011. The policy statement was made in the Scottish Parliament by the Cabinet Secretary for Rural Affairs and the Environment, Richard Lochhead. The policy outlines how higher activity wastes must not only be stored in near surface facilities, but that these should be located as near to the site where the waste is produced as possible. Developers must also demonstrate robust facility monitoring and that waste packaging, or the wastes within them, are retrievable. The policy also outlines the robust regulatory requirements, including the use of Strategic Environmental Assessment. This policy platform is unique amongst nuclear power producing nations, in that it doesn't recognise a role for final disposal underground, but rather emphasises ongoing stewardship of wastes. It is here that we can make a distinction between long-term radioactive waste management and radioactive waste disposal, although the distinction is not that clear when we factor in issues of retrievability of wastes from underground repositories. In UK policy for deep geological disposal there was a vogue for so-called 'stepwise' disposal. Basically, this meant that the construction of an underground facility would go ahead, but that once wastes had been emplaced there was a period in which this process could be reversed. The underlying principle behind this was that if future generations had discovered some way in which radioactive wastes could be used as a resource, or if they had found some other disposal method which was more sophisticated than geological disposal, then they could change their minds. In the Scottish policy case, *local* and above ground storage are the key facets. This is in direct opposition to the centralised and underground policy of Westminster. The specific significance of this difference of approach and geographical scale and distribution will be returned to in the final chapter.

On surface or near surface disposal of higher activity wastes with long-term community stewardship of the risks is a solution that involves active, rather than passive safety. However, since the early days of radioactive waste production a range of different radioactive waste management solutions that have sought to ensure passive safety have emerged in the scientific and technical literatures. These include burial in ice sheets or glaciers, allowing the heat produced from spent fuel to essentially melt through thick ice allowing the waste form to sink to the bottom, isolated from the human environment. Another solution might be to bury the wastes on the seabed, and indeed for many years the nuclear industry routinely buried intermediate level radioactive wastes at sea. Liquid wastes were disposed of by the principle of dilute and disperse, however, as discussed in Chapters 3 and 4, this caused widespread consternation and was later banned by International Convention. It would also be possible to dispose of radioactive wastes in subduction zones; this would involve emplacing wastes at points where tectonic plates meet, where the action of one plate sliding underneath another would draw wastes into the mantle of the earth. There was also some discussion of disposal of spent fuel in space, effectively allowing these radioactive wastes to leave the biosphere altogether. The big concern with this method, however, is the risk of a spacecraft-related disaster either on the launchpad, or worse, in the upper atmosphere. The risk of spreading high-level radioactive materials across high altitudes is a sobering thought. As we shall see in later discussions about the radioactive waste management options assessment process of the Managing Radioactive Waste Safely policy, the UK government did consider a range of these more esoteric options at one point, although they, like many other radioactive waste producing nations did finally settle on deep geological disposal as the preferred route. However, one strategy that has gained some traction is the disposal of higher activity wastes in deep boreholes 5 km below the surface in the bedrock granite. It is this disposal route that I argue for in Chapter 9, for a host of political as well as technical reasons discussed throughout this book.

For lower activity wastes, there are several different options available. As with the higher activity wastes, the aim is to minimise environmental exposure to radionuclides. Disposal of low-level wastes is comparatively straightforward, this is because it doesn't require specialist geology or technology. Rather, like municipal waste management, it requires space and site selection sensitivity, both in political terms to enhance social acceptability from locally affected site communities, and in terms of the potential environmental impacts that it might cause. Most LLW is typically sent to land-based disposal. First, it is packaged;

this involves separating the radioactively contaminated wastes into a containment package. Even under very low contamination very low level radioactive wastes (VLLW) are still separated from municipal landfill in many countries (including the UK). The disposal for low-level waste is usually either near surface disposal at ground level or sometimes in caverns below ground level. If disposed of in caverns this is usually at depths of tens of metres. In the United Kingdom, the Czech Republic, Sweden, Japan, the Netherlands, Spain, France and the United States of America, this type of near surface or below ground disposal of low-level waste has been implemented. Additionally, Finland and Sweden also store what are termed short-lived intermediate level wastes[5] in this fashion.

What we see, is that there is a settled consensus that a final disposal solution to HLW and ILW must involve a multiple engineered barrier system within host rock, but this has been implemented in various ways. Part of the variation in deep geological disposal concepts is about adaptation to the host geology of the respective countries in which it is to be buried. There are different variations of repository concepts for disposal in granite, salt and clay, for example. However, there are also considerable differences around any political processes surrounding the governance of these wastes and their associated management technologies. I shall explore four examples: The United States, Sweden, Finland and Canada through brief vignettes in the following section, subsequently followed by a more detailed description of the current situation in the United Kingdom.

International examples of radioactive waste management

The United States

The USA has 103 operating nuclear reactor units, with high-level radioactive wastes stored at 121 sites across the country (EIA, 2015). Collectively, these generate approximately 20 per cent of the total electricity production for the country. In the USA, the management of radioactive wastes has followed a familiar path of political controversy in the siting of facilities, although it is also an example of relative radioactive waste management policy success. As we shall see in the UK, early waste management processes involved piling up spent fuel and fuel cladding into storage ponds and silos. From the early development of the USA's nuclear weapons programme (the Manhattan Project) until the late 1980s, a site at Hanford in eastern Washington, on the Columbia River, was responsible for producing 20 million pieces of uranium metal for nine nuclear reactors. Five plants in the centre of the Hanford Site processed 110,000 tonnes of fuel from the reactors, and 67.4 tonnes of plutonium for the 60,000 plus nuclear weapons from the US nuclear arsenal at the height of the Cold War. The site was responsible for producing 200 million litres of solid and liquid radioactive waste. All of this waste material was stored in 177 underground storage tanks, and over 2 trillion litres of liquids from the nuclear reactors was discharged to soil disposal sites (Gerber, 1992; Office of Environmental Management, 2016; Rosso, 2016), creating one of the most expensive environmental cleanup operations on the planet.

By the 1980s liquid storage was recognised to be unsustainable. So, nuclear utilities began to put spent fuel into dry cask storage. All this means is that spent fuel is cooled and stored in steel cylinders for shielded storage (usually on site) on the surface as an interim measure. The radioactive waste problem is partly related to the policies stemming from 1977, which forbid reprocessing spent fuel, therefore, spent fuel was treated as high level waste, increasing the total waste burden. Nuclear utilities had been lax in taking actions towards the safe long-term management of radioactive wastes and so it was the federal government that took on responsibility for the final disposal of spent fuel products, and to search for a site for a geological repository. Two very important radioactive waste management sites subsequently became part of the mainstream political discourse of nuclear power: The Yucca Mountain project in Nevada and the Waste Isolation Pilot Plant, in Carlsbad New Mexico.

It was the Nuclear Waste Policy Act in 1982 that stipulated that the United States Department of Energy (DoE) should be responsible for disposal. Deep geological disposal was always the preferred option from the start. In 1957 the National Academy of Sciences recommended the deep disposal of wastes within host rock (National Research Council, 1957). And in 1978 the DoE began to examine the feasibility of Yucca Mountain to become the first long-term geological repository. In 1984 the DoE had shortlisted ten different locations to be considered as possible repository sites based upon desk research of the geological features of these sites. The findings were reported in 1985 and then-President Ronald Reagan approved three of those for further intensive scientific study. This involved what is termed site characterisation. However, by 1987 the Nuclear Waste Policy Act was amended specifically to designate the site at Yucca Mountain to be the final repository site. The original intention was that if the site characterisation process found Yucca Mountain to be unsuitable then studies would be halted, or a different site could then be investigated. It was originally intended that a repository siting process would be complete by 1998. In 2002 the option to halt investigations of the Yucca Mountain site and choose one of the others (which included Hanford in Washington and Smith County in Texas) expired. Therefore, President George W. Bush signed a House Joint Resolution in 2002, which then allowed the Department of Energy to proceed with Yucca Mountain (Bryan, 1987; United States Department of Energy, 2001; Nowlin, 2016).

Though the site is located on federal land adjacent to the Nevada test site in Nye County, approximately 130 km from Las Vegas (east of the Amargosa desert), it has remained a site of considerable political activism, legal challenge, contentious relations between the federal government and Native American Nations. Some of these concerns are on scientific grounds. They relate to issues such as the underlying geology of the site: notably a series of large and highly explosive volcanic eruptions occurred to the north of Yucca Mountain, and that the area itself is criss-crossed by a variety of geological fractures formed as a result of this volcanic activity. However, on the other hand it is this volcanic activity which allows us to think of the geology more favourably. Volcanic activity produced layers of rock called tuff which form the mountains and hills in that region (Swift & Bonano, 2016). This layered rock formation is potentially beneficial for preventing radionuclide migration to the surface, once a repository has been built and filled with radioactive wastes. Other environmental concerns relate specifically to the transportation of nuclear waste to the facility. It is an isolated location, which is good from the perspective of reducing the risks of radionuclide migration over long time frames, though it does require long transportation routes from populated and sometimes coastal areas where nuclear power stations produced the wastes. The risk of accidents or material theft increases the further the wastes must travel, so this remains a contentious issue (Rechard, Arnold, Robinson, & Houseworth, 2014). Other technical issues concern the rock formation itself and the problems associated with drilling and access (Long & Ewing, 2004; Rechard, Liu, Tsang, & Finsterle, 2014).

Other concerns are more political in nature, specifically contestation within Congress, and between the Department of Energy and Native American peoples. Yucca Mountain and it surrounding lands is essential to the cultural and religious practices of the Western Shoshone and Southern Paiute peoples. These lands are used for resource gathering, religious ceremony and as the site of associated social practices, remaining a sacred place of the Shoshoni people today (see Endres, 2013; Houston, 2013). The Yucca Mountain project is also deeply unpopular in the broader state of Nevada. Part of this is based upon a feeling amongst the citizenry that the project was forced upon them by Congress and by judicial wranglings, and that voters have consistently pressured state elected officials to oppose the project (Flynn, Slovic, Mertz, & Toma, 1990; Slovic, Layman, & Flynn, 1991; Ratliff, 1997; Macfarlane, 2003; Vandenbosch & Vandenbosch, 2007; Nowlin, 2016). State-wide opposition was led by Harry Reid who was the Senate Majority Leader in 2008 and was a junior senator when the Yucca Mountain was first designated in 1987. Reid devoted his political career trying to halt the project. In 2008 during a campaign speech in Las Vegas, former president Obama declared that the federal government should try to find 'some place other than right here at Yucca Mountain' for a GDF. This is politically significant because Barack Obama went on to win the state in the ensuing presidential election – an unusual feat for a Democrat in the state of Nevada. This symbolises the political power of site opposition scaled up from state concerns to the national political arena.

It was after the election that Senator Reid and President Obama then set about trying to halt the Yucca Mountain project. Importantly, President Obama appointed a blue-ribbon commission to come up with alternative proposals. It is notable that the commission argued that deep geological disposal was the best option, however, they also recommended the development of a regional interim storage process. The Waste Isolation Pilot Plant was to be operational by 2021, and this would serve as a site for spent nuclear fuel from shutdown reactors first.

Then by 2025 a larger full-scale interim store would open, followed in 2048 by an underground facility fully operable for final disposal. The commission also recommended that spent fuel should be managed by a new organisation outside the DoE (Hamilton, Scowcroft, Ayers, Bailey, Carnesale, & Domenici, 2012). From a political perspective, it is also important to note that they asserted the need for greater coordination between federal, state and local levels in finding a site suitable to host a deep geological disposal facility for wastes. In that sense, it was clear that the Obama administration made a commitment to a voluntarist model site of selection. Voluntarism will be discussed in more detail in Chapter 8, but simply put, it is a process by which the communities themselves buy in to the process of waste siting, rather than just simply having an imposed top-down solution from (in this case) the federal government. The shift away from Yucca Mountain was financially costly, because delays in implementing a GDF meant that nuclear utilities could not be relieved of their spent fuel as was legislated under the Nuclear Waste Policy Act. This meant that there were additional and supplementary costs associated with further dry cask storage at existing reactor sites. Approximately $1.2 billion was then paid to nuclear utilities by the end of 2012 to offset these additional costs. Under contract with the DOE, it is important to note that any new reactors must undertake to store their spent fuel on-site indefinitely. This largely removes the DOE's liability for any future delays in finding a site. New contracts specify what the Nuclear Regulatory Commission terms the Waste Confidence Rule – in other words, the licensing of new nuclear reactor sites is dependent upon utilities being able to prove to the Department of Energy that they can safely manage spent fuel and high-level radioactive waste through long-term interim on-site surface storage (specifically dry cask storage) (Kinsella, 2016).

The other important radioactive waste management facility is the Waste Isolation Pilot Plant (WIPP). WIPP is a repository located in a salt formation about 25 miles east of Carlsbad, New Mexico. WIPP has a licence for the permanent disposal of transuranic wastes (specifically from weapons manufacture). It exists within the cluster of nuclear-related research and waste disposal facilities: it is relatively close to a low-level waste disposal facility in Andrews, Texas, and is also close to the National Enrichment Facility, also in New Mexico. Geologically, WIPP is in the Delaware deep salt basin. The advantage of salt is that it is highly impermeable to water intrusion; it also has the property of plasticity, so that any openings created by mining and drilling activities would 'heal' over time. However, salt has several potential problems associated with it, for example caverns may form within the salt structure which may create structural instability (Chan, Munson, Bodner, & Fossum, 1996; Munson, 1997).

WIPP had been pushed by the DoE since 1973. Initially there was some political support for the radioactive waste facility amongst the southern New Mexico community. However, following the announcement of site selection, public unrest grew. The government response was to set up the New Mexico Environmental Evaluation Group (EEG) in 1978. This is an interesting political development. The EEG was encouraged to verify or refute, where appropriate, facts and findings produced by the Department of Energy regarding the site. This meant that a checks-and-balances system of government information appraisal was formed. There is good evidence that this group provided an effective oversight of the governance process for the waste site, and that this, in turn, built public support for the facility. It is notable, therefore, that the facility was constructed, and that progress was made relatively quickly – a sharp contrast to the protracted Yucca Mountain project. It is also notable that this sort of independent organisation can act in the interests of the developer (in this case the federal government). The EEG not only acted on behalf of the local community, but also provided an advisory role. For example, in 1981 during drilling, pressurised brine was discovered. This could have meant that the entire site was abandoned in favour of a different location, however, the EEG conducted further testing to reveal how the brine deposit was in fact smaller than was first anticipated and that it was isolated and unlikely to affect the facility itself (once constructed). Therefore, the independent safety evaluation that the EEG provided was valuable, allowing both sides in a potential environmental conflict to trust the organisation to work in the best interests of completing the project safely (see for example McCutcheon, 2002; Richter, 2013).

From a political perspective, the WIPP required Congressional approval before wastes could be moved to this facility. This meant that testing was delayed until that approval was given. Approval from the House of Representatives was given in 1992, and the Senate passed a bill which allowed the opening of the facility shortly after. The legislation required that the Environmental Protection Agency (EPA) would issue safety standards for the facility, and would approve testing plans for the facility. In 1994, Congress ordered that extensive evaluation of the facility against EPA standards should be conducted. This meant that after the testing phase, the facility had been under a total of 25 years of continuous evaluation. It was only at this point in 1999 that the WIPP received its first shipment of transuranic wastes from the Los Alamos National Laboratory – a nuclear weapons research centre.

The WIPP has remained in the headlines since its inauguration. On 5 February 2014, a salt hauling truck caught fire. This prompted an evacuation of the facility with some workers needing to be hospitalised due to smoke inhalation. At this point, there were no traces of radiological material found to have leaked beyond their containment. However, by 15 February 2014, air monitors detected unusually high levels of radiation. In total, 21 workers were exposed to the radiation leak. By 26 February the DoE announced that 13 above-ground workers had tested positive to radiation exposure. The situation had deteriorated by April 2014, when it was found that several radioactive waste containers within the underground repository had released radioactive compounds. Due to the location of the air filtration system, radioactive particles were spread through underground tunnels to the exhaust shaft which led to the above ground air supply. The source of contamination was found to be a barrel that exploded because contractors had packed it with organic cat litter instead of clay cat litter. It was then realised that other barrels containing the same material had been sealed into larger containers. Cat litter was used because it is a source of bentonite – a type of absorbent clay. It's useful for packaging radioactive wastes because it absorbs water, and holds it for long periods. The organic equivalent obviously did not contain this material and had chemically reacted with the components of the waste package, causing the explosion.

It must be noted that the WIPP with its now checkered safety history provided further political uncertainty for the long-term radioactive waste management strategy of the United States. This is because after the shutting down of the Yucca Mountain project the WIPP was a potential alternative. With the facility out of action whilst safety measures were put into place, a general public concern grew: that the WIPP could never be safe. This excoriated future developments in finding an alternative site for spent fuel and other higher activity wastes at a federal level, leaving further project uncertainty for future federal administrations.

Finland

Finland's nuclear power programme has four nuclear reactors at two sites. These are located on the shores of the Baltic Sea. Finland's nuclear programme first came into operation in 1977 and by 2007 it provided roughly 28 per cent of total electricity. Finland is unusual in that it is expanding its nuclear programme, the fifth reactor is currently under construction following a decision in 2002. It is significant because it was the first decision to build a new nuclear power station in Western Europe – the harbinger of the so-called 'nuclear renaissance' of the early 2000s. In 2010, the Finnish Government also granted permits for the construction of a sixth and seventh nuclear reactor. Though controversial for cost and environmental reasons, if these projects are completed, the total share of nuclear powered electricity in Finland could reach 60 per cent by 2025, effectively doubling their nuclear capacity.

Finland is notable in that it is the first country in the world to be actively constructing a GDF for the disposal of spent nuclear fuel. In 1994, the Finnish Nuclear Energy Act was amended to specify that all radioactive wastes produced domestically must be disposed of in Finland. This is an example of the trend towards domestic waste disposal amongst nuclear power-producing nations. It was the municipality of Eurajoki that granted a site licensing building permit for a permanent facility in 2003. The site that was selected for the final disposal of spent fuel is called the Onkalo repository. The total investment costs of the disposal facility are estimated to be 503 million (Kukkola & Saanio, 2005), and it is built in Olkiluoto: an island off the western coast of Finland. Geologically, Olkiluoto has granite host rock. The facility will involve packaging wastes in copper canisters within a network of tunnels cut out of this granite and packed with bentonite clay. These tunnels will run 400 m underground. This repository concept differs slightly from those in the United States, the United Kingdom, France or Belgium as the wastes will be stored directly in the host rock rather than within an engineered barrier system (repository). It follows closely the

Swedish model (termed *kärnbränslesäkerhet* or KBS-3): using copper canisters and direct emplacement into the host rock using the clay buffer (Pool, 2007).

The facility is constructed, operated and managed by Posiva a company jointly owned by two existing nuclear power producers: Teollisuuden Voima Oyj (TVO) and Fortum. One of the reasons that TVO managed to successfully site the repository, is that Olkiluoto already hosts a nuclear-powered facility. It is in that sense already a 'nuclear community'. According to Kojo (2009), the local municipal authority of the island was initially opposed to the proposals, however, TVO managed to successfully frame the project in terms of the financial benefits to the local community: this includes tax revenues and a municipal compensation package. They also used a sophisticated community engagement programme, including local consultation with government officials and with the affected community. So, by 1999 when the successor to TVO (Posiva) came to finalise the process of site selection, local council members were demonstrably enthusiastic. This relative success story for the nuclear industry was incredibly influential for nuclear waste politics across Europe, including that of the United Kingdom. As we shall see in this book, in 1997 the United Kingdom had failed to site their own GDF programme beginning with a rock characterisation facility (a test laboratory) in Sellafield in the northwest of England, despite it also being a nuclear community, and one that houses most the country's existing wastes. The factor of a supportive community who is willing to work with the developer is a crucial component of ensuring siting success, though this is a factor that had been overlooked in successive rounds of siting in the UK up to that point.

Sweden

In Sweden there are ten currently operating nuclear reactors producing approximately 45 per cent of total electricity, with two recently decommissioned reactors in Barsebäck on the western coast. It is notable that following the Three Mile Island (TMI) incident in the USA, in 1980 a referendum led to the parliamentary decision to phase out nuclear power, though advocacy for new nuclear build in the face of anthropogenic climate change is growing.

The Stipulation Act 1977 transferred responsibility for radioactive waste management directly from the government to the nuclear industry. This meant that radioactive waste became a private rather than public liability. Operators were required to present a long-term radioactive waste management plan to obtain an operating licence. When compared with countries such as the United Kingdom, this is a considerable act of foresight. The Stipulation Act ensures that Swedish nuclear power plants must manage radioactive waste in such a way as to secure maximum safety for human beings and the environment before permission is granted to commission a new reactor (even one already constructed) (Anshelm & Galis, 2009). It is an extensive and detailed piece of environmental protection legislation. The emphasis upon an 'absolutely safe' disposal route spurred the Swedish Nuclear Fuel and Waste Management Co. (SKB) to develop high cost engineering solutions. This includes engineered barriers which increase safety beyond the geological barrier, and the placement of copper clad iron canisters in granite host rock filled with bentonite clay to exclude water (as in the case of WIPP and Olkiluoto) and then emplaced in crystalline bedrock at a depth of 500m. As mentioned, this is the KBS-3 method (Hedin, 2006). The legislation required the setting up of an independent radioactive waste management organisation (RWMO). This responsibility is now held by the Swedish Nuclear Fuel and Waste Management Company (Svensk Kärnbränslehantering Aktiebolag, SKB), a company created in 1980 to be responsible for the facilities used to handle waste from all Swedish nuclear power plants. As was the case in most siting proposals, a considerable degree of local controversy emerged in the proposed sites for radioactive waste management facilities. Yet Sweden has, to a large degree, succeeded in implementing its policy for long-term radioactive waste management. Facilities for the final storage of low and intermediate level wastes and the interim storage for high-level waste have been located and constructed without strong opposition at either national or local levels; and work since the late 1990s to find a place for the final disposal of high-level waste and spent fuel, has also been done without any great impediments – the reason being that SKB paid specific attention to creating trust and social acceptance as part of their siting process; with conscious adaptation to demands and reactions from the network of stakeholder actors involved in the decision process (Lidskog & Sundqvist, 2004; Sundqvist, 2002). Sweden is thus held as a best-practice model for RWMOs throughout the world.

The responsibilities for SKB include operation of the monitored retrievable storage facility called the Central Interim Storage Facility for Spent Nuclear Fuel. This is situated near to the coastal city of Oskarshamn: about 250km south of Stockholm. At the beginning of the Swedish nuclear programme there were plans for exportation of spent fuel for reprocessing, and then later for a domestic reprocessing plant. However, neither of these proposals were successful, and so spent fuel is now currently designated as a waste product, under SKB's jurisdiction. All wastes are stored at the reactor site one year before transportation to Oskarshamn. The wastes are stored in excavated caverns filled with water for about 30 years for cooling before removal to a permanent repository. It is in this way that the Oskarshamn project is an interim store, rather than a permanent one. This is arguably one of the primary reasons why the project was politically successful. The interim store is not a final disposal site, and so can be potentially framed as an active (job creating) industrial facility, rather than as a burdensome 'waste dump'.

The 1997 Stipulation Act required nuclear utilities to prove that the engineered solution to radioactive waste management must be 'absolutely safe' in order for any reactors to gain a site licence. As Berkhout (1991) argues, this meant that SKB focused much of it early R&D efforts upon engineered barriers, rather than investigating specific sites and trying to prove the completeness of geological data. This strategy differs from the current emphasis upon geological screening as a precursor to GDF siting in current UK policy (see Chapter 9). As argued by Lidskog and Sundqvist (2004), this meant that SKB could demonstrate that the waste problem was solvable in principle, giving the RWM strategy a certain 'placelessness' – they de-emphasised the necessity of a safe geological barrier, and this proved successful in gaining social support amongst host communities. When a municipality volunteered to become involved in the siting process, its suitability as a candidate site was independent of the geological characteristics of the location, which aided site selection success.

Following this process of voluntarism, in 2009, SKB selected a site and applied for permission to build a repository for spent nuclear fuel near to Forsmark (the home of an existing nuclear reactor) and an encapsulation plant in Oskarshamn – thus creating the final disposal solution for the spent fuel from Swedish nuclear power plants. To get to that point, SKB had to choose between Forsmark in the municipality of Östhammar, and Laxemar in the municipality of Öskarshamn. When it chose Forsmark, it then sent in (in 2010) applications for permits to the Swedish Radiation Safety Authority and the Environmental Court, complete with environmental impact assessment (EIA) and a safety analysis for a spent fuel repository. In theory, this will be the first permanent disposal solution for high-level waste to be built in the world, yet it has recently come under fire from independent scientific scrutiny. The KBS-3 model, using copper canisters, has been shown under experimental conditions to be more susceptible to corrosion than was first thought. Corrosion was shown to be accelerated by heat and radiation emitted by radioactive waste, casting doubts over copper's suitability as a material for disposal. There was also concerned about the erosion of the bentonite clay over time. Moreover, in 2016 the Swedish National Council for nuclear waste, Kärnavfallsrådet, published a report which identified a range of project risks and uncertainties related to seismic impacts, issues of finance and the monitoring of the site's condition over the long-term (Kärnavfallsrådet, 2016). All-in-all the council's report as an independent scientific evaluation, has played an important role in revealingly KBS-3 project's flaws; leaving the future of the project in jeopardy.

Canada

In Canada, the nuclear industry produces approximately 15 per cent of its electricity. Nuclear power plants tend to use a domestic design, and Canada is a world leader in exporting nuclear reactor designs. It is also the world's largest exporter of uranium with the second largest proven reserves, and the largest exporter of radioactive isotopes for medical purposes. What we see, therefore, is that there is a broader national economic interest in the continuation of the nuclear industry. These factors are politically significant because they set a national context in which the continuation of the industry is needed for overall economic prosperity.

Much of Canada's radioactive wastes by volume emerge from the uranium mining process. Canada has a very long history of uranium mining, it used to provide uranium during the Second World War for the Manhattan Project: a joint United States–British–Canadian undertaking. Saskatchewan was once described as the Saudi Arabia of the uranium industry; it has active mines covering an area of nearly 200,000 km². In terms of power generation, most of the reactors are in Ontario. It has 16 operating reactors that provide 50 per cent of the province's electricity. There has been renewed interest in nuclear energy spurred by a demand specifically within Ontario, and a growing awareness of climate change and hence the need to decarbonise electricity systems further (Kuhn, 1998; Winfield, Jamison, Wong, & Czajkowski, 2006).

Radioactive waste management in Canada covers three main categories. The issue of low-level radioactive waste management and uranium mill tailings is much greater than in several other countries that just operate nuclear power stations. Spent fuel, like in the United States and United Kingdom, is stored at licensed facilities close to reactor locations. This on-site above-ground storage is an interim solution, as existing reactor sites were not originally designed to be permanent storage sites. There is also growing political pressure locally around these reactors for a final disposal solution, based upon a perceived long-term risk from radiation exposure. In 2002, therefore, the Canadian Government passed the Nuclear Fuel Waste Act, which required site licensed owners of the spent fuel to assess the options for long-term management of these materials. The act creates the Nuclear Waste Management Organisation; this body has a statutory duty to engage with a range of different stakeholders. These stakeholders include the citizens of the surrounding communities, technical and scientific specialists, environmental non-governmental organisations and other specialist stakeholders, and importantly, with First Nations peoples (Kuhn, 1998; Johnson, 2007). Canada is largely seen as a pioneer of this form of dialogue-related solution to the radioactive waste management problem. In 2005, the NWMO recommended a process of Adaptive Phased Management (APM) as the basis for their strategy. In many respects this is identical to that of other radioactive waste producing countries: the preference is for geological disposal. However, APM is significant in that it is a sequential and collaborative decision-making process; one that emphasises two main characteristics. The first is that the management of risks and uncertainties inherent to the very long time frames of spent fuel management requires potential retrievability, before a decision is made to seal the facility permanently. This effectively involves long-term community stewardship which transfers capacity for decision-making responsibility from current generations to future generations (see Johnson, 2008 for discussion of this point). The second is voluntarism, that the communities that will ultimately host the waste must step forward to be selected, rather than this being imposed in a top-down fashion. This approach had political backing within the Canadian government, and in 2007 was approved. The NWMO began implementation shortly after. This move to voluntarism also had bearing on the governance structures of waste decision-making in The United States, and in the United Kingdom, as recent developments in policy have emphasised sequential decision-making and voluntarism in radioactive waste disposal.

Drawing international comparisons

The case study countries discussed highlight a range of common themes internationally. The first of these is the move towards deep geological disposal for higher activity wastes, with some form of interim storage solution. There are of course technical differences in the way in which a geological disposal solution is enacted. For example, in Finland and Sweden the bedrock is granite, allowing direct emplacement of wastes packed in clay, whereas in other countries a further engineered barrier is used. However, the principle is fundamentally the same: wastes will be placed in a mined, underground repository, commonly between 500 m and 800 m below the surface. This repository will be joined to the surface by an access drift, with above-ground facilities for operations management, logistics (including access to transport networks), and for monitoring of repository safety and performance. Across these case countries, different repository concepts have emerged, but they share these common features.

The second comparison to highlight is the move to include public participation as a key element of the siting process. Sweden, Finland and Canada have been held in high regard by other RWMOs internationally. What these countries have done goes beyond the 'normal' consultation processes usually seen in the construction of large infrastructure projects. Specifically, there has been a move towards voluntarist site selection, which includes an element of partnership working between municipal authorities and central government/RWMOs. This means that the problems associated with imposing a facility on a community are alleviated to some extent. Voluntarism is a dialogue process. It requires bi-directional communication between technical authorities involved in GDF design and implementation, and with municipal authorities that represent local community interests. Voluntarism involves host communities 'stepping forward' to take the wastes on behalf of the broader society. In reality, it is not that simple. Voluntarism can often mask the behind-the-scenes complex negotiation and power relationships between central authorities and the communities that become the volunteers. There is, of course, a risk that voluntarism becomes a smokescreen for implicit coercion; particularly when voluntarism is combined with some form of compensation to alleviate risk concerns. These are issues that have been discussed in detail in relation to the Swedish, Finish and Canadian cases (Lidskog, 1992; Lidskog & Litmanen, 1997; Gunderson, 1999; Hunhold, 2002; Sundqvist, 2002, 2005; Anshelm & Galis, 2009; Kojo, 2009; Ozharovsky, 2016) with concerns expressed that the government–community interactions are not quite as egalitarian and progressive as may first appear.

What is notable for this book, is that the United Kingdom has followed the pattern of these four countries in adopting: first, a geological disposal strategy as the end point for radioactive waste disposal, alongside a period of interim storage. Second, over the period between 1988 and 2013 there was a slow progression towards a participatory–deliberative approach to radioactive waste politics. The emphasis has been on multi-stakeholder dialogue on technical, social, psychological, ethical and economic issues. This includes the different kinds of radioactive waste management options, site selection processes and frameworks for decision-making. The UK has to some extent, uncritically adopted a participatory–deliberative approach to siting a deep geological facility for housing wastes, based upon the relative success of the Swedish, Finnish and Canadian experiences. One of the aims of this book, is to highlight the influential factors that have shaped this move to the triumvirate of participation, voluntarism and geological disposal; to discuss the technical and political history of radioactive waste management processes in the United Kingdom, and to suggest ways in which the politics can be improved. To do this, however, I begin with a discussion of the core features of the United Kingdom's radioactive waste stockpile, and some of the technical and environmental challenges involved.

The radioactive waste management problem in the United Kingdom

In the UK, the problem of radioactive waste is felt most acutely at Sellafield – a site constructed along the west Cumbrian coast in north-west England in the late 1940s. It was built originally to manufacture plutonium for the UK's atomic bomb programme, and later housed the world's first commercial nuclear power station. As such it became a storage site for highly radioactive wastes from weapons manufacturing and the civilian electricity producing reactors that followed. This early history, discussed in detail in Chapter 3, is significant, because most of the highly radioactive wastes (and the most difficult and dangerous environmental management problems) are found at this Sellafield site. Since the 1950s wastes were simply dumped into ponds. These ponds are several times the size of an Olympic swimming pool. The hot wastes were cooled by constantly circulating water over them, but this caused corrosion of the metal alloys of some of the radioactive fission products (the elements produced by the nuclear reaction) and the metal cladding on the fuel assemblies. This means that the pools are now filled with hundreds of cubic metres of radiotoxic sludge. Moreover, the exact contents of these storage ponds and pools are difficult to discern. Simply characterising the inventory of nuclear wastes within these legacy ponds is a difficult, expensive and ongoing task for current scientific authorities.

In the early development of the atomic bomb project in the UK, Sellafield became the site of what were then termed atomic 'piles' (what we would now term reactors). They are significant because in 1957 one of the piles caught fire, releasing radiation into the atmosphere. Once the fire was extinguished the reactor core was sealed and is currently being left alone, though it remains a potentially dangerous source of radioactive material that has not been safely disposed of. From this early 1950s nuclear programme are also the pile fuel storage ponds which contain spent fuel from both the weapons reactors and the energy reactors. Radioactive waste and chemical sludge formed from the storage process sit in deteriorating concrete structures filled with water, the removal of this sludge is currently underway. Yet, there are other more recent, and perhaps more dangerous sites at Sellafield. Building 30 on the Sellafield site, home of the Magnox spent fuel storage pond was described by George Beveridge, Sellafield's deputy managing director as 'the most hazardous industrial building in Western Europe' (quoted in McKie, 2009). The Magnox storage ponds are 150 m long open-air ponds and are sometimes visited by birds (particularly seagulls and other coastal birds), which spread radioactive material across the local landscape. Cracks have also appeared in the storage pond, which is starting to leak radioactive materials into the surrounding soil. The Magnox swarf (chippings and filings) storage silo is just as dangerous. This silo stores magnesium fuel cladding from spent fuel assemblies. The cladding was stored underwater causing corrosion, which formed a sludge over time. So this sludge has leaked through cracks in concrete and there is a risk of explosion from hydrogen gas that is released from the corrosion of the storage vessels (Pearce, 2015). Clearly classifying, extracting, packaging and disposing of these materials safely is an urgent matter of environmental safety, and so we see the decommissioning and cleanup operations of our past nuclear history as part of an ongoing political discussion about how best to manage and dispose of these so called higher activity radioactive wastes over the long-term. So, although nuclear waste is an ongoing product of nuclear powered electricity it is this *legacy* problem that is the most expensive and difficult to manage.

These legacy wastes from poor environmental management practices of past generations are only one dimension of the radioactive waste problem. As mentioned in the introductory paragraph, the plutonium produced by reprocessing the 'spent' nuclear fuel in the on-site Thermal Oxide Reprocessing Facility could potentially be used in the manufacture of atomic bombs. Plutonium blurs the boundaries of classification when talking about what is waste and what is not. Waste implies that materials cannot (or should not) be used for another purpose, and so must be disposed of. However, this distinction is itself a political rather than solely technical decision. Plutonium has potential use in mixed oxide (MOX) fuel for further energy generation, though this has not been achieved under current policy. In countries including the UK, plutonium has an uncertain fate, not quite classified as waste for final disposal, but not yet classified as a resource for future use. Ensuring the safe management of radioactive materials from both environmental exposure and theft is therefore of paramount importance; and so, nuclear electricity generation in advanced economies such as the United States and those in Western Europe have some of the most stringent regulatory and security regimes of any industry (see for example Thomas, 1988; Duffy, 1997; Nuclear Energy Agency, 2001; Poslusny, 2002).

Waste locations

To date radioactive wastes are stored at 34 locations across Great Britain (major sites shown in Figure 1.2). These locations are primarily sites of waste generation (mainly nuclear reactors and the THORP facility), so the stockpiles of wastes are currently stored on-site awaiting a decision on a centralised final disposal solution.[6] By the late 1990s, nuclear power stations contributed around 25 per cent of total annual electricity generation in the UK, but this has gradually declined as old plants have been deactivated and ageing-related problems affect plant availability. At the time of writing, the UK has 15 operating reactors. In 2014, 335 billion kWh (TWh) of electricity was produced in the UK of which 63.75 TWh (19 per cent) came from nuclear sources. However, almost half of this capacity is to be retired by 2025 (World Nuclear Association, 2016). The issue of radioactive waste management has, therefore, been undergoing additional political pressure arising from the decommissioning process for this aging reactor fleet under the auspices of the Nuclear Decommissioning Authority (NDA). UK Magnox reactor decommissioning is the responsibility of the NDA, at an estimated cost of £12.6 billion.[7]

The shutdown of the last remaining Magnox station in the UK leaves seven operating twin-unit advanced gas-cooled (AGR) stations and one pressurised water reactor (PWR), all owned and operated by a subsidiary of France's state-owned energy provider, Électricité de France (called EDF Energy). The AGR reactor fleet will follow the Magnox decommissioning process at the end of their 25–35-year lifecycle – with the last predicted to shut down (Sizewell B) in 2035. See Table 1.1 for details of the proposed shutdowns.

The combined liability of Magnox, AGR and PWR-related radioactive wastes is currently managed on a total of 36 sites in the UK including research sites (Nuclear Decommissioning Authority, 2011), though it must be noted that a range of other non-nuclear power station sites also harbour wastes. These include research and development sites where the NDA is undertaking facility decommissioning and site clean-up including Harwell, Windscale, Dounreay and Winfrith. It also includes facilities that support the civil nuclear fuel cycle (Capenhurst, Sellafield and Springfields), the Joint European Torus (JET) fusion facility located at Culham; Ministry of Defence (MoD) owned sites supporting the nuclear weapons programme (notably Aldermaston) and the nuclear submarine propulsion programme (Barrow-in-Furness, Derby, HMNB Devonport, Clyde, Rosyth and Vulcan) and other nuclear related activities (Donnington, Eskmeals and HMNB Portsmouth). Finally, there is the previously mentioned

Table 1.1 Predicted shutdown dates of currently operating nuclear power stations

Currently operating power station	Year of first supply to grid	Predicted shutdown
Hunterston B 1 and 2 (AGR)	1976 and 1977	2023
Hinkley Point B 1 and 2 (AGR)	1976	2023
Heysham I 1 and 2 (AGR)	1983 and 1984	2024
Heysham II 1 and 2 (AGR)	1988	2030
Hartlepool 1 and 2 (AGR)	1983 and 1984	2024
Dungeness B 1 and 2 (AGR)	1983 and 1985	2028
Torness 1 and 2 (AGR)	1988 and 1989	2030
Sizewell B (PWR)	1995	2035

Source: derived from World Nuclear Association, 2016.

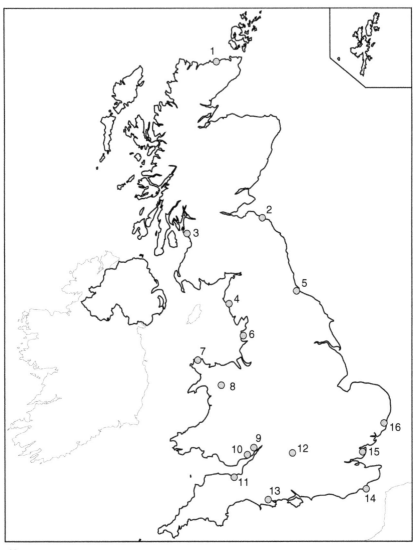

Key

1. Dounreay	2. Torness	3. Hunterston	4. Windscale/Sellafield
5. Hartlepool	6. Heysham	7. Wylfa	8. Trawsfynydd
9. Berkeley	10. Oldbury	11. Hinkley Point	12. Harwell nuclear labs
13. Winfrith	14. Dungeness	15. Bradwell	16. Sizewell

Figure 1.2 Map of major civilian nuclear sites in the United Kingdom.

Source: author, www.d-maps.com/carte.php?&num_car=2555&lang=en.

national Low Level Waste Repository for disposal near to Drigg in Cumbria (though LLW management is outside the scope of this book).

From a political perspective, the management of radioactive wastes is dependent upon four factors. The first is the current operation of existing nuclear reactors which produce spent fuel and associated waste products from normal operations (this includes plutonium, although as mentioned this doesn't currently count as a waste product). The second is the decommissioning of the ageing reactor fleet, which in its first incarnation was not designed to be decommissioned and thus represents a considerable technical challenge. The third is the decommissioning of the Thermal Oxide Reprocessing Facility (THORP) at Sellafield. This site was designed to extract usable products including uranium and plutonium from spent nuclear fuel. It is due to be brought off-line in 2018 once all existing contracts are fulfilled. The fourth is the potential waste arising from new nuclear build – the third generation of reactors currently supported by UK government energy policy. This includes the Hinkley Point C project discussed in Chapter 9. We can see, therefore, that there are different liabilities at stake. The politics and economics of the radioactive waste management process mixes private sector investment for contractors involved in the decommissioning process and ensuring the economic viability of new nuclear build, which incorporates a long-term decommissioning and radioactive waste management programme as part the licensing, with the public liabilities to ensure the cleanup of legacy wastes from the first power stations and the construction and development of a deep geological disposal facility. This complex pattern of investment, responsibilities and liabilities is discussed throughout this book.

Waste volumes and types

Though the nuclear industry is the largest producer of wastes, medical facilities, universities and other industrial processes that use radioactive materials in everyday operation produce waste materials, and from the list of Ministry of Defence sites listed above, it is notable that an approximate 2 per cent of waste sources stem from military activities such as nuclear weaponry production and the operations of nuclear powered submarines (Nuclear Decommissioning Authority, 2013). Approximately 88 per cent of the volume of wastes produced can be attributed to the nuclear power generation lifecycle from uranium mining to power production and reprocessing, with the remaining 12 per cent produced in the everyday processes of industrial, medical and research purposes. Other sources show waste volume percentage to be as high as 95 per cent from nuclear industry activities: including enrichment of uranium, the fabrication of nuclear fuel, reactor operations, spent fuel reprocessing and related research and development activities (Electrowatt-Ekono, 1999). Yet of concern is not simply the volume of waste but also its levels of radioactivity. Some of the wastes produced in the nuclear fuel cycle (and through other applications of radioactive materials) have levels of activity comparable with natural background levels. However, some of the wastes from the nuclear fuel cycle are highly radioactive and hence require long-term isolation from people and the environment, to protect human and non-human life. The hazard that the waste produces and therefore the steps that are required to prevent radioactive contamination of the human and non-human environment is determined in the first instance by the concentrations of radioactive material in the waste product, the half-life of the radioactive isotopes within the waste package, and the extent to which the waste form generates heat.[8]

In the United Kingdom, the total physical volume of radioactive waste has been estimated to fill the Royal Albert Hall approximately 20 times and of this volume, high level waste (HLW) represents a comparatively tiny proportion of the total. According the 2013 UK Radioactive Waste Inventory (Nuclear Decommissioning Authority, 2013) by volume of total radioactive waste is:

- 63.2 per cent VLLW (2,840,000 m^3)
- 30.5 per cent is LLW (1,370,000 m^3)
- 6.4 per cent is ILW (286,000 m^3)
- <0.1 per cent is HLW (1,080 m^3)

However, physical volume is not of course the only property of waste that poses a challenge to management decisions and the socially constructed nature of these volumes is discussed in the subsequent section of this chapter. For example, changes to waste management practices have altered the composition of waste types – i.e. decreasing ILW volumes have resulted in rapid growth in LLW volumes as shown in Figure 1.3. One of the issues discussed in this book, is the extent which the *scale* of this problem is socially constructed by different actors embedded within the policy process. Whereas the nuclear industry is keen to emphasise the comparatively small volumes of waste produced, particularly of

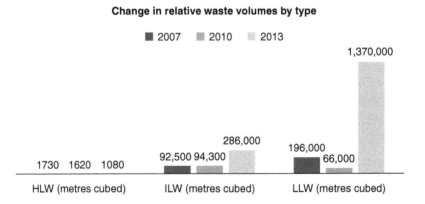

Figure 1.3 Relative waste volumes by type.

Note
Numbers derived from official radioactive waste inventory reports (Nuclear Decommissioning Authority, 2008, 2011, 2013).

spent fuel, environmental organisations have often argued the opposite. ENGOs commonly point to the very small amounts of highly active wastes needed to cause illness in an individual or a population. There is no single picture to which all actors within the debate adhere, and so the scale and nature of the problem is a matter of *social construction*.

The politics of radioactive waste management

With concerns about health risks, trust in the institutions involved in radio-active waste management and the nuclear industry more generally, and con-tinued failures of RWMOs to achieve socially acceptable outcomes within the communities in which they operate; the issue has remained deeply politically contentious for decades. Government and industry-proposed strategies to imple-ment final disposal and the selection of a location for the associated radioactive waste management (hereafter referred to as RWM) facilities have been continu-ally subject to political opposition, including protest actions by grass roots environmental movements composed of locally affected citizens and ENGOs, as well as opposition votes in county and district council decisions.

Inherent to the challenge of radioactive waste management is the shadow of what could be termed *technocratic* decision-making. Technocracy is a form of political structure. It is grounded in a belief that causal relationships can be established between technological and social progress within society. Technolo-gical innovation represents what Hennen (1999) describes as 'the last unques-tioned, transcendent, meta-societal principle of the "common good"': that technoscientific rationalism is the means to resolve social injustices and that science and technology are the principal mode of knowledge creation in society. By this I imply that historically, UK RWM policy has been approached from within scientific and technical organisations, which have served to exclude other forms of expertise from significantly influencing the decisions that have been made in previous iterations of facility siting. Radioactive wastes are pro-duced through industrial processes and their management has often been treated as a technical problem: involving research into disposal techniques followed by siting processes aimed at finding suitable locations for wastes based primarily on outcomes that presented the lowest potential 'risk' based upon current scientific understanding and technical criteria. Such an approach is technocratic in the sense that it has often failed to address significant concerns amongst com-munities affected by siting of waste facilities in their local area, alongside broader societal concerns about how best to manage wastes whilst maintaining value for money from government expenditure, and ensuring long-term public safety. However, this technocracy also hides a deeper need for political expedi-ency – that often the technical language of risk and safety masks a political desire to site wastes in unsuitable locations; i.e. is not truly technocratic, but is rather designed to give the appearance of being a *rational* decision, when no such rationality can be brought to bear (this is termed *synoptic rationality*, discussed in Chapter 2).

As Chapters 3 and 4 show, the emergence of local conflict over siting proposals has contributed to a repeated blocking of attempts to identify suitable sites, which has radically altered the institutional landscape of RWM policy, and has in turn had ripple effects in the governance of environmental risk and the management of controversial infrastructure projects beyond nuclear-related policy. The vehicle for this change occurred in the late 1990s, when the former RWMO Nirex (the Nuclear Industry Radioactive Waste Executive) failed to gain planning permission for a Rock Characterisation Facility (RCF) in a location close to Sellafield. This failure catalysed the adaptation of radioactive waste policy and the institutional changes to the structure of the UK's radioactive waste management organisations, with the implementation of the government-appointed Committee on Radioactive Waste Management (CoRWM); and an epistemological shift that reframed radioactive waste as a substantially 'socio-technical' policy issue. The issue of socio-technical radioactive waste management is discussed in Chapters 4, 5 and 6 – it involves opening RWM decision-making to a broader range of actors and viewpoints outside technical organisations and their associated experts. The socio-technical reframing of the problem shifted the emphasis towards incorporating political, psychological, social and ethical factors alongside scientific and technical ones. There has been a significant trend towards the use of 'analytic-deliberative' decision-support techniques designed to facilitate the integration of community and stakeholder values into governmental decision-making processes through an implicit political commitment to sustained and inclusive public and stakeholder engagement (PSE). Though I consider this attempt at a deliberative democratic policy process laudable, it has, however, remained broadly unsuccessful. In February 2013, the West Cumbrian Managing Radioactive Waste Safely Partnership, the only volunteer community for a GDF in the UK, voted to withdraw their support for further site investigations, leaving the UK again without a site for a deep geological disposal facility. It is this failure of a voluntarist and participatory model that has spurred me to write this book. I aim to examine the outcomes of the different forms of decision-making process that have occurred in the radioactive waste policy arena, and to both theorise and practically assess the political and philosophical implications of deliberative democratic decision-making both to future nuclear policy and to other environmental planning contexts. In essence to try to present some solutions to this intractable policy problem.

Notes

1 Waste production starts with the 'tailings' of raw uranium extraction. Uranium ore is mined, crushed and chemically treated to remove the valuable uranium-bearing compounds, and then the remaining waste products are stored in impoundments close to the mine or mill. These tailings can retain up to 85 per cent of the ore's original radioactivity. With global production of $938\times106\,m^3$ tailings from mining activities (Abdelouas, 2006) these wastes are a potential environmental threat – particularly as contamination also frequently includes heavy metals and other toxic materials, which

when entering water courses can produce a significant health and environmental threat. Once the uranium dioxide is extracted from the ore (called yellowcake), it is then enriched. The yellowcake (U_3O_3) itself has roughly equivalent radioactivity to the granite used as a building material (i.e. it is not significantly radioactive at this pre-processed stage). The yellowcake is first converted to uranium hexafluoride gas (UF_6). The enrichment at the gas stage increases the U-235 content from 0.7 per cent to about 4.4 per cent. It is then turned into a hard-ceramic oxide (UO_2) for assembly as reactor fuel elements. It is the enriched uranium-235 that is the principal component of nuclear reactor fuel assemblies that are used in commercial fission process for electricity generation. The by-product of the enrichment process is depleted uranium (though this has uses as a high density material, including the manufacture of the highly controversial weapons manufacture for tank shells for example; it also has potential use in mixed-oxide or MOX fuel assemblies) (Cochran, Lewis, Tsoulfanidis, & Miller, 1990). Depleted uranium is controversial primarily as its use in warfare creates additional radioactive contamination of the combat area. Significant concerns have been raised by veterans' associations around so-called Gulf War Syndrome and more recently Balkan Syndrome. In such cases, affected veterans of conflicts involving the use of depleted uranium (DU) munitions possess retained fragments of depleted uranium within their bodies. This has uncertain long-term health effects (Bleise, Danesi, & Burkart, 2003), though chronic systemic exposure to uranium remains a key health issue for those exposed (McDiarmid, Keogh, Hooper, McPhaul, Squibb, Kane, et al., 2000).

2 Many of the fission products are themselves neutron absorbers. As these build up within the fuel they eventually absorb so many neutrons that the chain reaction stops within the fuel assembly, and so the fuel rod must be replaced in the reactor with a fresh one. This is despite there being substantial quantities of uranium-235 and plutonium still present (McFarlane & Todd, 2013).

3 Other wastes are produced during the enrichment of uranium, the fabrication of nuclear fuel, irradiated fuel reprocessing and more recently from the decommissioning of nuclear reactors.

4 In countries including the USA, spent fuel rods are stored as a waste product, though in the UK there has been a substantial fuel reprocessing programme at the Thermal Oxide Reprocessing Facility (THORP). The reprocessing operations at THORP at the Sellafield site in Cumbria produce 57 per cent of the total wastes; from reprocessing fuel from the UK's Magnox reactors and Advanced Gas Cooled Reactors (AGR) together with fuels from overseas (Nirex, 2002). Originally, reprocessing was used solely to extract plutonium for weapons production, though it also has applications in mixed oxide fuel production and commercial applications for international fuel reprocessing contracts. Nuclear reprocessing reduces the volume of high-level waste, but by itself does not reduce radioactivity or heat generation and therefore does not eliminate the need for a long-term HLW management solution. It also carries significant political controversy, due in part to its relatively high economic cost compared with the once-through fuel cycle; but also, due to the possible negative impacts on nuclear proliferation of weapons grade nuclear materials (particularly plutonium), and the relative vulnerability of reprocessing installations to nuclear-related terrorism activities.

5 Short lived ILW is defined by containing radionuclides with a short half-life so that radiation levels decay to background levels very quickly.

6 In many cases, the problem is one of a lack of legacy planning. For example, at the Sellafield site there remain concrete tanks filled with the shavings from old Magnox nuclear fuel casings that have been corroding there since the 1960s. These give off hydrogen gas (making the legacy ponds potentially explosive) and thus require constant ventilation.

7 Of the 11 Magnox stations in the UK, none are currently operational, with the last Wylfa on the island of Anglesey shut down in 2015. All the UK's Magnox Reactor

Sites (apart from Calder Hall) are operated by Magnox Ltd a Site Licence Company (SLC) of the NDA, with Reactor Sites Management Company (RSMC) holding the contract to manage Magnox Ltd on behalf of the NDA. In 2007, RSMC was acquired by American nuclear fuel cycle service provider Energy Solutions and then separated into two nuclear licensed companies in 2008. These two companies Magnox North Ltd (covering the management of the Chapelcross, Hunterston, A, Oldbury, Wylfa and Trawsfynydd sites) and Magnox South Ltd (covering Berkeley, Bradwell, Hinkley Point A and Dungeness) were then recombined in 2011 to Magnox Ltd with Research Sites Restoration Limited and Magnox Limited then merging in 2015 to form a single organisation owned by Cavendish Fluor Partnership Limited on behalf of the Nuclear Decommissioning Authority and operating as Magnox Ltd (thus the combined business is responsible for 12 nuclear sites and one hydroelectric power station) (Magnox Ltd, 2015). The consolidation of these entities represents an organisational streamlining of the nuclear decommissioning liability in the UK, now that the Magnox reactor fleet moves from generating capacity to decommissioning and waste management liability to the tax payer.

8 Radioactive waste substances in the UK are commonly divided into four main classifications; very low level waste (VLLW), low level waste (LLW), intermediate level waste (ILW) and high level waste (HLW). The waste classifications themselves are largely a historical consequence of the labelling of various outputs of nuclear fuel reprocessing and are broadly based upon the increasing levels of radioactivity emitted and the heat produced (in the case of HLW) (Nutall, 2003). The waste classifications are as follows:

- Very low level waste – wastes that can be disposed of with ordinary refuse, each 0.1 cubic metre of material containing less than 400 kBq (kilobecquerels) of beta/gamma activity or single items containing less than 40 kBq. Much of this waste can come from sources such as hospitals in the form of contaminated gloves, paper etc.
- Low level wastes – Wastes other than those suitable for disposal with ordinary refuse but not exceeding 4 GBq (gigabecquerels) per tonne of alpha, or 12 GBq per tonne of beta/gamma activity. This type of waste often comes in the form of discarded protective clothing, equipment and building rubble and is disposed of in shallow burial at suitable sites such as Drigg in Cumbria.
- Intermediate level waste – wastes exceeding the upper boundaries for LLW, but which do not need heat to be taken into account in the design of storage or disposal facilities. The major components of ILW are metals and organic materials, with smaller quantities of cement, graphite, glass and ceramics. Wastes such as Magnox cladding and parts of decommissioned reactors make up the bulk of this waste stream. ILW requires shielding to provide radiation protection.
- High level waste – wastes in which the temperature may rise significantly because of their radioactivity, so this factor must be considered in the design of the management facilities. Most HLW comes from the vitrification of reprocessed fuel wastes in glass blocks. HLW requires complex technical procedures and substantial shielding for protection.

Bibliography

Abdelouas, A. (2006). Uranium mill tailings: geochemistry, mineralogy, and environmentalImpact. *Elements*, 2(6), 335–341. doi: 10.2113/gselements.2.6.335.

Anshelm, J., & Galis, V. (2009). The politics of high-level nuclear waste management in Sweden: confined research versus research in the wild. *Environmental Policy and Governance*, 19(4), 269–280. doi: 10.1002/eet.512.

Berkhout, F. (1991). *Radioactive waste: Politics and technology*. Abingdon: Routledge.

Bleise, A., Danesi, P., & Burkart, W. (2003). Properties, use and health effects of depleted uranium (DU): a general overview. *Journal of Environmental Radioactivity*, 64(2), 93–112.

Blowers, A., & Sundqvist, G. (2010). Radioactive waste management – technocratic dominance in an age of participation. *Journal of Integrative Environmental Sciences*, 7(3), 149–155.

Bryan, R. H. (1987). The politics and promises of nuclear waste disposal: The view from Nevada. *Environment: Science and Policy for Sustainable Development*, 29(8), 14–38.

Chan, K. S., Munson, D. E., Bodner, S. R., & Fossum, A. F. (1996). Cleavage and creep fracture of rock salt. *Acta Materialia*, 44(9), 3553–3565.

Cochran, G., Lewis, E. E., Tsoulfanidis, N., & Miller, W. F. (1990). *The nuclear fuel cycle: Analysis and management*. La Grange Park, IL: American Nuclear Society.

Cowan, G. A. (1976). A natural fission reactor. *Scientific American*, 235(36), 36–47.

Department of Energy and Climate Change. (2011). *Management of the UK's plutonium stocks: A consultation on the long-term management of UK owned separated civil plutonium*. London: Department of Energy and Climate Change.

Donald, I. W., Metcalfe, B. L., & Taylor, R. N. J. (1997). The immobilization of high level radioactive wastes using ceramics and glasses. *Journal of Materials Science*, 32(22), 5851–5887.

Duffy, R. J. (1997). *Nuclear politics in America: A history and theory of government regulation*. Lawrence, KS: University Press of Kansas.

EIA. (2015). Total Energy: Table 8.1. Nuclear Energy Overview, from www.eia.gov/totalenergy/data/browser/?tbl=T08.01 – /?f=A&start=200001.

Electrowatt-Ekono, U. (1999). *A review of the processes contributing to radioactive waste in the UK*. Horsham, West Sussex: Report prepared for the Department of the Environment, Transport and the Regions, and United Kingdom Nirex Limited.

Endres, D. (2013). Animist intersubjectivity as argumentation: Western Shoshone and southern Paiute arguments against a nuclear waste site at Yucca Mountain. *Argumentation*, 27(2), 183–200.

ENEF. (2009). *Roadmap to successful implementation of geological disposal in the EU*. Luxembourg: European Nuclear Energy Forum, Office for Official Publications of the European Communities.

Ewing, R. C. (2014). *Projecting risk into the future: Failure of a geologic repository and the sinking of the Titanic*. In MRS Proceedings. Cambridge: Cambridge University Press, 15–21.

Feiveson, H., Mian, Z., Ramana, M. V., & von Hippel, F. (2011). Managing nuclear spent fuel: Policy lessons from a 10-country study. *Bulletin of the Atomic Scientists*, 27, http://thebulletin.org/managing-nuclear-spent-fuel-policy-lessons-10-country-study.

Flynn, J. H., Slovic, P., Mertz, C. K., & Toma, J. (1990). Evaluations of Yucca Mountain: Survey findings about attitudes, opinions, and evaluations of nuclear waste disposal and Yucca Mountain, Nevada. Carson City, Nevada: Nevada Nuclear Waste Project Office.

Gerber, M. S. (1992). *On the home front: The Cold War of the Hanford Nuclear Site*. Lincoln: University of Nebraska Press.

Gunderson, W. C. (1999). Voluntarism and its limits: Canada's search for radioactive waste-siting candidates. *Canadian Public Administration*, 42(2), 193–214.

Hamilton, L. H., Scowcroft, B., Ayers, M. H., Bailey, V. A., Carnesale, A., Domenici, P. V., et al. (2012). *Blue Ribbon Commission on America's Nuclear Future: Report to the Secretary of Energy*. Washington, DC: Blue Ribbon Commission on America's Nuclear Future (BRC).

Hedin, A. (2006). *Long-term safety for KBS-3 repositories at Forsmark and Laxemar – a first evaluation*. Main Report of the SR-Can project: Swedish Nuclear Fuel and Waste Management Co.

Hennen, L. (1999). Uncertainty and modernity. Participatory technology assessment: a response to technical modernity? *Science and Public Policy, 26*(5), 303–312.

Hoornweg, D., & Bhada-Tata, P. (2012). *What a waste: A global review of solid waste management*. Washington D.C.: World Bank.

Houston, D. (2013). Environmental justice storytelling: Angels and isotopes at Yucca Mountain, Nevada. *Antipode, 45*(2), 417–435.

Hunhold, C. (2002). Canada's low-level radioactive waste disposal problem: Voluntarism reconsidered. *Environmental Politics, 11*(2), 49–72.

IAEA. (2001). *The use of scientific and technical results from underground research laboratory investigations for the geological disposal of radioactive waste*. IAEA-TECDOC-1243. Vienna: International Atomic Energy Agency.

IAEA. (2016). *The Power Reactor Information System (PRIS)*. Retrieved 6 July 2016.

Johnson, G. F. (2007). The discourse of democracy in Canadian nuclear waste management policy. *Policy Sciences, 40*(2), 79–99.

Johnson, G. F. (2008). *Deliberative democracy for the future: The case of nuclear waste management in Canada* (Vol. 29): Toronto: University of Toronto Press.

Kärnavfallsrådet. (2016). *Nuclear waste state-of-the-art report 2016. Risks, uncertainties and future challenges*. Stockholm: Kärnavfallsrådet – The Swedish Council for Nuclear Waste.

Kinsella, W. J. (2016). A question of confidence: Nuclear waste and public trust in the United States after Fukushima. In R. Hindmarsh, & R. Priestley (Eds.), *The Fukushima effect: Nuclear histories, representations and debates*. London: Routledge.

Kojo, M. (2009). The strategy of site selection for the spent nuclear fuel repository in Finland. In M. Kojo, & T. Litmanen (Eds.), *The renewal of nuclear power in Finland* (pp. 161–191). Berlin: Springer.

Kuhn, R. G. (1998). Social and political issues in siting a nuclear-fuel waste disposal facility in Ontario, Canada. *The Canadian Geographer/Le Géographe Canadien, 42*(1), 14–28.

Kukkola, T., & Saanio, T. (2005). *Cost estimate of Olkiluoto disposal facility for spent nuclear fuel*. Eurajoki, Finland: Posiva Oy.

Lee, W. E., Ojovan, M. I., Stennett, M. C., & Hyatt, N. C. (2013). Immobilisation of radioactive waste in glasses, glass composite materials and ceramics. *Advances in Applied Ceramics, 105*(1), 3–12.

Lidskog, A., & Litmanen, T. (1997). The social shaping of Radwaste Management: The case of Sweden and Finland. *Current Sociology, 45*(8), 59–79.

Lidskog, R. a. I. E. (1992). Reinterpreting locational conflicts: NIMBY and nuclear waste management in Sweden. *Policy and Politics, 20*(4), 249–264.

Lidskog, R., & Sundqvist, G. (2004). On the right track? Technology, geology and society in Swedish nuclear waste management. *Journal of Risk Research, 7*(2), 251–268.

Long, J. C. S., & Ewing, R. C. (2004). Yucca Mountain: Earth-science issues at a geologic repository for high-level nuclear waste. *Annual Review Earth and Planetary Sciences, 32*, 363–401.

Macfarlane, A. M. (2003). Underlying Yucca Mountain. The interplay of geology and policy in nuclear waste disposal. *Social Studies of Science, 33*(5), 783–807.

Magnox Ltd. (2015). *Magnox and RSRL merge to form one company*. Dursley: Cavendish Fluor Partnership Limited.

McCutcheon, C. (2002). *Nuclear reactions: The politics of opening a radioactive waste disposal site.* Albuquerque: University of New Mexico Press.

McDiarmid, M. A., Keogh, J. P., Hooper, F. J., McPhaul, K., Squibb, K., Kane, R., et al. (2000). Health effects of depleted uranium on exposed Gulf War veterans. *Environmental Research, 82*(2), 168–180. doi: http://dx.doi.org/10.1006/enrs.1999.4012.

McFarlane, H. F., & Todd, T. (2013). *Nuclear fuel reprocessing.* Idaho Falls: Idaho National Laboratory.

McKie, R. (2009, 19 April). Sellafield: The most hazardous place in Europe, *The Observer.*

Metlay, D. S. (2016). Selecting a site for a radioactive waste repository: A historical analysis. *Elements, 12*(4), 269–274.

Munson, D. E. (1997). Constitutive model of creep in rock salt applied to underground room closure. *International Journal of Rock Mechanics and Mining Sciences, 34*(2), 233–247.

National Research Council. (1957). *The disposal of radioactive waste on land.* Washington DC: National Academy Press.

NEI. (2016a). *World nuclear power plants in operation, 2016.* From www.nei.org/Knowledge-Center/Nuclear-Statistics/World-Statistics/World-Nuclear-Power-Plants-in-Operation.

NEI. (2016b). *World statistics: Nuclear energy around the world.* Retrieved 7 July 2016.

Nirex. (2002). *Radioactive wastes in the UK: A summary of the 2001 inventory.* Harwell: United Kingdom Nirex Limited.

Nowlin, M. C. (2016). Policy change, policy feedback, and interest mobilization: The politics of nuclear waste management. *Review of Policy Research, 33*(1), 51–70.

Nuclear Decommissioning Authority. (2008). *2007 UK radioactive waste inventory.* Harwell: Nuclear Decommissioning Authority.

Nuclear Decommissioning Authority. (2011). *UK radioactive waste inventory as at 1 April 2010.* Retrieved 10 September 2013, from www.nda.gov.uk/ukinventory/summaries/index.cfm.

Nuclear Decommissioning Authority. (2013). *2013 Radioactive waste inventory: Waste quantities from all sources.* Harwell: Pöyry Energy Limited and Amec plc for the Department of Energy and Climate Change and the Nuclear Decommissioning Authority.

Nuclear Energy Agency. (2000, 2001). *Investing in trust: Nuclear regulations and the public, workshop proceedings.* Paris, France.

Nutall, W. J. (2003). *Signs of consensus in nuclear waste management?* Cambridge: Judge Institute of Management.

Office of Environmental Management. (2016). Hanford Site, from https://energy.gov/em/hanford-site.

Ozharovsky, A. (2016). *When haste makes risky waste: Public involvement in radioactive and nuclear waste management in Sweden and Finland.* Retrieved from http://bellona.org/news/nuclear-issues/radioactive-waste-and-spent-nuclear-fuel/2016-08-21710.

Pearce, F. (2015). New delays hit Sellafield clean-up. *New Scientist, 225*(3005), 8–9.

Pool, R. (2007). Nuclear power waste-digging deep. *Power Engineer, 21*(3), 20–24.

Poslusny, C. (2002). Improving public confidence in the regulation of transport of nuclear materials. *RAMTRANS, 13*(3–4), 227–230.

Ratliff, J. N. (1997). The politics of nuclear waste: An analysis of a public hearing on the proposed Yucca Mountain nuclear waste repository. *Communication Studies, 48*(4), 359–380.

Rechard, R. P., Arnold, B. W., Robinson, B. A., & Houseworth, J. E. (2014). Transport modeling in performance assessments for the Yucca Mountain disposal system for spent nuclear fuel and high-level radioactive waste. *Reliability Engineering & System Safety, 122*, 189–206.

Rechard, R. P., Liu, H., Tsang, Y. W., & Finsterle, S. (2014). Site characterization of the Yucca Mountain disposal system for spent nuclear fuel and high-level radioactive waste. *Reliability Engineering & System Safety, 122*, 32–52.

Richter, J. (2013). *New Mexico's nuclear enchantment: Local politics, national imperatives, and radioactive waste disposal.* Albuquerque: The University of New Mexico.

Rosa, E. A. (1993). Prospects for public acceptance of a high-level nuclear waste repository in the United States: Summary and implications. In R. E. Dunlap, M. E. Kraft, & E. A. Rosa (Eds.), *Public reactions to nuclear waste.* Washington DC: Duke University Press.

Rosso, J. (2016). This issue: Global nuclear legacy. *Elements, 12*(4), 228.

Slovic, P., Layman, M., & Flynn, J. (1991). Risk perception, trust and nuclear waste: Lessons from Yucca Mountain. *Environment, 33*, 6–11.

Sundqvist, G. (2002). *The bedrock of opinion: Science, technology and society on the siting of high-level nuclear waste.* Dordrecht: Kluwer.

Sundqvist, G. (2005). *Stakeholder involvement in radioactive waste management.* Göteborg: Göteborg University.

Swift, P. N., & Bonano, E. J. (2016). Geological disposal of nuclear waste in Tuff: Yucca Mountain (USA). *Elements, 12*(4), 263–268.

Thomas, S. D. (1988). *The realities of nuclear power: International economic and regulatory experience.* Cambridge: Cambridge University Press.

United States Department of Energy. (2001). *Radioactive waste: An international concern.* Retrieved 2 June 2006, from www.ocrwm.doe.gov/factsheets/doeymp0405.shtml.

Vandenbosch, R., & Vandenbosch, S. E. (2007). *Nuclear waste stalemate: Political and scientific controversies.* Salt Lake City: University of Utah Press.

Winfield, M., Jamison, A., Wong, R., & Czajkowski, P. (2006). *Nuclear power in Canada: An examination of risks, impacts and sustainability.* Drayton Valley, Alberta: Pembina Institute.

WNA. (2016). *Radioactive waste management, 2016*, from www.world-nuclear.org/information-library/nuclear-fuel-cycle/nuclear-wastes/radioactive-waste-management.aspx.

World Nuclear Association. (2016). *Nuclear power in the United Kingdom*, from www.world-nuclear.org/information-library/country-profiles/countries-t-z/united-kingdom.aspx.

2 Inflexible technologies and incrementalism

Introduction

In this chapter I aim to outline the theoretical framework that informs my analysis of the radioactive waste management problem. In Chapter 1, I discussed the problem in terms of the different liabilities, waste volumes, costs and some of the cases of radioactive waste management practices in different countries. One of the things that ties these together is the sheer scale of operation. In the United States, Canada, Sweden, Finland and the United Kingdom, each country has, by different routes, come to settle on deep geological disposal as the eventual solution. Moreover, in each case there is a focus upon a single disposal site within national borders. I call this a single-site domestic solution. This means collecting the wastes produced by nuclear reactors (and other sources) within England and Wales, and after a period of interim storage on site at the place where they are produced, they will eventually come to rest in a single geological disposal facility (GDF) in either England or Wales.

The construction of a GDF is a massive financial undertaking. In the United Kingdom, the Nuclear Decommissioning Authority estimates that its share of the costs of a geological disposal facility come to £3.8 billion. It also prepared an estimated cost of the GDF in the government's National Infrastructure Plan published in 2011. It produced an undiscounted figure, which includes the total cost of disposing of waste in a GDF for which the NDA is not financially liable, (specifically the wastes from existing nuclear power stations operated by EDF Energy, rather than those from legacy operations, such as the piles at Sellafield). It gave the lifetime cost of a GDF as £11.5 billion (Nuclear Decommissioning Authority, 2012, p. 28). Projects of this size and scope have been labelled in different ways by social scientists: as major infrastructure projects, grand-scale projects, or (as is more common today) as *megaprojects*.

Megaprojects are significant because they provide some of the most enduring technical achievements created within society, and also some of the most costly or damaging mistakes (Genus, 2000). In this chapter, I explore the literature around megaprojects: the challenges faced by infrastructure developers in trying to realise such projects; the political processes by which such projects are 'greenlit' by policy-makers; and the implications for decision-making, mainly how local communities are affected by such projects, and their capacity to be involved in decisions that are made. Finally, I draw upon the concept of *inflexible technologies* to describe the problem that radioactive waste management processes share with other large scale technological programmes such as hydro-electric dams, major power stations, tunnels and airports (for example), and to offer potential solutions.

Inflexible technologies are high-stake, high cost, require specialist supporting infrastructure, involve considerable delays and cost overruns, and are socially and environmentally controversial (Collingridge, 1980). In this chapter I discuss how the problems associated with megaprojects (and radioactive waste management specifically) are not simply explained by their size and cost, but in the underlying philosophies of planning that underpin them. They are inflexible technologies because decision-makers assume that scientific and technical evidence can be brought to bear upon the decision over their implementation in such a way that problems can be foreseen, outcomes predicted, and solutions optimised. However, this ignores the limits of rationality that decision-makers can bring to bear, it ignores the limitations of evidence that can be gathered before the decision is made, and it ignores the scales of decision-making – that high cost, high-stakes solutions inevitably involve a high risk of project failure for reasons other than technical failure or poor science. The proposed solution, as per the work of David Collingridge (1980), is policy incrementalism. Incrementalism is both a *description* of how policy is made (in contrast to the assumption that a rational decision can be made based upon gathering all the evidence beforehand), and a *prescriptive solution*: that by dividing a project into a series of smaller, lower-stakes decisions, by integrating a broader range of voices in the decision-making process, and by 'de-scaling' megaprojects, we can achieve fairer and more successful project outcomes. The implications of this model of decision-making are discussed throughout this book, but the underlying precepts are presented in this chapter.

The problem of the megaproject

From the late 1960s in Western Europe, the United States and Canada, governments became increasingly engaged in promoting development, specifically in assisting local regions to realise development ambitions. However, this occurred within a context in which citizens had become increasingly empowered to constrain unwanted developments on environmental, public health and aesthetic grounds. As Altshuler and Luberoff (2004) argue, this prompted a change in tactics for governments faced with increasing opposition to public works development amongst affected citizens. Governments shifted their tactics towards encouraging major investors into infrastructure development through processes of privatisation of utilities, fiscal and regulatory inducements. It was through this process of politicising infrastructure development (and simultaneously privatising public works – shifting away from direct public investment towards, among other things, public–private partnerships) that the concept of the so-called 'grand scale project' or 'megaproject' emerged. Megaprojects soon became a form of symbolic urban revitalisation through economic growth, and since the 1990s became an increasingly common feature of economic develop-ment across both advanced and rapidly developing economies of the world.

The drivers of megaproject growth are partly explained in growing popula-tion numbers and an advancing middle class in countries that are transitioning from predominantly agrarian to industrial and service sector economic produc-tion – meaning that domestic users and businesses large and small require greater access to infrastructure networks for energy, water, sanitation, data com-munications, transport and service provision (such as health and education). In terms of a theoretical evaluation of this growth, we can describe this as a demand for infrastructure systems that compress *space–time* relationships; i.e. technological innovations that condense or elide spatial and temporal distances (mass communications, mass transit, ubiquitous computing, increased access to electricity, are all key examples) (Harvey, 1999). And as Massey (1992) argues, our globalised society 'speeds up' and 'spreads out', our demand for this process of space–time compression through infrastructure development. The mega-project is important, therefore, because it is commonly perceived by politicians as offering this type of time–space compression to publics en masse – that the lives of citizens will be fundamentally improved by big infrastructure. Yet, from an academic social science perspective, it is significant that until the early 2000s there was relatively little research in the operational management and planning of these megaprojects, despite their growing popularity across the world (see for example Shapira & Berndt, 1997).

Many infrastructure projects fall under the category of megaproject: nuclear power stations, major offshore wind energy developments, hydro-electric dams, tunnels and transnational bridges, motorway networks, harbours and airports are common examples. Flyvbjerg (2014) suggests that a project classification can be defined in cost terms – a megaproject typically costs a billion dollars or more, compared with a *major project* in hundreds of millions, and a *project* in millions or tens of millions. Megaprojects are also characterised by their long time frames. Many megaprojects take decades to develop and build, will involve agreement and cooperation from multiple public and private interests, and will impact upon millions of people either directly or indirectly (see also Flyvbjerg, Bruzelius, & Rothengatter, 2003). The form and function of megaproject devel-opment varies, and with it the cost scales. Some have regional impacts, but most have national or international-scale ramifications for societal development. It is in this way that we can think of radioactive waste management as falling within the megaproject concept, in part due to the size and scale of the technological intervention: the development of a GDF has high cost (in the billions) and long construction lifecycle (over decades). Take for example the now defunct Yucca Mountain geological disposal concept in Nevada. The estimated total cost (before the moratorium on the project under the Obama administration), was $96.2 billion in 2007 dollars (World Nuclear News, 2008). This is roughly comparable with some of the world's most expensive megaprojects such as poly-centric city development programmes or mass transit networks. For example King Abdullah Economic City in Saudi Arabia (at an inflation-adjusted cost: $95 billion), includes six cities aimed at housing four million people, with an estimated completion date of 2020 (see Moser, Swain, & Alkhabbaz, 2015); and California's High-Speed Rail network comes in at a similar estimated cost of $98.5 billion. Yucca Mountain outstrips 'Dubailand' launched in 2003 (aiming for completion by 2020), which would house a range of mass-scale theme parks and shopping districts (at a current cost of $64.5 billion) (Renaud, 2012); and comes in at nearly four times the cost of London's cross-rail project (at an estimated $23 billion), or the Three-Gorges Dam across the Yangtze river in China – the world's largest hydroelectric project at $22.5 billion (Wu, Huang, Han, Xie, & Gao, 2003).

In economic terms, megaprojects are characterised by three things. First, the megaprojects listed are all either private investment initiatives or public–private partnerships. The movement from government funded public works to mega-project infrastructure provision through industry finance is significant. Second, because of the private financing, they broadly aim for net profitability upon completion. Third, the broader social benefits from profit sharing, infrastructure provision and regional development are stressed by industry proponents to 'sell' the idea of a disruptive megaproject to sceptical public authorities. It is the potential mass profits and the supposed benefits that these bring in terms of employment and reducing 'economic friction' (Flyvbjerg et al., 2003) that justi-fies the investment risk to a policy-making audience. Radioactive waste man-agement differs from this model in the sense that it is, for many nuclear power producing nations, a national public liability rather than a privately owned asset.[1] Simply put, radioactive wastes are not a profitable resource, the construc-tion of facilities has few positive effects on broader community development (and indeed may actively harm it through processes of community stigmatisa-tion as discussed in Chapter 4), and the investment risk is usually held by the tax-payer. This investment risk commonly includes expenditure on *community benefits* – payments to communities to accept risks on behalf of a broader society. Clearly under these conditions radioactive waste management cannot be 'sold' to public authorities as a profit-making venture, and so under conditions of scarce public resources there is a potential risk of NIMTOO (not-in-my-term-of-office) thinking – where policy-makers actively try to slow down the process of decision-making to push the cost liability on to subsequent legislators in the future. This is essentially *non-agenda setting* – keeping a decision away from political process due to the cost and political capital expenditure required to implement the policy measure. We see, therefore, that because the aim of RWM is primarily public protection (and perhaps further nuclear expansion as a net end-result) rather than the frictionless economic growth promised by high speed rail networks or telecommunications infrastructure, it is unlikely to be cham-pioned as a grand-scale prestige project in the same way that a new hydro-dam, airport or telecommunications network might be. Megaprojects evidently have an unusually powerful appeal for political and symbolic as well as practical reasons (Szyliowicz & Goetz, 1995) due to their grand promises and iconic nature: a factor that is fundamentally appealing to politicians in search of a legacy. Yet radioactive waste management carries little of the political grandeur of a new Economic City, or land-of-theme-parks. In short, it's difficult to get a political 'win' out of radioactive waste, and so their symbolic appeal to politicians is limited.

Though the political psychology of supporting a GDF differs to that of other megaprojects, they do share a key similarity: that is, they are both characterised by *failure*. Indeed, the picture of actual megaproject development is considerably less rosy than that imagined by policy-makers and major private investors. Megaprojects have measurable practical impacts upon economic and social development of the affected region and the broader national economy, the destruction of the natural environment and upon public expenditure, and this is of course true of 'project-level' interventions at a smaller scale. However, there are two aspects that differentiate the megaproject from the smaller project. The first is that megaprojects commonly fail to achieve their stated objectives, often impose heavy cost overruns, project delays and unintended consequences, and these can only be absorbed with great pain and difficulty, often with little public support (Flyvbjerg et al., 2003). Thus, despite being pushed by promoters in terms of their positive implications for domestic economic and social development (and sometimes foreign policy) objectives, there is a deep ambivalence over the capacity of these projects to serve society. This is mirrored in the experience of RWM planning – they both share a problem of project failure, one that is based in the planning and policy processes that surround it; and this is what is of interest in this book.

Rational policy

In addition to the problem of *failure*, what both the megaproject and the radioactive waste management problem have in common is a grounding in what is termed the *comprehensive rational planning worldview*. This is an epistemic position on decision-making in which objectives are clear, outcomes are constant and predictable, risks and benefits are transparently and reliably calculated, the problem confronting decision-making authorities is well-specified, data analysis can be used to measure optimum solutions, and outcomes can be measured and evaluated (see for example Stuart, 1969). This model of planning has long-been debunked by policy and planning theorists, though it has remained curiously persistent in practice (Dalton, 1986), in part, because it is deeply embedded in the institutional contexts of how planning is achieved, in professional education and in the worldviews of policy-makers that desire straightforward solutions to complex problems. Comprehensive rational planning is a function of both *rationality-as-optimisation*, in which decision-making is conceived as a fully rational process of finding an optimal choice given the available information, and *bounded rationality* in which individuals make decisions based upon the tractability of the problem, cognitive abilities and other decision resources (such as time) that are available

(Simon, 1955; Gigerenzer & Selten, 2002). How this worldview has played out in radioactive waste management practice is discussed in Chapters 2, 3 and 4, but to summarise: in the comprehensive rational worldview, policy-makers and planners conceive of the problem of planning in straightforward terms – that the *right* decision can be achieved by utilising all available evidence and then weighing the options to select an optimal solution based upon this evidence. This allows policy-makers to argue that the decision is well-reasoned and to justify it within civil society. Such a model is commonly conceived as following discrete stages. I present (as per the work of Howlett, 1991; Howlett & Ramesh, 1995; Hayes, 2002, 2006) a four stage model of a rational planning model here: *problem identification, policy adoption, policy implementation,* and *policy evaluation*.

Problem identification involves the development of potential solutions by prioritising specific political agendas. Problems must be identified as important (or indeed urgent) given a finite amount of political resources (usually time and money). Problem identification, therefore, involves moving between a system-level agenda of government (all the issues that are advanced for consideration by policy-making authorities) and an institutional-level agenda (the shortlist of specific issues to be considered by any given political body) (Hayes, 2006). In the UK context, the systemic agenda is informed by the campaigning of a general election. Once elected with a majority in government, the legislative agenda is based upon the election manifesto of the winning party (or parties in the case of coalition governments). It is then a process by which ministers compete for political 'attention' that a legislative agenda is formed, with various outside influences from major events (in the case of nuclear energy and radioactive waste management policy, factors such as the Fukushima-Daichii nuclear disaster are pertinent, see Wittneben, 2012; Cotton, 2015; Hindmarsh & Priestley, 2015; Molyneux-Hodgson & Hietala, 2015) or specific interest groups, which shape this legislative agenda. Problem identification, therefore, moves between 'big picture thinking' of what direction the prevailing government aims to lead the allocation of values in society, and the smaller-scale institutional agenda of managing specific interest groups (the practical business of engaging with lobbyists and other stakeholder interests in managing policy issues under consideration). Radioactive waste policy is one such issue that has fallen foul of the problem identification issue within policy-making. Radioactive waste management is urgent in an environmental sense (if we are to prioritise long-term public health and environmental safety), it is also politically urgent in the sense that renewed nuclear energy generation is dependent upon having a plan for a safe long-term disposal solution. However, this urgency is at the systemic, rather than the institutional scale. Managing radioactive waste is perpetually a long-term goal of environmental management organisations within governments of nuclear power-producing countries, yet as Katz (2001) suggests, it lacks immediate political salience for most citizens, decreasing the need for urgent political action outside nuclear communities (those affected by or having an influence upon long-term nuclear renewal to support regional development or deactivation and decommissioning of existing facilities).

This brings us to the second element – *policy adoption*. For the purposes of this book, policy adoption is boiled down to the process by which government proceeds with typical legislative activity (though I recognise that this is a narrow definition). In the UK context, this has specific stages from policy proposal, to green paper, to white paper, bill and then act.[2] At each of these stages there are considerable opportunities for political deliberation upon the scope and aims of the proposed legislation, opposition amendments and consideration of the proposal between the House of Commons and House of Lords, as each essentially scrutinises the changes made by the other. In the legislative process, it is this process of amendment through which a policy is formed. However, the other aspect of policy adoption is often the creation of specific policy organisations or bodies. For example, in the UK radioactive waste management case in the 2000s, the government's main policy instrument was the Managing Radioactive Waste Safely Programme (DEFRA, 2001). Fundamental to this was the role of an advisory organisation: The Committee on Radioactive Waste Management (called CoRWM, pronounced 'quorum'). CoRWM was a quasi-autonomous non-governmental organisation, or quango. It was (and is) an independent expert advisory body appointed by government. In the 2000s its role was to appraise the different options for radioactive waste management, and then report back with recommendations. CoRWM was not a decision-making body. The decision on radioactive waste management policy lay with the then Labour Government, and subsequently with the Conservative–Liberal Democrat Coalition and then Conservative Governments. Yet at the point when decisions were made over the type of radioactive waste management option to be chosen, the policy-making process was heavily influenced by this non-governmental body. It is in this way that we can see the process of policy adoption for radioactive waste management occurs in concert with the agency of non-Parliamentary bodies – in essence, policy-making is not the sole purview of representative politicians but is depended upon broader networks of interest groups competing for legislative influence (as per the work of democratic pluralists, see Hirst, 1989; Polsby, 1960; Stevens & Foster, 1978).

The third aspect of *policy implementation* usually occurs after parliament has passed legislation. It is commonly understood as the execution of policy, or some other means of realising the legislative intent of an act. Sometimes it is also about the operationalisation of new governmental bodies, departments, commissions, organisations or executive agencies to carry out policy measures. In the UK, we can see at the outset of the Managing Radioactive Waste Safely Programme that the appointment of CoRWM was both an aspect of policy implementation and of policy adoption (as both an outcome and a tool for deciding amongst future policy options). This is one way in which the seemingly discrete stages become blurred, with policy-making moving within and between these stages. Legislation must be interpreted by the organisations that enact it, sometimes this means interpretation of legislation by the courts, and sometimes it means government or civil service agencies have some latitude in their enforcement of legislation.

This then relates to the fourth stage of policy evaluation and modification – the idea that those involved in the implementation of policy and those affected by it, have further input into the political process. For example, if a policy is unpopular amongst the citizenry then they will lobby their elected officials to raise the issue in parliament, they may protest, sign petitions, march on Westminster. Their actions may be effective in stimulating further policy change (often dependent upon when they are raised within the election cycle). Other changes of circumstances such as major shocks to the system or unforeseen consequences of policy implementation may result in change (Fukushima, again). Alternatively, those agencies involved in enacting policy may struggle to do so due to various financial or other resource constraints, which then prompts further change. Therefore, although I have divided policy-making into four relatively neat stages, the reality is far more blended and iterative.

What is significant about this four-stage model is that it presents the process as cyclical, analytical and straightforward. Within this is an assumption that *efficiency* is the measure of policy success – commonly measured by the least possible input of scarce resources per unit of valued output and that this can be decided in advance (discussed variously by: Rothblatt, 1971; Von Weizsäcker & Samuelson, 1971; Dalton, 1986; Marsh & McConnell, 2010). Essentially, the concern at the heart of this book is whether the political system can respond to public concerns about (in this case radioactive waste management) policy and is then able to enact changes. Thinking of radioactive waste management in terms of problem identification, policy adoption and implementation is fundamental to how successive siting processes for a GDF have occurred in the UK. This assumes that a decision on radioactive waste is something that starts with the adoption of a strategy, this is then formulated into action, which in turn is implemented, evaluated and amended. The rational worldview assumes that this process is neat and multi-staged, and importantly results in a specific endpoint – that a physical technological project is built after all this 'process'. This is the assumption made by technical authorities when they say that the problem has been 'solved' in technical terms, but simply lacks a political solution. Importantly, this epistemological position largely fails to understand the context-specific, recursive and iterative nature of policy-making and what that means for the actual building of a physical radioactive waste management facility.

Inflexible technologies

The discussion of policy-making models is pertinent to our understanding of megaproject failure (and of radioactive waste management specifically). Rational planning is problematic because megaprojects are complex and *front-end* loaded. The front-end phase of a project is when it exists conceptually, before it is planned and implemented. This phase includes all activities from the time the idea is conceived until the final decision to finance the project is made (Williams & Samset, 2010). Megaprojects are front-end-loaded because projected benefits in terms of socio-economic development can be over-emphasised by private investors and because public authorities tend to express an implicit and uncritical enthusiasm for technological progress (regardless of its ethical viability or socio-economic and environmental sustainability) (Stirling, 2007, 2008). Commonly, their conceptual benefits are overestimated and their risks and costs underestimated. If a project idea is accepted in principle, then it is at this point that technological inertia sets in. The decision on whether to build the proposed megaproject then becomes 'irreversible' (Douglas & Wildavsky, 1983), 'indivisible' (Schulman, 1975) or 'locked-in' (Cowan, 1990; Carrillo-Hermosilla, 2006): the sunk costs, political commitments and bargains that are made in order to get the project off the ground then reinforce the political rationale that the decision cannot be subsequently overturned.

Collingridge (1980) describes this as a problem of *inflexible technology*, a term synonymous with the megaproject. Specifically, inflexible technologies are funded by very large public and private organisations, require very long lead times, have massive unit size, high capital intensity and are ultimately dependent upon networks of specialised infrastructure to support them. They are inflexible technologies because the potential political glamour involved often creates an alliance between private and public interests that militate against less ostentatious technical alternatives, those that might be forwarded by policy actors who are marginalised or excluded from the policy process (Genus, 2000; Genus & Coles, 2005). The range of voices that can oppose such projects is, therefore, often small and those involved are often powerless to intervene. Inflexibility describes the conditions by which technologies such as radioactive waste management options reach the threshold point at which the decision cannot be reversed, significantly adapted, or new policy directions explored.

Inflexible technology is related to a problem of *social control* over technological performance. What Collingridge (1980) notices is a link between centralisation of decision-making and the selection of 'big' decisions regarding the scale of technologies that are implemented. With regards to the radioactive waste management processes of major advanced industrial economies, what we see is a fundamental preference for a single decision for an all-encompassing policy solution – a single (or small number) of site(s), and a single or small number of technologies (interim storage and a GDF). This is true not just nationally, but internationally, as we start to see the standardisation of the geological repository concepts through the process of international policy learning. In Chapters 3, 4 and 5, the reasons for this preference for big decisions, big technologies and standardisation are outlined in detail. But what I want to do here is to highlight the problem of *inflexibility*. In Chapters 6, 7 and 8 the changing nature of radioactive waste policy is discussed, revealing how greater levels of flexibility have entered into the politics of radioactive waste technologies, only to later be retracted, as discussed in Chapter 9.

At the heart of the radioactive waste policy problem is a dichotomy between *inflexibility* (centralisation, bounded rationality and high cost, large-scale technologies) and *flexibility* – the conditions that relate to the capacity of decision-makers to modify their strategies in light of new circumstances, new information, and the input of different kinds of policy actors. Genus (1995), in particular, describes flexibility within decision-making in terms of the degrees of freedom of manoeuvre that policy actors enjoy. And here he makes a distinction between the *content* of flexible decisions, i.e. the extent to which alternative decision options are kept open, and the flexibility of decision *processes*. He describes flexible decisions as being fundamentally adaptive and incremental, they are decisions which open up new possibilities and ideas, avoid stereotyped responses, routines and habits. Part of this is understanding the constraints connected to decision-makers' biases, cognitive structures, mental models etc. What these different barriers and biases do, is influence the thinking of decision-makers and ultimately the actions that they take. Some of these biases are to do with information processing, and others are to do with ideological perspectives, ignorance of available information, or lack of cooperation. We can understand flexibility, therefore, as having various facets.

Here I adapt Nelson, Nelson and Ghods's (1997) typology of flexibility facets. The first set is what could be termed *process flexibility*. This includes for example the rate of response to change. This refers to the ability of technology decisions to *transition* from one state to another. The capacity for technological reversal, to fundamentally change the direction of a technological path is one such measure of this type of flexibility. Another is *expertise*. Partly this is about the types of knowledge which are brought to bear on a decision; it is also about the facilitation of communication between different groups of interested parties, and the opportunity to construct inquiries that lead to additional knowledge of the problem or its solutions in response to changing conditions. This leads to a third facet which we might call *coordination of action*. This is the extent to which independent actors function according to the needs and requirements of the other actors and of the technological system in question. When groups of heterogeneous actors can be coordinated successfully then process flexibility can be enhanced.

The second set of facets could be described as *structural flexibility*. This includes *modularity* – the number of different arrangements that can be formed within the technological programme. Essentially this is breaking down a larger project into smaller parts that can be rearranged, certain aspects excluded, or new elements introduced. A second facet of structural flexibility is *consistency*. This is about the extent to which different potential solutions to a problem can be integrated; if you can integrate different data, different actor perspectives and different applications, then you can greatly affect the flexibility of the technology. This then relates to the final facet, which is *change acceptance*. This is the capacity or willingness of specific actors involved in the decision process to accept the modularity of the decision, and the integration of different solutions without conflict.

I argue that by adapting a radioactive waste management policy processes to better cope with process flexibility and structural flexibility, then the conditions under which some of the problems associated with technological inflexibility can be overcome. A lack of process flexibility manifests as technocracy – the exclusion of certain voices due to a lack of cooperation between different stakeholder groups. A lack of structural flexibility leads to technological determinism, a settled consensus and certainty that a megaproject-scale GDF is the best solution, and that consideration of alternatives is politically undesirable (factors illustrated in Chapters 3 and 4). As Collingridge and Genus have argued, this inflexibility is fundamentally bound up in the rational planning worldview, and with the sequential and bounded stages of policy-making. Importantly, we can see that it is the problematic nature of rational planning (indeed even the assumption that planning itself is rational) that makes this process and structural inflexibility occur.

The rational planning worldview and its associated inflexibility is obdurate; it pervades policy thinking despite its flaws. These flaws are numerous. First, rational decision-making commonly encounters technical problems (specifically a lack of resources and expertise) (Boyne, Gould-Williams, Law, & Walker, 2004). These technical problems include a lack of available data, a lack of specific resources or access to the right expertise. There is no perfect dataset which can be used to optimise a decision. Similarly, policymakers are rarely in a position to evaluate their own expertise, they are not always implicitly aware of their own biases in utilising data. (This is the bounded rationality problem, see Simon, 1982.) Moreover, this creates a fundamental disconnect between how policy-makers view the policy process, and how it is governed. Rather than solution-optimisation, what decision-makers are actually engaging in is *synoptic rationality* – one where decision-makers don't seek the most optimal overall solution, but instead apply data in support of a pre-given solution in order to justify the choice post hoc (Hudson, Galloway, & Kaufman, 1979; Carley, 2013). The third problem is that creative solutions to complex problems may be overlooked in favour of following rules and procedure, as Collingridge (1992, p. 5) argues:

> providing the right formula has been followed ... whatever might happen in the future, there will never be a need to recognise that the original choice was erroneous and in need of revision, hence no point in searching for mistakes.

This means that rational planning and policy remains an *idealised*, rather than actual model for the majority of decisions, and the fact that this is not explicitly recognised by policy-makers is why radioactive waste policy has continued to fail as we see in Chapters 3 and 4. We see that policy-makers in the UK have, up until 1997, fundamentally failed to *reflexively* learn that it is the *worldview* on decision-making that is wrong, and not simply the data used. The politics of radioactive waste up to 1997 was thus characterised by a cyclical process of retrying iterations of the same rational approach to siting a GDF. I contend that it is this problem of the underlying worldview of policy-making that remains 'broken' in radioactive waste management, that rational planning as the way to 'site' radioactive waste, and that a big decision and a big technology are the desirable solutions. I contend throughout this book, therefore, that the consideration of an alternative model is the route to political success – that decisions must be smaller, less front-loaded, serial, messier and ultimately more flexible.

Incrementalism to resolve inflexible technology problems

In Collingridge's work on inflexible technologies he built upon the work of the political theorist Charles Lindblom. Lindblom questioned the *capacity* of policy-makers to make major changes in relation to past policies. He suggests that major policy changes or significant departures from previous policies are circumscribed first by the limits of bounded rationality (Simon, 1982; Forester, 1984): the capacities of policy-makers to fully understand the problem, problem definitions and the range of available solutions; and second, by the necessity within representative democracy to bargain and compromise in order to achieve political support for novelty in the policy process (pluralism). It is here where we see the overlap between our understanding of megaproject planning/radioactive waste management planning, and the broader policy processes that surround technological inflexibility; and it is Collingridge's solution to technological inflexibility through an *incremental* process of decision-making that I consider here.

An incremental perspective posits that when it comes to institutional decision-making, it is rarely the case that root changes are made to the status quo. In the comprehensive rational planning model, the assumption is that decision-makers (can potentially) have access to all the important information that they require to make decisions. Lindblom (1959) recognises the limitations of this. There are always constraints on the information and the mental capacities of decision-makers to engage in a rational planning process. Rational decision-making assumes that broad changes can be made within policy because goals can be identified and objectives reached through the application of near-perfect knowledge about the problem and the potential solutions available. But Lindblom suggests that decision-making is more commonly characterised by processes of *seriality*. Seriality assumes that decision stakes are never truly finished, policy-making is an ongoing process. If a policy measure 'fails' then this is simply one step within a continual, iterative process. There is no single comprehensive decision that can be made to resolve a problem. Policies are, therefore, modified in successive stages. Lindblom calls this a *branch method* or alternatively *incrementalism*. In the incremental model, there only a limited number of courses of action, and each is only marginally different from the status quo. It is the ongoing process of option selection within a small range that creates change over time. Deciding amongst competing options involves bargaining and compromise among contending actors; a process that commonly leads to outcomes that differ only marginally from previous policies. It is in this way that the seriality of decision-making is revealed: incrementalism is dynamic, it doesn't resolve problems using a single decision but rather understands the nature of policy-making as an ongoing process of continual negotiation, alliance-building and trial-and-error. The advantage of this model is that it builds in experimentation into the policy-making process. This means that innovation within policy-making can be done in a small-scale way; decisions are reduced to a series of steps rather than one giant leap, and so *reversal* of undesirable changes is easier and less costly in political and financial terms. It is in this way that we can understand incrementalism as both a descriptive and a prescriptive model. Lindblom recognises that policy-making rarely strays from the status quo, and also advocates and models the way in which an open ended, trial and error, and serial policy process can be achieved.

Essential to the incrementalist model is the importance of political *participation*. Collingridge ascertained a link between non-incremental decision-making, inflexible technologies and a lack of social control over technological performance and implementation. Inflexible technologies have centralised decision-making structures, creating barriers for broader pluralistic civil society input into their governance. Understanding the role of incrementalism in technology governance inevitably, therefore, involves attention to the systems of democratic input into the technology choice, oversight, rejection and implementation. Building upon Lindblom (1959), what is needed is an imperfect though *intelligent* democracy that is best placed to attend to the difficulties of complex social problems. This involves the dispersal of the problem across a range of social actors, each focusing upon their own portion of the problem and then negotiating across partisan lines. The advantage of this is that partisan groups will gather a broader range of data, reducing the need for a centralised, comprehensive planning body. This is the pluralist democratic model in action – trust in the agonistic nature of political bargaining to reveal a range of options and counter-proposals, thus strengthening political debate around a range of alternative policy measures, but also (due to bargaining and negotiation) reducing the deviation from the status quo. Incrementalism stands opposed to rational planning as a model of policy-making, but the opposite of 'rational' is not 'irrational' or 'subjective'. Lindblom is particularly sceptical about the rationality of decision-making processes. He doesn't assume that there is a fundamentally rational answer to every policy problem, rather he has faith in the process of intelligent democracy in which partisan actors use data to persuade other protagonists through reasoned argumentation. Good-quality social problem-solving should focus upon trying to understand the different factors that contribute to an effective intelligent democracy. Part of this is an understanding and reflexive awareness of the partisan nature of policy-making processes, and that specific actors construe the problem in different ways and define solutions based upon their own heuristics, habits, perceptions and biases. This is not a weakness, but rather a realistic portrayal of how policy is made. Complex decisions such as those involved in radioactive waste management facility siting cannot be 'held in the mind' of a single decision-maker (such as a government minister), nor can the decision be optimised simply by applying all the available scientific evidence and then attaching metrics or evaluation criteria. Within an intelligent democracy different actors will be involved in the process of bargaining and negotiation, but rather than weakening the credibility of the scientifically sound solution, partisan actors break up the complex decision into meaningful parts. Their biases and competing worldviews draw different aspects of the technology proposal to the forefront of public dialogue. Then, through this process of bargaining and negotiation, a policy will be forged, but it will be one which does not stray too far from the status quo. Sometimes this takes the form of propaganda, vetoes or political threats of some kind which do not require others to be persuaded on the grounds of scientific merit (what Habermas would term 'strategic rationality', i.e. ends-justified reasoning; Habermas, 1984; Johnson, 1991). Nevertheless, this form of political interaction encourages accommodations among different parties, as decisions can only be taken when there is a working majority. It isn't necessary, therefore, to agree about problem definition, the rationality of the decision, or even the underlying facts involved. Indeed as a Genus (2000) argues, there may still be substantial differences in the formulations that various groups have over an issue or an option, or in the means that they favour for its resolution. It created what Hayes (2002) terms a *disjointed* process, because the same actors who disagree over policy problems are usually the ones that are involved in the process of evaluation of future change.[3] So, although the process is incremental that doesn't mean that it is smooth and uncomplicated. One important caveat to this incremental model is that it only works if adequate *social probing* is in operation – that partisan groups will interrogate alternative options effectively across a range of constituent interests. In situations where this is impaired (for instance where secrecy or lack of communication prevent understanding of alternative options – as is clearly the case in much nuclear policy history discussed in Chapter 3), there is a tendency to move back to centralised, rationally planned policy interventions. Incrementalism only works under conditions of democratic transparency.

The application of incrementalism to radioactive waste management policy

The significance of incremental theory for the case of radioactive waste management lies in the changing discourses or worldviews inherent in successive governmental attitudes towards the underlying science of geological disposal, attitudes towards host communities and the organisations appointed by government to manage these materials. Incrementalism was originally composed as a theory to compete with the variety of rational public administration approaches popularised after the Second World War. Neo-classical economics, hard systems theory, rational choice theory, cost benefit analysis and the statistics driven work used in operational research by the RAND Corporation™ are all examples of these rational models of policy-making. Lindblom argued that for all but the most routine tasks, it is virtually impossible to operationalise the kind of linear means-ends relationships that these models provide. He asserted that decision-making is less heroic, revolutionary and rational than policy-makers believe (Lindblom, 1959). Means and ends intertwine and continually adapt to one another in a process of trial and error; decision options are often limited, and the adoption of a decision option is commonly confined to an incremental change of the status quo. This is the descriptive element of the theory.

What we see in the next three chapters is that for environmental policy-makers and their associated radioactive waste management organisations, this lesson took a long time to learn. In Chapters 3 and 4, I detail the history of radioactive waste management from its early roots in the nuclear weapons pro-gramme, up to the decision in 1997 by the then Conservative Government to reject a planning application for a rock characterisation facility (an underground laboratory designed to test host rock through suitability for a deep geological disposal). From 1973 when the issue of radioactive waste became a significant public policy dilemma, to 1997 when RCF was rejected – the decision was con-sistently framed in rational planning terms rooted in a settled scientific consen-sus that geological disposal is safe and that it is only political intransigence that is preventing the construction of a GDF. For various reasons, I argue that the decisions over radioactive waste management remained inherently inflexible. These include technological optimism in the abilities of rational technical actors to provide the safest solution, the blanket secrecy that surrounded nuclear technologies of all kinds under Cold War conditions, and the type of techno-cratic decision-making structures that favoured centralised decisions made by political authorities that were geographically remote from affected local com-munities. There was little opportunity up until 2001 for anyone outside the circle of nuclear industry experts to question whether deep geological disposal was the best option, whether West Cumbria was the best site for a GDF, or how communities should be treated in this process – what rights, responsibilities they should hold, and what compensation they should receive.

I argue in this book that the inflexibility of the technology explains its repeated failure. By repeatedly thinking that the decision could be decided rationally in advance, and that a frontloaded megaproject is the best way to manage this problem, we see successive rounds of public opposition, public inquiries into failed siting processes, and ultimately no progress since the early 1950s in building repository. I argue, based upon Collingridge's (1980, 1983, 1992) work, that there are three elements of this technology policy process that need to be attended to. The first concerns the nature and *role of expertise* – how science and technology experts have dominated decision-making, and how they relate to non-specialist lay citizens. The second is the appropriateness of *decision-making structures and processes* – in this case to move away from decide–announce–defence strategies, whereby technical authorities made decisions based upon technical criteria and then communicate this in a one-way manner to locally affected communities. These first two elements have been subject to considerable academic policy analysis since the late 1980s. There has been a concerted effort to move towards participatory–deliberative models of scientific communication and policy-making. What has received much less attention is Collingridge's third element: that attention must be paid to the *scale and flex-ibility of decision-making*. By this I mean we must be concerned with both the from cost overruns and delays; but also the scales of decision-making (not just the process by which different stakeholders can become involved, but the relationship between different scales of political organisations, their geographic relationship with one another, and the different powers held by each). This means thinking about relationships between host communities and their surrounding regions, between local government at the borough and county level, and collectively their interaction with central government; it also means thinking about the scale of which technologies become 'imagined' in policy (either as national infrastructure projects, or as local environmental governance projects) and how the performance of scale can lead to environmental injustices, even when 'participation' is embedded within decision processes. It is here that incrementalism is posited not simply as the description of how complex policy processes are managed; but also as a normative position on how policy *should* be managed – proposing a model of *ethical incrementalism* as a guiding principle in the future development of radioactive waste management policy.

Notes

1 In the United Kingdom, 'The Nuclear Provision' was set up to deal with cleanup and waste management legacy from early nuclear technology development for military and civilian uses. Of the 17 sites that this covers, Sellafield takes up roughly three quarters of the total public funding. For the so-called second generation fleet commissioned in the 1970s and 1980s (operated by EDF, formerly British Energy), there are separate funds set aside by EDF towards their future waste management and decommissioning programmes through the Nuclear Liabilities Fund. All new build nuclear will be built by the private sector with waste management and decommissioning plans required before build commences (Ashworth, 2016).

2 The process of legislation in British government begins with proposals brought forward by government that address the specific problem (of in this case radioactive waste management), the source for this may come from within the party or recommendations for new legislation based upon input from parliamentary select committees, quasi-autonomous non-governmental organisations (quangos), or from public inquiries, civil servants or campaign/lobbyist groups. Proposals are usually only furthered in parliament with the backing of a minister who will champion this idea within government. Then a process of consultation commonly occurs within parliament, with input from expert bodies and sometimes direct consultation with citizens (public consultation), usually through commentary on a green paper which outlines the policy proposal. This commonly leads to the production of a white paper which is a more refined legislative proposal which states the government's intentions. To further this agenda the proposal must be agreed by cabinet members, and the approval of a Cabinet Committee before being selected by the Legislation Committee, which then presents the proposal to Parliament for scrutiny by Members. Proposals are thus made into bills, translated from political principles into specific legislation. Parliament scrutinises these bills, which then go through a series of readings first in the House of Commons and then the House of Lords. The first reading in the Commons goes to a second reading (sometimes in the Lords), then to a committee stage where amendments are proposed, then a report stage and a third reading in the Lords. A bill approved by one chamber is considered by the other so bills introduced by the Commons are approved by the Lords and vice versa where the opposing House can make changes to the bill. Thus, both Houses must agree on the final bill before it gains Royal Assent and becomes law.

3 Hayes discussed the disjointed nature of this incremental policy process with reference to the work of Jones (1974), who described a 'public satisfying' model that explains the relationship between incremental and non-incremental policy change. Jones's work has roots in the study of air pollution policy, which up until the 1970s was certainly incremental. There were low levels of public involvement in the issues, with participation limited primarily to business-related stakeholders as a special interest group. Similarly, few policymakers held an active interest in air pollution, and legislative proposal to curb emissions had to contend with other political resources on the legislative agenda. As Hayes argues, this is a problem of problem identification between the systemic and the institutional level – there was a need to build majorities within Congress and so this led to a process of bargaining. Bargaining involves compromise between competing interests and so policy programmes became diluted and amended as they moved through the legislative process, making changes incremental rather than revolutionary. Yet in 1970 Jones observed a significant shift in the policy landscape. The first factor was the increased number and diversity of stakeholders (or active participants) that became embroiled in the policy discourse: what Jones describes as 'potential groups' that mobilise to influence the policy process. Among these was a growth in the number and activity of environmental groups including civil-rights movement-related environmental justice organisations, and hence a corresponding increase in organisational activity on air pollution activities at the state and local levels as well as in national (federal) policy. This then fed into broader public concerns about environmental issues that were circulating at the time with the Club of Rome and The Limits to Growth Report (Meadows, Meadows, Randers, & Behrens III, 1972) and growing public opinion polling findings stressing the importance of air pollution as a national problem. Jones designates this dramatic rise in public attention and political involvement as a 'pre-formed majority', in political terms. This reduced the normal need for bargaining and compromise within the policy process, as politicians sense the increased appeal of the air pollution issues and then began competing for public attention in their policy response to it. What then happened was a process of 'policy escalation' as the perceived need to satisfy an aroused mass public leads to the adoption of strengthening amendments in the course of the legislative process, and so a substantial, non-incremental change to previous policies then occurs (including in this case the formation of the Environmental Protection Agency and the Council on Environmental Quality that significantly increased federal institutional capacity to respond to environmental pollution). What Jones argues is that this outcome is formed through a process of 'speculative augmentation' – it is a response to a politically aroused citizenry, not any breakthrough in the science or technical knowledge of the air pollution problem (Jones, 1974; Hayes, 1987). This is significant for the incremental model, because it shows that 'revolutionary' change in policy is dependent upon escalation of policy after a build-up of public support for change. Big changes can occur, not due to a new scientific/technical consensus on how to approach an issue, but rather a groundswell of public opinion that forces lots of rapid and successive changes.

Bibliography

Altshuler, A. A., & Luberoff, D. E. (2004). *Mega-projects: The changing politics of urban public investment.* Washington DC: Brookings Institution Press.

Ashworth, H. (2016). *Radioactive waste: Legacy versus new build.* Retrieved from www.niauk.org/media-centre/blog/radioactive-waste-legacy-versus-new-build/.

Boyne, G. A., Gould-Williams, J. S., Law, J., & Walker, R. M. (2004). Problems of rational planning in public organizations. An empirical assessment of the conventional wisdom. *Administration & Society, 36*(3), 328–350.

Carley, M. (2013). *Rational techniques in policy analysis: Policy Studies Institute.* Amsterdam: Elsevier.

Carrillo-Hermosilla, J. (2006). A policy approach to the environmental impacts of technological lock-in. *Ecological Economics*, 58(4), 717–742.

Collingridge, D. (1980). *The social control of technology*. London: Frances Pinter.

Collingridge, D. (1983). *Technology in the policy process: Controlling nuclear power*. London: Frances Pinter.

Collingridge, D. (1992). *The management of scale: Big organizations, big decisions, big mistakes*. Abingdon: Routledge.

Cotton, M. (2015). Structure, agency and post-Fukushima nuclear policy: An alliance-context-actantiality model of political change. *Journal of Risk Research*, 18(3), 317–332.

Cowan, R. (1990). Nuclear power reactors: A study in technological lock-in. *The Journal of Economic History*, 50(3), 541–567.

Dalton, L. C. (1986). Why the rational paradigm persists – The resistance of professional education and practice to alternative forms of planning. *Journal of Planning Education and Research*, 5(3), 147–153.

DEFRA. (2001). *Managing radioactive waste safely: Proposals for developing a policy for managing solid radioactive waste in the UK*. Retrieved from www.defra.gov.uk/environment/consult/radwaste/pdf/radwaste.pdf.

Douglas, M., & Wildavsky, A. (1983). Risk and culture: An essay on the selection of technological and environmental dangers. Berkeley, CA: University of California Press.

Flyvbjerg, B. (2014). What you should know about megaprojects and why: An overview. *Project Management Journal*, 45(2), 6–19.

Flyvbjerg, B., Bruzelius, N., & Rothengatter, W. (2003). *Megaprojects and risk: An anatomy of ambition*. Cambridge: Cambridge University Press.

Forester, J. (1984). Bounded rationality and the politics of muddling through. *Public Administration Review*, 44(1), 23–31.

Genus, A. (1995). *Flexible strategic management*. London: Chapman and Hall.

Genus, A. (2000). *Decisions, technology and organizations*. Aldershot: Gower.

Genus, A., & Coles, A. M. (2005). On constructive technology assessment and limitations on public participation in technology assessment. *Technology Analysis & Strategic Management*, 17(4), 433–443.

Gigerenzer, G., & Selten, R. (2002). *Bounded rationality: The adaptive toolbox*. Cambrdige MA: MIT press.

Habermas, J. (1984). *Theory of communicative action, Volume 1: Reason and the rationalization of society* (T. McCarthy, Trans.). Boston: Beacon Press.

Harvey, D. (1999). Time-space compression and the postmodern condition. *Modernity: Critical Concepts*, 4, 98–118.

Hayes, M. T. (1987). Incrementalism as dramaturgy: The case of the nuclear freeze. *Polity*, 19(3), 443–463. doi:10.2307/3234798.

Hayes, M. T. (2002). *The limits of policy change: Incrementalism, worldview, and the rule of law*. Washington DC: Georgetown University Press.

Hayes, M. T. (2006). *Incrementalism and public policy*. Lexington MA: University Press of America.

Hindmarsh, R. A., & Priestley, R. (2015). *The Fukushima effect: A new geopolitical terrain* (Vol. 29). New York: Routledge.

Hirst, P. (1989). *The pluralist theory of the state*. Pergammon: London.

Howlett, M. (1991). Policy instruments, policy styles, and policy implementation. *Policy Studies Journal*, 19(2), 1–21.

Howlett, M., & Ramesh, M. (1995). *Studying public policy: Policy cycles and policy subsystems* (Vol. 3). Cambridge, MA: Cambridge University Press.

Hudson, B. M., Galloway, T. D., & Kaufman, J. L. (1979). Comparison of current planning theories: Counterparts and contradictions. *Journal of the American Planning Association, 45*(4), 387–398.

Johnson, J. (1991). Habermas on strategic and communicative action. *Political Theory, 19*(2), 181–203.

Jones, C. O. (1974). Speculative augmentation in federal air pollution policy-making. *The Journal of Politics, 36*(2), 438–464.

Katz, J. L. (2001). A web of interests: Stalemate on the disposal of spent nuclear fuel. *Policy Studies Journal, 29*(3), 456–477.

Lindblom, C. E. (1959). The science of 'muddling through'. *Public Administration Review, 19*(2), 79–88.

Marsh, D., & McConnell, A. (2010). Towards a framework for establishing policy success. *Public administration, 88*(2), 564–583.

Massey, D. (1992). Politics and space/time. *New Left Review* (196), 65–84.

Meadows, D. H., Meadows, D. L., Randers, J., & Behrens III, W. W. (1972). *The limits to growth.* London: Universe Books.

Molyneux-Hodgson, S., & Hietala, M. (2015). Socio-technical imaginations of nuclear waste disposal in UK and Finland. In R. Hindmarsh, & R. Priestley (Eds.), *The Fukushima effect: A new geopolitical terrain* (Vol. 29, pp. 141–161). New York: Routledge.

Moser, S., Swain, M., & Alkhabbaz, M. H. (2015). King Abdullah Economic City: Engineering Saudi Arabia's post-oil future. *Cities, 45*, 71–80.

Nelson, K., Nelson, H. J., & Ghods, M. (1997). *Technology flexibility: Conceptualization, validation, and measurement.* Paper presented at the Proceedings of the Thirtieth Hawaii International Conference on System Sciences, 1997.

Nuclear Decommissioning Authority. (2012). *NDA annual report and accounts 2011–12.* Harwell: Nuclear Decommissioning Authority.

Polsby, N. W. (1960). How to study community power: The pluralist alternative. *The Journal of Politics, 22*(3), 474–484.

Renaud, B. (2012). Real estate bubble and financial crisis in Dubai: Dynamics and policy responses. *Journal of Real Estate Literature, 20*(1), 51–77.

Rothblatt, D. N. (1971). Rational planning reexamined. *Journal of the American Institute of Planners, 37*(1), 26–37.

Schulman, P. R. (1975). Nonincremental policy making: Notes toward an alternative paradigm. *American Political Science Review, 69*(4), 1354–1370.

Shapira, Z., & Berndt, D. J. (1997). Managing grand-scale construction projects – A risk-taking perspective. *Research in Organizational Behaviour, 19*, 303–360.

Simon, H. A. (1955). A behavioral model of rational choice. *Quarterly Journal of Economic Analysis, 69*, 99–118.

Simon, H. A. (1982). *Models of bounded rationality.* Cambridge, MA: The MIT Press.

Stevens, D. N., & Foster, J. E. (1978). The possibility of democratic pluralism. *Economica, 45*(180), 401–406.

Stirling, A. (2007). Deliberate futures: Precaution and progress in social choice of sustainable technology. *Sustainable Development, 15*(5), 286–295.

Stirling, A. (2008). Science, precaution, and the politics of technological risk. *Annals of the New York Academy of Sciences, 1128*(1), 95–110.

Stuart, D. G. (1969). Rational urban planning: Problems and prospects. *Urban Affairs Review, 5*(2), 151–182.

Szyliowicz, J. S., & Goetz, A. R. (1995). Getting realistic about megaproject planning: The case of the new Denver International Airport. *Policy Sciences, 28*(4), 347–367.

Von Weizsäcker, C. C., & Samuelson, P. A. (1971). A new labor theory of value for rational planning through use of the bourgeois profit rate. *Proceedings of the National Academy of Sciences, 68*(6), 1192–1194.

Williams, T., & Samset, K. (2010). Issues in front-end decision making on projects. *Project Management Journal, 41*(2), 38–49.

Wittneben, B. B. F. (2012). The impact of the Fukushima nuclear accident on European energy policy. *Environmental Science & Policy, 15*(1), 1–3. doi:10.1016/j.envsci.2011.09.002.

World Nuclear News. (2008). *Yucca Mountain cost estimate rises to $96 billion.* Retrieved from www.world-nuclear-news.org/wr-yucca_mountain_cost_estimate_rises_to_96_billion_dollars-0608085.html.

Wu, J., Huang, J., Han, X., Xie, Z., & Gao, X. (2003). Three-Gorges Dam – Experiment in habitat fragmentation? *Science, 300*(5623), 1239–1240.

3   Nuclear power and the problem of radioactive waste

Introduction

In the previous chapter I discussed radioactive waste management policy as a problem of technology *flexibility* – that centralised decision-making authorities prioritise comprehensive rational planning and 'big' technological systems requiring specialised infrastructure, precluding the examination of technological alternatives and reflexive examination of the underlying rationality of the decisions made. It is for this reason, I argue, that nuclear technologies have had a complex and contentious history in the socio-economic, environmental and military development of civil society in Western democratic nations. This chapter looks at the inflexibility problem in a historic context. I discuss the development of nuclear weapons research and the first civilian nuclear reactors in the 1940s and 1950s, how the problem of radioactive waste was largely ignored in policy circles in the 1960s, and the factors that drove it into a prominent position on the environmental policy agenda of the 1970s. The chapter begins, therefore, with a brief thumbnail sketch of the development of nuclear science and technology, and then focuses more specifically on the institutional factors that led to successive rounds of radioactive waste facility siting failures covering a period up to the late 1970s. Chapter 4 then examines the birth of the Nuclear Industry Radioactive Waste Executive (Nirex) set up to dispose of intermediate and high level wastes, and the new political challenges that Nirex's siting strategies created in the 1980s and 1990s.[1]

A brief history of nuclear science and technology

In basic terms, nuclear science concerns the properties of the atom nucleus. In 1789 the element uranium was discovered by the German chemist Martin Klaproth. However, it wasn't until more than a century later that Wilhelm Rontgen demonstrated that by passing an electric current through an evacuated glass tube it was possible to produce continuous X-rays. In the following year, Antoine Henri Becquerel discovered the phenomenon of radioactivity within pitchblende (a mixture of Uranium and Radium) caused a photographic plate to darken. Together, these two experiments demonstrated the presence of ionising radiation. The property of *radioactivity* is the phenomenon by which the instability of certain atomic nuclei reach stability by emitting excess energy or mass. These emissions are termed ionising *radiation* when they have the effect of producing charged particles (ions) in matter.

In 1902, Marie and Pierre Curie successfully isolated the two radioactive metals *radium* and *polonium* and during the following decade, the research of Ernest Rutherford and Niels Bohr detailed the structure of the atom, describing it as having a positively charged core, the nucleus, and negatively charged electrons that revolve around the nucleus. They subsequently detailed how radioactivity was a spontaneous event, whereby the nucleus of an unstable element emitted an *alpha* or *beta* particle and so created a different element. In 1934, the Italian scientist Enrico Fermi successfully disintegrated heavy atoms by spraying them with neutrons. In doing so he produced a controlled process of nuclear fission, a feat later advanced by Otto Hahn and Fritz Strassman in 1939, whose collective work involved the discovery that bombarding the nucleus of a uranium atom with neutrons causes the nucleus to split. This fission process produces fissile products (other elements) and more neutrons – as the uranium (U-235) atoms split, the aggregate fissile products have a smaller mass than the original uranium atom, as Einstein proved, the lost mass is released as energy. It was soon realised, therefore, that the development of controlled nuclear fission presented the opportunity to harness massive energy yields, and in August 1939, Einstein wrote a letter to President Franklin D. Roosevelt saying that it was possible to produce a controlled chain reaction of nuclear fission within a large mass of uranium, and hence a nuclear bomb. He urged Roosevelt to begin constructing a nuclear programme immediately. This desire manifested in nuclear fission as an industrial process: culminating in the development of two critically important technologies to twentieth-century military and economic development: namely, nuclear weaponry and civilian nuclear power for the generation of electricity. A full history of nuclear weapons development is largely beyond the scope of this book, however, another thumbnail sketch of military nuclear development is necessary to set the context of nuclear powered-electricity development and the political processes of radioactive waste management, as military secrecy is pertinent to civilian nuclear politics, particularly in the USA, Canada and the UK.

Nuclear weapons

In the 1940s during the Second World War under the auspices of the Manhattan Project a USA–UK–Canadian collaborative project emerged to develop, construct and test an atomic bomb. Many prominent American scientists were associated with the project, including the physicists Fermi and J. Robert Oppenheimer and the chemist Harold Urey. The programme was headed by a US Army engineer, then-Brigadier General Leslie R. Groves. In July 1945, the US government conducted their first atomic bomb test at Alamogordo in New Mexico. Shortly after, on 6 August 1945, the US aeroplane *Enola Gay* dropped the first atomic bomb ever used in warfare on the city of Hiroshima in Japan, killing (in total) more than 140,000 people. Three days later, the United States dropped a second bomb, this time on the Japanese city of Nagasaki. The drop fell one mile off target although still caused massive destruction and loss of life, with the bomb eventually killing more than 75,000 people.

The political ramifications of utilising this new nuclear science in such a destructive way were far reaching and deeply significant, not only to military strategy but to the political philosophy of war itself. Clearly, the development of the atom bomb irrevocably transformed the conduct of international politics by drawing the Second World War to a close and maintaining conditions of détente between the global superpowers throughout the Cold War. Yet as German-born American physicist and Nobel laureate Hans A. Bethe said:

> If we fight a war and win it with H-bombs, what history will remember is not the ideals we were fighting for but the methods we used to accomplish them. These methods will be compared to the warfare of Genghis Khan, who ruthlessly killed every last inhabitant of Persia.

Following the Manhattan project the UK came to develop its own military nuclear programme after World War II, with domestic military nuclear capability becoming a key research priority with firm political backing. This expertise culminated in the first test of a nuclear weapon on 3 October 1952 from HMS *Plymouth* anchored 600 metres off the coast of Trimouille Island in the Monte Bello Islands region, 80 miles off the north-west coast of Australia (Spinardi, 1997). With states developing nuclear technologies for military purposes, the potential capability to devastate military and civilian targets moved beyond anything previously seen in conventional warfare. This is illustrated by the fact that a single three-megaton hydrogen bomb had the same potential explosive capacity as all the conventional bombs dropped in the Second World War put together (Nye, 1986). The tremendous power released from the nuclear fission process is such that the full use of nuclear weapons in war has the potential to destroy modern civilisation and cause unprecedented anthropogenic ecological catastrophe. The ramifications of nuclear science for the structures and practices of international politics remain deeply controversial, and go beyond the scope of this book. However, the apocalyptic image of nuclear destruction remains influential in inter-state political and military relations into the twenty-first century, and this in turn influences the national and local scales of nuclear politics when communities consider the implications of a range of nuclear-fission related processes and industrial facilities. Nuclear science, therefore, underpins a particularly threatening form of politics; and despite international commitment to anti-nuclear proliferation legislation and enforcement, the threat of nuclear war cannot be fully eliminated. As Ahearne (2000, p. 769) succinctly argues:

> Like the contents of Pandora's box, knowledge about how to build a nuclear weapon is now part of the world's understanding – a continual problem we leave to the future. The world is riding a tiger and trying to figure out how to get off.

Though nuclear weapons are not the principal subject here, the imagery of widespread destruction contributes to a persistent socio-cultural discourse that influences public reactions to all forms of nuclear technologies: of radiation and its perceived risks – an issue I will discuss more thoroughly in Chapter 5. In parallel to the military application of nuclear science in weapons production in the 1940s and 1950s was a process of harnessing nuclear fission in a way that at first seemed comparatively benign: namely civilian nuclear power production for the commercial generation of electricity. In the United States, the initial goals of civilian nuclear power were embedded within a prevailing political philosophy aimed at projecting US hegemonic power on a global stage. The diplomatic power of nuclear technologies was a key factor in their development, alongside the domestic infrastructural development and the associated economic development advantages that this entails. In December 1953, President Dwight D. Eisenhower, delivered an address to the newly formed United Nations (UN) in New York entitled 'Atoms for Peace' (read the full speech in Eisenhower, 2003), in which he openly recognised the role that nuclear nations must bear in alleviating poverty and building peaceful relations through the deployment and application of nuclear technologies. The speech was squarely aimed at alleviating the growing fears within the international community over mounting international political tensions between the USA and the Soviet Union. Yet it also outlined a practical programme of measures to promulgate peaceful nuclear activities, such as the formation of the International Atomic Energy Agency (IAEA) under the auspices of the UN, and by later supplying equipment and information to schools, hospitals and research institutions within the USA and throughout the world to propagate nuclear technologies as 'harnessed' for the public good.

Though the Atoms for Peace programme highlighted the various uses for fission research and development, it became increasingly enamoured with the concept of nuclear *fusion* – the alternative form of atomic energy production through a process by which atomic nuclei collide to form a new type of nucleus (such as when two hydrogen atoms form a helium atom). In September 1958 in the former League of Nations building in Geneva, the first United Nations-sponsored *International Conference on the Peaceful Uses of Atomic Energy* was held. This nuclear 'world fair' brought together 5000 officials, scientists, and observers all hoping to hear about the promised revelation of secret nuclear fusion research by the United States, Great Britain and the Soviet Union (Herman, 2006). Nuclear fusion research, oft-touted as the paragon of alternative energy in a fossil fuel intensive world, has remained deeply contentious. In March 1989, Fleischmann and Pons announced they had discovered a novel method to produce significant nuclear energy without radiation. Nuclear fusion was claimed to take place between deuterons in palladium when subjected to electrolysis (Fleischmann & Pons, 1989). This phenomenon became known as cold fusion, or low energy nuclear reaction (LENR). However, such claims were widely rejected by conventional science with many academic journals refusing to publish findings on fusion research (Storms, 2015).

Despite early promising advances in the 1980s and early 1990s, intense controversy emerged within the scientific community, and consequently, a growing polarisation between 'believers' and 'non-believers' of the founding concepts. Such ambivalence is touted as primarily due to the non-reproducibility of the claimed results by many reputed research groups that have often used sophisticated experimental equipment (Srinivasan, 1991); and the replicability of these early results became a key area of social contestation within the fledgling field of nuclear fusion research (Simon, 2001). Though far from a proven and commercially viable option for energy production when compared with nuclear fission technologies, there remains a desire for fusion-related research amongst the governments of developed economies. Fossil fuels are self-evidently finite, and from a European/North American perspective, increasingly sourced from regions with complex geopolitics. There is, therefore, a growing political desire for alternative forms of energy that are abundant, politically and economically secure, and with climate change a growing policy priority, with minimal environmental impacts. Though the rise of new unconventional forms of fossil fuel extraction and processes such as horizontal drilling and hydraulic fracturing of shales, tight oil and coalbeds (so called 'fracking') mean that peak oil conditions of declining fossil fuel reserves are not an immediate global energy security concern (Asche, Oglend, & Osmundsen, 2012; Boersma & Johnson, 2012); there is still significant public support and expectations around alternative energy in general, and nuclear fusion energy specifically. This is couched in a persistent social narrative that, following some decades of research and technology, nuclear fusion will be the solution to many of our energy problems (Dittmar, 2012), despite the fact that existing awareness and knowledge of nuclear fusion amongst 'lay' public actors remains very limited (López, Horlick-Jones, Oltra, & Solá, 2008). Whether or not nuclear fusion will replace nuclear fission as an alternative to fossil fuel-based energy production is not something that is easy to predict from current trends, though it is important to note that in the 1950s this expectation of the long-term fusion scenario had significant impact upon the ways in which nuclear fission was planned for: as a comparatively 'dirty' stop-gap measure until *clean* nuclear fusion arrived (for discussion of fusion energy as a 'clean' alternative fuel see Ongena & Van Oost, 2004 in particular).

On a more practical level, the applications of fission research had domestic electricity production at the core. It was during the early 1950s that the first nuclear fission reactors began to emerge as viable producers within electricity markets. The first two examples were the 5 megawatt (MW) reactor at Obinsk in the USSR and the 2.4 MW reactor at Shippingport, Pennsylvania in the USA. In the UK by the 1950s, civilian nuclear power development was already underway, and perhaps in contrast to the loftier goals of the Atoms for Peace rhetoric, provided more mundane objectives for the post-war Labour Government. One of the key political challenges in the immediate rebuilding of the shattered UK economy in the late 1940s and 1950s was the establishment of secure energy services to domestic and industrial electricity users and the rebuilding of industrial infrastructure. The major hindrance to economic rehabilitation through energy distribution was the prospect of coal shortages and the increasing political power of the National Union of Mineworkers to restrict production and hence raise domestic energy costs. Against the backdrop of this economic conflict, the prospect of harnessing nuclear power had become an increasingly politically attractive option in stimulating social and economic development. In parallel to providing cheap electricity to the market, however, a nuclear programme also offered the alluring prospect of military prestige gained from the development of nuclear weapons. Together, therefore, the two goals became powerful motivating factors for successive governments to invest in nuclear research, development and deployment.

The development of civilian nuclear powered electricity in the UK

Initially, UK nuclear activity was directed towards both weapons manufacture and civilian power generation, leading to the construction of nuclear reactors together with facilities for nuclear fuel production and reprocessing to produce plutonium, the reactor-born radioactive material essential for weapon production (for a thorough examination of the relationship between nuclear power and civilan weapons production in the UK I recommend Gowing, 1974; Hall, 1986). The first civilian programme in the UK involved successive phases of construction throughout the 1950s and 1960s. At first, a site close to the town of Drigg in West Cumbria in the Northwest of England was intended for the construction of military reactors. By 1947 however, this site was replaced by the choice of Windscale further north along the Cumbrian coast. The Windscale site was a former ordinance factory (Sellafield). Construction activities on the two Windscale Piles (piles being another term for reactor) commenced shortly after, with the fuel produced at the Springfields nuclear fuel manufacturing facility in nearby Preston in the north-west of England, established by the Ministry of Supply in 1946. The two Piles (No. 1 and No. 2) were completed in 1950 and 1951, respectively. It is interesting to note that at the time there was little consultation or parliamentary debate around the development of this first civil nuclear power programme and it appears that the announcement in 1955 of its arrival seems to have taken many, including Members of Parliament, by surprise (see in particular Simmons, Bickerstaff, & Walls, 2007; Welsh, 2000).

Despite some localised opposition to the proposals, the first prototype Magnox nuclear facilities were constructed in the early 1950s. The term 'Magnox' refers to an early design of pressurised, carbon dioxide-cooled and graphite-moderated nuclear reactors that use unenriched natural uranium fuel and a magnesium oxide alloy to clad the fuel as it enters the reactor. The first Magnox reactor, Calder Hall at Windscale, went under construction in 1953 and was later connected to the national grid electricity transmission network in 1956, thus creating the UK's (and indeed the world's) first facility to provide commercially produced electricity (NDA, 2008). After the construction of Calder Hall, in 1954 the Atomic Energy Authority Act created the United Kingdom Atomic Energy Authority (UKAEA), an authority with the overall responsibility for the UK's nuclear energy programme, which included responsibility for developing civilian nuclear technology. The primary focus was the development of the so-called fast breeder reactor (FBR) – a design that worked on the principle of creating more fissile material than it consumes (Waltar & Reynolds, 1981), with the former Second World War wartime airfield at Dounreay in Caithness, in Northern Scotland, selected for this purpose (the Dounreay Fast Reactor [DFR] programme) in 1954.

Though the civilian applications and public benefits were stressed in the political rhetoric around the construction of the Windscale site and the proposed Dounreay site, the primary goal in both cases was the production of plutonium from uranium for nuclear weapons production. The process of irradiating uranium to produce plutonium generates significant amounts of heat. The waste heat requires disposal, and it was quickly realised that this could be used to generate steam within a steam-powered turbine. Therefore, electricity could be produced as a by-product of the weapon production process (Wynne, 1982; Department of Trade and Industry, 2005). From 1957 the government began to promote electricity generation by nuclear power as an alternative to coal fired power stations, and so reduced the bargaining power of the coal miners' unions (Gowing, 1974) and establishing an alternative energy technology pathway to (previously dominant) domestic coal production.

Though energy security and weapons prestige were powerful drivers for government cooperation in the development of a civilian nuclear programme, this began to shift towards the end of the decade. Williams (1980) asserts that it was during this initial period of nuclear development and expansion in the late 1940s and early 1950s that the government appeared to be rushing towards the development of a viable national nuclear technology platform due to military imperatives; but towards the end of the 1950s this had given way to a political desire to establish prestige through world leadership in civilian nuclear technology. Thus, nuclear development became a key component of the UK's global technological authority in the late 1950s. Two further prototype Magnox stations at Chapelcross in Dumfries and Galloway in the Southwest of Scotland were connected to the newly developed national grid in 1959; followed by nine full scale Magnox power stations. The development of advanced gas-cooled reactor technology (AGR) beginning in 1964 (to succeed the earlier Magnox gas cooled stations) resulted in the development of five further AGR stations in England and two in Scotland (Simmons et al., 2007; NDA, 2008). The growth of commercial nuclear power generation in Britain in total resulted in the creation of a total of 22 Magnox reactors across sites in Britain, which was then followed by a further 15 of the more efficient AGR stations (NDA, 2008).

In terms of nuclear technology governance, as Mackerron and Berkhout (2009) suggest, during this initial period of nuclear technological expansion, the governance strategy was to establish the industry and segregate political oversight from its production. To this end, when in 1954 the UKAEA was set up through the Atomic Energy Authority Act it had to manage the twin responsibilities for nuclear facility management and weapon development research. So,

UKAEA commissioned the first reactors in the 1950s; it was a special department within what was then the Ministry of Supply, responsible for both for nuclear power research and the production of both fissile material and a nuclear bomb. Hence the top-down creation of UKAEA through an Act of Parliament tied together civilian and military uses of nuclear technology from its inception. The culmination of these factors led to an early nuclear technology development process that consisted of government monopoly of the nuclear industry, close ties between weapon production and civilian electricity generation, secrecy contrasted with a governmental rhetoric of 'boosterism' (i.e. a highly supportive attitude) and a sense of unchallenged technological optimism within UK society (Blowers & Pepper, 1988). Civilian nuclear electricity has depended upon knowledge gained from weapons manufacture and this in turn has remained reliant upon reactor-born plutonium, hence the two processes remain intertwined in a number of nuclear power producing countries, despite continued political commitments to nuclear non-proliferation agreements (Garwin & Charpak, 2002).

Throughout the early technologically *optimistic* period of nuclear expansion, the problem of radioactive waste remained in the background of nuclear policy, despite some prominent voices in the nuclear industry expressing doubts over the technical feasibility of the disposal of fission products (Kemp, 1990; Blowers, Lowry, & Solomon, 1991). In the 1950s and 1960s the primary factors that went into site selection and evaluation of nuclear facilities were aspects such as access to cooling water, suitable geology for building foundations, proximity to the national grid and proximity to areas of demand, all of which took priority over the social and political dimensions of nuclear development (Carver & Openshaw, 1996). Moreover, it is only comparatively recently that the myriad environmental, technological and social implications of long-term radioactive waste management have been overtly addressed as a political issue.

Of critical importance to understanding why radioactive waste management policies and facility siting processes have remained so politically contentious is the combination of these factors. The culture of secrecy that persisted within the nuclear technology community in the 1990s long after the Soviet threat to the West had receded, and the residual optimism from the development of the civilian nuclear programme, collectively masked the problem from public scrutiny and controversy for a sustained period. Policy-makers in the 1960s and 1970s had confidence in the eventual development of a technical solution to wastes, as after all, engineers and scientists had demonstrated such technical competence in the development of the nuclear programme itself, so few doubted that eventually they 'would be able to deal with the nuclear garbage', as Rosa and Freudenburg (1993) put it. It was clear, therefore, that although the need for the political shielding of nuclear technology secrets from espionage had somewhat diminished along with the collapse of the USSR in the early 1990s, the governance of the industry remained hidden from public view. This obduracy in the political culture of nuclear institutions is what created the conditions of technological inflexibility discussed in Chapter 2 – it encouraged centrally planned radioactive waste management policy, heavily influenced by scientific and technical expertise to create a 'rational' solution. Under conditions of secrecy there was no opportunity for 'social probing' of technological alternatives. This created later political problems for civilian nuclear power production and radioactive waste management processes, as blanket secrecy and confidence in a technological solution exacerbated public mistrust in the civilian side of the industry, and the government's ability to protect the public from emergent health and environmental risks from radioactive wastes.

The Windscale pile fire

The continued expansion of nuclear technologies throughout the 1950s and 1960s simply meant a growing stockpile of radioactive wastes. Initially, concerns had been raised within Parliament that the disposal of radioactive wastes at the tail end of nuclear production would pose a limit to the continued expansion and operation of nuclear power, however, by 1952 this anxiety was scarcely mentioned in policy circles because the new commercial electricity generating Windscale scale site appeared to be working so well (Gowing, 1974). However, on 10 October 1957, Windscale became the centre of an important nuclear accident, ultimately damaging its reputation as a safe form of power generation. The Windscale Pile fire was an example of what is now known as a Level 5 nuclear event: an 'accident with wider consequences' on the International Nuclear Events Scale (INES). A fire in Pile Number 1: a nuclear reactor at the Windscale Works in Sellafield, resulted in the uncontrolled release of radionuclides into the atmosphere. It was caused by a graphite annealing process (heating the graphite to change its chemical properties), which made the metallic uranium fuel catch fire. This meant radioactive dust was released. The environmental effects were widespread. The fire burned for nearly three days, releasing a range of radioactive contaminants (including iodine and polonium) across a broad area of the north-west of England. This posed a significant health risk through inhalation and milk consumption from local dairy produce (Crick & Linsley, 1983). Milk from about 500 km^2 of nearby countryside was destroyed (diluted a thousandfold and dumped in the Irish Sea) for about a month afterwards. A special mention goes to two exhaust shafts above the Windscale piles. They were described as Cockcroft's Folly, providing expensive filtering that was not deemed necessary at the time of their construction (Arnold, 1992). However, the presence of the filters prevented as much as 95 per cent of the radioactive material from the fire from entering the atmosphere (Leatherdale, 2014), reducing the overall ecological impact of the fire. Yet the political significance of this incident was not felt during or immediately after this period. The details of the fire, and its impacts were not fully revealed at the time, and as Blowers argues, this accident early on in the development of nuclear power in Britain 'had little impact on public consciousness at the time and did not disturb the settled discourse' of pro-nuclear optimism (Blowers, 2016, p. 78). Even under conditions of a relative environmental shock, the effect on nuclear policy was incremental.

Nuclear waste and the end of nuclear optimism

Prior to 1976, very little thought had been given to the question of how the highly active wastes produced by military and nuclear electricity programmes were to be disposed of. Policy in this arena became piecemeal and inconsistent, as successive governments relied upon varying notions of what was the best scientific advice and were heavily conditioned by a perceived need to politically protect spent fuel reprocessing (Berkhout, 1991) and maintain Britain's military and economic regeneration interests. The aforementioned nuclear optimism coupled with the secrecy surrounding nuclear technologies, including that surrounding the Windscale fire, prevented the problem of radiation health effects, and specifically the management of long-lived radioactive wastes from generating significant public controversy in the 1950s. As a result, the Magnox and AGR programmes continued to develop into the 1960s relatively unchallenged, while waste was still treated as a relatively minor or residual concern (Welsh, 1993). Although part of the UKAEA's remit was to investigate the problem of RWM, as Hookway (1984, p. 123) states:

> the early stages of our nuclear programme had hanging over them an urgency which led to the shelving of problems if this were possible. At Windscale [...] the highly active liquors [what is now commonly classified as 'high level' radioactive wastes, or HLW] were kept in tanks without real thought being given to their eventual fate. Intermediate level wastes were put into silos, little more than crude concrete boxes without there being any plan to retrieve them, let alone process and eventually dispose of them.

By the beginning of the 1970s, the issue of long-term planning for site decommissioning and radioactive waste management had started to reach the broader environmental agenda. In part this was due to other geopolitical and energy policy concerns emerging at the time. With growing political concerns about oil dependence with the rise of the Organisation of the Petroleum Exporting Countries (OPEC) production cartel, this began to stimulate a political desire for spent fuel reprocessing: taking reactor fuels that had been through the fission process, and then separating out the HLW and fissile materials from the remaining uranium and reactor-produced plutonium. Reprocessing would substantially complicate the technical challenge of waste management, yet the government remained largely silent on the long-term technical and socio-economic impacts, health and environmental risks. As such, decisions on HLW (the heat-generating products of spent fuel reprocessing) remained unresolved. UKAEA did, however, begin to conduct experiments into waste vitrification in the late 1950s and 1960s (Berkhout, 1991). Vitrification is a process by which heat producing higher activity wastes can be stored for long periods of time, as the process stabilises the waste into a chemically non-reactive and largely waterproof state – bonding the waste materials into a glass matrix which is poured into stainless steel cylindrical containers which then solidify into glass (National

Research Council, 1996). Because the vitrified wastes produced at the Sellafield reprocessing site are heat producing they are stored for a period of 50 years to allow heat dissipation.

Though a solution to higher level activity wastes was not forthcoming in the 1950s, there was some degree of disposal activity for the lower level activity waste taking place throughout this period. Solid wastes such as radioactively contaminated cements were dumped at various locations in the Atlantic from 1949, and in the Irish Sea during the 1950s. Low level wastes were also dumped in the English Channel from 1950 until 1963, though UKAEA acknowledged at the time that this sea disposal process was not a suitable long-term solution to the problem (Saddington & Templeton, 1958). Some low and intermediate-level wastes were disposed of in deep ocean sites up until 1982. Between 1949 and 1982 an estimated $33,000 \, m^3$ of radioactive wastes were disposed of in the Atlantic and British coastal waters (Nuclear Decommissioning Authority and the Department for Energy and Climate Change, 2011). Data submitted to the International Atomic Energy Authority reveal UK disposal at sea took place between 1949 and 1982. A total of 34 disposal operations across 15 sites in the Atlantic Ocean for a total of 74,052 tons of waste were dumped, leading to a total additional radioactivity load to the marine environment of $3.51 \times 10^7 \, GBq$ (IAEA, 1999). As we see in Chapter 4, this practice became a significant source of contention within policy communities – particularly spurred by ENGOs and maritime trades union bodies. On-land and by-sea disposal routes thus began to compete within government policy strategy as potential options for long-term radioactive waste disposal.

It is significant that throughout this period, regulatory non-compliance, secrecy and cover-up were endemic to early sea-based solid radioactive waste disposal, raising questions of potential eco-crime. According to Walters (2007), there are numerous examples of suspicious radioactive waste dumping activities: citing, for example, Greenpeace's independent research giving evidence of 285,000 corroded barrels of radioactive waste rusting on the seabed of the Channel Islands, reportedly dumped between 1950 and 1963 in the Hurd Deep – a stretch of water 15 km north-west of Cap de la Hage in France. Walters (2007) also discusses other cases including UKAEA's release of radioactive particles into the environment, with subsequent cover-up; and the Scottish Environmental Protection Agency in 2005 reported that Dalgety Bay contained more than 100 radioactive contaminated sites where the Ministry of Defence had dumped dismantled technology (see also Harvie, 2005 on this latter point). It is also noteworthy that following the creation of the THORP at Sellafield, in addition to the solid waste disposal, reprocessing activities also produce liquid radioactive effluent. In the 1980s, UK practice in the operation of the British Nuclear Fuels nuclear plant at Sellafield was to dispose of large volumes of low-level liquid wastes, under authorisation, into the Irish Sea. Included in these wastes are trans-uranium nuclides (including plutonium) created following nuclear fission. Scientific assessment in the 1980s showed persistent uncertainties over the chemical nature of the effluents, their behaviour in sea water, their association with settled sediments on the sea bed, and their transfer back to the human environment via the ingestion of sea foods (see for example Pentreath, Lovett, Jefferies, Woodhead, Talbot, & Mitchell, 1983). These radioactive isotopes discharged (particularly into the Irish Sea) contributed to total doses of radioactivity received by local coastal populations, and so due to the action of contamination from fishing and shore-based activities, this creates critical groups of citizens with potential long-term exposure, requiring ongoing monitoring. We can see that health concerns about routine discharges of liquid waste at sea emerged and then persisted throughout the 1980s. In 1983, a local Yorkshire television report called *Windscale: The Nuclear Laundry* suggested that there was an excess cancer risk for residents living near to Sellafield. Perhaps most significantly, the programme claimed an apparent increase in the incidence of childhood leukaemia in pockets of affected populations in local communities. A number of leading epidemiological studies emerged at the time, and Black's (1984) review study showed that the town of Seascale (approximately 3 km from the Windscale/Sellafield site) had the third highest lymphoid malignancy rate during 1968 to 1982 in children under 15 in one study (entirely due to leukaemia incidence increase). The district ward – Millom Rural District (which includes the town of Seascale) had the second highest rate among 152 comparably sized districts in England and Wales, ranked by leukaemia mortality among under 25s during 1968 to 1978. Some studies pointed to factors such as fathers' pre-conception exposure to radiation (Gardner, 1991), though other later studies have shown either no increased incidence when compared with case control groups (Bithell, Murphy, Stiller, Toumpakari, Vincent, & Wakeford, 2013), or else alternative hypotheses including the *infection hypothesis* – that increased cancer incidence is related to an influx of construction and other workers from outside the region (for discussion of the data see Gardner, 1989; Gardner, Snee, Hall, Powell, Downes, & Terrell, 1990; Kinlen, Dickson, & Stiller, 1995).

Given the deeply contentious nature of sea disposal and the potential health impacts from routine discharges of radioactive materials and sea dumping of ILW, a growing political pressure emerged from environmental non-governmental organisations to force the government to act. Growing international pressure throughout the 1980s pushed the government to eventually accept, in 1993, an international ban commonly referred to as the *London Dumping Convention*. The main objective of this agreement was to prevent indiscriminate disposal at sea of wastes that could be liable for creating hazards to human health; harm living resources and marine life; damage amenities; or interfere with other legitimate uses of the sea ('The Convention on the Prevention of Marine Pollution by Dumping Wastes and Other Matters', 1972; World Nuclear Association, 2016). The government's capitulation in the 1990s was compelled by broader international environmental politics, particularly the Rio Declaration in 1992 that established the precautionary principle (UNEP, 1992). The precautionary principle changed the nature to which all forms of hazardous waste disposal practice were implemented, in this case by showing greater care for unknown (and potentially unknowable) environmental risks to the marine environment and to affected land populations.

Simultaneous to the sea dumping was the perhaps less controversial solid low-level waste disposal in a 120 hectare repository at the former Second World War munitions site at Drigg. This site came into operation in 1959 and it remains the primary site for the long-term disposal of Britain's low-level wastes (World Nuclear Association, 2016). It was shortly after, in 1960, that the disposal of radioactive wastes became subject to stronger legal and regulatory control under the Radioactive Substances Act of 1960 (RSA60) (later replaced by the Radioactive Substances Act 1993 – RSA93, and then incorporated into Schedule 23 of the Environmental Permitting regulations for England and Wales). What the legislation did was to prevent individuals or businesses from producing, accumulating or disposing of radioactive wastes without proper licence and registration to do so, further illustrating the importance of radioactive waste *management* as a key environmental and public health priority, in contrast to the dominant thinking of the 1950s (for further discussion of the implications of this legislation on the development of regulatory authorities and substance control see Chandler, 1998; Jackson, Baker, George, & Mobbs, 2013). Under the substance control legislation, LLW wastes including contaminated clothing, medical equipment or building materials were unsuitable for municipal landfill and required a separate disposal strategy. So, although some LLW was disposed of at sea, most wastes produced within the nuclear industry were simply accumulating on-site at the production facilities without a longer-term strategy in place.

In terms of broader policy and governance roles for radioactive waste management throughout the 1960s, the UKAEA had become a powerful and autonomous body in the nuclear programme. As Mackerron and Berkhout (2009) argue, UKAEA controlled research programmes in both military and civilian areas, and the organisation had become an essentially self-regulating entity. Though the Radioactive Substances Act in 1963 established some formal criteria against which to judge the safety and viability of radioactive waste management practices, UKAEA remained largely unregulated and unchecked, thus politically beyond parliamentary control and departmental oversight. Consequently, the government passed in 1965 The Nuclear Installations Act, which established the Nuclear Installations Inspectorate (NII) as regulator of safety and health issues on all nuclear sites as a means to curb the self-regulating and institutionally isolated powers of the UKAEA. By 1971, the UK civilian nuclear programme had begun to stall, and so UKAEA's political strength also began to falter. At this point, the government separated the military development responsibilities from the domestic civilian power production responsibilities. The former powers went to the Ministry of Defence (MOD), whilst a new publicly owned company, British Nuclear Fuels (BNFL) was formed to manage the supposedly *commercial activities*. (These activities included spent fuel reprocessing at Sellafield, which included plutonium production and management.) (See in particular Berkhout, 1991; Department of Trade and Industry, 2005; Mackerron & Berkhout, 2009.) Similarly, during this period up until the early

1970s, radioactive waste management fell under the rubric of commercial activities, and so government left this aspect primarily to industry bodies such as BNFL to manage what was largely seen as the back-end of a commercial production process.

The Windscale Inquiry and the Thermal Oxide Reprocessing Facility

In 1973 the Central Electricity Generating board (CEGB) announced a renewal of the nuclear reactor programme, with an emphasis upon the construction of AGR reactors. This was in part spurred by the growing international oil crisis that led the government into considering the opportunities of a new wave of nuclear reactors to ensure energy security at a time when economic development was severely hampered by spiralling energy costs. Two years later, government plans emerged to build an international nuclear fuel reprocessing facility at the Windscale site. However, the Windscale facility had suffered a leak in 1973 with the plant out of action (Patterson, 1978). Not only was this new proposed facility met with strong local public resistance (see in particular Wynne, 1982), but when combined with the proposed new wave of AGR reactors, this triggered an investigation into the environmental effects of nuclear technologies.

In the 1970s Windscale was the largest nuclear installation in the UK, and one of the largest in the world. It was owned and operated at the time by British Nuclear Fuels Ltd (BNFL): the commercial fuel-cycle company run as a subsidiary of UKAEA. The facilities in service at the Windscale site included spent-fuel storage ponds, a reprocessing plant for metal fuel, storage tanks for liquid high-level radioactive waste, plutonium stores and a plutonium-fuel fabrication plant. In September 1973, The Windscale Head-End Plant for oxide fuel suffered a leak of radioactivity which put it out of operation. This in turn prompted discussions with Japanese and other overseas customers over the planned construction of a new purpose built full-scale oxide fuel reprocessing facility. Under the existing planning legislation Cumbria County Council had the power to approve BNFL's new Thermal Oxide Reprocessing Plant (THORP) – a facility designed to deal with irradiated oxide nuclear fuel from both UK and foreign reactors by removing uranium and plutonium from the spent fuel for reuse in a new fuel cycle. In November 1976, the application was approved after a relatively straightforward decision-making process. However, upon completion this had the effect of spurring public opposition to the plans, and after some deliberation by the Secretary of State for the Environment, Peter Shore MP, government announced that the Windscale proposal would be made the subject of a planning inquiry.

The public inquiry aimed to answer three questions. The first regarded whether the UK should reprocess fuel at all. The second, considered whether such reprocessing should be carried out specifically at the Windscale facility. The third considered whether the reprocessing facility should be enlarged to accommodate foreign imported fuels. The inquiry was unique in that it considered both local and international aspects of the proposal, including the exchange of nuclear fuel materials with Japan. The inspector in charge of the inquiry reported directly to the Secretary of State for the Environment, who alongside Cabinet colleagues would then take responsibility for approval or rejection of the BNFL application (Patterson, 1978; Parker, 1979; Wynne, 1982). The inquiry began in June 1977. Though previous planning inquiries into reactor construction, for example at Bradwell in Essex and Trawsfynydd in Gwynedd Wales, had been routine examinations that focused exclusively on local environmental and socio-economic effects of plant construction, the international dimensions of this public inquiry made it unique among nuclear decision-making processes (Walker, 1999). This inquiry was broad reaching in scope, hearing 100 days of oral and written evidence and cross-examination, with sessions taking place in the media spotlight. The final inquiry transcript came in at over 4 million words, backed by 1500 documents at a total cost of over £1 million (additional costs borne by opponents for legal representation and outside expertise amounted in some instances up to £250,000) (Patterson, 1978; Williams, 1980). The eventual result of the inquiry was that the new THORP facility was green-lit in 1978; though construction wasn't completed until 1994. (It became operational in 1997.) The total cost of construction was £1.8 billion, making it one of the most expensive nuclear capital projects ever constructed.

To proponents of nuclear expansion within government, and among industry supporters, the outcomes of the process were viewed as a triumph of open democratic politics in resolving a technical controversy. Yet critics of the inquiry were less sanguine about the both the process and its outcomes. As Patterson (1978, p. 44) notes:

> For the past year the British government has been congratulating itself in public about its handling of civil nuclear controversy in Britain. But it may have taken its bows too soon. Government representatives have pointed repeatedly with pride to the country's longest nuclear planning inquiry, the Windscale Inquiry, as a model of open examination of a sensitive nuclear proposal. They have noted the ugly confrontations which have occurred elsewhere in Europe, implying that the British way has been far preferable. Unfortunately for the British government's self-satisfaction, however, the official Report of the Windscale Inquiry, published in March 1978, bears little relationship to the proceedings of the inquiry. Instead the Report is a heavy-handed nuclear apologia, so clumsily one-sided as to provoke unease even among many Britons previously unmoved by the issue which gave rise to the Inquiry.

Wynne specifically examined the processes by which agreement was reached. Contrary to the calls of resounding success, Wynne's (1982) book: *Rationality and Ritual* examines not only the underlying science used in the inquiry, but also the nature and concept of rationality mobilised in the inquiry process itself. He argues that the process of public inquiry was inherently structured to produce agreement, at least on the issues under consideration and the ways in which arguments were presented, if not on the actual outcomes of the process itself. This is because the scientific concepts mobilised in this legalistic inquiry process tended to prioritise and reify specific notions of 'truth', 'exactness', and 'justi-fication' as properties implicit in scientific discourse (and indeed as qualities of the scientists themselves) – in effect an underlying ritual of process that steered the inquiry towards a legitimating outcome for the technical authorities propos-ing the new THORP facility. This had the effect of excluding or diminishing lay conceptions of the problem, or other forms of moral judgements or value claims beyond the realm of science (Wynne, 1982, see also the updated version: 2010; Wallis, 2012; Landstrom, 2013). The inquiry served to socially construct the 'nuclear problem' within bounded technical rationality and a peculiar form of scientific and engineering ethics, to the exclusion of other forms of moral and political judgement. The inquiry served to 'technocratise' the deliberative process and marginalise lay actor voices – something which would become a template for nuclear decision-making processes for the next two decades. Wynne's anthropological analysis of the nuclear decision-making process was extremely powerful in revealing the nature of science as a self-sustaining ritual in decision-making: that technocracy emerged because of institutional forces that acted to reinforce the value of scientific information as the foundation for decision-making, to the exclusion of all other forms of evidence. As the book and its updated version in 2010 show, this was an ominous template for nuclear decision-making that persisted long after the deficiencies of technocratic methods had been revealed.

The Flowers report and the Radioactive Waste Management Advisory Committee

In 1976 the Sixth Report of the Royal Commission on Environmental Pollution (RCEP) into *Nuclear Power and the Environment* was published (Royal Commis-sion on Environmental Pollution, 1976). The report committee was chaired by physicist Brian Flowers (and is commonly referred to as the Flowers Report). It highlighted the significant environmental and policy concerns around current and future nuclear technology programmes. The comprehensive analysis uncov-ered issues related to energy policy strategy and environmental protection, the handling of nuclear material, the creation of plutonium in large quantities under Cold War conditions, the hazardous nature of plutonium as a substance, the potential for threat and blackmail against society that plutonium presents due to its radiotoxicity and its fissile properties, alongside issues concerning reactor design, siting, and radiation protection. It also raised concerns over the credible risk of construction of crude nuclear weapons by an 'illicit group' (what we might now call a *dirty bomb*: packing nuclear materials with conventional explo-sives to spread radioactive contamination). The report was critical of the gov-ernment for not fully appreciating the implications of this scenario, and that such security issues required wide public debate. Specifically, on the issue of radioactive waste management, the report recommended that formal responsibility for the management and eventual disposal of radioactive wastes should be given to the Department of the Environment. Before 1976 no such role had been given to a government department, so radioactive waste management was a de facto condition of nuclear industry business operations, with UKAEA taking the lead (Berkhout, 1991). This call was to make nuclear waste a public responsibility due to the lack of safe management practices in the industry.

The report had some significant impacts upon radioactive waste politics. First, it is significant that the report broke from previous political reassurances of the safe expansion of nuclear new build, recommending not only that the UK Government create a disposal site as a long-term solution to the radioactive waste problem, but also that continued expansion of the civilian nuclear power programme be conditional upon the safe disposal of wastes (Royal Commission on Environmental Pollution, 1976):

> There should be no commitment to a large programme of nuclear fission power until it has been demonstrated beyond reasonable doubt that a method exists to ensure the safe containment of long-lived, highly radioactive waste for the indefinite future.

The concept of futurity was made explicit within the report. The Flowers Report grounded its recommendation within a normative ethical assessment of the radioactive waste management problem, suggesting that:

> It would be morally wrong to commit future generations to the consequences of fission power on a massive scale ... unless it has been demonstrated beyond reasonable doubt that at least one method exists for the safe isolation of these wastes for the indefinite future.
> (Royal Commission on Environmental Pollution, 1976, p. 81)

The idea that *future generations* should be a significant consideration in current and future nuclear planning processes was novel in the context of the prevailing political thinking of the 1970s. These recommendations also came against a backdrop of emergent political interest in environmental futures, particularly in light of the publication of The Club of Rome's *Limits to Growth* (Meadows, Meadows, Randers, & Behrens III, 1972), where ecological capacities and their implications for human society had started to become increasingly visible within environmental politics.

The second major impact, is that the Royal Commission on Environmental Pollution report also recommended changes to the governance structure of the industry and within government, suggesting that a national disposal facility for radioactive waste should be built and operated by a specialised Nuclear Waste Disposal Corporation, independent of the industry (in contrast to prevailing policy). Together these two facets provided an important turning point for UK radioactive waste policy, as for the first time a leading institution independent of government, military and industry interests had examined the situation and publicly announced it to be highly unsatisfactory; contrary to the repeated reassurances of the nuclear policy community in the 1950s and 1960s. The Flowers Report laid the blame firmly on the government, highlighting the lack of satisfactory progress and the potential environmental and health risks to the public that this posed. The report brought a significant degree of urgency to the policy framework for managing radioactive wastes, making the problem increasingly prominent within the government's environmental agenda. As Berkhout (1991) suggests, the practical upshot of this report was to ensure that within the incumbent Labour Government the Department of Environment took a far more active role in planning for long-term radioactive waste management.

The Flowers Report recommendation of a total industry-independent radioactive waste management organisation with planning and siting responsibilities was not forthcoming, however, in addition to the reorganisation of radioactive waste governance within the DoE, was the setting up of a new independent expert committee – the Radioactive Waste Management Advisory Committee (RWMAC) in 1978. We can see this as an incremental policy change – responsibility was still held by industry, but government created a new advisory agency to shape future policy learning. RWMAC's role was to offer independent advice to ministers on a range of radioactive waste management related issues, though in practice its remit spread beyond issues solely associated with radioactive waste (Beveridge, 1998). Its initial membership was principally scientific and technical expert-driven, with members of the committee drawn from a wide range of backgrounds and specialisms.[2] Each year until 2004, RWMAC undertook work commissioned by government ministers on a range of nuclear-related issues. It also responded to consultations on relevant issues and maintained an active interest in all aspects of radioactive waste management activities undertaken by UK nuclear site operators and other users of radioactive materials (Radioactive Waste Management Advisory Committee, 2008a).

The creation of RWMAC in 1978 is indicative of a broader trend towards the development of independent advisory bodies on issues of technological risk. The concept of *Technology Assessment* (TA) emerged in the 1970s as governments sought independent advice on the political and technical ramifications of new and emerging scientific and technological trends. TA in practice became embodied in certain civil society institutions in Europe and the United States. The US Congress set a global institutional precedent by creating the (now defunct) Office of Technology Assessment (OTA) in 1972, and other similar models followed in Europe such as the Danish Board of Technology (DBT), the Swiss Centre for Technology Assessment, the UK Parliamentary Office of Science and Technology (POST), the Office of Technology Assessment at the German Parliament (TAB), and the Belgian Institute of Society and Technology (IST). The aim of these institutions was/is to enhance societal understanding of the broader implications of science and technology and, thereby, to improve the quality and efficacy of political deliberation in fields ranging from environmental management, science policy and military decision-making (Cotton, 2014). RWMAC is a smaller and more specific form of this kind of TA body – adopting an analytical approach that aims to speak-truth-to-power, gain advance knowledge of radioactive waste management technology options, their potential impacts and consequences, and hence provide a political early warning system to encourage governments to steer clear of potential future technological hazards, or else to minimise their harmful effects on society (Decker & Ladikas, 2004). Like other TA bodies at the time, RWMAC was constructed to fulfil an advisory capacity to the government, adopting a multi-disciplinary approach to the analysis and solving of technical problems caused by radioactive waste management technology development and siting. Thus, RWMAC in its early phase, falls into the category of what Van Eijndhoven (1997) calls the classical paradigm of TA: conceived of as an analytic activity, aimed at providing decision-makers with an objective analysis of effects of a technology. Its second role was to make its views public, presenting itself as an independent voice in public debate (Kemp, 1992). This classical model of TA embodied in RWMAC illustrates the political thinking at the time – that radioactive waste management is a technical and scientific activity and that technical authority (even when drawn from the nuclear industry), when expressed publicly, would be sufficient to alleviate public concerns on the potential environmental and health impacts.

UKAEA and HLW siting 1976–1981

In parallel to the RCEP report, in 1976, UKAEA continued to explore potential sites for HLW siting. It announced in the same year that the granite formations in areas within the Highlands and Islands and the Scottish Uplands were suitable for a disposal site for HLW. This declaration was somewhat premature, however, as the Institute of Geological Science had identified 127 locations, ranging in size from $5\,km^2$ to $6,000\,km^2$ (Mather, Gray, & Greenwood, 1979). This list of sites was reduced further through a process of desk studies to 24 potential sites. Following the desk studies, a series of field surveys revealed eight potential sites that were then shortlisted for complete investigation through test drilling of bore holes to evaluate the suitability of the potential host rock for the emplacement of radioactive waste containers. The problem that the UKAEA encountered, however, was that planning permission was necessary before such drilling begin, a continual sticking point throughout RWM assessment processes, and so planning applications were only ever submitted for three of the granite sites – two in Scotland and one in northern England. More specifically, in 1978 UKAEA put in an application to Kyle and Carrick District Council, in the south-west of Scotland, to implement a test drilling site on Mullwharchar Hill that borders Strathclyde and Dumfries and Galloway, near an area that is now Galloway forest park.

What is significant about this planning application is that the site became the centre of local political opposition from within the council, which spilled out into the popular media and then into energy and environmental politics at the national level. Following extensive and often heated deliberation on the proposals, Kyle and Carrick Council not only rejected the planning application, but went one step further. They declared that geological site investigations were prohibited, and went on to ban the geologists from putting up drilling rig equipment or parking their vehicles near to the site. Following the subsequent rejection of proposals, UKAEA lodged an appeal with the Secretary of State for Scotland in the Autumn of 1978. Then Secretary of State for Scotland George Younger acted as arbitrator in the planning application, though the national political implications for this site application were somewhat complicated by the fact that Younger was also the MP for Ayr, one of the affected regions. The appeal ran to a public inquiry. This was held between February and March of 1980. The application then became the centre point for the formation of three opposition groups – the Scottish Campaign to Resist the Atomic Menace (SCRAM); the Scottish Conservation Society and the Campaign Opposing Nuclear Dumping (COND), which together, mobilised massive organised public protest, spurring other opposition groups across Scotland including sites which had not even made it to the original shortlist (see No2NuclearPower, 2000 for an in-depth timeline of these events). The public inquiry is an inherently adversarial setting, and forms the main institutional arena within which public concerns about specific development proposals can be considered (Yearley, 1989). However, in this first inquiry into radioactive waste siting, it treated the issue as a local planning dispute rather than one arising from government policy. UKAEA's attempt to frame the issue solely as one of scientific investigation rather than potential repository siting was unsuccessful and the inquiry upheld the council's decision (Simmons & Bickerstaff, 2006).

In the wake of the inquiry, a new form of nationalistic political rhetoric was beginning to emerge, spurred by the radioactive waste siting problem in Scotland. This growing political discourse depicted conflict between English and Scottish interests. To give an example, in the local paper: the *Dumfries and Galloway Standard* called the inquiry into the Mullwharchar Hill site a 'Bannockburn for ordinary folk over the big battalions of politics, bureaucracy and science worship' (*The Economist*, 1980). The Bannockburn image was significant because it was one of the few battles against the English that the Scots actually won (ibid.). Thus, the public inquiry in 1980 which was ostensibly set up to assess the relative merits of borehole drilling for basic geological research became a platform for opponents to deliberate upon the government's broader nuclear policy priorities and a growing divide in North–South relationships between England and Scotland, rooted in this environmental controversy (Smith, 1985). As Simmons and Bickerstaff (2006) argue, the Mullwharchar inquiry had broader political significance because it highlighted the secrecy within which UKAEA operated, and so this characteristic came to be associated with later attempts to conduct siting investigations up to and including the Rock Characterisation Facility in 1997. So, whilst not all subsequent siting processes became embroiled in the official investigatory powers of a public inquiry, they all appeared to engender varying degrees of localised public opposition

(Simmons et al., 2007). This opposition began to spread across the Scottish regions, with SCRAM operating in Aberdeen to fight proposals in north-east Scotland, and then assisting in setting up and running further opposition groups across Scottish regions. Their tactics involved, for example, dispatching speakers to public meetings to openly protest the against the Institute of Geological Sciences' proposals for drilling tests in Glen Etive in Argyll. In England, opposition within the district councils spread, as applications in 1978 to Alnwick and Berwick District Councils in the north-east of England for test drillings were also rejected, leading to a second public inquiry in 1980 in Newcastle.

What we see, therefore, is a process of social movement adaptation and expansion, whereby the success of one social movement in Scotland (SCRAM) then subsequently shapes the trajectories of other movements for environmental opposition and social change, initiating a more widespread cycle of protest that creates new opportunities for activism to emerge within other constituencies (Tarrow, 1994). This is likely rooted in what is termed the 'demonstration effect' of one group's actions, i.e. successful or effective collective action by a small scale initial protest movement encourages protest by a growing number of new participants because early protest signals the potential vulnerability of political and scientific elites to opposition challenges (Conell & Cohn, 1995). Therefore, it is the dissemination of information about successful protest by nascent social movements that drives the development of broad-based cycles of protest (Minkoff, 1997), in this case, first across a range of Scottish radioactive waste management exploration process sites, and then more broadly spreading into England and Wales.

Planning applications for test drilling continued more broadly, including sites at Altnabreac in Strath Halladale: submitted to Caithness District Council in 1978 (No2NuclearPower, 2000). What was different in Caithness was that the nuclear industry was intrinsic to the economic stability of the region, as the population relied on the Dounreay nuclear power station for continued employment. This created complex conditions of socio-economic dependence upon the industry and hence a condition of what is termed nuclear *peripherality*, whereby the comparative economic strength of the industry coupled with low levels of social activism, socio-political marginalisation and the polluting and stigmatising nature of the industry, led to a crowding out of other potentially competitive clean industries and growing social and economic dependence within the affected community to create something of a *nuclear oasis* (Blowers & Leroy, 1994; Blowers, 2016). This peripheralisation process was a leading factor in the granting of planning permission for 27 borehole tests between November 1978 and May 1979, making Altnabreac in Caithness the only site to successfully carry out such test drillings. Concurrent to the processes of siting, refutation and protest that were occurring in Scotland during this period through the expanding cycles of social movement development, UKAEA also began to explore alternative rock formations, including salt rock and clay in England and Wales, in part to seek less politically heated arenas for radioactive waste site exploration. Some of the proposed sites focused upon former military locations such as an ordinance factory in Somerset, a former airfield in Leicestershire and a Royal Air Force base in Leicestershire. Others were proposed in areas currently occupied with civilian land uses such as the Brent Knoll service area near Bristol, and Radcliffe-on-Soar power station in Nottinghamshire, areas in the Worcester Basin, and Gwynedd and Powys in North Wales. However, all of these applications (including military sites) followed the now increasingly familiar pattern of localised protest and the formation of social movements of opposition, followed by the eventual denial of local planning permission in the period between 1980 and 1981 (Kemp, 1992; No2NuclearPower, 2000).

Given the continued failures of siting processes at this point, The government came to realise the sustained political difficulties in HLW site investigation from district council opposition and sustained and costly public inquiries in site investigations. These continued failures were creating an expensive (and increasingly embarrassing) barrier to successful policy implementation, and so they then abandoned test drilling programmes for HLW siting in December 1981 in favour of a new programme based upon desk research of geologically suitable locations, laboratory testing and the evaluation of data already available (Radioactive Waste Management Advisory Committee, 1982). Ultimately what this signalled was a significant policy failure, causing government to reconsider the long-term siting strategy, and the governance processes within the nuclear industry.

Conclusions

The development of the early nuclear industry in the United Kingdom is a story of shifting goals, rhetoric, governance patterns and incentives. The political viability of the early nuclear industry was judged on its military outputs. In the 1950s, electricity production was a secondary concern, though one which solved a growing problem of energy security in the post-war era and provided a sort of political cover for the industry, by demonstrating civilian as well as military–strategic benefits from nuclear science. In essence, what emerged in the 1950s at Windscale (now Sellafield) was something akin to Eisenhower's (1987) concept of the military–industrial complex: policy and monetary relationships between civilian industry and military research and development were intertwined, with murky and secretive governance relationships whereby oversight bodies were unable to fully separate military from civilian goals. Perhaps ironically, Eisenhower's Atoms For Peace programme actually cemented the political discourse of the civilian benefits of nuclear science through the political framing of it as a peaceful technology. This strategy specifically aimed to counter growing fears of the H-bomb following Hiroshima and Nagasaki bombings at the end of the Second World War, and the growing tensions and nuclear détente strategy between the USA and the USSR. What this did was to further inculcate the military–industrial nuclear complex into UK civil society.

In the UK global military strategy and domestic energy politics became almost politically indistinguishable to the outside observer, with the expansion of nuclear power capabilities in the UK through Magnox and then AGR technologies grounded in technological optimism and industry boosterism on the one hand, and the secrecy over objectives such as the Trident missile programme on the other. The underlying philosophy of early civilian nuclear power development is, to use Dryzek's (1997) environmental discourse terminology, distinctly *Promethian* – it represents a radical political orientation to energy and environmental policy that prioritises uranium as an exploitable natural resource, and the use of which is determined primarily by human needs and interests, whilst emergent environmental problems can be overcome through continued human innovation and the application of technology. Simultaneous to this Promethian discourse was the deepening of Cold War conditions that shrouded the actual nuclear production processes in administrative secrecy, which impaired the *social probing* necessary to encourage civil society examination of alternative technology options. The governance of the industry, through its ties to the military, created significant democratic deficits, lack of accountability, alongside clear evidence of environmental damage and the mismanagement of nuclear materials. Radioactive waste is one of the most significant outcomes of these political processes. It is, therefore, not simply a technical by-product of an industrial process, but is grounded in the discursive social construction of energy, power, military might, technical expertise, environmental values and post-war socio-economic development in the United Kingdom throughout this period.

What we see after the 1950s is that it is both the technical and *discursive* legacy of the nuclear industry that created the ongoing problem of waste: a problem widely recognised as the 'Achilles heel' of the nuclear industry (Sundqvist, 2002; Metlay, 2016). Successive government responses to this problem were first, to largely ignore it, second, to dispose of it in ways that caused growing public environmental controversy (by sea, specifically), and then third, to *reluctantly* recognise the growing threat of radiotoxicity in the human environment. The ever-expanding stockpile of radioactive materials was beginning to increase the socio-cultural visibility of radioactive waste; forcing the issue into mainstream environmental politics in the 1970s. With the Royal Commission on Environmental Pollution (RCEP) or 'Flowers Report' highlighting, among other aspects, the intergenerational nature of the threats posed, radioactive waste became an issue of environmental futurity and responsibility, not coincidentally at a time when environmental futures were becoming part of the international political agenda (the Limits to Growth report being the most obvious example, Meadows et al., 1972). The eventual reaction of the government to this growing concern was predictably technocentric in its approach, sustained by the underlying Promethian discourse of nuclear science. Experts and expertise have tremendous power in political decision-making, and given the prevailing conditions of political optimism about engineers' ability to deal with the complexities of nuclear power production and fuel reprocessing, confidence in similar ability to dispose of waste safely remained high during the 1970s.

Against central government confidence in the engineering capabilities of the industry to ultimately dispose of the wastes, there was considerably less attention paid to suitable processes of site selection, governance and oversight to ensure accountability, fairness and procedural justice of the political outcomes of waste disposal. When scientists from the Institute of Geological Science (the precursor to the British Geological Survey) came into communities to drill boreholes, they were repelled by local opposition. This occurred because of the growing effectiveness of social movements of technology opposition (particularly in Scotland) to both demonstrate their political power, and to mobilise and block successive siting applications. The effect is what Blowers (1999) terms a *landscape of defence*: whereby both the dependent communities act to defend their accustomed standards of living in the face of nuclear 'threat', and the nuclear industry and associated scientific authorities counter to defend economic interests in the face of opposition. Part of this defence process amongst the emergent social movements of opposition was an ongoing social learning process and multi-scalar engagement with political authorities. SCRAM, for example, lobbied ministers and local authorities to block applications and protect spaces and communities from intrusion by technical authorities and their associated scientific experts. Their relative capacity to share strategy and mobilise support within other affected communities (including those in England and Wales) showed the growing power of a grassroots environmental justice network in radioactive waste politics. This was a relatively unusual phenomenon in the UK at the time – with SCRAM creating a flow of information that then spread out among a growing social network of local opposition movements. Collectively, these networks became powerful enough to stymie government policy strategy – they provided social probing of a secretive policy landscape. What was clear in the subsequent decade is that government did not undergo a similar process of reflexive institutional learning about such social opposition. Lessons were not drawn about the importance of *procedural* fairness in waste siting; the government doubled-down on the streamlining of authoritarian control of radioactive waste governance through the development of the Nuclear Industry Radioactive Waste Executive (Nirex). What we see is that Nirex's processes of siting, rather than alleviating the political knot of long-term RWM policy, served to deepen divisions and mount growing social tension in a host of new communities over the next decade and a half. The development of Nirex as a constituent body of the nuclear industry and its role in radioactive waste governance (and successive policy failures) is discussed in the following chapter.

Notes

1   This historical narrative about the development of nuclear waste management policy up to and including the early 1990s provides a broad overview of the key decisions and political implications of these management processes. For an in-depth analysis of these issues within this historical period I recommend the following works. First Hall's 1988 book *Nuclear Politics: The History of Nuclear Power in Britain* (Penguin) covers the development of nuclear reactor technology; Kemp's 1992 book *The Politics of Radioactive Waste*

Disposal; Blowers et al.'s 1991 book *The International Politics of Nuclear Waste*; and Berkhout's 1991 book *Radioactive Waste: Politics and Technology* collectively examine the political processes of early attempts at radioactive waste siting. Chandler's (1998) *Radioactive Waste Control and Controversy: The History of Radioactive Waste Regulation in the UK* deals more specifically with the regulatory development of radioactive substances control.

2 To date, the expertise of RWMAC includes nuclear and radioactive waste management from the nuclear industry and associated consultancy organisations; geology, hydrology, geochemistry, chemical modelling from universities and research institutes; industrial waste management and pollution control; radiological protection from the National Radiological Protection Board; environmental and public health perspectives from the Medical Research Council, charities and hospital personnel; local government and regional planning perspectives from local authorities and non-governmental organisations; environmental and civil society perspectives from environmental non-governmental organisations; and health and safety from trades unions and regulators, and environmental law from private practice (Radioactive Waste Management Advisory Committee, 2008b).

Bibliography

Ahearne, J. F. (2000). Intergenerational issues regarding nuclear power, nuclear waste, and nuclear weapons. *Risk Analysis*, 20(6), 763–770.

Arnold, L. (1992). *Windscale 1957: Anatomy of a nuclear accident*. Basingstoke: Palgrave Macmillan.

Asche, F., Oglend, A., & Osmundsen, P. (2012). Gas versus oil prices the impact of shale gas. *Energy Policy*, 47, 117–124.

Berkhout, F. (1991). *Radioactive waste: Politics and technology*. Abingdon: Routledge.

Beveridge, G. (1998). The work of a radioactive waste management watchdog: The work of the Radioactive Waste Management Advisory Committee. *Interdisciplinary Science Reviews*, 23(3), 209–213. doi:10.1179/isr.1998.23.3.209.

Bithell, J. F., Murphy, M. F. G., Stiller, C. A., Toumpakari, E., Vincent, T., & Wakeford, R. (2013). Leukaemia in young children in the vicinity of British nuclear power plants: A case-control study [Epidemiology]. *British Journal of Cancer*, 109(11), 2880–2885. doi: 10.1038/bjc.2013.560.

Black, D. (1984). *Investigation of the possible increased incidence of cancer in West Cumbria*. London: HMSO.

Blowers, A. (1999). Nuclear waste and landscapes of risk. *Landscape Research*, 24(3), 241–264. doi:10.1080/01426399908706562.

Blowers, A. (2016). *The legacy of nuclear power*. Abingdon: Earthscan from Routledge.

Blowers, A., & Leroy, P. (1994). Power, politics and environmental inequality: A theoretical and empirical analysis of the process of peripheralisation. *Environmental Politics*, 3(2), 197–228.

Blowers, A., & Pepper, D. (1988). The politics of nuclear power and radioactive waste disposal: From state coercion to procedural justice? *Political Geography Quarterly*, 7(3), 291–298.

Blowers, A., Lowry, D., & Solomon, B. D. (1991). *The international politics of nuclear waste*. London: Macmillan.

Boersma, T., & Johnson, C. (2012). The shale gas revolution: U.S. and EU policy and research agendas. *Review of Policy Research*, 29(4), 570–576. doi:10.1111/j.1541-1338.2012.00575.x.

Carver, S., & Openshaw, S. (1996). *Using GIS to explore the technical and social aspects of site selection for radioactive waste disposal facilities.* Leeds: School of Geography Working Paper 96/18, University of Leeds.

Chandler, S. D. (1998). *Radioactive waste control and controversy: The history of radioactive waste regulation in the UK.* Florida: CRC Press.

Conell, C., & Cohn, S. (1995). Learning from other people's actions: Environmental variation and diffusion in French coal mining strikes, 1890–1935. *American Journal of Sociology, 101*(2), 366–403.

The Convention on the Prevention of Marine Pollution by Dumping Wastes and Other Matters (1972).

Cotton, M. (2014). *Ethics and technology assessment: A participatory approach.* Berlin: Springer-Verlag.

Crick, M. J., & Linsley, G. S. (1983). An assessment of the radiological impact of the Windscale reactor fire, October 1957. Harwell: National Radiological Protection Board.

Decker, M., & Ladikas, M. (Eds.). (2004). *Bridges between science, society and policy: Technology assesment – methods and impacts.* Berlin: Springer-Verlag.

Department of Trade and Industry. (2005). Nuclear power generation development and the UK industry. *Nuclear Energy.* Retrieved 28 January 2006, from www.dti.gov.uk/energy/nuclear/technology/history.shtml.

Dittmar, M. (2012). Nuclear energy: Status and future limitations. *Energy, 37*(1), 35–40.

Dryzek, J. S. (1997). *The politics of the earth: Environmental discourses.* Oxford: Oxford University Press.

The Economist. (1980, 23 February). Nuclear waste; not helping with inquiries. *The Economist,* 65.

Eisenhower, D. D. (1987). The military–industrial complex. *American Journal of Economics and Sociology, 46*(2), 150.

Eisenhower, D. D. (2003). Atoms for peace. *IAEA BULLETIN, 45*(2), 62–67.

Fleischmann, M., & Pons, S. (1989). Electrochemically induced nuclear fusion of deuterium. *Journal of Electroanalytical Chemistry and Interfacial Electrochemistry, 261*(2), 301–308.

Gardner, M. J. (1989). Review of reported increases of childhood cancer rates in the vicinity of nuclear installations in the UK. *Journal of the Royal Statistical Society. Series A (Statistics in Society), 152*(3), 307–325.

Gardner, M. J. (1991). Father's occupational exposure to radiation and the raised level of childhood leukemia near the Sellafield nuclear plant. *Environmental Health Perspectives, 94,* 5–7.

Gardner, M. J., Snee, M. P., Hall, A. J., Powell, C. A., Downes, S., & Terrell, J. D. (1990). Results of case-control study of leukaemia and lymphoma among young people near Sellafield nuclear plant in West Cumbria. *British Medical Journal, 300*(6722), 423–429.

Garwin, R. L., & Charpak, G. (2002). *Megawatts and megatons: The future of nuclear power and nuclear weapons.* Chicago: University of Chicago Press.

Gowing, M. (1974). *Independence and deterence: Britain and atomic energy, 1945–1952* (Vol. 2). London: Macmillan.

Hall, T. (1986). *Nuclear politics: The history of nuclear power in Britain.* London: Penguin.

Harvie, D. (2005). *Deadly sunshine: The history and fatal legacy of radium.* Stroud: Tempus.

Herman, R. (2006). *Fusion: The search for endless energy.* Cambridge: Cambridge University Press.

Hookway, B. R. (1984). Radioactive waste management: 1963–1984. *Journal of the Society for Radiological Protection*, 4(3), 122–126.

IAEA. (1999). *Inventory of radioactive waste disposals at sea*. Vienna: INIS Clearinghouse – International Atomic Energy Agency.

Jackson, D., Baker, A., George, R., & Mobbs, S. (2013). England and Wales: Experience of radioactive waste (RAW) management and contaminated site clean-up. In W. E. Lee, M. I. Ojovan, & C. Jantzen (Eds.), *Radioactive waste management and contaminated site clean-up: Processes, technologies and international experience*. Cambridge: Woodhead Publishing.

Kemp, R. (1990). Why not in my backyard? – A radical interpretation of public opposition to the deep disposal of radioactive-waste in the United Kingdom. *Environment and Planning A*, 22(9), 1239–1258.

Kemp, R. (1992). *The politics of radioactive waste disposal*. Manchester: Manchester University Press.

Kinlen, L. J., Dickson, M., & Stiller, C. A. (1995). Childhood leukaemia and non-Hodgkin's lymphoma near large rural construction sites, with a comparison with Sellafield nuclear site. *British Medical Journal*, 310(6982), 763–768.

Landstrom, C. (2013). Book review: Brian Wynne, *Rationality and ritual: Participation and exclusion in nuclear decision-making*. Second edition with a new introduction by the author and foreword by Gordon MacKerron. *Public Understanding of Science*, 22(1), 122.

Leatherdale, D. (2014). *Windscale piles: Cockcroft's follies avoided nuclear disaster*. Retrieved 7 July 2016, from www.bbc.co.uk/news/uk-england-cumbria-29803990.

López, A. P., Horlick-Jones, T., Oltra, C., & Solá, R. (2008). Lay perceptions of nuclear fusion: Multiple modes of understanding. *Science and Public Policy*, 35(2), 95–105.

Mackerron, G., & Berkhout, F. (2009). Learning to listen: Institutional change and legitimation in UK radioactive waste policy. *Journal of Risk Research*, 12(7–8), 989–1008.

Mather, J. D., Gray, D. A., Greenwood, P. B. (1979). Burying Britains's radioactive waste: The geological areas under investigation. *Nature*, 281(5730), 332–334.

Meadows, D. H., Meadows, D. L., Randers, J., & Behrens III, W. W. (1972). *The limits to growth*. London: Universe Books.

Metlay, D. S. (2016). Selecting a site for a radioactive waste repository: A historical analysis. *Elements*, 12(4), 269–274.

Minkoff, D. C. (1997). The sequencing of social movements. *American Sociological Review*, 62(5), 779–799.

National Research Council. (1996). *Nuclear wastes: Technologies for separation and transmutation*. Washington DC: National Academy Press.

NDA. (2008). *The Magnox story*. Harwell: Nuclear Decommissioning Authority.

No2NuclearPower. (2000). *History of nuclear waste disposal proposals in Britain*. Retrieved from www.no2nuclearpower.org.uk/reports/waste_disposal.php.

Nuclear Decommissioning Authority and the Department for Energy and Climate Change. (2011). *Radioactive wastes in the UK: A summary of the 2010 inventory*. Cumbria: Nuclear Decommissioning Authority.

Nye, J. S. (1986). *Nuclear ethics*. New York: The Free Press (Macmillan).

Ongena, J., & Van Oost, G. (2004). Energy for future centuries: Will fusion be an inexhaustible, safe, and clean energy source? *Fusion Science and Technology*, 45(2), 3–14.

Parker, R. J. (1979). *The Windscale inquiry: Report*. London: HM Stationery Office.

Patterson, W. C. (1978). The Windscale report: A nuclear apologia. *Bulletin of the Atomic Scientists*, 34(6), 44–46.

Pentreath, R., Lovett, M., Jefferies, D., Woodhead, D., Talbot, J., & Mitchell, N. (1983). *Impact on public radiation exposure of transuranium nuclides discharged in liquid wastes from fuel element reprocessing at Sellafield, United Kingdom.* Paper presented at the Radioactive waste management. V. 5, Seattle, 16–20 May.

Radioactive Waste Management Advisory Committee. (1982). Third annual report. London: Her Majesty's Stationery Office.

Radioactive Waste Management Advisory Committee. (2008a). The Radioactive Waste Management Advisory Committee. Retrieved 2 February 2015, from http://collections. europarchive.org/tna/20080727101330/http://defra.gov.uk/rwmac/index.htm.

Radioactive Waste Management Advisory Committee. (2008b). RWMAC membership (as at March 2004). Retrieved 2 February 2015, from http://collections.europarchive. org/tna/20080727101330/http://defra.gov.uk/rwmac/members.htm.

Rosa, E. A., & Freudenburg, W. R. (1993). The historical development of public reactions to nuclear power: Implications for nuclear waste policy. In R. E. Dunlap, M. E., Kraft, & E. A. Rosa (Eds.), *Public reactions to nuclear waste: Citizens' views of repository siting* (pp. 32–63). London: Duke University Press.

Royal Commission on Environmental Pollution. (1976). *Nuclear power and the environment.* London: Royal Commission on Environmental Pollution.

Saddington, K., & Templeton, W. L. (1958). *Disposal of radioactive waste.* London: George Newnes.

Simmons, P., & Bickerstaff, K. (2006). The participatory turn in UK radioactive waste management policy In K. Andersson (Ed.), *VALDOR 2006 – Values in decisions on risk conference proceedings* (pp. 530–537). Stockholm: Informationsbolaget Nyberg & Co, Stockholm.

Simmons, P., Bickerstaff, K., & Walls, J. (2007). *CARL country report – United Kingdom.* Norwich: University of East Anglia.

Simon, B. (2001). Public science: Media configuration and closure in the cold fusion controversy. *Public Understanding of Science, 10*(4), 383–402.

Smith, P. J. (1985, 3 May). Futures: How the waste was dumped, *The Guardian.*

Spinardi, G. (1997). Aldermaston and British nuclear weapons development: Testing the 'Zuckerman Thesis'. *Social Studies of Science, 27,* 547–582.

Srinivasan, M. (1991). Nuclear fusion in an atomic lattice: An update on the international status of cold fusion research. *Current Science, 60*(7), 417.

Storms, E. (2015). The present status of cold fusion and its expected influence on science and technology. *Innovative Energy Policies, 4*(1). doi: 10.4172/2090-5009.1000113.

Sundqvist, G. (2002). *The bedrock of opinion: Science, technology and society on the siting of High-Level Nuclear Waste.* Dordrecht: Kluwer.

Tarrow, S. (1994). *Power in movement: Social movements, collective action and politics.* Cambridge: Cambridge University Press.

UNEP. (1992). Rio Declaration on Environment and Development.

Van Eijndhoven, J. (1997). Technology assessment: Product or process? *Technological Forecasting and Social Change, 54*(2), 269–286.

Walker, W. (1999). *Nuclear entrapment: THORP and the politics of commitment.* London: IPPR.

Wallis, M. K. (2012). Review of rationality and ritual: Participation and exclusion in nuclear decision-making by Brian Wynne. *The British Journal for the History of Science, 45*(4), 708–709.

Waltar, A. E., & Reynolds, A. B. (1981). *Fast breeder reactors.* New York: Pergammon Press.

Walters, R. (2007). Crime, regulation and radioactive waste in the United Kingdom. In P. Beirne, & N. South (Eds.), *Issues in green criminology: Confronting harms against environments, humanity and other animals* (pp. 186–205). Portland: Willan Publishing.

Welsh, I. (1993). The NIMBY syndrome: Its significance in the history of the nuclear debate in Britain. *British Journal of the History of Science, 26,* 15–32.

Welsh, I. (2000). *Mobilising modernity: The nuclear moment.* London: Routledge.

Williams, R. (1980). *The nuclear power decisions.* London: Croom Helm.

World Nuclear Association. (2016). *Nuclear power in the United Kingdom,* from www.world-nuclear.org/information-library/country-profiles/countries-t-z/united-kingdom.aspx.

Wynne, B. (1982). *Rationality and ritual: The Windscale Inquiry and nuclear decisions in Britain.* Bucks: The British Society for the History of Science.

Wynne, B. (2010). *Rationality and ritual: Participation and exclusion in nuclear decision-making.* London: Routledge Earthscan.

Yearley, S. (1989). Bog standards: Science and conservation at a public inquiry. *Social Studies of Science, 19*(3), 421–438.

4   Nirex and the search for a site

Introduction

With continued failures to find a site for high level waste (HLW), UKAEA had lost a great deal of political legitimacy as an authority in radioactive waste siting by the end of 1981. The government quickly shifted direction again and declared that, given the stored cooling period for higher activity wastes was 50 years, there was no apparent urgency in the siting process for higher activity wastes (Department of the Environment, 1982). Secretary of the Environment Tom King then announced an end to the drilling programme for HLW site testing. This meant that onsite storage of spent fuel became the responsibility of BNFL for the foreseeable future, with no long-term deep geological disposal strategy on the horizon. Emphasis within the government moved from HLW towards a new search for low and intermediate-level waste (LLW and ILW) sites. This was due in part to the implicit (and naïve) expectation that ILW and LLW would be less likely to stimulate social opposition to facility proposals due to the potentially lower degree of environmental and public health threat (for discussion of this point see Berkhout, 1991 in particular).

Instrumental in this new shift to lower activity wastes was a new body set up in 1982 by government called the Nuclear Industry Radioactive Waste Executive (Nirex). It was first established as a private company by the component bodies of the British nuclear industry of the time: British Nuclear Fuels, Nuclear Electric, the Atomic Energy Authority (UKAEA) and Scottish Nuclear, with the Secretary of State for the Environment holding a special 'golden share'. It later became a limited company in 1985 (called United Kingdom Nirex Limited – hereafter both are simply referred to as 'Nirex' for simplicity). Nirex was based at Harwell in Oxfordshire, and became the principal body under government sanction with responsibility to implement a strategy for the disposal of LLW and ILW. It had statutory duties to:

> provide and manage facilities for the disposal of low and intermediate level radioactive waste ... operating within firm policy guidelines laid down by the government.
>
> (DoE, 1986)

In 1983 Nirex began its programme of work by announcing its new lower activity waste disposal strategy, one that focused upon two potential sites. The first was a site for ILW: a deep anhydrite mine under a site near to the town of Billingham in (what was then known as Cleveland, now the Tees Valley) and a clay pit in Oxfordshire for the shallow burial of LLW. Billingham was selected principally on the basis that the site itself was nearly derelict land (a brownfield site without existing planning permission for other forms of redevelopment). Yet as was seen in the 1970s, there was a swift mobilisation of social opposition in the region shortly after Nirex's announcement. The opposition group was called 'BAND' (Billingham Against Nuclear Dumping), chaired by local Reverend Peter Hirst. Nirex's scientific case for the site was premised on the geological suitability of the anhydrite mine, though Billingham itself is a relatively large population centre,[1] unlike other radioactive waste facility locations considered in previous siting processes. Initially, the site selection was supported by Imperial Chemical Industries (ICI), and Nirex stated in 1984 that the siting decision was a purely commercial matter between these two companies and was, therefore, immune to public requests for details (Openshaw, Carver, & Fernie, 1989). Nirex argued that it was a commercial organisation and as such, dealt with other commercial organisations in normal business confidence. Yet public opposition was intense, so much so that government officials required a police presence to attend local public meetings. ICI also was influenced by trade union pressure alongside local public opposition. ICI was at the time a large corporate presence in Cleveland, and the sale of this otherwise derelict land was damaging corporate–community relations in the region, in essence undermining ICI's social licence to operate within the region. ICI did eventually reverse its support for the siting application and government decided in early 1985 that it would not proceed with Billingham and would ask Nirex to instead nominate three alternative sites in addition to Elstow for a near-surface facility (Parker, Kasperson, Andersson, & Parker, 1986). Nirex then abandoned Billingham shortly afterwards, early in 1985.

The growing pressure to find a site for ILW and LLW

Nirex's first foray into the final disposal siting process for ILW had failed, and so by the mid-1980s there was yet again growing political pressure on the government (and by extension Nirex) to proceed quickly to secure a site. I argue that four principal factors began to drive an ever more urgent need for a resolution of the low and intermediate level waste problem:

The end to sea disposal

In February 1983, the Convention on the Prevention of Marine Pollution by Dumping Wastes and Other Matter met to consider a proposal to prohibit the dumping of radioactive wastes. Ultimately the proposal was defeated but a resolution calling for countries to voluntarily suspend sea dumping pending scientific review was passed following a vote. However, the UK delegation did not accept the validity of the resolution on the voluntary suspension action (claiming it was not based upon scientific evidence), though did support the need for a scientific review. The National Union of Seamen had been following the proceedings closely and acted to try and counter the government's position on sea dumping. The union's general secretary, in particular, was concerned about dumping activities and was generally sympathetic to Greenpeace's position on the issue (all from Holliday, 2005, pp. 53–54). The Trades Union Congress then met in September 1983 and endorsed the transport unions' actions to block radioactive waste dumping at sea off the west coast of France.

In the following year, the government had made a commitment to comply with the Paris Commission requirements for the gradual elimination of radioactive discharges into the Irish Sea from Sellafield, and to suspend the dumping of LLW in the Atlantic, 600 miles off the coast of Land's End in Cornwall in south-west England. Shortly after, as part of ongoing negotiations around the London Dumping Convention in 1985 (mentioned in Chapter 3), there was a significant growth in international pressure, particularly from Scandinavian countries, on the UK Government to eliminate sea disposal altogether. Government received ad hoc scientific advice on the risks of sea disposal, as well as a Ministry of Agriculture, Fisheries and Food (MAFF) publishing of a joint report with the Trades Union Congress, which independently reviewed the environmental impacts of radioactive waste disposal in the North Atlantic. The committee was chaired by marine biologist Professor Fred Holliday, former Chancellor of the University of Durham. The report examined the best practical environmental options for low and intermediate level waste disposal, recognising the important role that public opinion played in the acceptability of waste management options, and concluding that further research was necessary into the long-term effects of sea disposal. The report effectively called for the government to impose a moratorium on sea disposal activities in the interim period, closing off this route for ILW and thus stimulating the need for further safe on-land (effectively on site) storage at point of production.

The public inquiry into Sizewell B

Between 1983 and 1985 there was a public inquiry into the proposal by the CEGB to construct a Pressurised Water Reactor (PWR) nuclear power station at Sizewell, Suffolk. The inquiry was presided over by Sir Frank Layfield QC, appointed by the then Conservative Government. Sizewell already had a Magnox reactor (Sizewell A), and the second reactor (Sizewell B) was first announced in 1969 as an Advanced Gas-Cooled (AGR), then a steam-generating heavy water reactor (SHGWR) in 1974, and finally as a PWR in 1980. Before construction began, the reactor proposals were subject to a safety review by the NII, which ran in parallel to the public inquiry. The inquiry itself was significant in that it was the largest and most detailed of its kind, even more so than the Windscale inquiry before it: taking 340 days and hearing 16 million words worth of evidence. It revealed the underlying economics, design and con-struction safety issues, whilst highlighting a number of significant challenges. Some of these were technical: such as the methodology for balancing safety and cost during plant design. Others concerned governance practices, such as the inconsistent and uncoordinated involvement of numerous governmental depart-ments in the governance of nuclear safety procedures, the comparative lack of parliamentary scrutiny and approval of overall safety standards; and the pro-longed record of inefficient management in earlier nuclear projects (specifically previous AGR projects).

Perhaps, most significantly in the context of this book, the inquiry high-lighted the communication problems between engineers and their intended audience, specifically the capacity of technical specialists to explain their exper-tise to lay citizens, decision-makers and to other professionals (for detailed dis-cussion of the technical and governance issues highlighted see: Purdue, Kemp, & O'Riordan, 1984; O'Riordan, Kemp, & Purdue, 1985; Layfield, 1988). Though a wide range of issues were explored in the dialogue processes of the inquiry, the eventual outcome was approval of the application. Thus, though subject to a satisfactory safety case, the inquiry found no substantive reasons why the project should not proceed. The NII later accepted the Pre-Construction Safety Case and issued a licence to proceed with construction in August 1987. (For an in-depth examination of the aftermath of the inquiry and the broader socio-economic and governance issues surrounding the Sizewell B project, see: O'Riordan, 1984; O'Riordan, Kemp, & Purdue, 1988; Glasson, 2005.) From a waste management perspective, this new nuclear build emerging at the end of the 1980s (though Sizewell B of course remains, at the time of writing, the last new reactor to be built in the United Kingdom) signalled yet again an urgent political need for new waste disposal arrangements, driving the issue back into a prominent position on the environmental policy agenda in the middle of this decade.

The capacity issues of Drigg, the LLW repository

The third issue that affected radioactive waste policy at the time was the capa-city of the LLW repository at a site near to Drigg in Cumbria, a town close to the Sellafield site. The Drigg site was in operation for the disposal of LLW since 1959. Up until 1988, lower activity wastes (frequently garments or other routine materials which were lightly contaminated from use in the Sellafield plant) were loosely tipped into excavated trenches, cut into the glacial tills underlying the site (Miyasaka, 2003). In the early 1980s, therefore, there was concern raised that Drigg only had half the expected capacity (Kemp, 1989) and so the ques-tion of what to do when this was filled further exacerbated the pressures on ILW/LLW disposal siting. However, in 1988 the loose filling of trenches was phased out in favour of containers of compacted and conditioned wastes that were stored in concrete vaults, and the trenches capped with earth which incorporates an impermeable membrane to stop water leaking in (Coyle,

Grimwood, & Paul, 1997) as a short-to-medium term solution to the capacity issue. This new compaction process did successfully relieve the capacity stress on the existing site (for the short-to-medium term disposal of LLW at least). In 1995, a government review of radioactive waste management policy confirmed that Drigg would continue as the primary site for the disposal of LLW in the UK for as long as it has both the radiological and volumetric capacity to do so. It was recognised that the success of waste minimisation initiatives in recent years, together with the increased use of high force compaction of wastes, has potentially increased the duration of use to the middle of the twenty-first century (HMSO, 1995).[2]

Nuclear submarines

In addition to civilian waste production, one of the other important elements was military technology decommissioning and the processes of nuclear submarine dismantling and radioactive waste disposal. The used fuel cores from submarine reactors as part of the UK's Trident programme of nuclear weapons deterrent are a form of HLW. Routine production of ILW and LLW associated with Trident has been produced at a range of sites including Sellafield, Chapelcross, Faslane, Devonport and Aldermaston facilities. Further wastes (particularly ILW) will be produced when submarines are decommissioned, and new wastes produced under conditions of Trident renewal. In 1982, the nuclear submarine HMS Dreadnought was decommissioned following a process of De-fuel, De-equip and conduct of Lay-up Preparation (DDLP). The intention was to sink the submarine (based upon the dilute and disperse principle of radioactive disposal). However, two factors prevented this from occurring. First, as just mentioned, sea dumping of wastes was becoming an increasingly controversial aspect of nuclear waste policy in the UK. Second, the USA raised concerns that proprietary nuclear technology would be compromised under Cold War conditions of military secrecy, and under so under the 1958 USA–UK agreement the disposal programme was deferred, though concerns about this waste stream also increased pressure on the need for a solution to the ILW/LLW waste disposal route, and the political rhetoric at the time increasingly favoured a merging with the on-land deep geological disposal solution for civilian wastes. In 1998 following direction from the Secretary of State, the Ministry of Defence (MOD) revisited the issue, and led the Interim Storage of Laid-Up Submarines (ISOLUS) project for DDLP submarines. Under ISOLUS, nuclear submarines are currently stored afloat for at least 30 years to allow the radiation levels within the reactor compartment to decay prior to dismantling, and hence protecting worker safety and the quantity of ILW produced through decommissioning. At present there are 12 decommissioned submarines in afloat storage, and it is expected that the UK will have 27 decommissioned nuclear submarines awaiting final disposal by 2030.

With broader shifts within the deliberative democratic governance of radioactive wastes as discussed in later chapters, the MOD held two public consultations in 2001 and 2003 regarding the ISOLUS project. The Front End

Consultations (FEC) involved public and stakeholder engagement through a series of discussion groups held at a variety of locations both near to, and distant from, existing sites of nuclear and/or submarine activities; stakeholder workshops with key industry and policy actors in London, Plymouth, Manchester and Edinburgh, and a citizens' panel involving 12 members of the public from different occupational backgrounds, who met together for four days over two weekends, to examine the issue, become informed, question expert witnesses and produce a report identifying their key concerns. The report gave 65 recommendations covering a wide range of topics, including: influences and responsibilities; the role of the private sector; links to future submarine programmes; development of trust and understanding; risk management; concern for future generations, public consultation measures, institutional trust, technical and siting options and independent scrutiny of MOD practices. In practical terms, notable issues included a desire for desisting with the afloat storage programme, pursuit of interim on-land storage, and final disposal in an ILW long-term management facility (CSEC, 2001; Clark, 2004). The report was instrumental in shaping the final disposal policy for nuclear submarines in line with the Managing Radioactive Waste Safely Programme, whereby wastes are finally disposed of on land. Thus, military decommissioning became more dependent upon a civil radioactive waste disposal policy, dovetailing policy on the two issues.

The four-site saga – rescaling radioactive waste decisions

Growing pressures on the waste stream in the mid-1980s due to rapidly filling LLW trenches at Drigg, the curtailing of sea disposal for ILW, the prospect of further nuclear power expansion and military technology decommissioning joining civilian waste streams, combined with the failure of the Billingham proposal necessitated a new and increasingly urgent siting process. The strategy of shallow disposal of LLW and short-lived ILW was, at the time, considered the 'Best Practicable Environmental Option' in a report published in 1986 for the Department of Environment and Transport (Department of the Environment and Transport, 1986). As such, Nirex announced four sites for such a near surface storage facility. These were Killingholme and Fulbeck in Lincolnshire, Bradwell in Essex and Elstow in Bedfordshire. Government announced that only LLW could be stored in this form of near-surface facility, and there remained no official policy for the management of long-lived ILW and HLW. In light of the problems experienced in the 1970s for technical specialists to gain access to selected locations for site investigation, Parliament granted Special Development Orders (SDOs), which permitted survey engineers to gain access unimpeded by local councils. However, yet again, a highly committed and mobilised array of opposition groups emerged across the selected sites. An umbrella social movement organisation was formed: 'Britons Opposed to Nuclear Dumping' (BOND). BOND coordinated the actions of regional social movements in Bedfordshire, Lincolnshire, Humberside and Essex. Of perhaps greater significance was the formation of the Councils Coalition of Bedfordshire,

Lincolnshire and Humberside County Councils in opposition to the proposals. What effectively emerged was a powerful advocacy coalition of technological opposition, whereby:

> People from a variety of positions (elected and agency officials, interest group leaders, researchers) who share a particular belief system and who show a non-trivial degree of coordinated activity over time.
>
> (Sabatier, 1987)

This drawing together of similar political motivations and beliefs between social movements and local government officials was a powerful form of protest at the time. The strength of this advocacy coalition lay in its coordination across regional boundaries in opposing the technocratic authority of Nirex. We can understand this strategy in terms of Cox's (1998a, 1998b) conceptualisation of *scale* within local politics. Cox examines scale as a series of *spaces of engagement* grounded in networks of interaction. This is contrasted with *spaces of dependence* – broadly fixed, localised and geographically situated arenas within which individuals become embedded in socio-economic and/or (in this case) environmental interests. Spaces of engagement are sets of relations that extend into and beyond spaces of dependence as a means to construct relations: networks of association, exchange, and politics within 'broad fields of events and forces' (Cox, 1998b), that are relational and contingent upon the particular networks and associations in any given instance (see also Jones, 1998). For my purpose here, Cox's model can be used to explain the spatiality of the emergence of this advocacy coalition across geographically distinct political boundaries. The contingency of scale is the important facet – the idea that this coalition can effectively 'jump scales', shifting the nature of the political dialogue away from isolated site communities towards national level policy-making on waste, and the legitimacy of Nirex as a political institution. Thus, the advocacy coalition engaged in a political strategy of shifting between spaces and scales of engagement beyond the spaces of dependence defined by purely regional geographic siting practices.

In this case it was clear that the views of the local authorities in areas selected for waste disposal had little influence upon the decision-making process under the scalar relations defined by Nirex's siting process (Blowers & Lowry, 1987). Kemp (1990) argues that Nirex perhaps anticipated strong local authority opposition to their proposals, and thus neglected to nurture good relations with them prior to siting announcements in 1987. This approach inevitably damaged trust relationships, stimulating non-cooperation among the local councillors and officials. Moreover, the lack of adequate community consultation measures or effective means for citizen-centred decision-making control stimulated a shift towards what Chilvers (2010) terms *uninvited* forms of engagement: specifically pushing citizens into direct action and vocal social movements of opposition. The advocacy coalition between these groups was thus held together by a sense of common threat from Nirex, to create the 'battle of the dumps'

(Blowers, Lowry, & Solomon, 1991), and by jumping scales, the coalition became spatially coordinated across multiple spaces of dependence.

In practical terms, the battle of the dumps involved great animosity and direct protest action. For example, at the point when test borehole drilling was due to start at three of the sites in August 1986, campaigners occupied the sites. They formed human barricades that succeeded in preventing contractors from gaining access. As in the previous decade, contractors only gained access to the sites by use of court injunctions supported by a heavy police presence. This type of uninvited engagement is a good example of Cox's (1998b) concept of a 'jumping of scales' strategy. The coalition of local opposition movements coordinated across all four nuclear waste site regions with support from opposing councils, re-scaled the decision process – redefining the political boundaries that Nirex used to limit opposition (within spaces of dependence defined by clear geographical boundaries – i.e. the four sites) by creating a new space of collective engagement with Nirex across these spaces of dependence (a coalition under an umbrella opposition movement with coordinated local council support). Ultimately this proved to be a highly effective strategy of opposition. Given the growing public controversy in national news media over radioactive waste siting that emerged in response to the battle of the dumps, in 1986 the government changed tack again. They announced that in response to the views expressed by the House of Commons' Environment Committee and by the four communities around the potential near-surface disposal sites, 'a near-surface site should only be used for what is broadly described as low-level wastes' (DoE, 1986; Nirex, 2005b). Government then urgently called for the development of a deep disposal facility to deal with both the short-lived and long-lived ILW that remained in storage, awaiting disposal.

The shift in policy was also short lived, however, as in 1987 the government announced that policy would change direction again. ILW and HLW, it was decided, should be disposed of together deep underground in a mined GDF. The near-surface disposal facility in its later stages of development was denied planning permission by then Secretary of State Nicholas Ridley on 1 May 1987, just prior to the General Election; and so the four original selected sites for near-surface disposal were promptly abandoned, bringing the so-called four-site saga to a close (Kemp & O'Riordan, 1988; Berkhout, 1991; Kemp, 1992). Once again the pattern of site selection through technical criteria, the announcement to local authorities and the inevitable backlash against proposals emerged.

The 'four-site saga' or the 'battle of the dumps' followed what we now understand to be the Decide–Announce–Defend structure of site selection (see Susskind, 1985 in particular); whereby the decision on where to site the waste comes first, information is then released to the affected citizenry and local authorities. They, in turn, mobilise and attempt to obstruct or reverse the decision, with the whole process damaging citizen–state and citizen–scientist relationships along the way. What is striking about the situation in the mid-1980s is that Nirex followed a pattern of decision-making which was effectively identical to the failed siting processes in the previous decade. Nirex had failed to undergo any kind of reflexive institutional learning on the processes of site identification, information exchange or citizen engagement up to this point. Once the proposals for the four sites were dropped, Nirex released publications detailing how they had arrived at their selected locations. Openshaw et al. (1989) assert, however, that this was simply a post hoc justification for Nirex's actions, as these publications were not in full use during the selection of what could be termed the 'round-one' or the 'long-list' site selection process for a geological disposal facility. Government (and to an extent Nirex) began to recognise at the end of the four-site saga that this approach was simply drawing animosity from affected citizens, deepening the distrust of Nirex and undermining the legitimacy of government's waste management policy strategy, and the nuclear enterprise itself. A new approach to the *decision*-part of the siting process needed to be implemented. This was spurred, for the most part, by the findings of a House of Commons Select Committee on the Environment chaired by Sir Hugh Rossi. The report established that *transparency* should be a key component of effective future radioactive waste siting processes. This transparency principally related to the information given to potential host communities, clarity over the roles of planning inquiry and simplification of the regulatory regime for radioactive wastes. The government responded to the findings in a White Paper (DoE, 1986) stating:

> Any planning application (for a radioactive waste management facility) will be considered at a Public Inquiry, to which Nirex will be required to submit an environmental impact assessment in which the comparative merits of the proposed site, and those rejected, must be set out. This process will *allow the public to be involved in the site selection process* [my emphasis]....
> The Government will, equally, expect the industry to pursue a policy of openness and consultation ... Nirex have made it clear from the outset that they will make available the data gathered from the geological investigation of the four sites, which will enable its validity to be checked independently. They will also want to involve the public as fully as is practicable in their further work.

It was noted by commentators on the siting process from affected communities in Sellafield that this new policy approach, when combined with the 1984 Green Book on radioactive material regulation, provided a clear direction that assured 'proper consultation' as an integral aspect of subsequent siting processes, and so new optimism emerged in nuclear communities that adequate community legitimacy in siting would be a fundamental part of this new direction (Hetherington, 1998).

'The Way Forward'

After the policy failure of the four-site saga, combined with critique from the House of Lords Select Committee on the Environment and the subsequent Government White Paper criticising Nirex's approach, Nirex then embarked upon a new, more consultative approach to the siting process for LLW and ILW. We see therefore an incremental move away from technocracy towards a partic-ipatory–deliberative model of decision-making. Secretary of the Environment Nicholas Ridley MP gave a speech on 1 May 1987 that catalysed another incre-mental change in policy direction. He announced acceptance of Nirex's conclu-sions that disposal of low-level radioactive waste (LLW) in a multi-purpose underground repository (i.e. LLW disposal alongside ILW) would be preferable on economic grounds to near-surface disposal of LLW, thereby ending the investigations at Bradwell, Elstow, Fulbeck and Killingholme for a near-surface LLW repository. Ridley also explained that Nirex should, therefore, concentrate on identifying a 'suitable location for a deep multipurpose facility' for both ILW and LLW as the main priority (Hansard, 1987; Nirex, 2005b). The technology was consolidating – a bigger all-purpose repository was now the policy strategy. Ridley envisioned that this would require more community involvement as a salve to this new larger-scale and higher-risk project.

This ultimately meant another change in RWM policy and a new siting process. In response to the broader changing of the political platform on waste towards deep geological disposal, in September 1987, British Nuclear Fuels (BNFL) announced that it would start its own consultation process in the area around the Sellafield site on the issue of a deep geological repository. It began by initiating discussions with local authorities and certain community groups on the issue of preliminary investigation for site suitability for a GDF. BNFL wanted to locate the facility in a layer of anhydrite offshore that was thought to be accessible through an access tunnel from the Sellafield works. BNFL worked with the British Geological Survey (BGS), to conducted geophysical surveys and develop plans for an exploratory borehole (Nirex, 2005b). Nirex, however, redirected this action. Through the Nirex Board it agreed with BNFL-appointed directors that Nirex would be responsible for site investigations around Sell-afield, folding this local proposal into a broader national framework for site selection (and consistent with its desire for a 'more rational' approach to site selection). The data and plans that BNFL had obtained then subsequently became available to Nirex in the next phase of site selection.

In the early 2000s, Nirex undertook some social scientific work (see for example Nirex, 2004), including studies using qualitative interviews with parti-cipants in the ensuing process of selecting a potential deep disposal site. They found that in the 1980s the earlier setbacks of the 1970s and the experience of mass organised public opposition and loss of trust following both the failed Billingham proposal and the sites investigated for near-surface disposal in the four-site saga had deeply influenced Nirex's approach in two ways. First, Nirex had wanted to have a better understanding of public perception of, and attitudes towards, radioactive waste management in a general sense. Second, Nirex wanted to 'adopt a more rational approach to site selection, following more rig-orously the available, recommended best practice' (Nirex, 2005b). As Nirex began another siting process, it claims in the 2005 report that it had learnt some lessons about social engagement from the four-site saga and were keen to implement new forms of decision-making process. It states that the new process aimed to be less reliant upon desk-based evaluation of suitable sites using technical and geological criteria and more upon public perceptions of the organisation and the risks involved, whilst trying to design mechanisms that could choose between sites holistically, without showing apparent bias or coercion.

To this end, in November 1987, Nirex began the new national-level site selection process with the publication of a consultation document called 'The Way Forward' (TWF). This initiated a six-month consultation process during which a range of stakeholders including publics were invited to choose the 'best option' for dealing with LLW and ILW. Around 50,000 copies of the discussion document and the shorter summary document were distributed to a range of stakeholder organisations,[3] alongside broader discussion on television and radio on deep disposal concepts stimulated by a series of briefing seminars held by Nirex at sites around the country (principally for professional stakeholders directly affected by or interested in siting outcomes – what Nirex termed 'interested parties', such as environmental NGOs, local pressure group organisations, industry bodies and trades unions). Kemp (1990) notes that by inviting comment on these proposals, Nirex aimed to promote public understanding of the issues involved and to provide some feedback in a consultative manner to assist Nirex in developing more publicly acceptable proposals throughout their site selection process. Nirex's style was to keep everything relatively generic, in the sense that TWF and the associated briefings didn't mention specific sites or regions, though was informed by indication of 'areas of search' (Nirex, 2005b).

The multi-attribute decision analysis for site selection 1987–1991

In parallel to the public consultation exercises, Nirex based the process of siting upon guidelines for deep geological disposal established by the IAEA. Best practice was defined by the IAEA as site selection through three successive stages: *regional evaluation* (examining favourable characteristics for a repository), followed by *site identification* (naming candidate sites for comparative evaluation and physical exploration to confirm their suitability, such as by drilling boreholes) and then *site confirmation* (where a location is finally selected). The criteria for each stage included geological, ecological and societal considerations; examined in a sequential pattern from generic to specific assessments. Geological assessment and repository design operate concurrently and in connection with one another – in essence so that engineered barriers for radionuclides could operate within the host rock's geology and hydro-geochemistry (International Atomic Energy Agency, 1983). The geological criteria were principally based upon safety parameters including long groundwater return times, a predictable flow regime and slow rates of water movement to minimise the risks of radionuclides returning to the surface after a repository is sealed.

In 1988, Nirex moved through an internal selection exercise informed by multi-attribute decision analysis (MADA) techniques with the intention to narrow down the site selection criteria from a long list selected from broad areas of geologically suitable land (representing over 30 per cent of the landmass). The site selection process for deep geological followed the IAEA pattern, as Nirex began with initial regional evaluation based primarily upon geological criteria to the identification of 537 possible locations. The number of potential sites was then reduced using various selection criteria based on geological as well as non-geological criteria (such as planning considerations), moving sequentially down to 204, 165 and finally a shortlist of 10 (and 2 generic offshore) sites (Nirex, 2005b). MADA is unusual in that it is both an approach and a set of techniques, with the goal of providing an overall ordering of options, from the most preferred to the least preferred option. The options may differ in the extent to which they achieve several objectives, with no single option standing out as the best to achieve all objectives (Tompkins, 2000; Dodgson, Spackman, Pearman, & Phillips, 2001). In this case, the MADA of potential disposal facility sites was assessed on four primary branches of attributes (Nirex, 1989):

• Safety – conventional and radiological safety for both operational and 'post-closure periods' (once the repository has been sealed) of a disposal facility.
• Robustness – sustainability and verifiability of performance ratings in light of uncertainties, including geological predictability.
• Cost – capital and operating costs.
• Socio-economic and environmental impact – e.g. proximity to people, nature conservation, natural resources, transport, noise and visual impact.

The first phase of the siting process involved a regional evaluation of the geological make-up of potential sites. This contrasts with the experience in Sweden, mentioned in Chapter 1, where proving the safety of the engineered barrier for different geological contexts was the 'lead' to the process. Here geology 'led' the process. The design for the RWM system was based upon the natural safety barrier of geological formation, complemented and augmented by an engineered system designed to provide physical and chemical containment of the wastes. One of the key planning considerations was that Nirex did not have compulsory purchase powers to enable it to acquire a site for the development of a disposal facility through purely legal means. In light of this, Nirex primarily examined sites owned by the government or by Nirex's nuclear industry shareholders following a review process with input from the British Geological Survey (BGS).

The outcome of the MADA exercise was that where post-closure safety requirements were considered to be met then this attribute did not discriminate between the sites, hence cost emerged as the major discriminating factor between options (Nirex, 2005b). A series of 'weightings' were applied to these attributes, following 'sensitivity tests'. Consequently, an area known as the Borrowdale Volcanic Group (BVG), near to Sellafield ranked highly, as the costs associated with transporting wastes and the greater level of safety due to reduced transportation of wastes (most of which was stored at Sellafield) was judged to offset any greater margin of post-closure safety that might be achieved elsewhere (ibid.). It was primarily due to the MADA assessment that Nirex opted for the West Cumbrian region as the focus for further investigations. Nirex's Science Programme aimed to assess the suitability or otherwise of this location as the host for a geological disposal facility. Such an assessment included the requirement to develop an understanding of the physical characteristics of the area. This investigation of the geological structure was then added as a component to the multi-disciplinary MADA characterisation of the site (Nirex, 1997).

The political legitimacy of site selection 1987–1991

In some respects, The Way Forward represented an upstream consultation process on technology options rather than siting per se,[4] as consultation was sought on a range of alternative geological conditions for repository construction that would house multiple types of waste. However, despite consultative elements, it was not deemed to be satisfactorily *participatory* by Nirex's own admission, and failed to gain the political legitimacy needed for widespread stakeholder support of proposals. As Simmons and Bickerstaff (2006) note, the consultation responses to The Way Forward showed no overall consensus favouring any particular engineering approach or location, though they did highlight concerns about the retrievability of wastes from a deep waste repository in the post-closure period, whilst highlighting a link between geographical location of waste and public acceptance: locations with existing nuclear facilities were the only areas in which Nirex's proposals drew a measure of local support. Yet, respondents were worried about the potential stigmatising effects created by the presence of these technologies in the host communities, in a manner that mirrored the problems of the four-site saga. In addition, despite its broadly consultative approach, the technocratic design of the overall siting process was highly criticised by anti-nuclear groups, environmental NGOs and local authorities in Cumbria. First, criticism was levelled at the way in which consultation took place after the deep disposal option had been agreed by Nirex and the government, exemplifying a decision-making process that lacked transparency, and was conducted by an organisation that inspired intense public distrust (Kemp, 1990). Second, as Nirex admitted later, the underlying MADA process for decision-making lacked robust political legitimacy:

> Nirex believed that the process used (involving MADA) was technically sound, but it was conducted in secret and did not involve stakeholders, therefore, it was not a legitimate process.
>
> (Nirex, 2005a, p. 3)

MADA offers a powerful set of decision-support tools for holistically assessing complex social, technical, cost and environmental factors. The use of MADA methodologies was therefore congruent with Nirex's aim for rational decision-making that avoided bias or convenience for site selection as had been done in the 1970s and early 1980s with the four-site saga. Yet as Stirling (1996) argued in evidence submitted to the Planning Inquiry into the eventual Sellafield Rock Characterisation Proposal Facility application, effective use of MADA techniques requires the observance of a number of principles in order for it to be effective. Users must draw an explicit distinction between 'performance scores', which are technically derived, and 'importance weightings', which are more subjective, based upon expert opinion. MADA users must also publish the criteria for the scope for the analysis and invite outside stakeholders to contribute (thus incorporating a wider range of competing and contrasting perspectives). They must provide systematic sensitivity testing of the underlying assumptions and value judgements in the selection of data for inclusion, the optimisation of choice of options under each perspective and the explicit presentation of the data, underlying assumptions and methodologies deployed. Finally, accessible procedures for critical evaluation and peer review beyond the narrow scientific reviews of other technical experts (i.e. review by lay citizens) must also be provided. Stirling's (1996) robust critique of the Nirex MADA process concluded that it was largely deficient in most (if not all) of these aspects, fundamentally undermining both political and technical legitimacy of the process, contrary to Nirex's position.

More broadly, the MADA was criticised as running contrary to the spirit of the White Paper that emphasised transparency, accountability and local consultation because the underlying data were not made publicly available at the time (Hetherington, 1998; Western, 1998). Despite repeated requests for the details of the MADA process, these were for a long time immune to requests for disclosure in line with government policy. In 2005, however, the Freedom of Information Act came into force, effectively forcing Nirex to release the information into the public domain. The selection criteria for the site listing process were eventually released following a stakeholder consultation meeting in Manchester on 26 May 2005 for the 'old site list' to be put out into the public domain. (Nirex, 2005b provides a detailed summary discussion of the concepts used in the MADA process.) This was described as a 'managed release', intended, in the new spirit of transparency to show how the process used to operate, and how (under the government's Managing Radioactive Waste Safely programme) Nirex had become far more open and accountable than in the bad old days of the late 1980s and early 1990s. Nirex clearly stated that 'This historic list will not form the starting point of any future site selection process' (Nirex, 2005a), and then managing director of Nirex Chris Murray justified the release in 2005 stating (Nirex, 2005a):

> Radioactive waste exists and needs to be dealt with whether or not there is any programme of new build in the UK. Dealing with the waste is as much an ethical and social issue as a scientific and technical one. This is the key lesson we have learned from the past. Openness and transparency must underpin everything that is done in this area. We hope that the publication of the list, following consultation with our stakeholders, will help to move the debate away from past attempts to tackle this issue and on to the new

process, led by the Committee on Radioactive Waste Management (CoRWM), in which we would encourage everyone to get involved. Many things have changed since this old list was drawn up, but what has not changed is that the waste still exists and needs to be dealt with in a safe, environmentally sound and publicly acceptable way for the long-term. Responsibility lies with this generation to ensure this is done.

Greenpeace did note, however, that a BGS geologist in the meeting had stated that though a search for a deep disposal site for radioactive waste may use different criteria under the new decision-making process, many of the original sites on the list of 12 were likely to appear on any new list, along with sites on the list of 537, which were eliminated later in the process (Greenpeace, 2005). Nirex similarly admitted that 'the geology in the UK has not changed, so sites that were considered to be potentially suitable previously on geological grounds could be considered suitable in a future site selection process' (Nirex, 2005b). In 2005, therefore, there were concerns raised over the lock-in of the site selection process to follow similarly lines to that initiated in 1987–1991, due to the geological criteria necessary for safe repository design.

It must also be noted that within the MADA the options presented in The Way Forward were limited to some form of burial, either beneath the seabed via some kind of offshore platform; beneath the seabed accessed from land; or beneath UK land. Long-term storage of existing nuclear waste above ground and at the site of production, was not included as one of the consultation options in the original document. In this sense, The Way Forward was not a true 'upstream' consultation process, but rather a consultation upon a predefined set of technical options for a geological disposal strategy that Nirex had already decided upon, based upon the prevailing scientific wisdom that a geological option represented the state of the art solution. Because all of the consulted upon options involved some form of geological disposal solution, the opportunities for the stakeholder consultees to open up the discussion beyond the policy platform of deep geological disposal to a full participatory technology assessment were entirely curtailed, and this was one of the reasons for the lack of political legitimacy and ultimate failure of this round of siting. (Discussion of this issue can be found in Blowers & Lowry, 1987; Openshaw et al., 1989; Cotton, 2014; Kemp, 1990).

The turn to Caithness and Sellafield

In the end, The Way Forward led Nirex to recommend that it would carry out geological investigations at Dounreay (in Caithness, Scotland) and around Sellafield (in Cumbria) in advance of an application for planning permission for a combined ILW/LLW deep geological repository. In line with government policy of the time, Nirex did not announce any of the other sites that were considered, so this decision to focus on these two locations was (at the time) immune to public scrutiny.[5] Nirex later suggested that the rationale for Sellafield and

Dounreay was based upon the principle that these were existing 'nuclear communities' that hosted civilian power-related facilities and existing on-site waste stores and hence this would foster a degree of in-built acceptance within the community (Nirex, 2005b). In essence Nirex was implicitly utilising the nuclear oasis effect in their decision-making (Blowers, 2003): relying upon the culturally embedded nature of nuclear technology within those communities as a means to alleviate social movements of opposition and hence smooth the siting process for technical authorities, due to the ongoing economic peripheralisation and political marginalisation occurring within those communities. Such factors serve to pressure citizens into adopting further reliance on nuclear-related activities (in this case shifting from production and reprocessing to long-term waste stewardship) – and, consequently, deepen conditions of environmental injustice. What was clear, and indeed somewhat surprising in hindsight, was that this recommendation and the underlying siting rationale was accepted not only by the Secretary of State for the Environment which had called for greater transparency and public legitimacy in the previous White Paper (see Hansard, 1989); but also by RWMAC the independent advisory committee (Radioactive Waste Management Advisory Committee, 1989).

Nirex proceeded with the investigation of the two sites, later publishing preliminary site investigation reports. It was notable that Caithness District Council adopted a much different approach to this new siting process that when applications for test drilling in Altnabreac were proposed in 1978. This time, in November 1989 the council organised a local referendum on the application, which revealed a 74 per cent voter opposition to Nirex's plans. Then MP for Banff and Buchan, Alex Salmond criticised the move to test drilling in the Caithness region under the Secretary of State's consent, stating (Hansard, 1990):

> In granting planning permission to Nirex, the Government are overriding not only the decision of the elected representatives of Highland region but also the overwhelming vote against Nirex by the people of Caithness in the referendum last November. At that time, despite the attempt to buy votes with the deep pockets of Nirex and the claims that Caithness would be a soft touch for dumping, the people said no to Nirex by a majority of 3:1.
>
> At that time, even Nirex claimed that the views of the people would be taken into account along with other factors when the Secretary of State reached his decision. In fact, today, neither in the brief statement from the Scottish Office nor in the letter to the Nirex lawyers, is there any mention of the views of the people of Caithness. They have been dismissed as irrelevant to the consideration of the planning commission. Given that the only reason Nirex is investigating Caithness is that it claimed public support for its plans, this is a display of breath-taking hypocrisy.
>
> The Secretary of State may claim the fiction that test drilling for nuclear dumping is a separate matter from dumping itself, but nobody in Scotland is likely to be fooled. The Government and Nirex are lining Scotland up to

be Europe's No. 1 dumping ground for nuclear waste. As *Spitting Image* once noted, the Tory party seems to envisage an energy exchange between Scotland and England: we give England our oil and gas and England gives us its nuclear waste.

The opposition in Parliament is indicative of an emergent political discourse of inter-regional environmental justice between Scotland and England. Concepts of distributive injustice are mobilised in this political discourse. These have ramifications beyond the local community–national nuclear industry authority relationships that emerged in the four-site saga. With Salmond's criticism of the government's strategy for waste siting without community consent, it became an issue of Scottish nationalism. What we see is that Scottish energy politics and associated social opposition to waste *imposition* in Scotland evidently carried some weight with Nirex, as once the test drilling programme in both Caithness and Sellafield was complete, it announced in July 1991 that its preferred site was going to be near Sellafield, in part due to the intensification of anti-nuclear (specifically anti-Nirex) protest and MP lobbying in the Caithness region.

It is worth mentioning that energy has long been a contentious issue between Scotland and England. England, with its much larger population and greater urban density is a net energy consumer of Scottish electricity. In the quote above, electricity production and associated generation and waste technologies were construed in Scottish nationalist political discourse as inherently unjust – a factor that continues to shape Scottish–English energy politics. Indeed it is noteworthy that these energy justice debates have intensified in recent years, specifically around issues of oil and gas ownership in the run up to the Scottish Independence referendum (Armstrong & Ebell, 2014); the development of offshore wind development and potential nuclear new build and associated electricity transmission systems[6] (and waste which, as a devolved administration issue is managed differently in Scotland than England and Wales).

The Rock Characterisation Facility

Following the 1991 announcement, Nirex stated that it would aim for submission of a planning application for a geological disposal facility in the following year. Originally the intention was to submit a planning application in October 1992 though Nirex's announcement was delayed to 1993, and the application was scaled back to the development of a Rock Characterisation Facility (hereafter, RCF – a type of laboratory for testing the host rock for its suitability to house an engineered disposal facility),[7] rather than a complete repository proposal. A full planning application for the latter submitted by 1998 with an original hope that the disposal facility would be operational by the year 2007. However, due to ensuing delays based upon technical criteria, funding and transparency issues (discussed below), it then took until late in 1994 for Nirex to submit a planning application for the RCF. The RCF planning application was to build on land at Longlands Farm, Gosforth, in Cumbria – a site close to the Sellafield works and just outside the Lake District National Park boundary. The area was described in the inspector's report thus: 'The site lies in the undulating coastal belt between the Sea and the foothills of the Lake District' (McDonald, 1996). The RCF would have involved sinking two shafts to depths of up to 1020 m and opening out galleries in the Borrowdale Volcanic Group of rocks. The basis of this laboratory was to conduct extensive testing of the host rock, and the formation of engineered barriers for surface-level radiation protection.

The application, however, met with significant planning delays. First, there were delays in gaining approvals to drill boreholes for testing. The original target date for disposal facility operation was stated to be 2010, but this date was beginning to slip. Of great political significance was the action of Cumbria County Council in rejecting the proposal, which was later called in for public inquiry in 1995 under Section 78 of the Town & Country Planning Act 1990. The public inquiry lasted for 66 days over a period of five months to 1 February 1996. It directly pitted Nirex's legal counsel and technical expertise against local opponents and national environmental non-governmental organisations (namely Cumbria County Council, Friends of the Earth, Greenpeace and local opposition groups including Cumbrians Opposed to a Radioactive Environment, CORE). Nirex had an alleged budget of £10 million to prepare its case, with a much smaller budget for the opposing side. The inquiry itself had two components: the first examined issues of surface planning, and the second examined the science and policy issues. It was recognised that geology, hydrogeology, geophysics and engineering were the areas of expertise and technical knowledge upon which the debate would be won or lost, and so both sides gathered technical expertise from these field to aid them in the case (Haszeldine & Smythe, 1997).

Following the public inquiry, then Secretary of State for the Environment, John Gummer MP completed his consideration of the inspector's report into the RCF planning. The report recommended the refusal of the planning application based primarily upon planning matters that adversely affected the local environment and particular planning matters arising from the RCF design and implementation (SCST, 1999). The eventual outcome was, that on 17 March 1997, just prior to a general election, Gummer followed the recommendations and rejected Nirex's planning application, ending Nirex's Sellafield investigations. The unsuitability of the RCF site was based mostly on scientific and technical criteria, of which geology was the main concern. Nirex's proposal has been subject to continued academic debate over whether the BVG was a suitable candidate for a geological disposal facility based upon the host geology, hydrology and hydro-geochemistry, following extensive surveying both before and after the RCF proposal was submitted. For a full scientific assessment of the issues emerging in the assessment report it is worth examining the original sources and associated academic evaluation (Bath, McCartney, Richards, Metcalfe, & Crawford, 1996; Black & Brightman, 1996; Haszeldine & Smythe, 1997). For a brief overview, the main technical and environmental issues were:

- The adverse visual impact of the above ground RCF buildings and spoil heaps.
- Criticisms of road traffic and parking plans.
- Possible harm to local ecology including the habitat of a badger clan.
- Scientific uncertainty about the hydro-geology of the site. Of particular concern was the possibility of disturbing the rock and groundwater conditions by sinking the shaft for the RCF.
- The location of the RCF had not been shown to be the best one from the point of view of the location of the eventual repository facility, and concerns were raised that the 'potential repository zone' might be damaged by constructing the RCF.
- The technical assessor in the inquiry was of the view that the site was more geologically and hydro-geologically complex than would be expected of a choice based principally on scientific and technical grounds.

As a matter of political analysis, of greater consideration are the processes through which the science was utilised in decision-making. David Smythe, emeritus professor of geophysics was originally a consultant for Nirex, but worked to challenge the apparent consensus within technical communities that Sellafield was a suitable location for waste siting. The planning inquiry into the Sellafield site highlighted problems with the site selection process and Nirex's failure to optimise radiological protection using best available techniques. Smythe conducted 3D seismic surveys for Nirex in 1994. He was quoted in the *Observer* newspaper as being 'horrified' by what his study had revealed, describing the action to site waste in the region as 'irresponsible and dangerous', as 'It [the Borrowdale Volcanic Group] is manifestly unsuitable … Studies suggest there could be leaks in as little as 50 years, when the material needs to be held for between 100,000 and 1m years' (cited in Doward, 2014). Haszeldine and Smythe raised concerns that the BVG in the region where the waste was to be sited was highly fractured by previous seismic activity; and this would be further exacerbated by the drilling of boreholes and the construction of an eventual GDF. The net impact of this analysis was that they insisted the rock layer provided an insufficient geological barrier to water intrusion into a repository over the 100,000 plus year time frame necessary for safe storage of radionuclides to prevent their return to the surface. As they later concluded after the failure of the RCF proposal:

> Sellafield was always a long shot. The site was chosen for non-scientific reasons, in a decision-making process which [sic] concealed its true geological problems. Results of initial drilling were ignored by the Nirex management, in a culture of speed and over-optimism.
>
> (Haszeldine & Smythe, 1997)

Moreover, they argued that Nirex sought to conceal the area's true geological problems, leading them to conclude that the planning inspector's comprehensive dismissal of the site would make it hard to return to it in the future.

Simply put, the implications were that Nirex was trying to push the Sellafield site to get a swift resolution to the siting problem, even though the site in question was fundamentally geologically unsuitable; and that Sellafield had been comprehensively 'ruled out' as a suitable site for a geological repository.

Trust in Nirex

Moreover, there was a distinct lack of decision-making transparency in the process of site selection itself and the types of data that were utilised in this assessment process. Even taking aside the concerns about site suitability, the 1997 proposal illustrated the primarily techno-centric nature of the RWM planning process. The criteria used for assessing the suitability of the host site paid little attention to the social and political factors emerging from the communities in and around the Sellafield area. Throughout the site selection process in the 1990s there was continued public opposition from West Cumbrian communities towards the RWM planning process and towards Nirex itself. This key issue had extensive political ramifications for the nuclear industry and the UK Government in settling upon an agreed RWM strategy. As Nirex state:

> This signalled not just the demise of the national policy but also of Nirex. Nirex had been charged with delivering the policy. The policy had failed. So, it followed, Nirex had failed too.
>
> (Nirex, 2006, p. 7)

Opponents of the nuclear industry (and of Nirex itself) argued that the rejection of the RCF and the local opposition were instrumental in the failure to secure planning permission for that site and that this failure effectively amounted to a loss of 15 years of scientific and technical research and £450 million in costs, plus additional cost to the taxpayer in planning inquiry bills. To critics, the failure left the UK without firm plans for the long-term management of intermediate level radioactive waste and caused huge setbacks in the industry (Beveridge & Curtis, 1998). Supporters of nuclear (and indeed Nirex itself), framed the outcome in a more positive light, suggesting that the culmination of factors that led to the rejected proposal in turn provided an opportunity for a fresh start, going back to the beginning, and undertaking a fundamental policy review (CoRWM, 2006, p. 4). Nirex itself suffered as a result of the policy failure – it went from staffing levels of 250, 150, 88 and then 67 employees, and had its budget cut from £50 million to £11 million. However, much of the scientific and technical expertise gained pre-1997 by Nirex (and more recently the NDA's Radioactive Waste Management Directorate and Radioactive Waste Management Ltd) remained transferable to the further development of new RWM strategies, risk and safety assessment models and packaging designs, all of which supported the subsequent policy overhaul that occurred under the incoming Labour Government in 1997.

Conclusions

With the creation of Nirex, the government had only partially fulfilled the promise of the 1976 Flowers Report. Within broader stakeholder networks there had long been calls for the creation of a radioactive waste management organisation that was independent of nuclear industry interests, yet Nirex was built from component elements of the industry itself. It lacked financial independence and yet also lacked the political power for compulsory purchase of land for siting. It had a rather hazy authority on siting issues, reliant upon local government support for its siting processes. However, as the four-site saga shows, Nirex failed to develop the social licence with local authorities that might have assisted them in convincing locally affected site communities to accept waste in their regions.

The turn to the more consultative 'Way Forward' approach to site consultation was perhaps a step in the right direction. It went some way to dispelling the blanket secrecy and cover-up of nuclear industry operations at a time when the Cold War was ending. It showed that Nirex had undergone some incremental policy learning as a result of past failures, and was indicative of a new mood for dialogue. However, it was inadequate as a consultation tool, pre-empting the technical choice of deep geological disposal and providing very limited opportunities for participatory evaluation of alternative options, sites or management processes. As such, this rather piecemeal consultation had the opposite effect to that intended – it exacerbated social opposition due to perceived democratic deficits in the siting process, alongside a tone-deaf approach to understanding the different sort of values embedded in public perceptions of waste technologies. The accompanying MADA tool represented what Nirex termed a 'rational' form of decision-making that emphasised transportation costs and risks as key criteria in the weighting process. As such, Sellafield scored highly in the MADA as it held the bulk quantity of wastes. Yet criticisms of the weighting criteria as based upon subjective judgement rather than scientific analysis undermined the claims of impartial rationality. Indeed, it is clear in hindsight that the rational decision-making was bounded in specific notions of expertise and technical merit rather than objective assessment. Together these two decision-making tools were intended to narrow down the range of geographical options, but were inherently problematic (involved synoptic rationality) and prioritised certain types of input from certain technical specialists and criteria (predominantly technical, economic and risk criteria).

We can see this as *technocratic* decision-making. Such technocracy is inherently procedurally unjust, in the sense that it places limits not only on who can be involved in the decision, but also the types of evidence considered and the access of citizens to information about the proposals. *Engagement* with the decision-making was through 'invited' platforms which constrained the options available. These limited opportunities for citizen-stakeholders to challenge proposals, to question the underlying rationality of the decision, to defend their communities and have access to due process in a public decision-making forum.

Similarly, as Nirex in the end chose two sites, one in England and one in Scotland, they put pressure on cross-border diplomatic relations on similar environmental justice grounds. The notion of energy justice (as a form of distributive justice between beneficiaries and those that bear the burdens and risks) is a recurrent theme, and these emerge again as Nirex settled on the Sellafield site and began to apply for planning permission to pursue its deep geological disposal platform. When this too failed, with the rejection of the 1997 RCF proposal, this catalysed a cultural shift within government. The incoming Environment Secretary for the then Labour Government, headed by John Prescott MP found that the RCF application rejection 'inevitably meant that there was a need for a period of reflection' (cited in Nirex, 2006), and Nirex similarly underwent an internal governance review. The general outcome was an understanding that greater levels of transparency and early involvement of non-nuclear industry actors in the processes of decision-making was necessary to secure a solution that had sufficient political legitimacy to be implemented, and thus stop the cycle of continued policy failure. They learnt that the process of technology policy was fundamentally *inflexible* – it was based upon high stakes decision-making from centralised industry and government authorities, which excluded broader participation in radioactive waste politics. What became clear following the developments of 1997 was that the culmination of failed siting processes since the 1970s required a complete overhaul in the nature of radioactive waste decision-making, taking into account the social, psychological and ethical dimensions of the problem (Atherton & Poole, 2001). In essence improving its decision-making flexibility: creating a new role for philosophical and social scientific expertise in the policy-making process, and much greater opportunities for citizen-stakeholder involvement.

Notes

1 Billingham's current population is 35,765 inhabitants based upon most recent census data.
2 It must be noted that Drigg is currently undergoing a public consultation in the summer of 2015 upon the further expansion of the site through an application led by the site's management company LLW Repository Limited. Steve Hardy (2015) of the Environment Agency's Nuclear Regulation group stated of the expansion plans that:

> LLW Repository Ltd wants to dispose of more radioactive waste at its site and has applied to us for an environmental permit. We will only issue a permit once we're satisfied that further disposals at the site are safe for people and the environment, both now and in the future. We've assessed LLW Repository Ltd's environmental safety case and consider it demonstrates that future waste disposal is safe within the limits we have set. Before we make a final decision, we want to consider the views of local people and other organisations.

3 These stakeholders included statutory consultees, environmental NGOs, political organisations, trades unions, industry associations and local authorities. Further copies were made available to public libraries and free copies were also sent to members of the public on request, following advertisements for the document in the national print media.

4 There is a growing literature on the upstream engagement concept; whereby stake-holders are included in decisions over technology choice prior to actual implementation or design, rather than simply at the point of locating the technology or in the period after implementation impacts have occurred (see Wilsdon & Willis, 2004; Pidgeon & Rogers-Hayden, 2007; Cotton, 2010; Corner, Pidgeon, & Parkhill, 2012 for further discussion).

5 During the later rock characterisation facility proposal inquiry, the proofs of evidence for the selection of these two sites did emerge; specifically that two different sites close to Sellafield were under consideration, alongside sites in Caithness and Dounreay.

6 Of note in relation to energy diplomacy controversies is the installation of cross-border electricity transmission lines. One line runs from the north of Scotland to grid connections in the south of Scotland with the intention of supplying England. This is the so-called Beauly–Denny line project that has been particularly politically controversial (Tobiasson, Beestermöller, & Jamasb, 2015).

7 The application for the RCF was to build (McDonald, 1996):

> Construction of 2 shafts (5 m diameter, not exceeding 1020 m depth), galleries (none exceeding 5 m height and width and 975 m length), exploratory drilling from underground; construction of engineered platform and associated buildings and works for the purpose of carrying out searches and tests of the Borrowdale Volcanic Group (BVG) and overlying geological strata, including use for carrying out scientific investigations, measurements and experiments in and from the said shafts and galleries; storage of topsoil and subsoil, deposit of underground spoil, internal access road, services, landscaping and restoration.

Bibliography

Armstrong, A., & Ebell, M. (2014). Assets and liabilities and Scottish independence. *Oxford Review of Economic Policy*, 30(2), 297–309.

Atherton, E., & Poole, M. (2001). The problem of the UK's radioactive waste: What have we learnt? *Interdisciplinary Science Reviews*, 26, 296–302.

Bath, A. H., McCartney, A. R. A., Richards, H. G., Metcalfe, R., & Crawford, M. B. (1996). Groundwater chemistry in the Sellafield area: A preliminary interpretation. *Quarterly Journal of Engineering Geology and Hydrogeology*, 29(1), 39–57.

Berkhout, F. (1991). *Radioactive waste: Politics and technology*. Abingdon: Routledge.

Beveridge, G., & Curtis, C. (1998). *Radioactive waste disposal – Where do we go from here?* Paper presented at the Nuclear Free Local Authorities Annual Conference, Caernarfon.

Black, J. H., & Brightman, M. A. (1996). Conceptual model of the hydrogeology of Sellafield. *Quarterly Journal of Engineering Geology*, 29(1), 83–93.

Blowers, A. (2003). Inequality and community and the challenge to modernization: Evidence from the nuclear oases. In J. Agyeman (Ed.), *Just sustainabilities: Development in an unequal world* (pp. 64–80). Cambridge MA: MIT Press.

Blowers, A., & Lowry, D. (1987). Out of sight, out of mind: The politics of nuclear waste in the United Kingdom. In A. Blowers, & D. Pepper (Eds.), *Nuclear power in crisis: Politics and planning for the nuclear state* (pp. 129–163). London: Croom Helm.

Blowers, A., Lowry, D., & Solomon, B. D. (1991). *The international politics of nuclear waste*. London: Macmillan.

Chilvers, J. (2010). *Sustainable participation? Mapping out and reflecting on the field of public dialogue on science and technology*. Harwell: Nirex.

Clark, S. M. (2004). Public participation in decisions relating to the environmental management of Ministry of Defence sites. In K. Mahutova, J. J. I. Barich, & R. A.

Kreizenbeck (Eds.), *Defense and the environment: Effective scientific communication* (Vol. 39, pp. 65–70). Dordrecht: Springer Netherlands.

Corner, A., Pidgeon, N., & Parkhill, K. (2012). Perceptions of geoengineering: Public attitudes, stakeholder perspectives, and the challenge of 'upstream' engagement. *Wiley Interdisciplinary Reviews: Climate Change, 3*(5), 451–466.

CoRWM. (2006). *Managing our radioactive waste safely: CoRWM's recommendations to government*. London: Department for Environment Food and Rural Affairs and the Committee on Radioactive Waste Management.

Cotton, M. (2010). Discourse, upstream public engagement and the governance of human life extension research. *Poiesis & Praxis, 7*(1–2), 135–150.

Cotton, M. (2014). *Ethics and technology assessment: A participatory approach*. Berlin: Springer-Verlag.

Cox, K. R. (1998a). Representation and power in the politics of scale. *Political Geography, 17*(1), 41–44.

Cox, K. R. (1998b). Spaces of dependence, spaces of engagement and the politics of scale, or: Looking for local politics. *Political Geography, 17*(1), 1–23.

Coyle, A., Grimwood, P. D., & Paul, W. J. (1997). Waste acceptance policy and operational developments at the UK's Drigg LLW disposal site. *Planning and Operation of Low Level Waste Disposal Facilities: Proceedings of a Symposium, Vienna, 17–21 June 1996* (pp. 339–351). Vienna: International Atomic Energy Agency.

CSEC. (2001). *Project ISOLUS front end consultation: Final report*. Lancaster: University of Lancaster.

Department of the Environment and Transport. (1986). *Assessment of best practicable environmental options (BPEOs) for management of low and intermediate-level solid radioactive wastes*. London: Department of the Environment and Transport.

Dodgson, J., Spackman, M., Pearman, A., Phillips, L. (2001). *DTLR multi-criteria analysis manual*. London: Department of Transport, London and the Regions.

DoE. (1982). *Radioactive waste management*. Cmnd 8607. London: Department of the Environment.

DoE. (1986). *Radioactive waste: The government's response to the Environment Committee's report*. Cmnd 9852. London: Department of the Environment.

Doward, J. (2014, 18 January). Nuclear waste site consultation was rigged to favour Sellafield, say experts. *The Observer*. Retrieved from www.theguardian.com/environment/2014/jan/18/nuclear-waste-consultation-sellafield-radioactive.

Glasson, J. (2005). Better monitoring for better impact management: The local socio-economic impacts of constructing Sizewell B nuclear power station. *Impact Assessment and Project Appraisal, 23*(3), 215–226.

Greenpeace. (2005). *How did the secret Nirex list of potential nuclear waste dump sites come about?* Retrieved from www.greenpeace.org.uk/MultimediaFiles/Live/FullReport/7219.pdf.

Hansard. (1987). Parliamentary statement by the Secretary of State for the Environment, Mr Nicholas Ridley, Vol. 115, HC Deb., 1 May, Col. 504.

Hansard. (1989). Written answer 21 March 1989 from Mr Nicholas Ridley, Secretary of State for the Environment, Vol. 149, HC Deb., 21 March, WA Col. 506.

Hansard. (1990). Nuclear dumping (Dounreay). HC Deb., 15 May, 172, 741–742.

Hardy, S. (2015). *Environment Agency confident nuclear waste plan is 'safe'*. Retrieved from www.itv.com/news/border/story/2015-06-18/consultation-over-plans-to-expand-nuclear-repository/.

Haszeldine, S., & Smythe, D. (1997). Why was Sellafield rejected as a disposal site for radioactive waste? *Geoscientist, 7*(7), 18–20.

Hetherington, J. (1998). Nirex and deep disposal: The Cumbrian experience. In F. Barker (Ed.), *Management of radioactive wastes: Issues for local authorities* (pp. 17–32). London: ICE Publishing.

HMSO. (1995). *Review of radioactive waste management policy: Final conclusions*, Cm 2919. London: Her Majesty's Stationery Office.

Holliday, F. G. T. (2005). The dumping of radioactive waste in the deep ocean: Scientific advice and ideological persuasion. In D. E. Cooper, & J. A. Palmer (Eds.), *The environment in questions* (pp. 51–64). London: Routledge.

International Atomic Energy Agency. (1983). *Disposal of low and intermediate level solid wastes in rock cavities: A guidebook.* Vienna: IAEA Safety Series.

Jones, K. T. (1998). Scale as epistemology. *Political Geography, 17*(1), 25–28. doi: http://dx.doi.org/10.1016/S0962-6298(97)00049-8.

Kemp, R. (1989). *Planning and consultation procedures for low level radioactive waste disposal: A comparative analysis of international experience (1).* Norwich: University of East Anglia.

Kemp, R. (1990). Why not in my backyard? – A radical interpretation of public opposition to the deep disposal of radioactive-waste in the United Kingdom. *Environment and Planning A, 22*(9), 1239–1258.

Kemp, R. (1992). *The politics of radioactive waste disposal.* Manchester: Manchester University Press.

Kemp, R., & O'Riordan, T. (1988). Planning for radioactive waste disposal: Some central considerations. *Land Use Policy, 5,* 37–44.

Layfield, F. (1988). The Sizewell B public inquiry. *Nuclear Energy, 27*(3), 165–169.

McDonald, C. S. (1996). *Inspector's report: Cumbrian County Council appeal by United Kingdom Nirex Limited.* Bristol: File APPIH0900/A194/247019. Retrieved 2 June 2016, from http://davidsmythe.org/nuclear/inspector%27s_report_A.pdf.

Miyasaka, Y. (2003). Trends of radioactive waste management policy and disposal of LLW/ILW in the UK. *Dekomisshoningu Giho, 28,* 10–22.

Nirex. (1989). *Deep repository project: Preliminary environmental and radiological assessment and preliminary safety report (71).* Harwell: Nirex.

Nirex. (1997). *Sellafield geological and hydrogeological investigations: The geological structure of the Sellafield site (S/97/007).* Retrieved from www.nirex.co.uk/educate/343765.pdf.

Nirex. (2004). *The Foundation Report on the Nirex Involvement Program and social science research.* Harwell: Nirex.

Nirex. (2005a). *Historic list of possible locations for a radioactive waste repository, June 2005.* Harwell: Nirex.

Nirex. (2005b). *Review of 1987–1991 site selection for an ILW/LLW repository (477002).* Harwell: Nirex.

Nirex. (2006). *A new way of thinking – Nirex's story: 1997–2005.* Harwell: Nirex.

O'Riordan, T. (1984). The Sizewell B inquiry and a national energy strategy. *Geographical Journal, 150*(2), 171–182.

O'Riordan, T., Kemp, R., & Purdue, M. (1985). How the Sizewell B inquiry is grappling with the concept of acceptable risk. *Journal of Environmental Psychology, 5*(1), 69–85.

O'Riordan, T., Kemp, R., & Purdue, M. (1988). *Sizewell B: An anatomy of the inquiry.* Basingstoke: Macmillan.

Openshaw, S., Carver, S., & Fernie, J. (1989). *Britain's nuclear waste: Safety and siting.* London: Belhaven Press.

Parker, F. L., Kasperson, R. E., Andersson, T. E., & Parker, S. A. (1986). *Technical and socio-political issues in radioactive waste disposal.* Stockholm: Swedish National Board for Spent Nuclear Fuel.

Pidgeon, N., & Rogers-Hayden, T. (2007). Opening up nanotechnology dialogue with the publics: Risk communication or 'upstream engagement'? *Health, Risk & Society, 9*(2), 191–210.

Purdue, M., Kemp, R., & O'Riordan, T. (1984). The context and conduct of the Sizewell B Inquiry. *Energy Policy, 12*(3), 276–282.

Radioactive Waste Management Advisory Committee. (1989). *Tenth Annual Report, Appendix C*. London: Radioactive Waste Management Advisory Committee.

Sabatier, P. A. (1987). Knowledge, policy-oriented learning, and policy change. An advocacy coalition framework. *Science Communication, 8*(4), 649–692.

SCST. (1999). *Management of nuclear waste: Third report*. Retrieved from www.parliament.the-stationery-office.co.uk/pa/ld199899/ldselect/ldsctech/41/4102.htm.

Simmons, P., & Bickerstaff, K. (2006). The participatory turn in UK radioactive waste management policy. In K. Andersson (Ed.), *VALDOR 2006 – Values in decisions on risk conference proceedings* (pp. 530–537). Stockholm: Informationsbolaget Nyberg & Co.

Stirling, A. (1996). On the Nirex MADA [Multi-Attribute Decision Analysis]. Proof of evidence. In R. S. Haszeldine, & D. K. Smythe (Eds.), *Radioactive waste disposal at Sellafield, UK: Site selection, geological and engineering problems*. Glasgow: University of Glasgow.

Susskind, L. E. (1985). The siting puzzle: Balancing economic and environmental gains and losses. *Environmental Impact Assessment Review, 5*(2), 157–163.

Tobiasson, W., Beestermöller, C., & Jamasb, T. (2015). *Public engagement in electricity network development: A case study of the Beauly–Denny Project in Scotland*. Cambridge: Cambridge University Press.

Tompkins, E. L. (2000). *Using stakeholder preferences in multi-attribute decision-making: Elicitation and aggregation issues*. CSERGE working papers, (ECM 03–13). Norwich.

Western, R. (1998). The UK Nuclear waste crisis. In F. Barker (Ed.), *Management of radioactive wastes: Issues for local authorities*. London: ICE Publishing.

Wilsdon, J., & Willis, R. (2004). *See-through science: Why public engagement needs to move upstream*. London: Demos.

5 Health, environmental risks and the social construction of radioactive waste

Introduction

In this chapter, I pause the historical account to consider some of the social and psychological factors that influence citizen–stakeholder engagements with radioactive waste management. With the failure of the 1997 RCF proposal, the resulting shift towards participatory–deliberative dialogue as a decision-making tool meant that the inflexible, centralised and technocratic approach to radioactive waste siting was being replaced with a more 'bottom-up' and 'values-led' approach. In this chapter, I explore some of the different ways in which radioactive wastes are perceived, their risks negotiating, and how the technologies associated with the geological disposal are socially constructed.

The scale of the waste problem

The separation of wastes into different sources, streams, types and volumes, alongside estimations of current wastes and predictions about future wastes, not only presents a set of technical challenges, but also a number of socio-cultural challenges in the process of establishing a coherent picture of the 'seriousness' and scale of the radioactive waste issue to broader civil society. Actors on both the pro- and anti-nuclear sides of the debate have at times sought to assert the discursive dominance of their perspective, appealing to a wider civil society that theirs is the coherent and objective picture of the hazards involved, thus aiming to frame the terms of the debate by presenting the opponent as untrustworthy, fallible or biased in the reporting of the risks. However, the different material streams with their comparative volumes and levels of radioactivity present two contrasting conceptions of the waste problem. This in turn leads to widely differing interpretations between competing representations of the scales of nuclear waste, and the obstacles that it presents to institutions involved in managing these materials. Thus, the volumes of radioactive waste, their relative risk properties and dosage implications are inevitably matters of context and interpretation, and hence can be described as *socially constructed* (see in Bijker, Hughes, & Pinch, 1987 for discussion of the social construction of technologies in this manner), and this is the primary focus of this chapter.

The Nuclear Decommissioning Authority states that the total volume of radioactive waste that exists today or is forecast over the next century or so from existing facilities is about 4.5 million cubic metres. A further 1 million cubic metres of radioactive waste has already been disposed of.[1] Some 96 per cent (4.3 million cubic metres) of this total volume is made up of existing or legacy wastes from past and current civil and military nuclear programmes, leaving 4 per cent of future waste arising from future nuclear power industry activities, ongoing defence programmes (called Trident) and from the continued use of radio-activity for medical and industrial purposes. The NDA states that (Nuclear Decommissioning Authority, 2013, p. 10):

> Although 4.9 million tonnes of radioactive waste is a large amount, it is small when compared to other wastes the UK produces annually. Over 300 million tonnes of other wastes are produced annually in the UK, which includes about 6 million tonnes of hazardous waste.

This is an example of how the scale of the problem is socially constructed. To further illustrate, consider the contrasting description from Shrader-Frechette (1991), who states that at the nuclear industry's zenith worldwide each year every 1000-megawatt reactor discharged around 25.4 metric tons of HLW in the form of spent fuel. For 300 commercial reactors worldwide, the annual HLW production would be 7,620 metric tons per year. Shrader-Frechette then com-pares this volume with the 10 μ-grams of plutonium that would almost certainly induce cancer if inhaled or consumed by an individual, suggesting that several grams of plutonium dispersed in a ventilation system would be enough to cause thousands of deaths. The figure of 7,620 metric tons invokes a discourse of material scale that frames the problem as unmanageably large when compared with the comparatively tiny portions of nuclear material that pose a health risk. This is what is termed a framing effect: specifically, an *emphasis frame*. Frames are, in essence, a means by which individuals interpret and ascribe meaning to social phenomena (Chong & Druckman, 2007). An emphasis frame is a type of persuasion technique whereby focus is placed upon specific aspects of a problem and/or its potential solutions in a way that encourages the receiver of the frame to adopt certain interpretations of the meaningful context, and discourage certain others (Duchon, Dunegan, & Barton, 1989; Schon & Rein, 1994; Hom, Plaza, & Palmén, 2011). In this case the framing of waste volumes may spur the receiver of the framing into action to reduce the material production of wastes, influenced by a social discourse of comparative framing between the relatively tiny dose needed for radiotoxic contamination with the large volumes produced (for discussion of similar framing effects in nuclear discourse see for example Bickerstaff, Lorenzoni, Pidgeon, Poortinga, & Simmons, 2008; Henwood, Pidgeon, Sarre, Simmons, & Smith, 2008; Hunt, 2001). Alternatively, it might encourage inaction when a different emphasis frame is applied. For example the size and scale of the radioactive waste problem may seem small when compared (what the NDA put at 300 million tonnes across the UK) with what DEFRA states as 228 million tonnes of municipal landfill waste generated every year in England alone (DEFRA, 2013), invoking a frame of technical management and safe amelioration of the problem. My point is that this is a matter of interpretation through a process of framing, rather than an intrinsic feature of the wastes and their respective volumes in isolation from the social construction of the *meaning* of these figures.

Of course, one cannot easily compare radioactive wastes with other wastes on volume alone (including hazardous materials such as chemical wastes) given the unique capacity of radionuclides to emit ionising radiation and thus potentially cause harm beyond the physical space that they occupy. Given the differences in volume and radioactivity between waste streams, the homogenised group 'radioactive waste' is a catch-all term that complicates rather than clarifies the issue. Furthermore, radioactive wastes are not a homogeneous collection of materials, and treating them as such is highly problematic. The potential for these differing perceptions of the materiality of radioactive waste to shape the efficacy of debates over its management is an obstacle that has continued to permeate such management practices throughout nuclear producing countries. The relative size and make-up of wastes thus remains a problem of interpretation of both scale and impact, one that is dependent upon the pre-existing psychological characteristics of the participants within political debate and the prevailing social discourses that influence such interpretations (and vice versa). The subsequent task faced by UK institutions responsible for managing such a mix of potentially harmful materials from such a range of sources, (with differing chemical, radiological and physical characteristics along with varying perceptions around their safety and manageability) is one that is continually fraught with complex scientific, technical, environmental, political, social, economic and ethical difficulties. If we understand these elements as framing effects then it is important to understand the context in which concepts of scale, risk and safety are mobilised in social discourse, rather than trying to find an objective and uncontroversial framing to which all participants can agree, with the hope of reaching a political consensus upon the issue of their long-term management.

Radioactivity and health

By far the most important issue that relates to the framing of nuclear risk governance is the management of the public and environmental health implications of nuclear technologies, and the radionuclides that they produce. As mentioned in Chapter 1, radioactive substances undergo a process of nuclear decay whereby the nucleus of an unstable atom loses energy by emitting ionising radiation. In living cells ionising radiation can produce harmful effects in living tissue. In acute and sufficiently high doses this can cause radiation sickness and even death. Ionising radiation can potentially kill cells directly, or if they don't die, it can cause genetic damage (i.e. to the DNA molecules within cells). Acute radiation syndrome (ARS), also known as radiation poisoning, radiation sickness or radiation toxicity, is a set of health effects that usually present within

24 hours of exposure to high doses of radiation. These include burn effects, nausea and other gastrointestinal injury, headaches, drowsiness and dizziness, a drop in the blood cell count leading to poor wound healing and infection prevention. In low, chronic doses, the radiation doesn't directly kill the cells, but the genetic damage can cause cell mutations, leading to the later formation of cancerous cells and tumour development (Donnelly, Nemhauser, Smith, Kazzi, Farfan, & Chang et al., 2010).

The adverse effects of high dose radiation were first identified shortly after the discovery of radioactivity and x-rays in the 1890s. Early research on the health effects of radioactivity in the early 1900s reported the development of skin cancers amongst users of radioactive materials (who were largely unaware of the potential health effects from radiation exposure and thus took no precautions to protect themselves). The occupational hazards of working directly with radioactive materials became increasingly apparent in the early twentieth century. For example, reports on radium dial painters described cases of bone cancer in women who wet their brushes on their tongues to get a good 'point' for painting radium on watch dials (Martland & Humphries, 1929; Aub, Evans, Hempelmann, & Martland, 1952). In March 1932, a renowned American industrialist named Eben Byers died from cancer as a result of radium poisoning from drinking 'Radithor': a 'radium water' that was nationally advertised and available across America; designed essentially as a quack cure for a variety of ailments (Macklis, 1990). Byers' death prompted a nationwide inquiry into the sale of these radioactive 'health tonics', and served to dispel the popular myth that radioactive substances were a healthy thing to consume on a regular basis. Shortly after, in 1934 Physics Nobel laureate Marie Curie died of leukaemia. Her death was almost certainly caused by overexposure to the radioactive elements that she studied throughout her career (Quinn, 1995). The specific link between radiation exposure and the development of leukaemia in humans was first reported in 1944 by physicians and radiologists, however, the greatest source of knowledge on the effects of radiation exposure come from data collected following the bombs at Hiroshima and Nagasaki.[2] The percentage of cancers related to radiation depends on the dose received. On average about 12 per cent of all the cancers that have developed among those survivors within the post-bomb study group were estimated to be related to radiation (and around 9 per cent of the fatal cancers in this study population are estimated radiation-related) (IAEA, 1991).

However, the health dangers of radiation are dependent upon several factors, including the type of radiation and the route of exposure. Most importantly, the degree of damage to the human body depends upon:

- the amount of radiation absorbed by the body (the dose);
- the type of radiation (alpha, beta, gamma);
- the route of exposure (through the skin, ingestion, inhalation etc.);
- the length of time a person is exposed.

Health risk impacts from radioactive materials cannot therefore be simply mapped to the total *amount* of radiation produced by the radioactive source. A large dose received through the skin may be potentially less harmful than a smaller dose that is inhaled (and this lodged within the internal organs) for example. The possible health effects from radiation exposure are a complex science, and as new data emerges the accepted understanding of how radiation interacts with the human body alters. It is also important to note that radiation exposure is a part of human interaction with the natural environment and not simply an additional risk factor from man-made activities such as nuclear power generation. The World Health Organisation illustrates the sources of radiation in our environment and what proportion of our total exposure they make up, shown in Figure 5.1. It is important to note that on a population level, non-medical or food related radiation exposures account for less than 1 per cent of annual exposures, giving some indication of the relative scale of nuclear power and waste related threat ordinarily experienced by the UK public (concepts of scale and threat are discussed in greater detail in the subsequent sections).

Overall, as Figure 5.1 shows, the man-made sources of radiation account for around 1 per cent of total human exposure. As a health risk issue the International Commission on Radiological Protection (ICRP) affirms a paradigm whereby such low doses of radiation have a very weak effect on causing cancer in individuals exposed to radioactive isotopes. Since 1959 there has been an

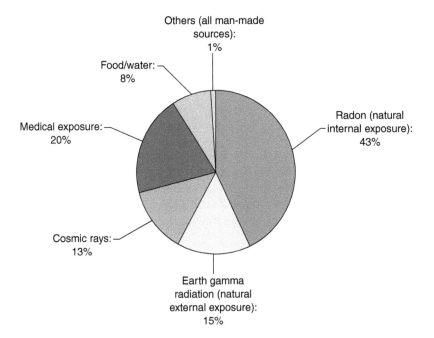

Figure 5.1 Sources of radiation exposure.

Source: World Health Organisation.

assumption that the health impacts of low dose radiation can be derived from linear extrapolation of the effects of high dose radiation, such as those seen following the exposure of Japanese citizens to the fallout from nuclear bombs at the end of the Second World War. This theory is the 'Linear No Threshold Hypothesis' (LNTH) and remains the current basis for setting radiation–protection standards worldwide. Yet concerns remain amongst some scientific communities regarding continuous or intermittent exposure to radiation over a long period of time. With chronic low dose exposure there is, in effect, a delay between the start of the exposure and the observed health effect (whether this is cataracts, benign growths or tumours, or the potentially more harmful genetic changes that cause malignant cancers). The US Environmental Protection Agency guidelines on radiation exposure assert that there is some cancer risk from any level of exposure to radiation, though at low doses it is difficult to distinguish whether a particular cancer in any given individual was specifically caused by chronic very low doses of radiation or by some other factor. There is also disagreement about what the exact definition of 'low dose' actually is. EPA defined radiation protection standards are based on the premise that any radiation dose carries some risk, and that risk increases directly with dose, and this is based upon the LNTH: the underlying assumption is that the risk of cancer increases linearly as radiation dose increases. Therefore, we might expect that doubling the dose of radiation in turn doubles the risk. Small doses are therefore assumed to carry a correspondingly small (but significant) health risk – though this risk is in turn contingent upon the sex, age and other contiguous health and environmental risk factors such as chemical exposure, lifestyle factors (such as smoking), exposure to UV light, and underlying genetics (US Environmental Protection Agency, 2015). In short, low dose radiation-induced cancer in humans depends on several variables, and most of these variables are not possible to correct for in any epidemiologic study (Prasad, Cole, & Hasse, 2004) so ascertaining low-dose radiation health risks is difficult. It is important to note that some researchers vigorously challenge the LNTH as one that leads to exaggerated predictions of the adverse health consequences of low-level exposures (Pollycove, 1995). To such critics, the LNTH leads to unjustified levels of public fear concerning low-level radiation, unnecessarily large expenditures of (limited) public resources and misconceptions with respect to the overall safety of nuclear materials (including nuclear reactors and radioactive wastes). Others, however, have asserted that there is insufficient scientific evidence to warrant a change from the LNTH and thus it must remain as a standard principle in radiation health impact assessment (Garrick, 1999).

Alternatives to the LNTH include some comparatively controversial theories such as the hormesis theory that postulates that low doses of radiation are potentially beneficial to the human body (Romerio, 2002) as living organisms develop adaptive protection – stimulation from low-dose radiation encouraging cells to undergo DNA damage prevention and immune system stimulation (Feinendegen, 2005). The scientific uncertainty is propagated by challenges to the epidemiological evidence of low-dose response. Yet, from a social science perspective we can understand this too as a contrast in *framing* the low-dose problem. More specifically we can understand this as a *paradigmatic* clash between adherents to competing bio-physical models. Advocates of hormesis assert that low-dose radiation risks are overemphasised – causing public fear of radiation that is scientifically unfounded. Advocates of the LNTH assert a more precautionary approach to the management of nuclear risks. To lay communities concerned about risk management these debates may seem remote and contingent. The fact that there is disagreement may serve to diminish trust that lay citizens have in the information coming from a community of professionals socio-culturally framed as the 'scientific experts'. Additionally, disagreements such as this between members of scientific communities can often be trans-scientific rather than upon solely scientific concerns (such as the dose response of cells to ionising radiation), raising questions which cannot be decided upon using science alone, either because crucial experiments cannot be performed, because the problems are 'undisciplined' or the judgements required are of a moral or aesthetic character. Decision-making bodies may seek to gain authority from relying on scientific models and experiments to define appropriate environmental management practices. However, expert prescriptions involve judgements about environmental and social benefits and frequently disguise the disagreement amongst scientists about precisely what features of nature or society may benefit from any given management practices (Burgess, 2000, pp. 273–274).

In addition to internal disagreement within scientific communities, direct conflict may also emerge between scientific specialists and so-called 'lay' citizens. These disagreements can be about the status of specific knowledge claims when negotiating between competing interests. This type of conflict has emerged in past governmental decisions regarding post-Chernobyl environmental remediation; the communication of science to local sheep farmers affected by radioactive fallout was initially hindered by governmental organisations ignoring or denying the relevant scientific facts and then even further by recommending impractical solutions stemming simply from their ignorance of hill sheep farming (Wynne, 1989). Wynne thus called for more two-way dialogic forms of scientific communicative activity that directly involve lay public and lay knowledge in decision-making processes as a potential means to ameliorate such disagreements.

The challenges to what constitutes the scientific 'truth' about radioactive waste risks become challenges to the identities and the social networks of trust in which these supposed truths about radioactive waste are embedded, blurring the distinction between 'hard' scientific objectivity and 'soft' political subjectivity. Within these disagreements are significant relationships between scientific framing, health and importantly the concept of *risk*.

Risk

The concept of *risk* is integral to the understanding of how societies engage with the processes of managing the environmental and health implications of radioactive materials. What is clear is that the terminology of *risk* is commonly employed in decision-making contexts over a host of environmental problems, and consequently it has been extensively and divergently theorised, with no commonly accepted or wholly objective definition existing either in the scientific, social scientific or popular 'lay' understanding (Renn, 1998). Studying the phenomenon of risk therefore requires a holistic conceptualisation of its myriad definitions using a trans-disciplinary approach (Renn, 2008).

We can start simply, however, by understanding health and environmental risks such as those related to radioactive wastes, as being intrinsically linked to the possibility of an undesirable state of reality (Kates, Hohenemser, & Kasperson, 1985). Such 'undesirable states' are commonly associated with physical hazards: the products, processes and other external conditions that threaten the safety and wellbeing of individuals, social groups and non-human entities. Hazards are typically categorised as external or environmental, such as in the case of earthquakes, droughts or floods; or else anthropogenic, i.e. resulting from human actions, such as the generation of radioactive wastes, oil spills or airborne pollutants from manufacturing or fossil fuel use. In understanding the concept of risk, however, it is important to note that it is through human involvement that events or objects that threaten human or non-human safety are transformed into hazards. Without a direct or indirect consequence to the human environment events might not be categorised as hazards. Consider for example an earthquake or flood on an uninhabited island. Without a measurable cost to people, the geological/hydrological event is likely not considered hazardous. Moreover, as our understanding of how human actions alter the structure of environmental systems and their properties such as in the case of greenhouse gas-emission related climate change, the neat epistemological distinction of hazards into 'natural' and 'man-made' is problematic. Risk theorists within the social sciences have therefore often sought to explore a more dialectical relationship between natural and man-made risks (see for example Cotton, 2015). To simplify, however, the concept of *environmental risk* is the collective contingent effects of anthropogenic technological and developmental processes that generate hazards, and hence human actions and social values are integral to understanding how risks can be identified, calculated and consequently managed and mitigated.

In the 1980s, there was a rapid expansion of technical and largely quantitative approaches to assessing risk. Fundamentally, quantitative risk assessment involves an understanding of three elements: What can happen? How likely is it to happen? And what are the consequences? (Kaplan & Garrick, 1981). Resultant models for quantifying these factors commonly focus upon measuring the likelihood of possible outcomes that result from human decisions. Risk 'exists' when known probabilities can be assigned to these outcomes. Therefore, the severity of risks can be judged using probability-weighted averages of the severity of potential outcomes. A simple technical definition of risk, therefore, is as the 'product of the probability and consequences (magnitude and severity) of an adverse event (i.e. a hazard)' (Bradbury, 1989, p. 382) leading to risk calculation using relatively simple metrics (such as for example, Risk = Threat*Vulnerability* Impact). In this equation 'Threat' is the frequency of potentially adverse events; 'Vulnerability' is the likelihood of success of a particular threat category against a particular group, individual or organisation; and 'Impact' is the total cost of a particular threat experienced by a vulnerable target (Haimes, Moser, & Stakhiv, 2003).

A whole range of human activities can fit within this rubric of risk assessment. Efforts to avoid risks can generate countervailing risks, which may be of greater probability or magnitude and hence be more dangerous to human and non-human targets. Thus, risk management becomes a question of choosing between competing risks, rather than the absolute elimination of specific risks. By adopting this approach, the process of risk assessment focuses upon questions of how well risks can be calculated, the level of seriousness that they pose, the accuracy of the underlying science and the inclusiveness of the causal or predictive models used to understand why risks occur and why people respond to them in certain ways (Lupton, 1999). In practical terms, such models aid decision-makers in estimating the expected harms (whether these are physical or financial), and provide an empirical summary using the best knowledge available of the probability of damage linked with each action (Bradbury, 1989; Renn, 2008).

In the subsequent decades since the development of the risk analysis paradigm, social scientists and philosophers have significantly broadened their conception of risks from purely calculable phenomena. Of particular note was Beck's seminal Risk Society thesis, which argued that definitions of risk are not objective categories, but rather communicative claims that have constitutive force (Beck, 1992). Defining risk is therefore a process of social construction, whereby actors involved in risk management and communication reflexively create the very uncertainty they purport to describe, and so risk constructs inevitably 'rationalise and reinforce many societal, political, and economic structures' thus requiring the need for evaluation in terms of the environmental, social, political, and economic realities they create for us to inhabit (Russell & Babrow, 2011, p. 244). The supposed objectivity in quantitative risk assessment has been subject to a sustained philosophical challenge: the role of human agents, their thought processes, heuristic biases, the underlying mathematical assumptions, and the broader socialisation of risk phenomena mean that the study of risk must elucidate its complexity. This involves the wider context of individuals' beliefs, morals, attitudes, perceptions, judgements and emotions (Wynne, 1985; Slovic, 1987; Fischhoff, 1995; National Research Council, 1996; Sjöberg, 2003). As a consequence, social scientists and philosophers of risk have consistently called for the incorporation of broader cultural, social and moral values into the process of risk analysis and management, and thus new methodological tools have emerged to expand the comparatively narrow technical definitions of risk to produce qualitatively richer and potentially more epistemologically *robust* risk management practices.

Radiation risks as a psychological and cultural phenomenon

At the heart of radioactive waste management planning is the problem of radiological hazard-related risks. In relation to this, one might consider a rhetorical question arising from Beck's (1992) work. In *Risk Society: Towards a New Modernity* Beck asks, 'what would happen if radiation itched?' i.e. what effect would occur if radiation caused instantly noticeable physical side effects in individuals. The problem of radiological risk stems in part from its physical nature; it is not directly observable (without appropriate detection equipment) and is largely imperceptible to the human senses (unless of course illness occurs). The invisibility of radiation is not solely a physical property, but a socio-cultural one. Beck describes environmental and technological risks as being:

> 'piggy back products' which are inhaled or ingested with other things [...] stowaways of normal consumption. They travel on the wind and in the water. They can be in anything and everything [...] air to breathe, food, clothing, home furnishings – they pass through all the otherwise strictly controlled protective areas of modernity.
>
> (Beck, 1992, p. 40)

In part, the 'invisibility' is a physical property of chemical or radiological hazards. However, it is the pervasive 'normality' of risk throughout everyday modern living that renders it socio-culturally invisible. The processes of managing radiation risks have lain in the hands of technical experts, scientists and government organisations that reside outside the direct influence of the citizenry affected by the radiological risk. Beck argued that natural hazards, such as floods, droughts, disease and famine, are readily perceptible to our senses, but that it is the transformation of these external and often unchangeable physical events into socially determined hazards that produces the socio-cultural invisibility of risk, and hence the need to measure and manage risks in new ways (Beck, 1996). The generation of civilian nuclear power (and by extension, radioactive wastes) is a clear example of how such risks are socially constructed. Beck argued for instance that fear about radiation is not linked to clear scientific evidence that nuclear power generation is more dangerous than any other energy source; it results from a more generalised and perceived sense of risk that is grounded in the broader cultural practices of risk management within society.

This apparent socio-cultural invisibility means that the perception of risk is cognitively detached from the probabilistic, empirical assessment of the radiation hazard constructed by risk assessment practitioners. This is particularly true in the event of major environmental catastrophes. Beck asks us to consider widely reported risk events like the Chernobyl disaster of April 1986. In the aftermath of this disaster and its broad reaching environmental and health effects, nuclear-related activities such as electricity generation and the management of radioactive wastes cease to be simply technical processes; rather, they become transformed into iconic representations of risk in (broadly speaking,

Western) culture. In reference to this, Beck argued that Chernobyl was particularly significant as it reflected a fundamental relationship between industrialised modernity and the production of risk. He described Chernobyl as causing 'anthropological shock'; arguing that the reactor meltdown and subsequent fire that spread radioactive particles across Northern Europe symbolised the hubris of Cold War industrialisation. Consequently, Chernobyl was perceived by citizens as a product of modernity itself, rather than simply an anomaly or accident (Beck, 1987) – a problem that we see re-emerging as a result of the Fukushima disaster of 2011 (for discussion of these issues see Hindmarsh, 2013; Rieu, 2013; Cotton, 2015; Hindmarsh & Priestley, 2015). Thus technological risk emerges as a consequence of industrial modernity, and not only generates harm in a physical, biological sense, but also creates the conditions for the emergence of a new kind of 'reflexive' modernity (Giddens, 1991; Beck, 1992) that is characterised by broad and popular critique of the goals and methods of scientific and technological development. This emergence of reflexive modernity stems from 'the failure of techno-scientific rationality in the face of growing risks and threats from civilisation' (Beck, 1992, p. 59). Beck and Giddens asserted that modern citizens have become less trusting of scientific authorities as 'the public' has begun to recognise that scientific advancement is the cause of new technological risks and that both current scientific and governmental institutions are ill-equipped to solve the problems that result.

It is worth reiterating the notion that risks are never fully eliminated, they are only transferred. Eradicating one risk either introduces or increases another (Nakayachi, 1998). In this case, for example, if nuclear power is stopped altogether and all reactors are decommissioned, then the risks of a cataclysmic nuclear power station operating disaster as in the Chernobyl scenario or the more recent Fukushima Daichii disaster effectively drop to zero (or close to zero). However, in doing so certain risks are exchanged. If as a society we 'denuclearise' electricity systems and move to greater use of fossil fuels to plug an energy gap between supply and demand, then we potentially transfer the risk of nuclear catastrophe to another catastrophic risk – that of anthropogenic climate change. Hillman and Fawcett (2004) argue in line with other 'pro-nuclear environmentalists', such as James Lovelock and George Monbiot (see for example McCalman & Connelly, 2015), that if we remove the risks of nuclear power we will create some form of 'Faustian Pact' whereby radiation risks are replaced with climate change risks (or vice versa). Paradoxically, the lure of a zero-risk scenario (i.e. one of complete risk elimination rather than transference) remains desirable for a range of stakeholder actors including citizen-stakeholders and governmental decision-makers. The behavioural economists Tversky and Kahneman (1981) call this the *pseudo-certainty effect*: a cognitive bias whereby individuals tend to perceive outcomes as certain when they are in fact uncertain. In relation to risks, this meant that individuals tend to prefer options which eliminate risks when decision tasks are framed conditionally; therefore protective actions which reduce the probability of harm from 1 per cent to 0 per cent are valued more highly than those that reduce risks from 2 per cent to 1 per cent. Individuals' understanding and interpretation of probability often leads them to 'over-weight' sure things and improbable events, relative to events of moderate probability. Moreover, people's understanding and attitude towards decision problems is influenced by the way in which such problems are described or *framed*. Differences in the framing of decisions give rise to different preferences, whether or not the probabilities are the same (Kahneman & Tversky, 1984; Malenka, Baron, Johansen, Wahrenberger, & Ross, 1993). We can see that this effect will stimulate political pressure to eliminate risks, yet because this is nearly impossible to do, the pseudo-certainty (along with other biases and heuristics involved in the mental risk calculations that individuals undergo) creates a paradox within environmental politics. Risks are intangible, transferable and uncertain, and certain problem frames encourage publics to desire their elimination. When this can't happen citizen-stakeholders will then likely react negatively against political and technical authorities that fail to eliminate risks. To summarise: the socio-cultural invisibility of risks is influenced by the cognitive biases and risk preferences held by individuals which differ substantially to those chosen based upon mathematical criteria alone.

The problem of socio-cultural invisibility in the radioactive waste management case is then further compounded by the time horizons of risk exposure, and the transference of risk from current generations to those in the future. Given the long half-lives of many radioactive substances, long-term RWM facilities (such as geological repositories) are designed to immobilise, contain and shield wastes from the biosphere, preventing, or at least delaying the migration of radioactive particles until their decay has reached biologically safe levels (however this may be defined). However, as waste shielding disintegrates over time and the uses of land around such facilities inevitably change, this causes problems in assessing the potential future impacts of radiation risks on humans and the environment. Compounding this problem is the fact that judgements made about the containment performance of radioactive waste packages are inevitably based upon short-term data. This is highly controversial, due in part to the time horizon for long-term waste management being hundreds of thousands of years. This time span far exceeds the dynasty of any known civilisation (Rosa & Short, 2004), and indeed it expands beyond our political capacity to imagine such futures, meaning that political authorities operating under short windows of decision-making control dictated by election cycles tend towards interim, ad hoc solutions and temporary fixes (see for example Leroy, 2006). Furthermore, if the requirement to think in terms of thousands of years has proved daunting in looking at areas of physical science and quantitative risk analysis then it is even more daunting when examining the human dimensions of the radioactive waste management process. In fact, the technical predictions of the stability and change of the physical environment despite their uncertainties are likely far more accurate than predictions on the evolution of the social and political conditions for surface dwellers over comparably long time frames (Buser, 1997); this is because physical properties of radionuclides and migration through different materials can be modelled on natural analogues found in the natural environment (Ewing & Jercinovic, 1986; Alexander, Chapman, McKinley, Smellie, & Miller, 2000). Also our observations of how man-made structures of the past (such as ancient monuments for example) have behaved in relation to both social and physical changes of millennia have been of great use to the design of future radioactive waste management facilities. However, the issue of uncertainty in the socio-political changes that will occur within future societies, and how questions of uncertainty are framed in the public sphere, what ethics we mobilise in the consideration of future generational interests affected by a radiation-polluted environment (see in particular Okrent, 1999; Shrader-Frechette, 2000; Cotton, 2013) remain crucial factors in assessing both the physical safety and public tolerability for risk decisions surrounding the construction of RWM solutions.

We can conclude, therefore, that the *tolerablility* of risk scenarios in public policy is a critical concern. When we combine issues of risk invisibility, pseudo-certainty effects, transferability between risk domains and between generations, problems of scale definition and of defining an objective materiality of wastes and of risks, the wicked nature of radioactive waste risks is revealed. The simplification of these risks through quantitative risk assessment and one-way risk communication from expert to public has thus only exacerbated negative public reactions, as the historical examples of radioactive waste policy failure mentioned in Chapters 3 and 4 can attest.

Empirical research on radiation risk perceptions

When trying to understand the tolerance that lay citizen actors have for RWM risk scenarios, the relative *perceptions* of radiation risks become important. There is ample research into the social and psychological context in which radioactive waste policy is formed. Notable early work on the issue was performed within the *psychometric paradigm* notably defined by the work of Slovic, Layman and Flynn. In broad survey work in the USA respondents were asked to associate freely about the concept of a deep geological radioactive waste repository. The method of continued association was used to evoke images, perceptions and affective states related to a repository siting (Flynn, Slovic, Mertz, & Toma, 1990; Slovic, Layman, & Flynn, 1991; Slovic, Flynn, & Layman, 2000). From a total of 3334 respondents and 10,000 word-association images a total of 13 general categories were created (with a total of 92 distinct subcategories). It is interesting to note from their study that the two largest categories, entitled 'negative consequences' and 'negative concepts' accounted for more than 56 per cent of the total number of images. The dominant image of subcategories labelled 'dangerous/toxic, death/sickness, environmental damage, bad/negative and scary' accounted for more than 42 per cent of the total number of images. The four most frequent single associations were the labels 'dangerous', 'danger', 'death' and 'pollution' (ibid.). Despite decades of reassurance from the nuclear industry's technical experts about the safety of their radioactive waste facility designs, the overwhelming level of negative imagery and the almost non-existent positive imagery (the category labelled 'positive' accounted for only 1 per cent of total images), illustrates the ineffectiveness of such strategies. Indeed, radioactive waste management facilities can be regarded as the most undesirable facilities to live beside. They beat oil refineries, chemical plants, landfill sites and (perhaps ironically) even nuclear power stations in this respect (Slovic, Layman, & Flynn, 1993). Hinman, Rosa, Kleinhesselink and Lowinger's (1993) work confirmed this finding; their pan Japanese–American comparative public survey revealed that fears around radioactive waste management were as intense as the dread of a nuclear accident or even nuclear war. It must be noted also that this fear is independent of the RWM strategy as either geological disposal in a repository (perceived as presenting a risk of involuntary exposure for current and future generations to 'catastrophic effects') (Kraft & Clary, 1993, p. 107), or indeed on-surface facilities are also perceived as highly risky to residents of neighbouring communities (Guillaume & Charron, 2004).

The overwhelmingly negative picture of public perceptions of RWM facilities has been interpreted in different ways. There are those that argue that fear of radiation has proved to be far more detrimental to public health than radiation itself. Threats to public health and safety such as deaths from pathogens resulting from regulations that prevent food irradiation, people avoiding medical procedures because they involve radiation and regulatory road blocks regarding low-level waste that result in the closure of radio-medical treatment centres. Furthermore as Maxey (1997, p. 1) states with regard to the proposed waste facilities at Yucca Mountain:

> Moreover billions of dollars have already been spent on trivial radiation risks based on grotesque scenarios about single atoms destined to travel through miles of desert soil to contaminate a potential water source in some distant future.

Representatives within the nuclear industry have sometimes gone on record criticising 'the general public' as being irrational, forcing it to waste its money on seemingly trivial risks as citizens seek the pseudo-certainty of risk elimination – money which might theoretically be spent more efficiently saving other lives in different risk scenarios. To give an example, the US Department of Energy awarded $85,000 in the early 1980s to psychiatrist Robert DuPont to help counter the so-called 'irrational fear' about nuclear power, in a study described as an attempt to demonstrate that opponents to nuclear power are mentally ill (Holden, 1984; Shrader-Frechette, 1998). Although decision-makers no longer deal with public risk perceptions in quite such a politically reactionary way, thirty years later, broadly speaking, there are those that feel exasperated by the obsession with public-focused risk management strategies that ask people what they *feel* about the risk of harm rather than telling them the about the probability of them *actually* suffering harm. Public engagement with risk can lead to certain outcomes being over-valued and over-discussed in deliberative processes involving the public. To such critics, decisive policy-making may seem to pander to the fears of ill-informed lay people. In relation to this problem, Grimstone remarks that certain commentators on RWM express the view that the 'problem' of disposal has been solved by the technical community and that 'only intransigence or a lack of courage on the part of the political establishment is preventing progress' (Grimstone, 2004, p. 4). To the nuclear engineer viewing the siting process in terms of technical criteria, factors such as safety, design and cost are imperative – everything else is just incidental. Public acceptability is normatively construed as irrelevant if the objective is to build a carefully engineered disposal that must be completely safe (Openshaw, Carver, & Fernie, 1989). Ergo, if science-based criteria come under attack from public sentiment then this would be detrimental to the success (and safety) of the chosen RWM strategy. As such some nuclear technical specialists have expressed concern over what they perceive as a weakening in the quality of primarily techno-scientific decisions by sacrificing scientific accuracy in favour of political expediency (Alario, 2001; Bäckstrand, 2003; Lock & McCall, 2001).

However, I contend that a detailed understanding of *why* radiation fears persist is key to understanding the tolerability of nuclear risk: and the acceptability and support of a siting procedure that technical experts tend to seek. These issues are objects of study and their integration into nuclear risk management is paramount. I take the normative position that engaging the public on issues of the social values inherent in risk management practices should be the ethical foundation of public engagement on science and technology; a strategy that is preferable to simply deploring how the 'uneducated masses' fear what they don't understand. In addition, accusations that the public are 'ill-informed' are an over-simplistic portrayal of public perceptions of risk. The critiques of this viewpoint come from diverse sources. Economists highlight the difficult issues raised in nuclear technologies, pointing out that it is rational to be averse to a risk of harm to which there is no clear individual benefit. Environmentalists assert the potential harm of a catastrophic accident rather than small routine doses; and ethicists warn we should not be too hasty in dismissing the inequity of risk distribution across generations, or between communities as irrational as they are clearly grounded in ethical norms (Oughton, 2001). The previous failures at siting long-term RWM technologies have come about due to a combination of pervasive fear and mistrust of nuclear installations and because of technocratic and top-down policy processes that have either tended to dismiss or misjudge these fears as being irrational, un-scientific and simply a nuisance to the planning process. As Joffe argues, when 'lay people' think about nuclear technologies they do not merely process information concerning the 'hard facts' utilising various biases and heuristics. Nuclear power is a highly emotive issue. It carries symbols of scientific and technological hubris and of environmental destruction. The emotive, symbol-laden response to nuclear power is as legitimate as the scientific take on it, rather than a delusional deviation from 'objective reality' (Joffe, 2003). Allowing individuals that are affected by developments to have a voice in the decision-making process is a normative ideal. Such voices must be free to speak of emotions: the fear and apprehension that they feel, without being labelled as irrational and thus detracting from the objectivity of facility siting. This means that those voices that remain marginalised by a technocratic process can have influence upon decision outcomes.

Social constructionism, history and imagery of nuclear technologies

The perceptions of radioactive waste technologies by 'the public' frequently do not mirror those of 'the experts'; something that has been explored by social constructionists in the field of technology assessment. Since the 1960's debate about many technologies (including nuclear technologies) especially their risk and acceptability, has exposed many to the question of the embedded public understanding of the intrinsic nature of scientific and technological advancement (Rip, 1986; Wynne, 1988). As mentioned previously, a social constructionist perspective questions the objectivity of scientific and technological developmental. Social constructionism is based upon the assertion that individuals create and assign meanings to their natural environments through filters that are provided to them by their different group-based values, beliefs and expectations (Albrecht & Amey, 1999; Kukla, 2000; Parker, 1998). By understanding the implementation of radioactive waste management technologies as a practice that has social, political, cultural and ethical ramifications, we can understand RWM as a problem of the social construction of risk. In essence, the objects and events surrounding RWM have the potential to embody multiple definitions for those who encounter them (Grieder & Garkovich, 1994). Artefacts such as radioactive waste management repositories have interpretive flexibilities, meaning that different individuals or indeed social groups associate different meanings to such artefacts (Kline, 1999). What results is that different individuals will select among alternative definitions of the technology that are most compatible with their own unique experiences, values and expectations (Albrecht & Amey, 1999). Therefore, the social effects of technologies are not pre-determined but are rather determined by the social relationships that vary from case to case (Feenberg, 1995). It makes sense to discuss radioactive waste technologies as 'social constructions' because they exist within in a particular time and space, are tied to human experiences of risk, values and expectations and have varying social, political and ethical impacts for different social groups. What is interesting in light of the Slovic et al. (2000) study is that these perceptions are comparatively uniform across demographic categories; men and women of different ages, incomes, education levels and political persuasions all hold similar negative perceptions of radioactive waste technologies. Conflict then arises between the powerful minority of the political and technical community that insists upon the safety, expediency and practicality of long-term RWM measures and the affected public majority that construct negative conceptions of danger and pollution and then challenge technocratic decision-making.

Pervasive negative nuclear imagery has grounding in the cultural history of nuclear science. Weart's (1988) historical analysis of nuclear technology argues that public 'nuclear fears' are deeply rooted in cultural consciousness. Nuclear power and radiation elicit images drawn from age-old beliefs and symbols associated with the concept of transmutation – the passage through destruction to rebirth, symbolised by the phoenix that is reborn from ashes. Images of radiation have proliferated in the popular culture of the twentieth century. Radiation is often drawn along the lines of 'uncanny rays' that transmute the body, bringing hideous death or miraculous new life. The image of new life is used in very diverse ways. Jaworowski (1999) argues that is through a variety of cultural forms that nuclear issues enter the public consciousness; individuals watch television programmes about nuclear disasters, or see films with villains threatening to explode atomic bombs in populated cities. Whether in fiction or in reality, the key image is that of change to life; if the recipient of radiation is not killed then they become irrevocably transformed by the experience. In a recent study on the cultural metaphors that emerge in relation to nuclear power, Renzi et al. (2016) find that these concepts of rebirth persist in the twenty-first century discussion of nuclear technologies in both positive framing (such as a 'nuclear renaissance') and in negative framing (as transmutation and sickness). These metaphors are themselves grounded in both religious and scientific domains of language and in turn shape publics' understanding and engagement with the science.

Of particularly significant historic consequence in this regard, were the bombings in Hiroshima and Nagasaki. These bombs did of course have immediate geopolitical ramifications at the end of the war, but they also showed the world images of instant devastation followed by long-term suffering in the aftermath – from cancers, blood and thyroid disorders. Despite this, the period of positive nuclear optimism following the Atoms for Peace rhetoric discussed in Chapter 3 persisted. This confidence in the safety of nuclear technologies was, however, damaged in the Spring of 1979 following the release of the film *The China Syndrome*, which centred on the discovery of a flaw in the design of a nuclear plant and the efforts of a television news reporter and a nuclear engineer to expose an official cover-up. The film stirred public concerns over the security and safety of nuclear power, which was confirmed, perhaps ironically, two weeks after the release of *The China Syndrome* early in the morning of the 28th March 1979, when the Three Mile Island (TMI) accident occurred at the nuclear power plant in Harrisburg, Pennsylvania. TMI remains the worst nuclear accident in U.S. history (Walker, 2004). It was rated at point five on the seven-point International Nuclear Event Scale (INES): i.e. an 'Accident With Wider Consequences'. Up to the Three Mile Island incident, the majority of the American public apparently believed that the generation of nuclear power rested upon proven and fundamentally safe technology (McCutcheon, 2002). The effect on the public from the release of radioactive materials after the incident produced a shift from a 2-to-1 margin in support of nuclear power before the incident, to a roughly even split between supporters and opponents immediately afterwards (Rosa & Freudenburg, 1993). As a point of context, it must also be noted that this occurred the year after the Love Canal disaster in

New York state, when a housing estate was built over a toxic waste dump and 2500 people had to be evacuated (Levine, 1982), so issues of environmental pollution and health risks were certainly salient political topics at the time.

In 1986 the Chernobyl disaster had the same effect in Europe, severely damaging the image of nuclear power. Nearly 7 tons of irradiated reactor fuel was released into the environment following the critical explosion of the reactor. Approximately 340 million Curies worth of radiation was released into the atmosphere, including some elements with a half-life of 16 million years. In the six years after the accident there was a hundredfold increase in thyroid cancers in Belarus, Russia and the Ukraine (K. Shrader-Frechette, 1999), and the long-term health and cultural memory of the effects of this event persist well into the twenty-first century.

There are other salient cases of radiation explosure that have meaningful social impacts. For example in 1987 Goiana in Brazil, two men searching for scrap metal came into an abandoned hospital and found a cancer therapy device that contained a blue glowing material. Although the material was contained inside protective shielding, the locals broke the shielding to get at the shiny material. The material in question turned out to be 28 grams of highly radioactive caesium chloride. Children and workers nearby were also attracted to the glowing material and began to play with it. Before the inhabitants knew the danger, several hundred people had been contaminated and four people eventually died from acute radiation poisoning. Publicity about the incident led to significant stigmatisation of the region and its residents (Petterson, 1988), leading to inhabitants being verbally abused and even assaulted out of the fear that they themselves may be dangerous to outsiders. The concept of *stigma* is an important one when examining the risks of RWM from the perspective of facility host communities. As the Goiana example demonstrates, radiation risk refers to something that is not only perceived as dangerous, but is seen to actively overturn or destroy a positive condition, i.e. converts a welcome facility or technology into an unwelcome one (Castán Broto, Burningham, Carter, & Elghali, 2010; J. H. Flynn, 2001; Gregory, Flynn, & Slovic, 2000; Peters, Burraston, & Mertz, 2004). Radioactive waste is not simply perceived as a potential danger but is often perceived to actively 'spoil' the community to which the association is attached. Stigmatisation can cause cultural and psychological stresses within communities; some members may feel stressed by the prospect of living close to such facilities (Dunlap, 1993; Edelstein, 1988, 2004); leading to suggestions that counselling, health education and monitoring of stress within site communities could be beneficial to alleviating such stigma (K. S. Shrader-Frechette, 1993; Wilson, 2000).

The impact of radiation-related deaths is often perceived as qualitatively different in nature from other risks. This is because radiation contaminates rather than merely damages; it pollutes, befouls and taints rather than just creates wreckage (Erikson, 1991). Images such as radiation sickness, cancer, physical deformities and genetic mutations often come to mind when thinking about radioactive waste risks (Slovic et al., 1991). Radiation appears to generate 'unnatural' attacks on the human body and the thought of bearing children with radiation-induced birth defects can generate tremendous personal anxiety (Easterling, 1995). As seen in the Hiroshima and Nagasaki example or in the contamination of areas of Belarus and the Ukraine, it is not just the initial accident/ disaster but the lingering harm that has no conceivable end that leads to unprecedented fear of radiation and thus the technologies that deal in radiation, whether that is its generation or containment.

By combining this pattern of radiological trauma and stigma with the institutional failures to site radioactive waste due to secrecy and technocracy, a simple but overwhelmingly negative picture begins to build. Death due to inexperience and misinformation about radiation risks; the destruction and long-term suffering of nuclear bomb victims; mismanagement, pollution, death and destruction from badly operated nuclear reactors; social stigma resulting from localised radiological exposure; and a failure to site radioactive waste due (in part) to secrecy and top-down rationalist decision making, have all presented the public with negative images of the management of nuclear materials. The compounding influence of these images and practices has contributed to pervasive fear and mistrust of nuclear technologies. The following section explores some of the reasons why such 'nuclear fears' are not easily alleviated through reassurances of safety by technical and scientific specialists.

The role of science in risk communication

As mentioned before, to some within scientific and technical communities, the problems of public risk perception, 'radio-phobia' and mistrust of scientific authority are based upon a fundamental public misunderstanding about the physical processes of radiation, due to insufficient knowledge of scientific concepts. A study by Miller (2004) examined public understanding of science survey results in the USA. The conclusion was that 10 per cent of American adults have what could be considered a scientifically correct understanding of radiation. When asked an open-ended question to explain the meaning of radiation, approximately 11 per cent of respondents provided information that involved the emission of energy as particles or waves. 10 per cent could mention the effect that radiation had, but were unable to name a source or explanation of the meaning of radiation. Frequent studies by the US National Science Board show that only 10 per cent of Americans can correctly define 'molecule', and that more than half believe that humans and dinosaurs lived on the Earth at the same time (National Science Board, 2002). These studies, revealing the public's general inaccuracy to describe fundamental scientific concepts, have often led scientific specialists and science policy-makers to decry the lack of knowledge and then call for new programmes to educate or provide information to fill the perceived knowledge gap (Ziman, 1991; Miller, 1998; Miller, 2001).

Returning to Beck's rhetorical question about itchy radiation, we can see that on a simple level he is calling for more information in the management of radiological risks. Because of the socio-cultural imperceptibility that radiological risks present, this lack of information, or more precisely the uncertainty involved is mediated through scientists, technical experts and professional risk managers. Uncertainty pervades the probabilistic and other quantitative risk models employed in radioactive waste management and so assumptions are inevitably made; decisions on how to frame the problem and break it into manageable and meaningful experimental models, each with distinct political and ethical ramifications (see in particular K. S. Shrader-Frechette, 1993). Overall, scientific and technical information has played an extensive role in shaping political decisions on radioactive waste management and the status of scientific and technical knowledge often lies at the centre of political disputes. Political actors in radioactive waste management policy-making will often claim a scientific justification for their position, and those that oppose the action will either invoke scientific uncertainty or a competing set of scientific results to support their opposition. Examining how radioactive waste management organisations and technical specialists conceive of local community actors is important – a concept that could be described as 'science's understanding of the public'. In a range of empirical studies it is revealed that scientific and technical specialists often characterise publics as being ignorant about scientific facts; as polarised for or against technological developments; demanding of zero-risk scenarios; basing their opposition upon non-scientific, ethical or political factors; or else as simply the malleable victims of a distorting and sensationalist media (Simmons & Walker, 1999; Marris, Wynne, Simmons, & Weldon, 2001; Burningham, Barnett, & Thrush, 2006; Burningham, Barnett, Carr, Clift, & Wehrmeyer, 2007; Cotton & Devine-Wright, 2012).

Together, these ideas about lay public actors are characterised by what is commonly termed a *deficit model* assumption about public understanding of science and technology, which are linked to concepts of scientific and technical literacy, i.e. the ability to understand scientific and technical matters 'correctly' in the manner in which it is communicated by experts (Bucchi, 1996; Sturgis & Allum, 2004). Deficit model thinking construes the public as being opposed to specific technological developments due to an inadequate knowledge base and an inability to think about the strategic relevance of technical matters beyond their immediate self-interested concerns (Cotton & Devine-Wright, 2012). Such a framing of the public posits citizen actors as fundamentally misunderstanding the risks, environmental and economic benefits involved across regional, national or international scales. The deficit model has informed the communication efforts of various scientific, technical and policy institutions because the problem of public reactions against science and technology was conceived as rooted in this scientific knowledge deficit among lay people (Frewer, Scholderer, & Bredahl, 2003). Scientists are by contrast framed as knowledgeable and benevolent experts, the public are (to varying degrees) ignorant lay people, and to follow that logic to its conclusion the key task becomes more and better communication of expert knowledge to the public. Under deficit model thinking if the public has more knowledge about how radiation and risk modelling works, then this will help to allay their misinformed and irrational fears and hence encourage them to adopt a more positive attitude towards the technology in question (Royal Society and Bodmer, 1985; Allum, Boy, & Bauer, 2002). The model thus prioritises the flow of information from the knowledge 'producers' i.e. the scientific elite, and their audience in a unidirectional manner. Deficit models are, in turn, based upon what is termed *bounded rationality*. Expert assessments are assumed to be objective because they involve 'hard' evidence such as costs, safety and environmental performance, rather than prioritised over 'soft', 'subjective' and 'irrational' public values, sentiments, emotions, aesthetics and morals (Forester, 1984; Bell, 1999; Grove-White, Kearnes, Macnaghten, & Wynne, 2006).

On the other side of the equation is the problem that heterogeneous publics have an increasing lack of confidence in scientists' ability to diagnose relevant risks accurately. In fact there is a growing concern by lay citizens in advanced Western economies that the risks associated with technologies such as radioactive waste management may not be well understood so there is little reason to trust the experts at all (Kasperson, Golding, & Tuler, 1992; Kunreuther, 2001). The basis of this criticism lies in the scientific experts' liability to disagree, a problem that the philosopher of science T. S. Kuhn examined in detail. Kuhn identifies the problem as a matter of paradigmatic conflict. It begins with the *normal scientific paradigm*, which represents a stable pattern of scientific norms, methods and analyses which in turn defines the identity of the community that shares in it. As the social identity of a scientific community is dependent upon the stability of the existing normal paradigm, anything that disrupts this stable pattern (thus forging a new paradigm) will always provoke a strong opposition from the partisans of the previous one. However, when fundamental changes in the basic underlying concepts and practices of the discipline (of in this case radioactive waste management) occur, this represents a *scientific revolution*, which if successful in overturning the pre-existing paradigm results in a paradigm shift and the establishment of a new normal paradigm (all from Kuhn, 1962). The growing concern for science-policy practitioners within central governments of advanced economies, is that this paradigmatic shift is, in turn, perceived by outsiders (such as non-specialist lay citizens) as contingent, temporary or unreliable. Science is portrayed as a sort of moveable feast where the fundamental precepts are ever shifting thus contingency and uncertainty are poorly tolerated, and scientific and media reporting of risks seems contradictory from one week to the next (see for example Goldacre, 2010 for a discussion of this problem). This has led many scientific commentators to reflect upon the declining public trust in science and its potential remedies (see for example Haerlin & Parr, 1999; Wynne, 2006).

Remedying public distrust of science has been a key concern of successive public authorities in the USA and Europe. The deficit model, as mentioned, is grounded in an assumption that public understanding of science (or scientific literacy as it is sometimes known) is the root cause of public distrust. Ergo, the improvement of more general public science literacy will improve public trust in scientific authority. Public understanding of science is the underlying philosophy to the deficit model of science communication emerging in the 1990s. For radioactive waste management, this issue is particularly significant. As discussed in Chapter 4, RWM processes have tended to involve action planning based upon expert judgment, followed by transmission of information to 'the public' through public relations mechanisms. Thus, if the public has more knowledge then this will naturally lead to a more positive attitude towards technology implementation plans. The difficulty remains, however, that the communication of risk is not solely a direct and unidirectional communicative process of transmitting knowledge from the experts to the lay people (see Douglas, 1986). If a policy decision on radioactive waste is announced, the decision-makers have historically ended up defending the project against the public backlash that occurs from a confused and distrustful public. Frequently we see that the mechanisms through which this defence occurs employ the same types of public relations techniques used to 'transmit' the technical information in the first place. Applying this approach to build public trust and confidence in a RWM siting process is fundamentally flawed and explains a lot of the continued policy failure for public authorities up to and including the 1997 failure to site the RCF in Cumbria.

The reaction against radioactive waste facilities by citizen-stakeholders often remain independent of the reactions (both in support and opposition) of official government entities. Indeed, support for nuclear facilities is an interesting and important facet of society–technology interactions in this field. At the local community level it is sometimes found that those most negatively affected by nuclear facilities are also the strongest supporters of nuclear industry renewal not only because of the employment opportunities, but also out of a personal identification with the technology and a political identity of patriotism (Malin, 2013). Yet strong opposition from the imposition of nuclear facilities from the top down, led by government authorities is, in the UK context, bound up with what former UK Government Chief Scientific Advisor Sir Richard May called the 'patina of distrust' (May, 1999, p. 18). The patina of distrust refers to how the public may not fully grasp all the scientific complexities of the RWM process but are nevertheless aware of the commercial imperatives, sceptical about politics and distrustful of the competence and impartiality of independent regulatory frameworks (see Owens, 2000). The type and severity of the resultant reaction to official decisions is largely dependent upon the level of trust that publics have in the institutions (both private industry and governmental) involved in the siting process. This trust is closely tied to the risk perceptions that accompany the radioactive waste technology; and the trust and confidence that the public has both in the safety of the technologies and the institutions that put them into practice can often be interpreted as a statement about the public's recognition of its legitimacy. As Miller (1973) argues, if citizens perceive the institutions, procedures and governing groups as legitimate then the tensions arising from gaps between official and individual interpretations of these radioactive waste management technologies can be absorbed. The affected site communities must have confidence in both the technical solution and the implementation, the management institutions involved must, therefore, not only comply with the existing legislation with regards to safety and regulatory control, but must be able to build public trust and therefore gain democratic legitimacy. Thus, in a democratic society such as that of the UK, public support for (or at the very least a lack of overt hostility towards) such a large scale technological project as this, is an important ingredient of eventual policy success.

The status of science in siting decisions – from technocratic to postnormal?

The status of science is not just a matter for public education, it is inherently a matter of political discourse. As mentioned earlier, to some critics of the public-centred approach to RWM, local participation in siting proposals leads to decision-making controlled by 'public sentiment' rather than scientifically defined safety (see North, 1999). Such an argument is not just about scientific literacy, but about how decision-making itself should be politically structured: an issue of what is commonly referred to as the science-policy interface. As Dryzek argues, concerns about public sentiment undermining techno-scientific authority are characteristic of *administrative rationalism*, whereby the role of the expert is placed in primacy in social problem solving, which leads to a political process where social relationships of hierarchy are stressed over those of equality or competition (Dryzek, 1997). Within this discourse, the criticism that radioactive waste management is too public-focused is a reaction against a perceived rise in the prominence of cultural relativism, whereby a core notion of truth is rejected in favour of experiential ways of knowing; and that such relativism propagates the view that science is in some way discredited, or somehow less relevant for policy decisions than it once was.

By contrast, there are those that see the requirement for transparency and democratic accountability as vital interests that must be protected from being overruled by the unidirectional input from a community of scientific and political 'experts'. Moreover, it is functionally impossible to separate facts from values as both are intertwined, at least in all issues that matter for the people (Kaiser, 2015). With regard to the nuclear policy debate Denenberg (1974, p. 3) insists: 'nuclear safety is too important to be left to the experts. It is an issue that should be resolved from the point of view of the public interest, which requires a broader perspective than the tunnel-visioned technicians'. Here, there is a clear tension between technocratic and deliberative-democratic paradigms of technology decision-making. The technocracy of regulatory science in environmental decision-making is embedded in the prevailing discourses of scientific optimism and ecological modernisation that stress technical rather than social solutions to siting processes – clashing with the new wave of deliberative science, stressing the role of *civic competence* in technical matters, one that incorporates new ideas of transparency, accountability and participation. Adherents to administrative rationalist decision-making express concern over weakening the quality of primarily techno-scientific decisions by sacrificing scientific accuracy in favour of political expediency, whereas advocates of participatory–deliberative democratic governance of science seek to support the protection of communities' rights to control their environment and society – providing defence against the indifference and exclusion resulting from techno-centric processes. To the latter, the technologies of radioactive waste management have the potential to become agents of oppression, in the sense that they foster large centralised authority structures while sacrificing the smaller units of government in which direct participation is possible (Fischer, 1993; Stirling, 2001; Bäckstrand, 2004). Thus, the RWM decision-making process is not simply a question of understanding or engaging with local risks, but one of democratic rights for affected communities when presented with a utilitarian decision – should a community accept the risk on behalf of society as a whole, and if so, under what conditions should they accept or reject such a decision? The issue of centralised power over the affected parties in environmental decision-making is a key political issue. Proponents of deliberative democratic approaches to technology planning insist that the power to make decisions must be placed as far as possible in the hands of the persons who are the most directly influenced by the decision concerned, and not in the hands of individual decision-makers and the associated experts. Within this is a geographic dimension to this problem. Decisions over RWM are made by governmental authorities in Westminster. The RWM decision, in the UK at least, raises ethical questions about core–periphery relationships and urban–rural relationships. The Sellafield site is geographically remote from London, and indeed from other major population centres in the north of England, such as Manchester and Liverpool. Hernández (2015) notes that rural (and in the nuclear case largely coastal) communities often become 'sacrifice zones', whereby centralised urban decision-makers and planning authorities are all too willing to site hazardous or otherwise unwanted facilities that benefit urban populations (by proxy through nuclear energy production and directly through removing the risk-bearing wastes from the vicinity of urban centres) in areas that are of relatively low population density under the utilitarian principle of minimising harm to the greatest number. However, these rural places commonly have poor access to urban political networks and have a correspondingly weak representation in democratic political forums. Therefore, an essentially *fair* decision-making process must find ways to counter these political imbalances, and this is an issue which I return to in Chapter 7.

Returning to the role of knowledge specifically, though scientific knowledge should not be ignored (especially regarding its contributions to understanding safety through a technically sound solution), there are powerful arguments for the inclusion of other knowledge, particularly so-called lay knowledge. Under these circumstances citizens are themselves involved in technological assessment of scientific and technical knowledge, and the reasons are largely pragmatic. The systems involved in the interaction of radioactive wastes in the natural, physical and social environment are complex, not merely complicated;

by their nature they involve deep uncertainties and a plurality of legitimate perspectives. At the risk of oversimplifying, science generates a picture of reality designed for controlled experimentation and abstract theory building. As previously stated, Kuhn (1962) showed that the scientific model 'normally' consists of puzzle solving within an unquestionable paradigm that provides a framework for all forms of enquiry. The normal scientific model can be very effective with complex phenomena reduced to their simple atomic elements, but it is not always best suited for the tasks of complex environmental decision-making (Bäckstrand, 2004; Funtowicz & Ravetz, 1999). This is because scientists are primarily trained with an eye to the 'technical agenda of science' (Funtowicz & Ravetz, 1993), whereby the practical upshot of theoretical knowledge is the central focus. In what Fox (1995) terms *Mode 1 Science*, there is a rhetoric of, 'if you want to achieve this result, then do X': the scientific mindset fosters expectations of regularity, simplicity and certainty in the phenomena and in our interventions, but these can inhibit the growth of our understanding of the problems and of appropriate methods to their solution. Hence, the methodologies of traditional laboratory-based science, modelling and risk assessment are of restricted effectiveness in this new context of decision-making complexity, and the conventional mode of science involves very little re-thinking of what scientific knowledge means and what actually counts as expertise (Wynne, 1996, 2002).

The concept of integrating so-called lay expertise in RWM decision-making has considerable merit in light of the policy failures of past administrations. Local citizens may know more about certain characteristics of local sites for radioactive waste facilities than will be available within aggregated environmental performance or spatial data (such as that used by risk analysts, geologists or geographical information scientists). This can lead to conversations along the lines of, 'If this is supposed to be a scientific process, how could you have overlooked something that everyone [here] knows?' (Freudenberg, 2004, p. 157). Though it is easy to espouse a principle of lay knowledge integration into a socio-technical decision, actually developing a satisfactory relationship between technical expertise and lay expertise is by no means a simple process. There are cases when the public either is not, or does not feel (or does not want to feel) qualified to make well informed decisions and take responsibility for action; in other cases, they believe they are the experts and don't want to hear the advice of outside authorities. This is based in part upon the relationship that is built between experts and associated publics, the trust that is implicit within those relationships and where public actors perceive the responsibility to lie, their personal experience of hazards and the messages that they interpret from broader cultural sources such as formal print and televised media, and social media. Citizens may want their elected political authorities and their associated experts to step in and solve the problem, or they may want a greater role for individual involvement. It can be difficult for decision-making authorities to know which it is in advance of a decision. Thus, the expert–lay divide, as it is known, is contingent upon the context of the individual, the situation in which

competing actor interests are negotiated, and the knowledge under consideration, and this has been a central concern of social scientific study of risk management and technology politics. As a potential solution to the challenging
nature of these dialogues between the technical and non-technical specialists,
Funtowicz and Ravetz (1993, 1999) postulate the idea of incorporating *postnormal science* into decision-making processes.

'Postnormal' is a label that relates to the aforementioned Kuhnian normal
scientific paradigm, for issues where facts are uncertain, values are in dispute and
the stakes are high: 'this involves going beyond traditional assumptions that
science is both certain and value-free, it makes system certainties and decision
stakes the essential elements of its analysis' (Ravetz, 1999, p. 647). If we understand RWM as a wicked policy problem, it certainly exhibits these qualities. A
postnormal radioactive waste management process moves beyond the sole use of
the traditional tools of science and technological management (i.e. research
into safety performance and probabilistic risk assessment, hydrogeology, geology
and geochemistry in assessing the conditions beneath the surface); to a method
where the quality of the process of research, planning and siting in a holistic
manner becomes paramount. In situations of risk and uncertainty, scientists
commonly believe that their job is to provide the proof that society needs in
order to make informed decisions. Kuhn's (1962) normal or puzzle-solving mode
of science generates a picture of reality designed for controlled experimentation
and abstract theory building. In the Popperian (Popper, 1959) tradition, scientific expertise is an objective and rational pursuit that explains physical reality
through empirical falsification using hypothesis testing of causal generalisations.
Science does not produce logically indisputable proofs about the natural world,
rather it provides a degree of consensus grounded in empirical evidence within a
process of inquiry, that is itself contingent. Science allows for scrutiny, re-
examination, and revision. Within any given scientific community, different
individuals may weigh evidence differently and adhere to different standards of
demonstration, and these differences are likely to be amplified when the results
of inquiry have political, religious, economic, aesthetic or moral ramifications
(Oreskes, 2004).

Postnormal science is dependent upon three principal criteria. The first is
that the decision stakes are high and there is urgency for a decision to be made,
whereby the potential costs and benefits of both action and inaction are significant. The second is that the decision stakes reflect conflicting strategies, purposes or values between different stakeholders. The third is that there are deep
uncertainties present within the systems and processes studied; uncertainties
which are not only technical, or methodological (and thus 'normal') but are
fundamentally epistemological or moral in character (Funtowicz & Ravetz,
1993; Saloranta, 2001). The making of decisions under such conditions should,
from a postnormal philosophical perspective, avoid using scientific inquiry as a
baseline form of 'proof' upon which to make robust decisions (hard evidence for
soft decisions). Rather, postnormality is defined by a recognition of inherent
complexity and the interwoven nature of these supposed hard and soft elements.

Like many other environmental issues, such as climate change, biodiversity loss or natural resource depletion, the problems inherent in long-term radioactive waste management will never be fully understood before action is needed to address them. A postnormal decision-making process includes enabling rapid action through joint learning and joint planning with those who will carry out the actions. This means participation by stakeholders as well as scientific and technical specialists – including those people that are specifically affected by an issue but that lie outside the communities of traditional expertise associated with the task. Postnormality ensures a grounding or contextualisation of radioactive waste management implementation within the practical context in which it is applied. The role of experiential or 'lay' knowledge therefore has a greatly elevated status. Science is no longer beyond the critique of lay people suffering under a knowledge deficit. Citizens become part of *extended peer communities* (Ravetz, 1999) providing alternative information and critique of the knowledge of technical experts. The process of planning is a true dialogue between science and policy, the experts and the affected. To achieve this however, the social, political, ethical and scientific processes must be both comprehensive and holistically integrated into a decision process without defining hierarchies of knowledge with science given primacy.

Within the postnormal paradigm one of the primary methods is that of meaningful and constructive public participation in science-centred issues. The goal is, to borrow Latour's (2004) expression, 'to bring science into democracy'. Postnormal decision-making requires deliberation in the public sphere, not techno-centric information provision shrouded as public involvement (Funtowicz & Ravetz, 1999; Luks, 1999). Participatory–deliberative approaches that encourage the involvement of citizens in the evaluation of scientific information and the institutional process through which science is used, are a primary means through which the postnormal evaluation of RWM can be achieved. As I shall discuss in the next chapter, this element of participatory dialogue has become an institutionalised practice in RWM, reflecting broader changes in policy-making on environmental issues that posit (at the very least) consultation with the public as a minimal level of good practice. Consultation is not the only requirement, however. Increasingly, environmental management decisions are involving public and stakeholder actors at earlier stages of policy development than the 'downstream' stage of site selection, in favour of more strategic 'upstream' dialogue processes (Wilsdon & Willis, 2004). The underlying ethos of this trend towards more influential public and stakeholder involvement involved recognising that environmental decisions are political (with a small 'p') as well as techno-scientific.

The resolution of environmental problems requires addressing the interests and values of the public in ways that cannot be resolved through the sole recourse to quantitative tools such as risk assessment and cost-benefit analysis. Effective participation requires active involvement on non-technical actors in decision-making at stages at which they can influence outcomes, not an abstract 'arms-length' consultation which may or may not be ignored when it comes to planning a facility site. By including stakeholder and community preferences and values, important information may be obtained that is otherwise overlooked in a technical analysis, therefore leading to more political support for the decision-making processes and resulting siting decisions. Allowing individuals both access to a range of information sources and the opportunity to express their 'emotional and subjective' perceptions, interests and values they hold towards radioactive waste facilities outside of the bounded administrative rationalist discourse of knowledge deficits and techno-centrism, may even help to alleviate some of the difficulties involved in gaining public trust. However, the processes of active citizen engagement must contend with corralling diverse stakeholder interests into a coherent dialogue process, and contend with the challenges of differing risk perceptions, low levels of trust in institutions, stig-matised and disenfranchised communities, and the representation of environ-mental and future generational interests that have no 'voice' in such dialogue processes. Moreover, doing so without diminishing or sidelining scientific know-ledge in a way that is truly postnormal, will remain hotly contested issue. These factors have deeply influenced the development of post-1997 RWM policy-making, and the following chapter discusses the practical 'turn' towards partici-patory dialogue processes and their pitfalls, followed by a discussion of this turn in practice with the development of the *Managing Radioactive Waste Safely* policy programme.

Notes

1 Though not explicitly stated, this includes wastes disposed of at sea.
2 Studies from within the United States Department of Energy and the Japanese Minis-try of Health and Welfare continue to evaluate the long-term effects of radiation on the survivors of the bombs.

Bibliography

Alario, M. (2001). A turn to scientific analysis and democratic deliberation in environ-mental policy: Political risk, legitimation crisis or policy imperative? *Theory and Science, 2*(2).

Albrecht, S. L., & Amey, R. G. (1999). Myth-making, moral communities, and policy failure in solving the radioactive waste problem. *Society and Natural Resources, 12,* 741–761.

Alexander, R., Chapman, N., McKinley, I., Smellie, J., & Miller, W. (2000). *Geological disposal of radioactive wastes and natural analogues* (1st ed.). London: Pergamon.

Allum, N., Boy, D., & Bauer, M. (2002). European regions and the knowledge deficit model. In M. W. Bauer, & G. Gaskell (Eds.), *Biotechnology: The making of a global con-troversy* (pp. 224–243). Cambridge: Cambridge University Press.

Aub, J. C., Evans, R. D., Hempelmann, L. H., & Martland, H. S. (1952). The late effects of internally-deposited radioactive materials in man. *Medicine, 31,* 221–329.

Bäckstrand, K. (2003). Civic science for sustainability. Reframing the role of experts, policymakers and citizens in environmental governance. *Global Environmental Politics, 3*(4), 24–41.

Bäckstrand, K. (2004). Scientisation vs civic expertise in environmental governance: Eco-feminist, eco-modern and post-modern responses. *Environmental Politics, 13*(4), 695–714.

Beck U. (1987). The anthropological shock: Chernobyl and the contours of the risk society. *Berkeley Journal of Sociology, 32,* 1 January, 153–165.

Beck, U. (1992). *Risk society: Towards a new modernity.* London: Sage.

Beck, U. (1996). *Risk society: Towards a new modernity.* London: Sage.

Bell, M. M. (1999). *The rationalization of risk.* Iowa State University, Ames, Iowa.

Bickerstaff, K., Lorenzoni, I., Pidgeon, N. F., Poortinga, W., & Simmons, P. (2008). Reframing nuclear power in the UK energy debate: Nuclear power, climate change mitigation and radioactive waste. *Public Understanding of Science, 17*(2), 145–169.

Bijker, W. E., Hughes, T. P., & Pinch, T. (Eds.). (1987). *The social construction of technological systems.* Cambridge MA: MIT Press.

Bradbury, J. (1989). The policy implications of differing concepts of risk. *Science, Technology & Human Values, 14*(4), 380–399.

Bucchi, M. (1996). When scientists turn to the public: Alternative routes in science communication. *Public Understanding of Science, 5,* 375–394.

Burgess, J. (2000). *Situating knowledges, sharing values and reaching collective decisions: The cultural turn in environmental decision-making.* In: *Cultural turns/geographical turns* (pp. 273–287). Harlow: Prentice Hall.

Burningham, K., Barnett, J., Carr, A., Clift, R., & Wehrmeyer, W. (2007). Industrial constructions of publics and public knowledge: A qualitative investigation of practice in the UK chemicals industry. *Public Understanding of Science, 16*(1), 23–43.

Burningham, K., Barnett, J., & Thrush, D. (2006). *The limitations of the NIMBY concept for understanding public engagement with renewable energy technologies: A literature review.* Retrieved from www.sed.manchester.ac.uk/research/beyond_nimbyism/.

Buser, M. (1997). Which is more stable: A rock formation or a social structure? *Nagra Bulletin, 30*(August).

Castán Broto, V., Burningham, K., Carter, C., & Elghali, L. (2010). Stigma and attachment: Performance of identity in an environmentally degraded place. *Society & Natural Resources, 23*(10), 952–968. doi:10.1080/08941920802705776.

Chong, D., & Druckman, J. N. (2007). Framing theory. *Annual Review of Political Science, 10*(1), 103–126.

Cotton, M. (2013). Deliberating intergenerational environmental equity: A pragmatic, future studies approach. *Environmental Values, 22*(3), 317–337.

Cotton, M. (2015). Structure, agency and post-Fukushima nuclear policy: An alliance-context-actantiality model of political change. *Journal of Risk Research, 18*(3), 317–332.

Cotton, M., & Devine-Wright, P. (2012). Making electricity networks 'visible': Industry actor representations of 'publics' and public engagement in infrastructure planning. *Public Understanding of Science, 21*(1), 17–35.

DEFRA. (2013). Reducing and managing waste. Retrieved from www.gov.uk/government/policies/reducing-and-managing-waste.

Denenberg, H. S. (1974, 25 November). Nuclear power: Uninsurable. *Congressional Record.* Washington DC.

Donnelly, E. H., Nemhauser, J. B., Smith, J. M., Kazzi, Z. N., Farfan, E. B., Chang, A. S., & Naeem, S. F. (2010). Acute radiation syndrome: Assessment and management. *Southern Medical Journal, 103*(6), 541–546.

Douglas, M. (1986). *Risk acceptability according to the social sciences.* London: Sage.

Dryzek, J. S. (1997). *The politics of the earth: Environmental discourses.* Oxford: Oxford University Press.

Duchon, D., Dunegan, K. J., & Barton, S. L. (1989). Framing the problem and making decisions: The facts are not enough. *IEEE Transactions on Engineering Management,* 36(1), 25–27.

Dunlap, R. E., Kraft, M. E., & Rosa, E. A. (1993). *Public reactions to nuclear waste.* Durham, NC: Duke University Press.

Easterling, D., & Kunreuther, H. (1995). *The dilemma of siting a high-level nuclear waste repository.* Boston: Kluwer Academic Publishers.

Edelstein, M. R. (1988). *Contaminated communities: The social and psychological impacts of residential toxic exposure.* Boulder, Colorado: Westview Press.

Edelstein, M. R. (2004). Sustainable innovation and the siting dilemma: Thoughts on the stigmatization of projects and proponents, good and bad. *Journal of Risk Research,* 7(2), 233–250.

Erikson, K. (1991). Radiation's lingering dread. *The Bulletin of the Atomic Scientists,* 34–39.

Ewing, R. C., & Jercinovic, M. J. (1986). *Natural analogues: Their application to the prediction of the long-term behavior of nuclear waste forms.* MRS Proceedings. Vol. 84. Cambridge: Cambridge University Press.

Feenberg, A. (1995). *Alternative modernity: The technical turn in philosophy and social theory.* Berkley: University of California Press.

Feinendegen, L. E. (2005). Evidence for beneficial low level radiation effects and radiation hormesis. *The British Journal of Radiology,* 78(925), 3–7. doi:10.1259/bjr/63353075.

Fischer, F. (1993). Citizen participation and the democratization of policy expertise: From theoretical inquiry to practical cases. *Policy Sciences,* 26, 165–187.

Fischhoff, B. (1995). Risk perception and communication unplugged: 20 years of process. *Risk Analysis,* 15(2), 137–146.

Flynn, J. H. (2001). *Risk, media and stigma: Understanding public challenges to modern science and technology.* London: Earthscan.

Flynn, J., Slovic, P., Mertz, C. K., & Toma, J. (1990). *Evaluations of Yucca Mountain: Survey findings.* Carson City, NV: Nevada Nuclear Waste Project Office.

Forester, J. (1984). Bounded rationality and the politics of muddling through. *Public Administration Review,* 44(1), 23–31.

Fox, W. (1995). Education, the interpretive agenda of science, and the obligation of scientists to promote this agenda. *Environmental Values,* 4, 109–114.

Freudenberg, W. R. (2004). Can we learn from failure? Examining US experiences with nuclear repository siting. *Journal of Risk Research,* 7(2), 153–169.

Frewer, L. J., Scholderer, J., & Bredahl, L. (2003). Communicating about the risks and benefits of genetically modified foods: The mediating role of trust. *Risk analysis,* 23(6), 1117–1133.

Funtowicz, S., & Ravetz, J. (1993). Science for the post-normal age. *Futures,* 25(7), 739–755.

Funtowicz, S., & Ravetz, J. (1999). Post-normal science – environmental policy under conditions of complexity. *Robust knowledge for sustainability.* Retrieved from www.nusap.net/sections.php?op=viewarticle&artid=13.

Garrick, J. B. (1999). *Linear no threshold hypothesis.* Washington, DC: United States Regulatory Commission.

Giddens, A. (1991). *Modernity and self-identity: Self and society in the late modern age.* Cambridge: Polity.

Goldacre, B. (2010). *Bad science: Quacks, hacks, and big pharma flacks*. London: McClelland & Stewart.

Gregory, R., Flynn, J., & Slovic, P. (2000). Technological stigma. In P. Slovic (Ed.), *The perception of risk*. London: Earthscan.

Grieder, T., & Garkovich, L. (1994). Landscapes: The social construction of nature and the environment. *Rural Sociology, 59*, 1–24.

Grimstone, M. (2004). *Ethical and environmental principles: A review of the influence of ethical and environmental considerations in the formulation and implementation of radioactive waste management policy* (670). London: Committee on Radioactive Waste Management.

Grove-White, R., Kearnes, M. B., Macnaghten, P. M., & Wynne, B. (2006). Nuclear futures: Assessing public attitudes to new nuclear power. *Political Quarterly, 77*(2), 238–246.

Guillaume, B., & Charron, S. (2004). *Exploring implicit dimensions underlying risk perception of waste from mining of uranium ores in France*. Retrieved from Fontenay-aux-Roses, France: www.irpa.net/irpa10/cdrom/00613.pdf.

Haerlin, B., & Parr, D. (1999). How to restore public trust in science. *Nature, 400*(6744), 499–499.

Haimes, Y. Y., Moser, D. A., & Stakhiv, E. Z. (2003). *Risk-based decisionmaking in water resources X*. Paper presented at the Tenth United Engineering Foundation Conference.

Henwood, K., Pidgeon, N., Sarre, S., Simmons, P., & Smith, N. (2008). Risk, framing and everyday life: Epistemological and methodological reflections from three socio-cultural projects. *Health, Risk & Society, 10*(5), 42 –438.

Hernández, D. (2015). Sacrifice along the energy continuum: A call for energy justice. *Environmental Justice, 8*(4), 151–156.

Hillman, M., & Fawcett, T. (2004). *How we can save the planet*. London: Penguin.

Hindmarsh, R. (2013). *Nuclear disaster at Fukushima Daiichi: Social, political and environmental Issues*. Abingdon: Routledge.

Hindmarsh, R. A., & Priestley, R. (2015). *The Fukushima effect: A new geopolitical terrain* (Vol. 29). Abingdon: Routledge.

Hinman, G. W., Rosa, E. A., Kleinhesselink, R. R., & Lowinger, T. C. (1993). Perceptions of nuclear and other risks in Japan and the United States. *Risk Analysis, 13*(4), 449–455.

Holden, C. (1984). Fear of nuclear power: A phobia? *Science, 226*(4676), 814–815.

Hom, A. G., Plaza, R. M., & Palmén, R. (2011). The framing of risk and implications for policy and governance: The case of EMF. *Public Understanding of Science, 20*(3), 319–333. doi:10.1177/0963662509336712.

Hunt, J. (2001). *Framing the problem of radioactive waste: Public and institutional perspectives*. Paper presented at the Values in Decisions on Risk (VALDOR), Stockholm.

IAEA. (1991). *The international Chernobyl project – assessment of radiological consequences and evaluation of protective measures* (91-03254). Vienna: International Atomic Energy Agency.

Joffe, H. (2003). Risk: From perception to social representation. *British Journal of Social Psychology, 42*, 55–73.

Kahneman, D., & Tversky, A. (1984). Choices, values, and frames. *American Psychologist, 39*(4), 341.

Kaiser, M. (2015). Ethics of science and a new social contract for knowledge. In S. Meisch, J. L. Lunderhausen, L. Bossert, & M. Rockoff (Eds.), *Ethics of science in the research for sustainable development* (pp. 153–177). Baden-Baden: Nomos Verlag.

Kaplan, S., & Garrick, B. J. (1981). On the quantitative definition of risk. *Risk Analysis, 1*(1), 11–27.

Kasperson, R. E., Golding, D., Tuler, S. (1992). Siting hazardous facilities and communicating risks under conditions of high social distrust. *Journal of Social Issues*, 48, 161–167.

Kates, R. W., Hohenemser, C., & Kasperson, J. X. (1985). *Perilous progress: Managing the hazards of technology*. Boulder CO: Westview Press.

Kline, R., & Pinch, T. (1999). Users as agents of technological change. In D. MacKenzie, & J. Wajcman (Eds.), *The social shaping of technology* (2nd ed.). Buckenham: Open University Press.

Kraft, M. E., & Clary, B. B. (1993). Public testimony in nuclear waste repository hearings: A content analysis. In R. E. Dunlap, M. E. Kraft, & E. A. Rosa (Eds.), *Public reactions to nuclear waste*. Durham, NC: Duke University Press.

Kuhn, T. S. (1962). *The structure of scientific revolutions*. Chicago, IL: University of Chicago Press.

Kukla, A. (2000). *Social constructivism and the philosophy of science*. New York: Routledge.

Latour, B. (2004). *Politics of nature: How to bring the sciences into democracy*. Cambridge MA: Harvard University Press.

Leroy, D. (2006). Political life and half-life: The future formulation of nuclear waste public policy in the United States. *Health Physics*, 91(5), 502–507.

Levine, A. G. (1982). *Love canal: Science, politics, and people*. Lexington, MA: Lexington Books.

Lock, P., & McCall, A. (2001). A coherent approach to the long-term management of radioactive waste. *Interdisciplinary Science Reviews*, 26(4), 307–312.

Luks, F. (1999). Post-normal science and the rhetoric of inquiry: Deconstructing normal science? *Futures*, 31, 705–719.

Lupton, D. (1999). *Risk and sociocultural theory: New directions and perspectives*. Cambridge: Cambridge University Press.

Macklis, R. M. (1990). Radithor and the era of mild radium therapy. *Jama*, 264(5), 614–618.

Malenka, D. J., Baron, J. A., Johansen, S., Wahrenberger, J. W., & Ross, J. M. (1993). The framing effect of relative and absolute risk. *Journal of General Internal Medicine*, 8(10), 543–548.

Malin, S. (2013). *The price of nuclear power: Uranium communities and environmental justice*. Rutgers, NJ: Rutgers University Press.

Marris, C., Wynne, B., Simmons, P., & Weldon, S. (2001). *Public perceptions of agricultural biotechnologies in Europe final report*. Retrieved from http://csec.lancs.ac.uk/pabe/docs.htm.

Martland, H. S. & Humphries, R. E. (1929). Osteogenic sarcoma in dial painters using luminous paint. *Archives of Pathology*, 7, 406–417.

Maxey, M. (1997). *The LNT (linear, no-threshold) hypothesis: Ethical travesties*. Paper presented at the Wingspread Conference, Racine, Wisconsin.

May, R. (1999). *Genetically modified foods: Facts, worries, policies and public confidence*. London: Office of Science and Technology.

McCalman, C., & Connelly, S. (2015). Destabilizing environmentalism: Epiphanal change and the emergence of pro-nuclear environmentalism. *Journal of Environmental Policy & Planning*, 1–18. doi:10.1080/1523908X.2015.1119675.

McCutcheon, C. (2002). *Nuclear reactions: The politics of opening a radioactive waste disposal site*. Albuquerque: University of New Mexico Press.

Miller, C. (1973). *The politics of communication*. New York: Oxford University Press.

Miller, J. D. (1998). The measurement of civic scientific literacy. *Public Understanding of Science*, 7(3), 203–223. doi:10.1088/0963-6625/7/3/001.

Miller, J. D. (2004). Public understanding of, and attitudes toward scientific research: What we know and what we need to know. *Public Understanding of Science, 13*(3), 273–294.

Miller, S. (2001). Public understanding of science at the crossroads. *Public Understanding of Science, 10*(1), 115–120.

Nakayachi, K. (1998). How do people evaluate risk reduction when they are told zero risk is impossible? *Risk Analysis, 18*(3), 235–242.

National Research Council. (1996). *Understanding risk: Informing decisions in a democratic society.* Washington DC: National Research Council.

National Science Board. (2002). Science and technology: Public attitudes and public understanding. *Science & Engineering Indicators.* Washington DC: US Government Printing Office.

North, W. D. (1999). A perspective on nuclear waste. *Risk Analysis, 19*(4), 751–758.

Nuclear Decommissioning Authority. (2013). *2013 radioactive waste inventory: Waste quantities from all sources.* Retrieved from www.nda.gov.uk/ukinventory/wp-content/uploads/sites/2/2014/02/14D042_NDASTSTY140010_-_Waste_Quantities_from_all_Sources.pdf.

Okrent, D. (1999). On intergenerational equity and its clash with intergenerational equity on the need for policies to guide the regulation of disposal of wastes and other activities posing very long-term risks. *Risk Analysis, 19*(5), 877–902.

Openshaw, S., Carver, S., & Fernie, J. (1989). *Britain's nuclear waste: Safety and siting.* London: Belhaven Press.

Oreskes, N. (2004). Science and public policy: What's proof got to do with it? *Environmental Science & Policy, 7*(5), 369–383. doi:http://dx.doi.org/10.1016/j.envsci.2004.06.002.

Oughton, D. (2001). *Ethical issues in nuclear waste management.* Paper presented at the Values in Decision on Risks (VALIDOR), Stockholm.

Owens, S. (2000). 'Engaging the public': Information and deliberation in environmental policy. *Environment and Planning, 32*(7), 1141–1148.

Parker, I. (1998). *Social constructionism, discourse and realism.* London: Sage.

Peters, E. M., Burraston, B., & Mertz, C. K. (2004). An emotion-based model of risk perception and stigma susceptibility: Cognitive appraisals of emotion, affective reactivity, worldviews, and risk perceptions in the generation of technological stigma. *Risk Analysis, 24*(5), 1349–1367.

Petterson, J. S. (1988). Perception vs reality of radiological impact: The Goiana Model. *Nuclear News, 31*(14), 84–90.

Pollycove, M. (1995). The issue of the decade: Hormesis. *European Journal of Nuclear Medicine, 22*(5), 399–401. doi:10.1007/bf00839052.

Popper, K. (1959). *The logic of scientific discovery.* London: Heineman.

Prasad, K. N., Cole, W. C., & Hasse, G. M. (2004). Health risks of low dose ionizing radiation in humans: A review. *Experimental Biology and Medicine, 229*(5), 378–382.

Quinn, S. (1995). *Marie Curie: A life.* Simon and Schuster, London.

Ravetz, J. R. (1999). What is post-normal science? *Futures, 31*, 647–653.

Renn, O. (1998). Three decades of risk research: Accomplishments and new challenges. *Journal of Risk Research, 1*(1), 49–71.

Renn, O. (2008). *Risk governance: Coping with uncertainty in a complex world.* Abingdon: Routledge Earthscan.

Renzi, B. G., Cotton, M., Napolitano, G., & Barkemeyer, R. (2016). Rebirth, devastation and sickness: Analyzing the role of metaphor in media discourses of nuclear power. *Environmental Communication.* doi:10.1080/17524032.2016.1157506.

Rieu, A.-M. (2013). Thinking after Fukushima. Epistemic shift in social sciences. *Asia Europe Journal, 11*(1), 65–78. doi:10.1007/s10308-013-0344-8.

Rip, A. (1986). Controversies as informal technology assessment. *Knowledge: Creation, Diffusion, Utilization, 8*(2), 349–371.

Romerio, F. (2002). Which paradigm for managing the risk of ionizing radiation? *Risk Analysis, 22*(1), 59–66.

Rosa, E. A., & Freudenburg, W. R. (1993). The historical development of public reactions to nuclear power: Implications for nuclear waste policy. In R. E. Dunlap, M. E. Kraft, & E. A. Rosa (Eds.), *Public reactions to nuclear waste: Citizens' views of repository siting* (pp. 32–63). London: Duke University Press.

Rosa, E. A., & Short, J. F. (2004). The importance of context in siting controversies: The case of high-level nuclear waste disposal in the U.S. In A. Boholm, & R. Löfstedt, (Eds.), *Facility siting: Risk, power and identity in land use planning.* London: Earthscan.

Royal Society (Great Britain), & Bodmer, W. F. (1985). *The public understanding of science: Report of a Royal Society ad hoc group endorsed by the Council of the Royal Society.* London: Royal Society.

Russell, L., & Babrow, A. (2011). Risk in the making: Narrative, problematic integration, and the social construction of risk. *Communication Theory, 21*(3), 239–260.

Saloranta, T. M. (2001). Post-normal science and the global climate change issue. *Climatic Change, 50*(4), 395–404.

Schon, D. A., & Rein, M. (1994). *Frame reflection: Toward the resolution of intractable policy controversies.* New York: Basic Books.

Shrader-Frechette, K. (1991). Ethical dilemmas and radioactive waste: A survey of the issues. *Environmental Ethics, 13*(4), 327–343.

Shrader-Frechette, K. (1998). Scientific method, Anti-foundationalism and public decision making. In R. Löfxstedt, & L. Frewer (Eds.), *Risk and modern society.* London: Earthscan.

Shrader-Frechette, K. (1999). Chernobyl, global injustice and mutagenic threats. In N. Low (Ed.), *Global ethics and environment.* London: Taylor and Francis.

Shrader-Frechette, K. (2000). Duties to future generations. Proxy consent, intra-intergenerational equity: The case of nuclear waste. *Risk Analysis, 20*(6), 771–778.

Shrader-Frechette, K. S. (1993). *Burying uncertainty: Risk and the case against geological disposal of waste.* Berkeley: University of California Press.

Simmons, P., & Walker, G. (1999). Tolerating risk: Policy principles and public perceptions. *Risk, Decision and Policy, 4*(3), 179–190.

Sjöberg, L. (2003). *Risk perception is not what it seems: The psychometric paradigm revisited.* Paper presented at the Values in Decisions on Risk (VALDOR), Stockholm.

Slovic, P. (1987). Perception of risk. *Science, 236*(4799), 280–285.

Slovic, P., Flynn, J., & Layman, M. (2000). Perceived risk, trust and the politics of nuclear waste. In P. Slovic (Ed.), *The perception of risk.* London: Earthscan.

Slovic, P., Kunreuther, H., e. a. & Flynn, J. (2001). *Risk, media and stigma: Understanding challenges to modern science and technology.* London: Earthscan.

Slovic, P., Layman, M., & Flynn, J. (1991). Risk perception, trust and nuclear waste: Lessons from Yucca Mountain. *Environment, 33*, 6–11.

Slovic, P., Layman, M., & Flynn, J. (1993). Received risk, trust and nuclear waste: Lessons from Yucca Mountain. In R. E. Dunlap, , M. E. Kraft, & E. A. Rosa (Eds.), *Public reactions to nuclear waste.* Durham, NC: Duke University Press.

Stirling, A. (2001). Participatory processes and scientific expertise: Precaution, diversity and transparency in the governance of risk. *Participatory Learning and Action, 40*(February), 66–71.

Sturgis, P., & Allum, N. (2004). Science in society: re-evaluating the deficit model of public attitudes. *Public Understanding of Science, 13*(1), 55–74.

Tversky, A., & Kahneman, D. (1981). The framing of decisions and the psychology of choice. *Science, 211*, 281–299.

US Environmental Protection Agency. (2015). *Radiation health effects.* Retrieved from www.epa.gov/radiation/radiation-health-effects.

Walker, J. S. (2004). *Three Mile Island: A nuclear crisis in historical perspective.* Berkeley University of California Press.

Wilsdon, J., & Willis, R. (2004). *See-through science: Why public engagement needs to move upstream.* London: Demos.

Wilson, L. M. (2000). *Nuclear waste: Exploring the ethical dilemmas.* Toronto, Ontario: United Church Publishing House.

Wynne, B. (1985). From public perception of risk to technology as cultural process. In V. Covello (Ed.), *Environmental impact assessment technology and risk analysis.* Berlin: Springer.

Wynne, B. (1988). Unruly technology: Practical rules, impractical discourses and public understanding. *Social Studies of Science, 18*, 147–168.

Wynne, B. (1989). Sheepfarming after Chernobyl: A case study in communicating scientific information. *Environment: Science and Policy for Sustainable Development, 31*(2), 10–39.

Wynne, B. (1996). May the sheep safely graze? A reflexive view of the expert-lay knowledge divide. In S. Lash, B. Szerszynski, & B. Wynne (Eds.), *Risk, environment and modernity.* London: Sage Publications.

Wynne, B. (2002). Risk and environment as legitimatory discourses of technology: Reflexivity inside out? *Current Sociology, 50*(3), 459–477.

Wynne, B. (2006). Public engagement as a means of restoring public trust in science – hitting the notes, but missing the music? *Public Health Genomics, 9*(3), 211–220.

Ziman, J. (1991). Public understanding of science. *Science, Technology & Human Values, 16*(1), 99–105.

6 The participatory–deliberative turn

Introduction

In Chapter 5, I discussed the social and psychological factors around risk and public understanding of science that directly or indirectly influence citizen– stakeholder reactions to radioactive wastes and decision-making over their long- term management. We can understand changes to the decision-making context for RWM as an adaptive political process, one that has been influenced by broader changes in thinking within the field of risk management since the late 1990s. Environmental and technological risks have, since the early 1990s been re-articulated within the critical social sciences as social constructions. Under- standing risks and citizen–stakeholder reactions to them, in terms of social movements of opposition, involves exploring a broad range of socio-cultural, psychological and moral positions, rather than simply treating risks as calculable phenomena, independent from observer interaction and thus simply explana- tions of the likelihood of harm that can be correctly or incorrectly understood by those subject to them. Perceptions and broader cultural values towards risk involve the interaction of biases and heuristics, aesthetic values, moral prin- ciples and cultural influences, as well as political factors such as decision-framing and trust in the authority of science and politicians. As an issue of risk epi- stemology there has been a concerted move to reject unqualified statistical cri- teria in risk evaluation – and the interpretive social sciences have been influential in shaping political institutions' conception of risk management as a complex and multi-dimensional phenomenon (Bradbury, 1989; Renn, 1998; Guehlstorf & Hallstrom, 2005). RWM has been a key driver and test case in this regard (Slovic, Layman, & Flynn, 1993; Jenkins-Smith & Silva, 1998; Blowers, 1999; Atherton, 2001; Hunt, 2001; Mackerron & Berkhout, 2009); not only in the UK but internationally – with pioneering forms of multi- dimensional environmental risk governance in a range of RWM national con- texts. Case studies in Sweden, Finland and Belgium (Lidskog, 1992; Lidskog & Litmanen, 1997; Litmanen, 1999; Nuclear Energy Agency, 2002, 2005), and the USA and Canada (Rabe, 1994; Kuhn, 1998; Gunderson, 1999; McCarty & Power, 2000; Nuclear Energy Agency, 2003), are particularly worth exploring in this regard. What is clear is that risks are interpreted and acted upon in myriad ways by different actors – and understanding why simply *more* science communication has not stopped adverse community reactions to RWM facilities has been a slow learning curve for nuclear site decision-making authorities in the United Kingdom.

Radioactive waste as a not in my back yard (NIMBY) problem

At the heart of a multi-dimensional risk governance approach is an understanding of the geographic and scalar nature of RWM politics. Specifically, the relationship between local and national scales of risk governance. In 2000 a pan-European network on radioactive waste governance called the Community Waste Management (COWAM) project was established. The focus of the first initiative in the COWAM network was to examine the role of local actors, as local communities were seen to be isolated within the political processes of RWM. Within COWAM the project leads suggested that local communities have a genuine interest in governance because they consider not only the issue of radioactive waste as a technical problem, but as a 'key challenge for the development of their territories and the life equilibrium of the population'. The chair of COWAM, Dubreuil (2001), described the radioactive waste issue as a 'global problem looking for a local solution', asserting that the need for national level engagement on the structure and processes of radioactive waste management decision-making must always be taken within the context of an ultimate host site. Across Europe, political deliberation over radioactive waste management has traditionally taken place within the national-scale decision-making structures of central government, yet the siting of waste will always in essence be a local issue. It is as the ethicist of nuclear waste Rawles (2000) states:

> Whatever decision is made about the management of nuclear waste, the waste will be located in a specific place, in, or under, a specific community. It is produced in particular sites and it must be disposed in particular sites.

Decision-making authorities in the development of hazardous facility sites have frequently cited the not in my back yard (or NIMBY) problem as a core consideration in planning and siting processes. The term NIMBY refers to a certain type of opposition towards facilities that are deemed undesirable or unwanted (sometimes referred to as locally unwanted land uses – LULUs) and the protectionist attitudes of, and oppositional tactics adopted by, community groups facing what they deem to be unwelcome developments in their vicinity. Given the capacity of local opposition to halt development, the NIMBY concept has become a familiar and oft-discussed concept in the field of environmental planning. LULUs are often hazardous, noxious or visually intrusive facilities or technologies. In the social science literature, these commonly include nuclear or other hazardous chemical waste treatment facilities, or else energy and transport infrastructures such as wind farms, motorways or airports. NIMBY responses are also documented in relation to facilities that house or facilitate the needs of politically or socio-economically marginalised individuals and community groups – such as drug treatment centres, refugee centres, mental health facilities, prisons and detention centres, affordable housing and homeless shelters.

The origins of the NIMBY term are difficult to pin down. It was likely coined by Emilie Travel Livezey (1980) in an article about hazardous waste for *The Christian Science Monitor* magazine. In the UK, it was then later popularised by Nicholas Ridley towards the end of the 1980s, during his term as Environment Secretary under Margaret Thatcher's Conservative Government. Ridley used the term NIMBY as a rhetorical device to attack the rural middle classes for their opposition to local housing development, calling it 'crude Nimbyism', rooted in a belief that those who were protesting against the building of houses in rural locations put their own interests ahead of the needs of society; motivated by selfish rather than principled objections (Welsh, 1993).[1] The NIMBY concept has become an iconic representation of citizen reactions to unwanted facilities, which characterises local community actors that oppose project proposals as being able to recognise the societal value of an unwanted facility so long as it is not planned for near to where they personally live. The typical characterisation of NIMBY opposition is that residents will assert that these facilities are noxious, polluting or in some other way economically and/or environmentally damaging. They will concede that the facilities are in some way necessary for society but assert that they should not be built near to their own homes, schools or places of work or worship.

Some theorists on planning for unwanted land uses have posited that a clearer understanding of why NIMBYism occurs and the types of arguments used to support such attitudes, can be used to counter such 'self-centred' opposition, and thus overcome the associated planning problems that occur. Dear (1992) in particular, presents a model of a NIMBY response to an unwanted development in three stages. He argues that conflict over locally unwanted land uses such as RWM facilities is both progressive and predictable, moving sequentially through different modes of argumentation and bargaining. Dear's model begins with *youth* – whereby small vocal minorities that oppose development light the fuse of conflict, expressing opposition in blunt terms reflecting 'an irrational, unthinking response by opponents'. This is followed by *maturity*, whereby battle lines are solidified with opponents and proponents of developments assembling ranks of supporters. At this stage the forum of debate moves from the private to the public sphere, and so the rhetoric of opposition becomes 'more rational and objective', voicing concerns over property value decline, increased traffic volumes, environmental impacts etc. Finally, is the period of *old age*. Conflict resolution becomes drawn-out and in some cases, inconclusive. Victory tends to go to those with the greatest resources and persistence. In this final stage the tenor of the opposition moves from conflict to arbitration, with both sides making concessions; though if positions become sufficiently entrenched a stalemate can persist which is costly and damaging to both sides.

In some respects, Dear's model is apt for describing the sequential nature of local protest over controversial RWM facility siting. For example, Kuhn's

(1998) study of nuclear waste repository siting reveals a correlation amongst those who supported a proposed facility in principle, between perception of risk and acceptable distance of the facility from their place of residence, implying that proximity to unwanted facilities is a crucial aspect of their public acceptability on a local level. Devine-Wright (2005) notes, however, that there is a general assumption within the literatures on the NIMBY concept that those living in closest proximity to developments are likely to have the most negative attitudes, though in fact the empirical evidence undermines this assumption. Kuhn's study shows a correlation between proximity and acceptance of radioactive waste management facilities, however, Krannich, Little, and Cramer (1993) researched the NIMBY phenomenon relating to the Yucca Mountain radioactive waste repository in Nevada and found that opposition and concern are strongest in the communities furthest from Yucca Mountain. This finding has been mirrored in similar facility siting studies that have shown that individuals living closer to developments tend to have more positive attitudes towards development projects in comparison with those living further away (Braunholtz, 2003; Devine-Wright, 2005; Warren, Lumsden, O'Dowd, & Birnie, 2005; Walker, 2009).

A more fundamental problem than the 'proximity assumption' of a NIMBY attitude, is a concern that rather than being an objective assessment of public attitudes, the NIMBY label is mobilised as a social construction of lay public actors by nuclear industry professionals and planners to reify public opposition as a selfish act. By socially constructing the notion of the public as NIMBY, protestors become people who fail to see the 'bigger picture' of the benefits of 'safe' siting processes to society, preferring instead to focus on a purely local, neighbourhood-level protectionism (Barnett, Burningham, Walker, & Cass, 2012; Cotton & Devine-Wright, 2012). The notion that the NIMBY response is selfish, is a key aspect of the framing of public opposition, one that 'symbolises a perverse form of antisocial activism' (Hornblower, 1988). However, recent developments in the academic literature on NIMBYism have focused upon how the label is problematic for both developers and local community interests, as it often used by proponents of LULU development projects to discredit all forms of project opposition, regardless of motivation (Davy, 1996; Burningham, 2000; Devine-Wright, 2009). NIMBY labels are used in a negative and blaming sense, and the term is often strategically deployed as a rhetorical device to characterise non-technical specialists as worried, irrational, ignorant of scientific technical facts and risks, self-interested and concerned primarily with the protection of local amenities and household property values (Devine-Wright, 2005; Cotton & Devine-Wright, 2010). This characterisation of local people persists even when specific evidence for these attitudes is lacking in the political discourse surrounding siting proposals. Inherent to the NIMBY label, therefore, are assumptions often made by technical specialists about the emotive behaviours of public actors and the characterisations of their opposition as lacking in technical sophistication. However, this again is unsupported by evidence, as studies into public testimony in radioactive waste management hearings have shown that non-expert individuals and groups present testimony around facility planning which is often of comparable technical sophistication to that of the experts (Martin, 1996). Rather than an accurate characterisation of public opposition, the social representation of local community activists as NIMBY activists has been used primarily to discredit opposition groups in the political processes of nuclear technology development (broadly) and radioactive waste management (specifically), by undermining their credibility as legitimate stakeholder actors (Luloff, Albrecht, & Bourke, 1998; Burningham, 2000; Wolsink, 2000; Burningham, Barnett, & Thrush, 2006; Devine-Wright, 2009). Such critique has been levelled at the concept itself. NIMBY theorists such as Devine-Wright and Burningham have shown empirically that the NIMBY label is an inaccurate portrayal of how and why people react negatively to environmental change at the local level, and one that the opposition movements themselves do not recognise. Research into how local stakeholders characterise their own opposition, and the types of arguments that they put forward in relation to project developments such as wind farms, electricity transmission lines and radioactive waste management facilities, has revealed that opposition to energy project developments is frequently scientifically grounded, broad-reaching and ethically reasoned, in contrast to the assumptions that their arguments are based upon selfishness, ignorance and a myopic obsession with local house prices or amenity values. Though it is true that project opponents may perceive developments as risky, costly or visually unattractive, this often leads locally affected community members not to a knee-jerk concern with house prices or personal risks, but to broader questioning of issues of community-level fairness, energy and waste strategy, utility and place identity (Michaud, Carlisle, & Smith, 2008; Devine-Wright, 2009).

As well as the empirical evidence, NIMBY is also criticised on philosophical grounds. In the RWM case, the risks are borne by specific communities, yet a utilitarian moral case is made by the RWMO that implements siting (whereby the greatest good is maximised for the greatest number of people). Site communities are expected to think beyond individual interests and think towards broader, national, environmental policy goals (as mentioned previously, a national problem with a local solution). However, this is problematic for two reasons. First, because asking individuals to accept risks generated by a profit-making nuclear industry without providing financial compensation or other benefits in kind has been shown by both economists and philosophers as a *supererogatory act* – i.e. beyond the call of duty for any group of individuals to bear without adequate recompense (Peterson & Hansson, 2004). Second, host communities seek both *procedural* and *distributive* fairness in the decision-making process. Procedural fairness concerns how the site is chosen, what the alternatives might be, who regulates the industry, and who is involved in process; whereas distributive fairness concerns how positive and negative outcomes are shared between those that profit and those that bear the impacts (Walker, 2012). Both of these procedural and distributive fairness aspects have been shown to be key drivers of public acceptability in energy project siting, because even if the outcomes of a siting process remain unwanted by opponents, they are more likely to be accepted if the process of deciding is perceived to be fair and transparent (Gross, 2007).

To alleviate distributive unfairness, in some cases community opposition can be assuaged by providing the right package of compensation or community benefits. Some effective means of achieving local acceptance of projects that have proved successful in the wind sector are profit sharing with local communities (through distributing stocks/shares); partnership working (allowing local community representation at board meetings and the AGM); and lower cost energy (through gas and/or electricity subsidies) (Devlin, 2005; Cass, Walker, & Devine-Wright, 2010). Though such benefits are key tools in achieving public acceptance, they may not always be effective because there are a number of intangible, soft social and cultural factors that lead to localised public opposition, and these cannot be easily valued and compensated for monetarily (Severson, 2012). These factors often link to a *sense of place* (Boholm & Löfstedt, 2004). Quantitative and qualitative social science research into social movements of opposition against unwanted land use development has shown that a key issue that stimulates public opposition is that the presence of industrial facilities in rural, peri-urban/suburban places can change the character of the place in which residents of those communities live. Rural places can become industrial places by the introduction of the technology – affecting not only how individuals perceive the landscape and the local environs, but also their own identity as rural people. This can cause a type of 'moral shock' where pre-existing emotions and experiences channel the interpretation of announcements about things like an RWM facility. For example, in the case of wind farms or electricity transmission systems it has been shown that a pre-existing personal reverence for the beauty of the countryside or suspicions about a local electricity utility, will increase the level of shock that individuals experience at hearing about a new proposal (Jasper, 1998; Cass & Walker, 2009). These shocks can disrupt an individual's sense of *place attachment* causing (in some instances) a desire to move away from the area, an anger towards the perceived unfairness of the implementation process and lost trust in implementing authorities. This in turn stimulates opposition groups to form in an attempt to prevent that disruption from occurring as a form of place-protective action (Devine-Wright, 2009). This factor isn't easy to gauge in advance of a development proposal, nor easy to value monetarily using tools like cost-benefit analysis or risk assessment.

There also remains the problem of bribery. It is difficult for a RWMO to argue both from a moral position (specifically the utilitarian position of expecting a community to bear risks on behalf of the greater good for the environmental safety and military security of the nation), and simultaneously provide monetary compensation – as this fundamentally undermines the authority of the moral claim (Cotton, 2013). When it comes to public acceptance of risks the key issue is to build trust relationships between institutions and communities (Wachinger, Renn, Begg, & Kuhlicke, 2012). Monetary compensation can damage trust, as it changes the form of incentive offered to the community; altering the fundamental relationship from one of national interest and moral stewardship for the RWM facility, to one of a transactional relationship (Cotton, 2013).

Despite the problems associated with the use of the NIMBY label, it persists within policy and planning discourse within and outside nuclear planning policy, and thus influences the ways in which technical specialists conceive of 'the public' and thus how to communicate information to them, and how to engage with them on the substantive issues that underlie their opposition (Burningham, Barnett, Carr, Clift, & Wehrmeyer, 2007; Cass & Walker, 2009; Barnett et al., 2012; Cotton & Devine-Wright, 2012). As Burningham et al. (2007) suggest, understanding how technical specialists construct the concept of different public actors is crucial in any attempt to understand how developers engage with local communities, and how they either involve or exclude them from decisions. This is because 'imagining publics' i.e. understanding the under-lying social construction of who the public are (the audience) and what assump-tions you might make about what that audience is like, is crucial for formulating a communicative strategy (Maranta, Guggenheim, Gisler, & Pohl, 2003; Burn-ingham et al., 2007). Research has shown that experts in science and industry tend to imagine publics in different categories. These can be as simple as sup-porters, opponents and those that do not have a view (Barnett et al., 2012); or else as customers, voters, neighbours, opponents, nimbies, the man in the street, lay people, migrants, stakeholders, citizens etc. When these different imaginings are taken into account, the design of a communicative strategy must incorp-orate and reflect upon the underlying assumptions made by technical authorities about what the public interest actually is and how this can be incorporated (Burningham et al., 2007; Cotton, 2013). Importantly for RWM, this leads us to consider how one might bring together technical specialists and citizen-stakeholders in a manner that takes account of differing constructions of the public and public interest in a manner that is balanced, technically grounded, well facilitated and fair.

Public engagement with radioactive wastes

If we understand RWM as a fundamentally scalar problem between national-level decisions (and decision-making authorities) and locally affected 'host' communities, then we must also understand it as one of conflicting disciplinary expertise – that the task of bringing the disparate social and technical elements of nuclear risk management together into a hybrid *socio-technical* understanding of the problem, i.e. one that relates engineering and safety criteria to the context of public values in which they are expressed (see in particular Flüeler & Scholz, 2004; Flüeler, 2006) must involve a process of integration through dia-logue. The local and socio-technical characterisation of RWM has, in turn, spurred a surge in the development of dialogue processes that involve a range of affected stakeholders including site communities and broader publics in decision-making. Dialogue is a mechanism through which the postnormal science of RWM mentioned in the previous chapter can emerge: creating conditions of decision-making that incorporate a range of non-technical and *local* knowledge and diverse actors alongside scientific and technical decision criteria. The blending of 'hard' technical and 'soft' value considerations through an integrated dialogue platform is alternatively referred to as an *analytic-deliberative* decision-making process (Renn, 1999, 2004; Chilvers, 2007), and the effects of this change in the fundamental philosophy of decision-making are detailed in this section. I discuss in the next part how RWM has been subject to a broader 'turn' towards participatory–deliberative dialogue processes as fundamental to the development of policy (Simmons & Bickerstaff, 2006), which in the professional radioactive waste management field is commonly referred to as *public and stakeholder engagement* (hereafter PSE – this terminology is used in this chapter). PSE-focused decision-making stands in contrast to the techno-centric politics of RWM in the UK up to and including the RCF proposal failure in 1997. In this regard, I focus upon two key decision points. The first is the development of the *Managing Radioactive Waste Safely* programme and the assessment of radioactive waste management options under the auspices of the Committee on Radioactive Waste Management (CoRWM). The second is the subsequent decision on the implementation framework for a long-term radioactive waste management solution based upon a voluntary site selection process and the its consequences (examined in Chapter 7).

The turn to participation

As discussed in previous chapters, the move towards PSE within RWM reflects broader changes in the nature of science and technology policy in the UK. The practice of involving public and stakeholder actors in technology decision-making processes has arisen primarily as a means to ameliorate what are seen by some scientific authorities as problems of scepticism, cynicism, and mistrust amongst publics towards science and scientists and the subsequent impact upon scientific discovery and technology development policy; and also as a means to make science more *local* in the sense of understanding how developments impact upon the daily lives of individuals and the communities in which they live. Failures to implement grand technology programmes in UK society and growing public fears over widespread health and environmental risks grew substantially in the 1990s. The Chernobyl example is key in understanding the effect of a global technological catastrophe on a local place: specifically, the impact upon farming in the northwest of England from the radioactive fallout from the dust cloud that travelled across Europe in the aftermath of the reactor explosion. Another is the public fear over the spread of Bovine Spongiform Encephalopathy (BSE). BSE caused the development of variant Creutzfeldt-Jakob Disease (vCJD) – a fatal neurodegenerative prion disease contracted from the ingestion of infected meat products. As a risk factor vCJD was deeply concerning in part because there was no cure, but also because the long incubation period meant that victims often developed the symptoms decades after the original infection – an insidious, low probability-high impact, 'dread' risk in psychological terms (see Gigerenzer, 2004). These failures of public scientific authorities to keep the public safe, so to speak, from such risks led to declining levels of trust in science and scientists in the UK, and the resolution of this problem became an important focus for leading scientific institutions.

Notable in the fight to regain public trust in science was the 1997 Royal Society conference on Science, Trust and Social Change that identified a greater role for *dialogue* between scientists and lay publics that moved beyond the deficit model assumptions of public science education, towards a more bi-directional examination of science in society (see in particular Grove-White, 1997). The concept of routine engagement between the public and scientific institutions then grew significantly within UK science and technology policy, bolstered by the House of Lords Select Committee on Science and Technology report that identified a 'new mood for dialogue' whereby direct engagement with the public over science-based policy-making was encouraged to shift from being an 'optional add-on' towards being a 'normal and integral part of the process' (House of Lords Select Committee on Science and Technology, 2000). The implications of the report were as Irwin (2001) puts it, a move towards genuine changes in the cultures and constitutions of key decision-making institutions in the UK.

This change in thinking had a profound effect upon the underlying policy and decision-making processes for RWM. In short, it represented an epistemic shift in RWM policy away from the nation-scaled, broadly utilitarian and technocratic approach that characterised government and industry decisions up to and including the 1997 RCF proposal. The shift is rooted in a broader level of political discourse that reveals how, to some extent at least, decision-making processes for complex environmental policy issues are challenging *representative* democratic norms. The concept that elected officials respond to their constituents' interests has come under scrutiny from academic social scientists, NGOs, think tanks and grassroots organisations protesting risk-bearing technologies. Though scientific communities themselves were shifting towards a new 'mood for dialogue', there has been a simultaneous collective effort by these organisations to pressure public authorities to hold participatory–deliberative processes as a routine aspect of technology governance (Sclove, 1995; Genus & Coles, 2005; Parkins & Mitchell, 2005; Bergmans, Sundqvist, Kos, & Simmons, 2015).

Bringing technology into the democratic sphere requires deliberation upon project proposals in an open manner, and not simply the one-way transmission of information from experts to the public, or project planning involving the Decide–Announce–Defend strategies mentioned in Chapter 5 (and discussed variously in Arnstein, 1969; A. G. Gunderson, 1995; Halvorsen, 2003; Barney, 2006; Snider, 2009). RWM has, internationally, shifted its political philosophy to recognise that at least *some* form of deliberation on technical planning processes should occur, and that this is not the exclusive purview of technical specialists. The ascendance of participatory–deliberative decision-support processes is, therefore, reflective of changes in the context of risk management as discussed in Chapter 5. Analytic–deliberative risk management processes are the means to combine and contrast technical and social knowledge (Stern & Fineberg, 1996). Participation has, in risk management circles as Fischhoff (1995) argues, restructured decision-making from 'all we have to do is get the numbers right' to 'all we have to do is make them partners', and this has come to be understood in some academic and policy circles as a kind of 'gold standard' for decision-making (Felt & Fochler, 2008), with a strong push from critical policy theorists and allied public policy actors to institutionalise this as best practice in planning and environmental governance (Burgess & Clark, 2006) of which RWM is a critical case.

The *turn* reveals how decision-making legitimacy has been construed by citizen-stakeholders as being based upon the ability and opportunity of non-elected public actors to participate in effective deliberation and represent, by proxy, those who are subject to collective decisions (Dryzek, 2000, 2006). The 'aggregative', vote-centric modes of democratic participation through the act of electoral voting or referenda gave way to a more 'talk-centric', deliberative and participatory model of individual involvement in decision-making (Gutmann & Thompson, 2004). Under these conditions citizens effectively take on the role of public representatives, albeit in a selected (or often self-selected) basis, rather than in an elected capacity. This occurs either alongside or in place of public interest representation through elected officials within traditional democratic forums (in the UK this includes parish, city, borough and county council representation, elected mayors and police commissioners, Members of Parliament, Members of the European Parliament and elected members of devolved administrations in Scotland, Wales and Northern Ireland). It must be noted, however, that participatory–deliberative democratic processes can generate political conflict, particularly when responses from citizens in direct democratic process are perceived as being overridden or ignored by elected authorities, or public values differ substantially from the policy platform of the prevailing majority in government. Despite this inevitable tension the participatory–deliberative turn has, to some extent, standardised and embedded public involvement in the policy-making processes within the machinery of government, and private sector organisations have also increasingly become accustomed to PSE as a statutory requirement in planning processes for big technology and infrastructure projects (Owens & Cowell, 2002; Cotton, 2011; Groves, Munday, & Yakovleva, 2013). The latter are commonly required as part of public authority-led permitting and planning processes. Whereas for personal/domestic technologies, user input in commercial application and development is a common practice. It therefore was recognised within academic and policy circles that deliberation on technology-based issues provided a test bed for new participatory–deliberative structures and methods to enable involvement of a broad range of actors including input from heterogeneous publics (Irwin & Wynne, 1996; Hunsberger & Kenyon, 2008). During the late 1990s to early/mid 2000s academic social scientists responded to the turn by developing a broad range of novel decision-support models, structures, 'toolkits' and handbooks for designing and implementing such dialogue processes (for example Wates, 2000; Lotov, 2003; Rockloff & Lockie, 2004; Creighton, 2005; Elliott, Heesterbeek, Lukensmeyer, & Slocum, 2005; Flüeler, 2005; Cotton, 2014), and the methods and models for the subsequent evaluation of such tools (Petts & Leach, 2000; Rowe & Frewer, 2000). In RWM a notable example was the trial of the Deliberative Mapping (DM) methodology in the radioactive waste management options assessment process (which is discussed below). DM integrates two independent but complementary approaches to informing decision-making. The first is stakeholder decision analysis (SDA): a qualitative group-based discussion process amongst citizen-stakeholders, and the second is Multi-Criteria Mapping (MCM): a quantitative, computer-assisted interview process for scoring different options. Though the methodology was not taken up by CoRWM in its appraisal of radioactive waste management options, the trialling of the methodology is indicative of an experimental attitude to deliberation that emerged at this time, and a willingness amongst public authorities to try these things on a live policy outside the purely 'academic' setting (see Burgess, Chilvers, Clark, Day, Hunt, King et al., 2004; Burgess, Stirling, Clark, Davies, Eames, Staley et al., 2007).

In addition to a proliferation of methods, there has also been an expansion in terms and concepts that stem from the participatory–deliberative turn. The related (and often interchangeable) terminology of *participation, postnormal science, deliberation, inclusion, engagement, civil, civic, stakeholder, citizen* and *democratic science* represent a set of catchwords to signify the ascendancy of this paradigm in environmental, scientific and technological policy (Bäckstrand, 2003). However, this masks great diversity and internal contradiction. These terms are loosely defined and often inconsistently applied – sometimes when authorities refer to participation or citizen deliberation, the underlying meaning is a strategic mechanism to try and speed up planning and implementation processes (often defined as a panacea to the 'NIMBY problem' discussed previously). In other cases, (particularly when discussed by academic social scientists and NGO actors), citizen deliberation means a bottom-up, community-focused means to critique, and some cases ultimately oppose, technological developments. There is risk that the use of such terms can encourage different actors to talk across purposes – leading to frustration as different visions of 'deliberation' do not meet the needs of the stakeholders engaged in such processes. As such, the myriad motivations for the participatory–deliberative turn have been subject to significant academic evaluation.

The motivations for participation

The different motivations or rationales for participation can be grouped into *normative/ethical* motivations, *strategic* motivations and *substantive* motivations (Fiorino, 1990). Normative/ethical motivations are intended to reinforce social justice by fostering greater community support and the alleviation of procedural decision-making injustices, whereby certain voices are excluded from having any input into decision-making. Participation is 'the right thing to do' because it encourages informed consent on decisions that directly affect local community interests and heterogeneous publics. It can also improve the fairness in the distribution of outcomes from decisions, and empower the participants in their own learning about the issues under deliberation. Strategic motivations aim to reduce costs and planning delays from opposition movements (Petts, 1999). Substantive motivations are about finding a means to resolve intractable stakeholder conflicts, restore trust in political institutions (Bloomfield, Collins, Fry, & Munton, 2001), render decision-making processes and resultant policies as legitimate in the eyes of decision-makers (Cohen, 1989; Beierle & Koninsky, 2000; Grunwald, 2004), and to improve the quality of decisions through collaborative participation to solve complex, contentious problems (Innes & Booher, 2004) by including not only stakeholder and local community preferences and values, but also by eliciting important information pertinent to the planning process from 'lay experts' (Wynne, 1996; Petts & Brooks, 2005), thus making technical decisions more 'socially robust' (Beierle, 1999; Flüeler & Scholz, 2004). The substantive value of public engagement stems from a recognition that broader deliberation with those not affiliated with science, technology, governmental politics and the planning profession can reveal new kinds of information relevant to the decision that may otherwise be overlooked: such as risk-based, geographical, social impact, economic and moral issues that are pertinent to the local community, the area in which they live and the decision at hand (Lidskog, 1996; Wynne, 1996; Yearly, 2000; Nowotny, 2001; Petts & Brooks, 2005; Cotton, 2009).

In addition to the potential benefits to the outcomes of policy decisions through deliberative dialogue (whether they are fairer, faster or more robust), there are several potential benefits felt by the communities themselves. Jin (2013) notes that researchers of direct citizen engagement in policy decisions report the *developmental* benefits of participation: that individuals who engage in dialogue processes become better able to realise their *personal* potential in various ways. Participants contribute to PSE programmes in part because it serves their own purposes as self-interested stakeholder groups or as private citizens with a 'stake' in the outcome of a decision; but also, often under moral motivation to represent their community, their social group or broader society beyond individual interests. This is what Goodin (1986) terms the 'laundering preferences', whereby the private self-interests of participants are filtered out from dialogue and more public-oriented preferences are expressed. This has potential benefits for the outcomes of decisions, but this process of laundering preferences potentially has other effects. On a personal and community level, it also allows opportunities for improvement of the moral and intellectual qualities of the participants (Fearon, 1998), encouraging them to undergo reflexive social learning (Tuler, 1998; Daniels & Walker, 2001). Community involvement is oft-cited as providing opportunities to foster the conditions of social and technical learning, and thus to promote active citizenship through a transformation of values and preferences in response to encounters with other deliberators

(D'Entrèves, 2002, p. 25). This might be technical or institutional knowledge about the issue, greater involvement with peers, skills in organising knowledge or stimulating creativity. In the case of nuclear power, it might also encourage pro-environmental behaviours, as participants make the link between their energy consumptive lifestyles and the generation of wastes. Moreover, it may prompt a change in the understanding of the community as different members come together to speak about the place in which they live. Social learning has been subject to significant academic evaluation. Thus, an important aspect of the evaluation of deliberative processes is to empirically investigate the transformative power of engagement to produce long-term 'beyond process' learning (Bull, Petts, & Evans, 2008) such as the effects of taking part upon transforming public responses to RWM policy proposals under consideration.

We can conclude, at this stage, that the participatory–deliberative turn in environmental policy and technology assessment has involved a great deal of public advocacy for the status of publics and a desire to improve their status relative to technical specialists and elected representatives. Advocates of deliberative approaches often argue that because deliberation involves reasoned and critical discussion rather than presumed cultural consensus, technical authority or political deal-making, it is therefore arguably 'superior' to aggregative political (Gutmann, 1993; Johnson, 1998) or technocratic, science-centred decision-making. The inclusion of individuals in the political and moral discussion of technology implementation remains important because the implicit consent involved in technocratic decision-making or aggregative voting (in electoral politics and representative forms of democratic process) is insufficient to legitimately expose individuals to additional or elevated risks resulting from living in proximity to RWM facilities. Inclusive participatory–deliberative process design is thus required so that consent can be obtained explicitly and transparently from those affected, improving the procedural fairness of decision-making and the ethical validity of the implementation selection process (for discussion of participation and consent in environmental decisions see Shrader-Frechette, 2002 in particular).

The participatory–deliberative turn in UK policy

Outside the academic literature on PSE and the underlying deliberative democratic theory that underpins it, is clear evidence that engaging publics at different stages in policy development became an accepted and legitimated practice within broader UK policy-making during the period of the early 2000s across a range of policy domains, particulalry regarding the governance of what could be termed 'socially contentious technologies' such as RWM (Cotton, 2014), and the achievement of sustainable development goals in particular changed as PSE became institutionalised across government departments (Chilvers & Burgess, 2008).

The institutionalisation of a participatory–deliberative turn in RWM also has its roots in the political agenda of sustainable development at the time. The

Rio World Summit on Sustainable Development (UNEP, 1992) called upon the scientific and technological communities and state and non-state actors, to begin to form partnerships to achieve the goals of sustainability. Of the Principles of Sustainable Development that emerged, Principle 10 has had significant influence upon the role of stakeholders. It states that concerned citizens at 'the relevant level' should be involved and given the necessary information to encourage their participation to achieve sustainability. As Cramer (2009) notes, citizen oversight is necessary for the public to contribute to environmental protection, and so access to information about governmental and non-governmental environmental activities is an imperative for environmental justice. The UNECE *Convention on Access to Information, Public Participation and Access to Justice in Environmental Matters* (UNECE, 1998) is particularly significant in this regard. It was signed in June 1998 in the Danish City of Aarhus. The *Aarhus Convention*, as it is known, began with the Environment for Europe process beginning in 1991, following the first Conference of European Environmental Ministers in the former Czechoslovakian city of Dobris. Many developed nations have enacted statutory or constitutional environmental protection laws, and have in parallel, enacted laws for government transparency and citizen access to information, however, most of these national laws do not reflect a commitment to inalienable human rights, and there are still numerous legal and practical obstructions for citizens to access information about how institutions are interacting with the natural environment. The Convention was, therefore, developed in response to growing demands among human rights activists, particularly in Europe, for public environmental protection, participation in decision-making on a local level and access to relevant information to be enshrined as basic human rights. Thus, with the active participation of environmental non-governmental organisations from the USA, Central, Eastern and Western Europe the Convention was eventually signed at the fourth Conference of European Environmental Ministers by 36 European and Central Asian governments. The Convention sets a precedent as the world's first multilateral agreement to establish a firm set of environmental rights for citizens of developed and developing nations, and links the protection of the natural environment with social and legal justice, all within a broadly participatory–deliberative democratic framework. The Convention was signed by the European Community in 1998 and it came into force in 2001. European Union law has thus adapted to the Aarhus Convention's three pillars of legal reform that collectively accord individuals 'environmental rights'; linking environmental planning with human rights conventions, establishing that sustainable development can be achieved only through the involvement of stakeholders (UNECE, 2004). Figure 6.1 shows these three pillars. What we see overall is that the Aarhus Convention aims to create more transparent and accountable regulatory processes for environmental governance (Mason, 2014), and crucially, The Convention asserts that authorities must not penalise, persecute or harass in any way any individual who exercises his or her rights under the Convention (Stec, 2003) thus providing legal protection for communities.

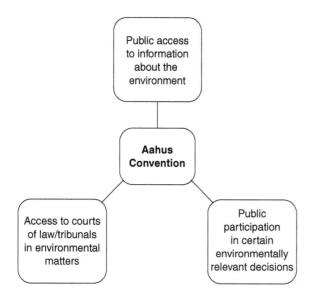

Figure 6.1 The three pillars of the Aarhus Convention.
Source: author.

The 'access to environmental information' pillar of the Convention was addressed in European Directive 2003/4/EC (EC, 2003). Article 1 of the Convention affirms the 'right of every person of present and future generations to live in an environment adequate to his or her health or well-being', and then uses this as justification for public actors to be provided with wider and easier access to environmental information, to participate in decisions and have access to legal redress from environmental injustices. The first pillar of the Convention's environmental justice framework regulates access to information about the environment by inferring that citizens have broad entitlement to access to information about aspects such as the public health effects of environmental plans, pollution risks, conservation and natural resource use plans, without the requirement to prove a special interest in the outcomes of such plans. This right exists towards 'authorities', which are broadly defined as both administrative authorities, such as judicial and legislative bodies and environmental protection agencies, and also (under certain circumstances) private entities that exercise public responsibility in environmental matters through public administrative functions or providing public services, such as, for example: RWMOs, mineral resource extraction providers, generators of electricity or managers of water sewage services. In terms of information access, the right is both passive, in that authorities should respond to citizen requests for information and be active, in the sense that it calls for authorities to directly act upon disseminating information amongst citizen-stakeholders, illustrating the need for transparency and equity of access to information for those that lack the resources to request information. Examples of active information dissemination include keeping publicly accessible lists or databases of environmental information and providing access to these free of charge, as reasonable measures that authorities could take. In practice, in terms of access to information for example, in the UK local authorities are required to respond to requests from the public for information within two months and will also be required to make information available in a wide range of formats. The first pillar promotes a philosophy of transparency in information exchange in environmental matters, in contrast to the secrecy experienced in previous rounds of RWM siting.

The second pillar regulates public participation in certain decision-making processes that could have an impact on the environment. Here the Convention sets out the mechanisms of public participation, particularly with respect to its time, form and scope. The European Commission strongly advocates public participation in environmental governance, arguing that it increases the legitimacy and transparency of decision-making processes. However, debate continues about exactly how to undertake public participation and confusion remains about when it should commence, the methods that should be used and how exactly 'the public' should be represented and engaged with, though there is a strong preference for participation to occur as part of an environmental assessment process (as discussed below).

The third pillar of 'access to justice in environmental matters' has been addressed through a proposal for a directive (Hartley & Wood, 2005) providing the right to recourse to administrative or judicial procedures to dispute acts and omissions violating the provisions of environmental law (UNECE, 1998). Thus, providing legal recourse to affected communities that suffer environmental injustices where disputes cannot be resolved through other (participatory) means. One notable example in the UK nuclear industry was Greenpeace's challenge to the UK Government over the consultation process for new nuclear power in 2007. In 2006 the former Labour Government had put into place an Energy Review in advance of a new Energy White Paper – one which would include new build nuclear power in contrast to the previous anti-nuclear policy agenda. As part of this the government employed a public consultation process, however, several parties, including the Trade and Industry Select Committee, the Environment Agency and Sustainable Development Commission, were deeply critical of the transparency, depth and scope of the consultation process. As Greenpeace argues, the process was not viewed as being the 'fullest public consultation' that the government had promised to conduct in 2003 before giving the go-ahead on new nuclear power. Greenpeace then took the government to the High Court, and on 15 February 2007 Mr Justice Sullivan found in favour of Greenpeace and ruled that the government's pro-nuclear decision was 'unlawful', describing the consultation as 'seriously flawed' and 'manifestly inadequate and unfair' because insufficient and 'misleading' information had been made available by the government for consultees to make an 'intelligent response' (Greenpeace, 2007). Here we can see that an NGO successfully challenged the government in court over issues pertaining to the first two pillars of the Convention: transparent information access and adequate public participation. Where these were violated it led to a legal redress upon environmental justice grounds.

These facets are themselves reflective of a broader policy shift within national government at the time. When the UK Labour administration came to power in 1997 they pushed forward a policy agenda around local community involvement as an 'essential component' of planning processes for achieving sustainable development objectives (see DETR, 1999), which was then embedded in planning system reform (DTLR, 2001). The value of public participation in city/regional and infrastructure planning in particular was stressed as a means to meet strategic objectives such as achieving 'lower costs, fewer delays and less uncertainty in the planning process' (Department for Trade and Industry, 2007, p. 259). Strategic Environmental Assessment (SEA) and Environmental Impact Assessment (EIA) are two tools that gained credence under this policy paradigm, and in relation to the Aarhus Convention. Both SEA and EIA have implications for the deliberative turn in the decision-making processes for RWM. SEA is the evaluation of the impacts of policies, plans and programmes upon the environment. It can be applied at different levels: sectoral (RWM, forestry, energy etc.), regional (to a city or borough for example) or indirect (applied to science and technology, finance or justice for example) (Staib, 2005). The aim is to apply impact assessment criteria across a broad area of environmental decision-making, though this of course leads to issues around problem definition, particularly what counts as 'strategic' and what doesn't (Noble, 2000). SEA is closely related to EIA, which is fundamentally the evaluation of environmental impacts at the *project* level. In theory, SEA should strengthen EIA (which is often applied late in the decision-making process) because it addresses impacts at higher or earlier levels of the process and thereby aims to avoid them at the lower levels or at a later stage (Marsden & Mulder, 2005). It also specifically advocates integrating environmental factors into decision-making, to advance sustainability. SEA and EIA require continuous citizen–stakeholder involvement throughout the process, including defining the scope of the decision and the issues to be addressed and considering the impact of proposals on affected communities in terms of social, ethical, environmental, economic, scientific and safety impacts (Bartlett & Kurian, 1999; Runhaar, 2009; Hourdequin, Landres, Hanson, & Craig, 2012). Public participation is a fundamental component of EIA in a range of different cultural and institutional contexts (Bartlett & Kurian, 1999; Cotton & Mahroos-Alsaiari, 2014). Indeed Wood (2002, p. 277) states that 'EIA is not EIA without consultation and participation', though there is significant regional differentiation in what that means as these tools get applied in different governance contexts and planning systems.

RWM decision-making has explored the use of Environmental Assessment planning tools; particularly SEA, Sustainability Appraisal (SA) and EIA; all of which involve participation from stakeholders and the public at different stages

(EC, 2001; Marsden & Mulder, 2005; Wesolowski, 2006), strengthened by the Aarhus Convention, current regulations and successive rounds of European planning policy and legislation (EC, 1985, 1997, 2001, 2003). The latter requires that both an SEA and an EIA be done as part of the implementation process of planning and siting an RWM facility (Miller, Richardson, Wylie, & Bond, 2006). The European SEA Directive (EC, 2001) states that:

> Authorities with environmental responsibility and the public, shall be given an early and effective opportunity within appropriate time frames to express their opinion on the draft plan or programme and the accompanying environmental report before the adoption of the plan or programme.

The Directive codifies specific opportunities for participant input at different stages of environmental assessment. In relation to RWM, Miller et al. (2006) argue that the SEA process provides a suitable framework specifically for streamlined decision-making early on in the process, when national site selection decisions are to be made, and SEA can incorporate a wide range of affected stakeholders. Similarly, they suggest that EIA can provide a suitable decision-making framework when specific local planning decisions over facilities are to be made. One difficulty remains, however, that directives on SEA and EIA are somewhat unclear regarding how and when participation should be incorporated into planning, implementation and monitoring of decisions, and hence additional guidance is needed to implement participatory procedures under these directives (Wood, 2002). Moreover, it remains difficult to assess how such provisions are interpreted in a policy context (Palerm, 1999) and what the implications will be in real terms: a problem that has still not been satisfactorily addressed in research (Heffron & Haynes, 2014); and at the time of writing remains even more uncertain given the referendum result on the UK's exit from the European Union and potential overturning of EU legislative instruments.

Conclusions

In summary, what we can see is that beyond specific requirements for participatory–deliberative processes in certain controversial technology decisions, the paradigm of *inclusion* has many facets across both national and international environmental policy. The Aarhus Convention and the strengthening of stakeholder participation provision through SEA and EIA in environmental politics, illustrate how processes of environmental planning and policy-making shifted away from science-centred technocratic decision-making towards public involvement using participatory–deliberative methods. The participatory–deliberative turn presents a unique opportunity for public participation procedures to be integrated into environmental planning and policy-making thus having significant implications for how the process of RWM takes place – reinforcing the requirements for transparent stakeholder and public engagement. With the failure of the 1997 RCF proposal, the prevailing epistemological shift in analytic–deliberative governance of risk, the need for transparency and participation in the meeting of sustainable development goals, and increasing requirements for participation in environmental governance across Europe, we can see that a range of 'push factors' were occurring simultaneously in environmental governance in the early 2000s, and RWM moved into this political space – adopting an overtly participatory governance approach, front and centre of the decision-making process.

Note

1 This was ironic, given that Ridley was later found to oppose the building of new houses which he would have been able to see from his Cotswold country home.

Bibliography

Arnstein, S. R. (1969). A ladder of citizen participation. *Journal of the American Institute of Planners*, 35(4), 216–224.

Atherton, E. (2001). *Getting stakeholder issues into the management of radioactive waste.* Paper presented at the Values in Decision-Making on Risk (VALDOR), Stockholm.

Bäckstrand, K. (2003). Civic science for sustainability. Reframing the role of experts, policymakers and citizens in environmental governance. *Global Environmental Politics*, 3(4), 24–41.

Barnett, J., Burningham, K., Walker, G., & Cass, N. (2012). Imagined publics and engagement around renewable energy technologies in the UK. *Public Understanding of Science*, 21(1), 36–50. doi:10.1177/0963662510365663.

Barney, D. (2006). The morning after: Citizen engagement in technological society. *Techné: Research in Philosophy and Technology*, 9(3), 23–31.

Bartlett, R. V., & Kurian, P. A. (1999). The theory of environmental impact assessment: Implicit models of policy making. *Policy & Politics*, 27(4), 415–433. doi:10.1332/030557399782218371.

Beierle, T. C. (1999). Using social goals to evaluate public participation in environmental decisions. *Policy Studies Journal*, 3(4), 75–103.

Beierle, T. J., & Koninsky, D. M. (2000). Values, conflict, and trust in participatory environmental planning. *Journal of Policy Analysis and Management*, 19(4), 587–602.

Bergmans, A., Sundqvist, G., Kos, D., & Simmons, P. (2015). The participatory turn in radioactive waste management: Deliberation and the social–technical divide. *Journal of Risk Research*, 18(3), 347–363.

Bloomfield, D., Collins, K., Fry, C., & Munton, R. (2001). Deliberation and inclusion: Vehicles for increasing trust in UK public governance? *Environment and Planning C: Government and Policy*, 19(4), 501–513.

Blowers, A. (1999). Nuclear waste and landscapes of risk. *Landscape Research*, 24(3), 241–264. doi:10.1080/01426399908706562.

Boholm, A., & Löfstedt, R. (Eds.). (2004). *Facility siting: Risk, power and identity in land use planning.* London: Earthscan.

Bradbury, J. (1989). The policy implications of differing concepts of risk. *Science, Technology & Human Values*, 14(4), 380–399.

Braunholtz, S. (2003). *Public attitudes to windfarms: A survey of local residents in Scotland.* Retrieved from www.scotland.gov.uk/library5/environment/pawslr.pdf.

Bull, R., Petts, J., & Evans, J. (2008). Social learning from public engagement: Dreaming the impossible? *Journal of Environmental Planning and Management, 51*(5), 701–716.

Burgess, J., & Clark, J. (2006). Evaluating public and stakeholder engagement strategies in environmental governance. In A. G. Peirez, S. G. Vas, & S. Tognetti (Eds.), *Interfaces between science and society*. London: Greenleaf Press.

Burgess, J., Chilvers, J., Clark, J., Day, R., Hunt, J., King, S., & Stirling, A. (2004). *Citizens' and specialists' deliberate options for mapping the UK's legacy intermediate and high level radioactive waste: A report of the Deliberative Mapping Trial, June–July 2004.* London: Department for Environment Food and Rural Affairs.

Burgess, J., Stirling, A., Clark, J., Davies, G., Eames, M., Staley, K., & Williamson, S. (2007). Deliberative mapping: A novel analytic–deliberative methodology to support contested science-policy decisions. *Public Understanding of Science, 16*(3), 299–322.

Burningham, K. (2000). Using the language of NIMBY: A topic for research, not an activity for researchers. *Local Environment, 5*(1), 55–67.

Burningham, K., Barnett, J., & Thrush, D. (2006). *The limitations of the NIMBY concept for understanding public engagement with renewable energy technologies: A literature.* Guildford: University of Surrey.

Burningham, K., Barnett, J., Carr, A., Clift, R., & Wehrmeyer, W. (2007). Industrial constructions of publics and public knowledge: A qualitative investigation of practice in the UK chemicals industry. *Public Understanding of Science, 16*(1), 23–43.

Cass, N., & Walker, G. (2009). Emotion and rationality: Characterising and understanding opposition to renewable energy projects. *Emotion, Space and Society, 2*(1), 62–69.

Cass, N., Walker, G., & Devine-Wright, P. (2010). Good neighbours, public relations and bribes: The politics and perceptions of community benefit provision in renewable energy development in the UK. *Journal of Environmental Policy & Planning, 12*(3), 255–275.

Chilvers, J. (2007). Toward analytic–deliberative forms of risk governance in the UK? Reflecting on learning in radioactive waste. *Journal of Risk Research, 10*(2), 197–222.

Chilvers, J., & Burgess, J. (2008). Power relations: The politics of risk and procedure in nuclear waste governance. *Environment and Planning A, 40*(8), 1881–1900.

Cohen, J. (1989). Deliberation and democratic legitimacy. In A. Hamlin, & P. Pettit (Eds.), *The good polity: Normative analysis of the state.* Oxford: Blackwell.

Cotton, M. (2009). Ethical assessment in radioactive waste management: A proposed reflective equilibrium-based deliberative approach. *Journal of Risk Research, 12*(5), 603–618.

Cotton, M. (2011). Public participation in UK infrastructure planning: Democracy, technology and environmental justice. In M. Cotton, & B. H. Motta (Eds.), *Engaging with environmental justice: Governance, education and citizenship.* Oxford: Inter-Disciplinary Press.

Cotton, M. (2013). NIMBY or not? Integrating social factors into shale gas community engagements. *Natural Gas & Electricity, 29*(9), 8–12.

Cotton, M. (2014). *Ethics and technology assessment: A participatory approach.* Berlin: Springer-Verlag.

Cotton, M., & Devine-Wright, P. (2010). NIMBYism and community consultation in electricity transmission network planning. In P. Devine-Wright (Ed.), *Renewable energy and the public: From NIMBY to participation* (pp. 115–130). London: Routledge.

Cotton, M., & Devine-Wright, P. (2012). Making electricity networks 'visible': Industry actor representations of 'publics' and public engagement in infrastructure planning. *Public Understanding of Science, 21*(1), 17–35.

Cotton, M. D., & Mahroos-Alsaiari, A. A. (2014). Key actor perspectives on stakeholder engagement in Omani environmental impact assessment: An application of Q-Methodology. *Journal of Environmental Planning and Management*, 1–22. doi:10.1080/09640568.2013.847822.

Cramer, B. W. (2009). The human right to information, the environment and information about the environment: From the Universal Declaration to the Aarhus Convention. *Communication Law and Policy*, 14(1), 73–103.

Creighton, J. L. (2005). *The public participation handbook: Making better decisions through citizen involvement.* London: John Wiley & Sons.

Daniels, S. E., & Walker, G.B., Working through environmental conflict: The collaborative learning approach. Westport, CT: Praeger.

Davy, B. (1996). Fairness as compassion: Towards a less unfair facility siting policy *Risk – Health Safety & Environment*, 7(2), 99–108.

Dear, M. (1992). Understanding and overcoming the NIMBY syndrome. *Journal of the American Planners Association*, 58(3), 288–300.

D'Entrèves, M. P. (2002). Political legitimacy and democratic deliberation. In M. P. D'Entrèves (Ed.), *Democracy as public deliberation: New perspectives.* Manchester: Manchester University Press.

Department for Trade and Industry. (2007). *Energy White Paper: Meeting the energy challenge.* London: DTI.

DETR. (1999). *A better quality of life: A strategy for sustainable development in the United Kingdom.* London: Department for Transport and the Regions.

Devine-Wright, P. (2005). Beyond NIMBYism: Towards an integrated framework for understanding public perceptions of wind energy. *Wind Energy*, 8(2), 125–139.

Devine-Wright, P. (2009). Rethinking NIMBYism: The role of place attachment and place identity in explaining place-protective action. *Journal of Community and Applied Social Psychology*, 19(6), 426–441. doi:DOI: 10.1002/casp. 1004.

Devlin, E. (2005). Factors affecting public acceptance of wind turbines in Sweden. *Wind Engineering*, 29(6), 503–511. doi:10.1260/030952405776234580.

Dryzek, J. (2000). *Deliberative democracy and beyond: Liberals, critics, contestations.* Oxford: Oxford University Press.

Dryzek, J. (2006). *Deliberative global politics: Discourse and democracy in a divided world.* Cambridge: Polity Press.

DTLR. (2001). *Planning: Delivering fundamental change.* London: Department for Transport, Local Government and the Regions.

Dubreuil, G. H. (2001). *Oskashamn seminar report: September 2001.* Paris: Cowam.

European Commission. (2001). Council Directive 2001/42/EC/, On the assessment of the effects of certain plans and programmes on the environment. *Official Journal L197*.

European Commission. (2003). Directive 2003/4/EC of the European Parliament and of the Council of 28 January 2003 on public access to environmental information and repealing Council Directive 90/313/EEC. *Official Journal* L 041, 14 February 2003, 26–32.

European Council. (1985). Environmental Impact Assessment Directive 85/337/EC.

European Council. (1997). Environmental Impact Assessment Directive 97/11/EC.

European Council. (2001). Council Directive 2001/42/EC/. On the assessment of the effects of certain plans and programmes on the environment. *Official Journal L197*.

European Council. (2003). Environmental Impact Assessment Directive 2003/35/EC.

Elliott, J., Heesterbeek, S., Lukensmeyer, C. J., & Slocum, N. (2005). *Participatory methods toolkit: A practitioner's manual.* Brussels: King Baudouin Foundation.

Fearon, J. D. (1998) Deliberation as discussion. In J. Elster (Ed.), *Deliberative democracy* (pp. 44–68). Cambridge: Cambridge University Press.

Felt, U., & Fochler, M. (2008). The bottom-up meanings of the concept of public participation in science and technology. *Science and Public Policy*, 35(7), 489–499.

Fiorino, D. (1990). Citizen participation and environmental risk: A survey of institutional mechanisms. *Science, Technology & Human Values*, 15(2), 226–243.

Fischhoff, B. (1995). Risk perception and communication unplugged: 20 years of process. *Risk Analysis*, 15(2), 137–146.

Flüeler, T. (2005). *Tools for local stakeholder in radioactive waste governance: Challenges and benefits of selected participatory technology assessment techniques.* Zurich: Institute of Human-Environment Systems.

Flüeler, T. (2006). *Decision making for complex socio-technical systems: Robustness from lessons learned in long term radioactive waste governance.* Dordrecht: Springer.

Flüeler, T., & Scholz, R. W. (2004). Socio-technical knowledge for robust decision making in radioactive waste management. *Risk, Decision and Policy*, 9(2), 129–159.

Genus, A., & Coles, A. M. (2005). On constructive technology assessment and limitations on public participation in technology assessment. *Technology Analysis & Strategic Management*, 17(4), 433–443.

Gigerenzer, G. (2004). Dread risk, September 11, and fatal traffic accidents. *Psychological science*, 15(4), 286–287.

Goodin, R. E. (1986). Laundering preferences. In J. Elster, & A. Hylland (Eds.), *Foundations of social choice theory.* Cambridge: Cambridge University Press.

Greenpeace. (2007). *Talking nonsense – The 2007 nuclear consultation.* Retrieved from www.greenpeace.org.uk/files/pdfs/nuclear/2007-consultation-nuclear-dossier.pdf.

Gross, C. (2007). Community perspectives of wind energy in Australia: The application of a justice and community fairness framework to increase social acceptance. *Energy Policy*, 35(5), 2727–2736. doi:10.1016/j.enpol.2006.12.013.

Groves, C., Munday, M., & Yakovleva, N. (2013). Fighting the pipe: Neo-liberal governance and barriers to effective community participation in energy infrastructure planning. *Environment and Planning C: Government and Policy*, 31(2), 340–356.

Grove-White, R. (1997). Science, trust and social change. In *Science, Policy and Risk* (pp. 53–58). A discussion meeting held at the Royal Society on Tuesday 18 March 1997. London: The Society.

Grunwald, A. (2004). Participation as a means of enhancing the legitimacy of decisions on technology? A sceptical analysis. *Poiesis & Praxis*, 3(1–2), 106–122.

Guehlstorf, N. P., & Hallstrom, L. K. (2005). The role of culture in risk regulations: A comparative case study of genetically modified corn in the United States of America and European Union. *Environmental Science & Policy*, 8(4), 327–342. doi:http://dx.doi.org/10.1016/j.envsci.2005.04.007.

Gunderson, A. G. (1995). *The environmental promise of democratic deliberation.* Madison, Wisconsin: University of Wisconsin Press.

Gunderson, W. C. (1999). Voluntarism and its limits: Canada's search for radioactive waste-siting candidates. *Canadian Public Administration*, 42(2), 193–214.

Gutmann, A. (1993). The challenge of multiculturalism in political ethics. *Philosophy & Public Affairs*, 22(3), 171–206.

Gutmann, A., & Thompson, D. (2004). *Why deliberative democracy?* Oxford: Princeton University Press.

Halvorsen, K. E. (2003). Assessing the effects of public participation. *Public Administration Review*, 63(5), 535–543.

Hartley, N., & Wood, C. (2005). Public participation in environmental impact assessment – implementing the Aarhus Convention. *Environmental Impact Assessment Review, 25*(4), 319–340.

Heffron, R., & Haynes, P. (2014). Challenges to the Aarhus Convention: Public participation in the energy planning process in the United Kingdom. *Journal of Contemporary European Research, 10*(2), 236–247.

Hornblower, M. (1988, 27 June). Ethics: Not in my backyard, you don't. *Time Magazine.*

Hourdequin, M., Landres, P., Hanson, M. J., & Craig, D. R. (2012). Ethical implications of democratic theory for U.S. public participation in environmental impact assessment. *Environmental Impact Assessment Review, 35*(0), 37–44. doi:http://dx.doi.org/10.1016/j.eiar.2012.02.001.

House of Lords Select Committee on Science and Technology. (2000). *Science and Society 3rd Report.* London: House of Lords Select Committee on Science and Technology.

Hunsberger, C., & Kenyon, W. (2008). Action planning to improve issues of effectiveness, representation and scale in public participation: A conference report. *Journal of Public Deliberation, 4*(1), Article 1.

Hunt, J. (2001). *Framing the problem of radioactive waste public and institutional perspectives.* Paper presented at the Values in Decisions on Risk (VALDOR), Stockholm.

Innes, J., & Booher, D. (2004). Reframing public participation: strategies for the 21st century. *Planning Theory & Practice, 5*(4), 419–436

Irwin, A. (2001). Constructing the scientific citizen: Science and democracy in the biosciences. *Public Understanding of Science, 10*(1), 1–18.

Irwin, A., & Wynne, B. (1996). *Misunderstanding science: The public reconstruction of science and technology.* Cambridge: Cambridge University Press.

Jasper, J. M. (1998). *The emotions of protest: Affective and reactive emotions in and around social movements.* Paper presented at the Sociological Forum.

Jenkins-Smith, H. C., & Silva, C. L. (1998). The role of risk perception and technical information in scientific debates over nuclear waste storage. *Reliability Engineering and System Safety, 59,* 107–122.

Jin, M. (2013). Citizen participation, trust, and literacy on government legitimacy: The case of environmental governance. *Journal of Social Change, 5*(1), 11–25.

Johnson, J. (1998). Arguing for deliberation: Some skeptical considerations. In J. Elster (Ed.), *Deliberative democracy* (pp. 161–184). (Cambridge University Press, Cambridge.

Krannich, R. S., Little, R. L., & Cramer, L. A. (1993). Rural community residents' views of nuclear waste repository siting in Nevada. In R. E. Dunlap, M. E. Kraft, & E. A. Rosa (Eds.), *Public reactions to nuclear waste* (pp. 263–287). Durham, NC: Duke University Press.

Kuhn, R. G. (1998). Social and political issues in siting a nuclear-fuel waste disposal facility in Ontario, Canada. *Canadian Geographer, 42*(1), 14–28.

Lidskog, A., & Litmanen, T. (1997). The social shaping of radwaste management: The case of Sweden and Finland. *Current Sociology, 45*(8), 59–79.

Lidskog, R. a. I. E. (1992). Reinterpreting locational conflicts: NIMBY and nuclear waste management in Sweden. *Policy and Politics, 20*(4), 249–264.

Lidskog, R. (1996). In science we trust? On the relation between scientific knowledge, risk consciousness and public trust. *Acta Sociologica, 39*(1), 31–58.

Litmanen, T. (1999). From the golden age to the valley of despair: How did nuclear waste become a problem? In E. Konttinen, T. Litmanen, M. Nieminen, & M. Ylönen (Eds.), *All shades of green: The environmentalisation of Finnish Society* (pp.111–128). University of Jyväskylä, Finland: SoPhi.

Livezey, E. T. (1980, 6 November). Hazardous waste. *The Christian Science Monitor.*

Lotov, A. V. (2003). Internet tools for supporting of lay stakeholders in the framework of the democratic paradigm of environmental decision making. *Journal of Multi-Criteria Decision Analysis, 12,* 145–162.

Luloff, A. E., Albrecht, S. L., & Bourke, L. (1998). NIMBY and the hazardous and toxic waste siting dilemma: The need for concept clarification. *Society & Natural Resources, 11*(1), 81–98.

Mackerron, G., & Berkhout, F. (2009). Learning to listen: Institutional change and legitimation in UK radioactive waste policy. *Journal of Risk Research, 12*(7–8), 989–1008.

Maranta, A., Guggenheim, M., Gisler, P., & Pohl, C. (2003). The reality of experts and the imagined lay person. *Acta Sociologica, 46*(2), 150–165.

Marsden, S., & Mulder, J. D. (2005). Strategic environmental assessment and sustainability in Europe – How bright is the future? *RECIEL, 14*(1), 50–62.

Martin, B. (1996). *Confronting the experts.* Albany: SUNY Press.

Mason, M. (2014). So far but no further? Transparency and disclosure in the Aarhus Convention. In A. Gupta & M. Mason (Eds.), *Transparency in global environmental governance: Critical perspectives.* Cambridge, MA: MIT Press.

McCarty, L. S., & Power, M. (2000). Approaches to developing risk management objectives: An analysis of international strategies. *Environmental Science & Policy, 3*(6), 311–319. doi:http://dx.doi.org/10.1016/S1462-9011(00)00103-9.

Michaud, K., Carlisle, J. E., & Smith, E. (2008). NIMBYism vs environmentalism in attitudes towards energy development. *Environmental Politics, 17*(1), 20–39.

Miller, B., Richardson, P., Wylie, R., & Bond, A. (2006). *The implementation of a national radioactive waste management programme in the UK: Implications for local communities and local authorities.* Cumbria: Nuclear Legacy Advisory Forum, NuLeaf.

Noble, B. F. (2000). Strategic environmental assessment: What is it? & what makes it strategic? *Journal of Environmental Assessment Policy and Management, 2*(2), 203–224.

Nowotny, H. (2001). *Re-thinking science. Knowledge and the public in an age on uncertainty.* Cambridge, UK: Polity Press.

Nuclear Energy Agency. (2002, 15–16 November 2001). *Stepwise decision making in Finland for the disposal of spent nuclear fuel, Workshop Proceedings.* Turku, Finland.

Nuclear Energy Agency. (2003, 14 October 2002). *Public confidence in the management of radioactive waste: The Canadian context, Workshop Proceedings,* Ottawa, Canada.

Nuclear Energy Agency. (2005). *The regulatory control of radioactive waste in Finland.* Vienna: Nuclear Energy Agency.

Owens, S., & Cowell, R. (2002). *Land and limits: Interpreting sustainability in the planning process.* London: Routledge.

Palerm, J. R. (1999). Public participation in environmental decision making: examining the Aarhus convention. *Journal of Environmental Assessment Policy and Management, 1*(2), 229–244.

Parkins, J. R., & Mitchell, R. E. (2005). Public participation as public debate: A deliberative turn in natural resource management. *Society and Natural Resources, 18*(6), 529–540.

Peterson, M., & Hansson, S. O. (2004). On the application of rights-based moral theories to siting controversies. *Journal of Risk Research, 7*(2), 269–275.

Petts, J. (Ed.). (1999). *Handbook of environmental impact assessment.* Oxford: Blackwell Science.

Petts, J., & Brooks, C. (2005). Expert conceptualisations of the role of lay knowledge in environmental decisionmaking: challenges for deliberative democracy. *Environment and Planning A, 38,* 1045–1059.

Petts, J., & Leach, B. (2000). *Evaluating methods for public participation: Literature review.* Bristol: Environment Agency.

Rabe, B. G. (1994). *Beyond NIMBY: Hazardous waste siting in Canada and the United States*: Brookings Institute.

Rawles, K. (2000). *Ethical issues in the disposal of radioactive waste.* Harwell: Nirex.

Renn, O. (1998). The role of risk communication and public dialogue for improving risk management. *Risk Decision and Policy, 3*(1), 5–30.

Renn, O. (1999). A model for an analytic-deliberative process in risk management. *Environmental Science and Technology, 33*(18), 3049–3055.

Renn, O. (2004). *Analytic-deliberative processes of decision-making: Linking expertise, stakeholder experience and public values.* Stuttgart: University of Stuttgart and DIALOGIK GmbH.

Rockloff, S. F., & Lockie, S. (2004). Participatory tools for coastal zone management: Use of stakeholder analysis and social mapping in Australia. *Journal of Coastal Conservation, 10*(1), 81–92.

Rowe, G., & Frewer, L. J. (2000). Public participation methods: A framework for evaluation. *Science, Technology & Human Values, 25*(1), 3–29.

Runhaar, H. (2009). Putting SEA in context: A discourse perspective on how SEA contributes to decision-making. *Environmental Impact Assessment Review, 29*(3), 200–209. doi:http://dx.doi.org/10.1016/j.eiar.2008.09.003.

Sclove, R. (1995). *Democracy and technology.* London: Guilford Publications.

Severson, G. (2012). Public relations: Managing NIMBY issues before they manage you. *Natural Gas & Electricity, 29*(5), 18–22. doi:10.1002/gas.21653.

Shrader-Frechette, K. S. (2002). *Environmental justice: Creating equality, reclaiming democracy.* Oxford: Oxford University Press.

Simmons, P., & Bickerstaff, K. (2006). The participatory turn in UK radioactive waste management policy In K. Andersson (Ed.), *VALDOR 2006 – Values in decisions on risk conference proceedings* (pp. 530–537). Stockholm: Informationsbolaget Nyberg & Co.

Slovic, P., Layman, M., & Flynn, J. (1993). Received risk, trust and nuclear waste: Lessons from Yucca Mountain. In R. E. Dunlap, M. E. Kraft, & E. A. Rosa (Eds.), *Public reactions to nuclear waste.* Durham, NC: Duke University Press.

Snider, J. H. (2009). Deterring fake public participation. *International Journal of Public Participation, 4*(1), 89–102.

Staib, R. (2005). Government environmental decisions. In R. Staib (Ed.), *Environmental management and decision-making for business.* Palgrave: Hampshire.

Stec, S. (Ed.) (2003). *Handbook on access to justice under the Aarhus Convention.* Szentendre, Hungary: Ministry of the Environment, Republic of Estonia.

Stern, P. C., & Fineberg, H. V. (1996). *Understanding risk: Informing decisions in a democratic society.* Washington DC: National Academy Press.

Tuler, S., 1998. Learning through participation. *Human Ecology Review, 5*(1), 58–60.

United Nations Economic Commission for Europe. (1998) *Convention on access to information, public participation and access to justice in environmental matters.* Geneva: UNECE

United Nations Economic Commission for Europe. (2004). Introducing the Aarhus Convention. Geneva: UNECE.

United Nations Environment Program. (1992). The Rio Declaration on Environment and Development (1992). *The United Nations Conference on Environment and Development,* 3–14 June 1992, Rio De Janeiro.

Wachinger, G., Renn, O., Begg, C., & Kuhlicke, C. (2012). The risk perception paradox – implications for governance and communication of natural hazards. *Risk Analysis, 33*(6), 1049–1065. doi:10.1111/j.1539-6924.2012.01942.x.

Walker, G. (2009). Beyond distribution and proximity: Exploring the multiple spatialities of environmental justice. *Antipode*, *41*(4), 614–636.

Walker, G. (2012). *Environmental justice: Concepts, evidence and politics*. London: Routledge

Warren, C. R., Lumsden, C., O'Dowd, S., & Birnie, R. V. (2005). 'Green on Green': Public perceptions wind power in Scotland and Ireland. *Journal of Environmental Planning and Management*, *48*(6), 853–875.

Wates, N. (2000). *The community planning handbook*. London: Earthscan.

Welsh, I. (1993). The NIMBY syndrome: Its significance in the history of the nuclear debate in Britain. *British Journal of the History of Science*, *26*, 15–32.

Wesolowski, C. (2006). *Environmental assessments and stakeholder involvement*. Paper presented at the Values in Decisions On Risk (VALDOR), Stockholm.

Wolsink, M. (2000). Wind power and the NIMBY-myth: Institutional capacity and the limited significance of public support. *Renewable Energy*, *21*(1), 49–64.

Wood, C. M. (2002). *Environmental impact assessment: A comparative review*. Harlow: Prentice Hall.

Wynne, B. (1996). May the sheep safely graze? A reflexive view of the expert-lay knowledge divide. In S. Lash, B. Szerszynski, & B. Wynne (Eds.), *Risk, environment and modernity*. London: Sage Publications.

Yearly, S. (2000). Making systematic sense of public discontents with expert knowledge: Two analytic approaches and a case study. *Public Understanding of Science*, *9*, 105–122.

7 Managing radioactive waste safely

Introduction – the failure of Nirex

The rejection of the Rock Characterisation Facility (RCF) proposal was a serious blow to the UK nuclear industry (and specifically to Nirex). The RCF was intended to push forward government plans for the long-term management of intermediate-level and high-level radioactive wastes and thus resolve decades of political deadlock. When the proposal for the RCF failed to gain planning permission, this action then had extensive political ramifications for the nuclear industry (particularly towards the prospect of further new nuclear build, industry expansion and the decommissioning of existing sites) and the UK Government in settling upon an agreed way forward for long-term RWM strategy. As Nirex state (Nirex, 2006, p. 7):

> This signalled not just the demise of the national policy but also of Nirex. Nirex had been charged with delivering the policy. The policy had failed. So, it followed, Nirex had failed too.

The consequences for Nirex were immediate and severe. It was quickly reformed as a smaller organisation. Its nuclear industry shareholders cut its budget from £50 million to £11 million with a resulting loss of staff. Almost overnight they went from 250 employees to 67. Managing director Michael Folger was replaced by Chris Murray. This signalled a period of reflection and a change in direction for the organisation. Post-1997, as Nirex itself shrank in both size and stature, it became subject to significant change. Nirex launched an internal inquiry into the organisational failures leading up to the 1997 RCF failure, the main conclusions of which were (derived from Nirex, 2006):

- There was lack of transparency in the site selection process (up to and including the choice of sites close to Sellafield for an RCF).
- There were scientific concerns about the site selection itself – the suitability of Sellafield particularly on geological and hydrological grounds given concerns raised about the suitability of the Borrowdale volcanic group.
- There were unresolved scientific issues that imply the need for a review of all waste management options, not just geological disposal.

- The programme running up to the RCF was being driven too quickly to try and create a rapid political resolution to the problem.
- The scientific information made available to stakeholders was not supporting decisions – there needed to be a clearer audit trail for major decisions and greater transparency in the reporting of this.
- Nirex's own behaviour was not sufficiently inclusive and transparent – there was a closed culture within the company. This approach alienated even its natural allies within industry and local government.
- There was a lack of recognition of ethical and social issues – there needed to be greater consideration and expertise mobilised within the social sciences.

Nirex's comprehensive review involved input from its opponents including Friends of the Earth, as well as from their more established stakeholder networks (for discussion of this point see Western, 1996, 1998). This review was the basis for a new corporate strategy for dealing with radioactive wastes. Nirex subsequently identified some broad areas of policy construction, described as a radical new approach (as Atherton & Poole, 2001 argued):

1   The process through which any possible management solution was to be reached, needed to be reformulated in terms of openness, transparency, and public engagement.
2   The structure of the organisations charged with overseeing and implementing the solution required thorough re-evaluation.
3   The behaviour of those organisations and the individuals within them requires new formulation in line with these two ideals.

Yet during this period, Nirex's very future was uncertain. It had lost credibility and political support. It quickly went from being in charge of the process to being a smaller player – the management responsibility was effectively taken out of its hands, and it became something akin to a consultancy organisation rather than an RWMO. It continued its work on what was called a Phased Geological Repository Concept (PGRC) – a multi-barrier concept where geology, the physical repository store and the waste containment package provide multiple layers of protection. It is phased in the sense that there is monitoring of repository performance and there is maintained retrievability of waste for a period once the repository is filled (Nirex, 2002). This provides opportunities for future generations to 'change their minds' if further uses or solutions to the waste problem could be found based upon future technological progress. As such, Nirex's expertise in technical matters remained invaluable, and they continued to provide what were termed Letters of Comfort (later called Letters of Compliance) to waste producers. These LoC were given to site licensees based upon whether their proposed form of waste packaging conformed to the PGRC. Interestingly, therefore, as the political process on radioactive waste management options progressed (as discussed in this chapter), there was an underlying path dependency of the geological disposal concept – an assumption that a repository, in some shape or form, was going to be the proposed solution.

More broadly the failure of the RCF proposal effectively amounted to a loss of 15 years of scientific and technical research, £450 million in direct costs, plus additional cost to the taxpayer in planning inquiry bills (Beveridge & Curtis, 1998). This policy failure pushed RWM back into the realm of political uncertainty, an instrumental step in changing the political culture of the broader nuclear industry and its attitude to the waste problem, and catalysing a cultural shift within government and Nirex towards greater levels of transparency and early involvement of non-nuclear industry actors in the processes of decision-making as necessary to secure a solution which would stand up to stakeholder scrutiny. Though the outcomes were ultimately extremely costly to the Treasury, we can see that it had positive benefits in terms of environmental justice. The failure of the process brought the activities of Nirex into a national public discursive arena, providing much needed political visibility to the problem and a fresh start to the planning process. And as mentioned in previous chapters, this occurred at a time also of a change of government and a broader institutional shift towards participatory–deliberative governance in environmental matters, so there were multiple 'push' factors occurring simultaneously.

A new government and a new approach

In May 1997 the Conservative Government was defeated following a general election, and a Labour Government was elected under Prime Minister Tony Blair. This period of political renewal provided a space for a fundamental policy review and the adoption of a new approach to the decision-making process for RWM. Then Deputy Prime Minister John Prescott was given an expanded brief to become Secretary of State for Environment, Transport and the Regions (heading the Department of Environment, Transport and the Regions – DETR), and oversaw the new radioactive waste management policy formulation in the wake of the failure of the RCF proposal. Initially there were strong calls within government to restart the search for a disposal site, however, internal disagreements led to the delay of a decision on RWM policy until after a House of Lords Select Committee on Science and Technology investigation. The ensuing report: *Management of Nuclear Waste*, published in 1999 (House of Lords, 1999) was the first major assessment of RWM following the public inquiry in 1997. The Lords recommended that the government produce a Green Paper on radioactive waste management, and after a period of consultation a White Paper (Grove-White, 2000; RWMAC, 2001). In the report the Select Committee considered various methods for managing nuclear waste and concluded that disposal in a deep geological repository was the most feasible and desirable method of dealing with radioactive waste. In 2000 the Minister of State for the Environment within DETR, Michael Meacher MP spoke in the House of Commons, stating that a new consultation process would begin, one that highlighted the need for a more open and transparent review of radioactive waste management options, with greater involvement of the public in the decision-making process. In his speech he rejected the House of Lords Select Committee recommendation of a new siting process for deep geological disposal under a new Radioactive Waste Management Organisation, and instead opted for a 'back to the drawing board' solution. This raised some criticism from the House of Lords Science and Technology Committee that published a follow up report in 2001: *Managing Radioactive Waste: the Government's Consultation*, which expressed their collective disappointment that the recommendation of deep geological disposal was not taken up, and the 'slow progress' to date on a new policy; noting that the minister seemed to feel 'little sense of urgency' about the need for progress (House of Lords Science and Technology Committee, 2001). The political debate recognised that no overall panacea, single technical or political consensus had emerged over the siting of radioactive wastes, and the UK (alongside other waste producing countries) had consistently tried to address the problem within the context of its own national policy-making structures, cultural expectations and energy and environmental priorities (see for example Kemp, 1992). Up until 1997, although vast resource expenditure had been allocated to the technical options for RWM processes, the development of equally efficacious political processes and institutions required to develop a credible and publicly legitimate strategy had not been under the same scrutiny. What Michael Meacher's speech did was to publicly acknowledge, within Parliament, the necessity of a politically legitimate and not solely technically robust solution as the way forward.

The need for transparency and independence

This need for transparency was a key consideration laid out in the 1999 report. The Lords recognised that 'openness and transparency in decision-making are necessary in order to gain public trust' and that mechanisms for inclusive decision-making would be necessary (House of Lords, 1999). The report proposed setting up a Nuclear Waste Commission with the initial task of consulting on a comprehensive policy – a sentiment echoed in a Royal Society report that called for the creation of a body whose independence and stature would command public confidence in developing proposals for a UK policy for the long-term management and disposal of radioactive wastes, and that would manage the process irrespective of whether new nuclear power stations were built (Royal Society, 2002). These calls for an independent committee to oversee the process drew back to the 1976 Flowers Commission report (Royal Commission on Environmental Pollution, 1976, p. 162):

> responsibility for developing the best strategy for dealing with radioactive wastes is one for the Government, and specifically for a department concerned to protect the environment, not one concerned to promote nuclear power ... We recommend that there should be established a Nuclear Waste Management Advisory Council to advise the Secretary of State.

Clearly the strategy to allow Nirex oversight over the RWM process had repeatedly failed. In part this was because Nirex was not an independent advisory body beholden to the Secretary of State: it was set up from the constituent parts of the nuclear industry that oversaw the back end of the waste management process, and it failed to shift this perception amongst a diverse range of stakeholders. Clearly there were concerns that Nirex operated in the interests of the industry rather than broader civil society when they went into negotiations with Cumbrian communities and local government, and they failed to command trust and respect from those stakeholders. The behaviour of key personnel during those community and local government engagement processes in and around the Sellafield area further alienated those stakeholders, and undermined broader trust in the fairness of the process. With the diminished role and budget that Nirex commanded after the failure of the 1997 RCF proposal, its very future looked uncertain. As mentioned previously, it lacked support even amongst its allies and had failed in its job at great public cost. The shift in thinking was that future policy could not be overseen by an organisation that lacked accountability to government or to the communities that would ultimately host a facility. As such, the longstanding Radioactive Waste Management Advisory Committee (RWMAC) then set out the key guiding principles for the process of developing a new policy. Notably they stated that (Select Committee on Environment, 2002):

> The policy formulation process should be overseen by an independent or at least balanced-interest body that is widely accepted as being capable of representing the broader public interest. The remit of this body should, in the first instance, be limited to overseeing the process and transparently drawing together its findings in the form of policy recommendations to Government. The overseeing body must be adequately resourced for the inevitably demanding work programme that it will be required to undertake and/or manage.

And Defra agreed, declaring that, 'most people are not familiar with current institutional arrangements, but seem to want an independent, inclusive body overseeing RWM, operating openly' (DEFRA, 2001, p. 48). RWMAC's position was the closest recommendation to that made in the 1976 Flowers report: the formation of an independent advisory committee with oversight over policy *process*, which would draw together findings from the broad range of technical and scientific expertise whilst remaining independent of industry interests and constraints. However, it was clear that the call was for an advisory rather than decision-making body. Thus this would avoid the undemocratic, centralised and techno-centric approaches that characterised all prior successive RWM policy failures made by government under the auspices of Nirex's planning application.

Managing Radioactive Waste Safely

The alignment of these different factors: the push to analytic–deliberative forms of risk governance, the emphasis upon community involvement in planning decisions and policy formation within the New Labour Government, the broader EU legislation on participation in sustainable development and the urgent political need for transparency and an independent committee to advise government on RWM, culminated in a new policy process termed 'Managing Radioactive Waste Safely' (MRWS). The MRWS policy platform had a number of key features summarised as (DEFRA, 2001, p. 48):

> UK Government and the Devolved Administrations ... are launching a national debate ... to develop, and implement, a UK nuclear waste management programme which *inspires public support and confidence*. To do this, we propose a major programme of research and *public discussion*, using many techniques – some traditional, some relatively new – to *stimulate informed discussion*, and to *involve as many people and groups as possible* ... to *inspire public confidence* in the decisions and the way in which they are implemented. To do that, we have to demonstrate that all options are considered; that choices between them are made in a clear and logical way; that *people's values and concerns* are fully reflected in this process ... So we propose to set up *a strong, independent and authoritative* body...
>
> [Emphasis my own]

I draw attention to the concepts outlined in italic text. We might consider these descriptor concepts in the formulation of the MRWS policy as something akin to discursive *storylines* (in a manner akin espoused by Hajer, 1995). Public support, confidence, discussion, involvement, values, independence – these are ensembles of thematic ideas, concepts and categories through which meaning is given to this new policy platform in a way that breaks from the practices embodied in previous policy failures. The writing is deliberately intended to contrast with past experience. It implicitly frames the Nirex-led proposal as authoritarian, technocratic and unjust; whilst proposing a new alternative based upon a discursive dialogue tradition, independent facilitation of the decision from outside industry interests, and a concomitant need for evidence-based policymaking at the heart of a government decision.

The independent review body in question, was the Committee on Radioactive Waste Management: an advisory non-departmental public body. Its acronym CoRWM is pronounced as a homophone of 'quorum' – a term that connotes a dialogue tradition of assembly, group-based deliberation and inclusion. CoRWM had a remit to assess RWM options in the manner laid out in the MRWS document: to review the options for safely managing the UK's higher activity waste and to make recommendations on the long-term solutions. As part of the MRWS, CoRWM was set up with a set of *Terms of Reference* (hereafter ToR) derived from Department of Environment, Food and Rural Affairs (DEFRA) consultations and workshops. The ToR stipulated the appointment of the committee by ministers of government and devolved administrations following a joint announcement by the Secretary of State for Environment, Food and Rural Affairs to the UK Parliament, and by the devolved administrations on 29

July 2002. The ToR specifies CoRWM's responsibility to deliver recommendations to ministers along agreed work plans. The initial deadline was to be the end of 2005 (though this deadline was later put back). The recommendations were to be drafted for ministers, and then it would be up to the elected officials, with reference to their respective Parliaments and assemblies to then finally *decide* future policy for long-term RWM. Therefore it was clear from the outset that the CoRWM process was a decision-*support* rather than decision-*making* process to 'recommend to Ministers the best option, or combination of options for managing the UK's solid radioactive waste' (CoRWM, 2006c). CoRWM's independent review made extensive use of PSE – in its final recommendations to government, CoRWM insists that it chose a deliberative approach and claims to democratic and 'holistic' integration intending to 'inspire public support and confidence' and thus aimed to meet the ToR by demonstrating:

> That all options are considered; that choices between them are made in a clear and logical way; that people's values and concerns are fully reflected in this process; and that information we provide is clear, accurate, unbiased and complete.
>
> (DEFRA, 2001)

The ToR also specified the composition of the committee – that it should include a broad membership, offering a range of relevant expertise on technical, scientific, environmental, social and public perspectives. CoRWM was set up with an initial membership of 13 'experts' from a wide range of backgrounds including human rights, social science and environmental activism as well as radiological protection and geology.[1] They were tasked with the delivery, review and overall responsibility for the reports and other outputs delivered under CoRWM's name, though were not in charge of the day to day activities of collecting and disseminating the information. It must be noted that though the initial membership was 13, two of these initial members parted company with CoRWM (for reasons discussed later on in this chapter).

Also of significance were the Guiding Principles that underpinned CoRWM's ethos and attitude to the assessment process. CoRWM recognised that ethical considerations would inevitably have an important part to play in its decision making process, and so ethical issues were a key aspect of these *Guiding Principles* (CoRWM, 2004; Grimstone, 2004). The Guiding Principles were described as statements of fundamental core values (Blowers, 2006). They applied very broadly to CoRWM's working practices, intentions and their approach to the PSE process (Blowers, 2006; CoRWM, 2004):

1 to be open and transparent;
2 to uphold the public interest by taking full account of public and stakeholder views in our decision making;
3 to achieve fairness with respect to procedures, communities and future generations;

4   to aim for a safe and sustainable environment both now and in the future;
5   to ensure an efficient, cost-effective and conclusive process.

As mentioned before, this set of Guiding Principles embodies a process of policy learning. It encapsulates not only a new set of policy measures and operating rules for technical assessment, but an underlying shift in emphasis towards a public-facing and analytic-deliberative decision-support procedure. In practice, under the ToR, CoRWM was charged with an extensive work package of analytic-deliberative options assessment, namely to:

- evaluate different technical options for RWM;
- identify scientific knowledge and uncertainties;
- learn from international experience;
- consider ethical issues;
- engage with the public and stakeholders.

At the heart of these guiding principles were an underlying set of ethical values, specifically codified as working practices. However, these principles are in essence simply, 'codes of conduct'. It was important for CoRWM's to clearly state the principles that underpinned their procedures. However these principles alone were insufficient ethical 'tools' for assessing the wide ranging issues involved in RWM options assessment (Cotton, 2009). Thus part of CoRWM undertook specific work in this area of ethical assessment, as discussed later in the chapter.

The CoRWM options assessment process

In essence what CoRWM did was to put together a package of analytic-deliberative methods that, though methodologically innovative and wide ranging in scope, was nonetheless recognisable as a Multi-Criteria Decision Analysis (Dietz, 2011). CoRWM's remit and the initial stages of the MRWS programme highlighted the need to develop a generic long-term RWM option (or set of options). CoRWM therefore committed to undertake a multi-phased assessment process and relay its recommendation(s) to government. The phases were as follows (Collier, 2005):

- Phase 1 – involved the preparation and trialing of different RWM policy options, framing and initial shortlisting of those options.
- Phase 2 – an options assessment procedure.
- Phase 3 – reporting to government and closure.

The first phases concerned the preparation of information and the framing of different RWM options. This was a tabula rasa for options assessment. CoRWM did not preclude any potential RWM options a priori from their analysis and discussion. This initial phase ran until September 2004 and was primarily focused on information gathering, testing methods, drawing up the long list of potential options for managing radioactive waste, and deciding how to undertake a shortlisting process (Collier, 2006). The structure of the PSE process as it relates to this options assessment process is shown in Figure 7.1.

CoRWM initially considered a full range of radioactive waste management options (CoRWM, 2006c; Nirex, 2003):

- interim or indefinite storage on or below the surface;
- near surface disposal, a few metres or tens of metres down;
- deep disposal, with the surrounding geology providing a further barrier;
- phased deep disposal, with storage and monitoring for a period;
- direct injection of liquid wastes into rock strata;
- disposal at sea sub-seabed disposal;
- disposal in ice sheets;
- disposal in subduction zones;
- disposal in space, into high orbit, or propelled into the sun;
- dilution and dispersal of radioactivity in the environment;
- partitioning of wastes and transmutation of radionuclides;
- burning of plutonium and uranium in reactors;
- incineration to reduce waste volumes;
- melting of metals in furnaces to reduce waste volumes.

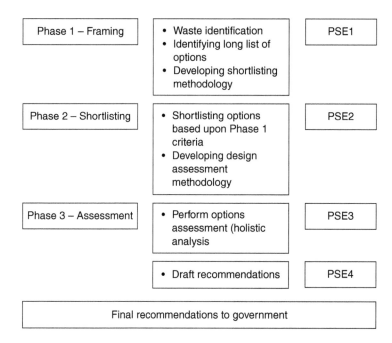

Figure 7.1 The structure of CoRWM's public and stakeholder engagement process.
Source: author.

Some of these options were relatively easy to rule out of the long list. For example, disposal in ice sheets in Antarctica would be technically feasible at a depth range of 20–100 m under the surface of either the Antarctic or the Greenland ice sheet. If the ice sheet remains stable then this would prevent widespread radioactive contamination (Philberth, 1977). However, The Antarctic Treaty for protection of this as a pristine environment precludes waste disposal in the Antarctic ice sheet, and so this option from the long list could be ruled out on international legal grounds. Similarly, disposal in space, though it would permanently remove wastes from the biosphere, nonetheless presents a significant risk from explosion of the delivery vehicle on the launch pad or in the upper atmosphere, potentially spreading radioactive contaminants across a broad area. The political significance of these options is that their consideration on the long list caused considerable ire amongst technical authorities on the issue. There were those on the committee that saw this list of esoteric options to be a distraction that lacked scientific credibility, thus causing internal conflict on the issue.

Nevertheless, these options were left on the long list, and a second shortlisting phase ran from September 2004 until July 2005. It was shortlisting in the sense of assessing the criteria against which the different options performed, ruling out certain RWM strategies (so some were based upon legal requirements, and others on risk grounds). So the bulk of this phase was dedicated to actually deciding how to draw up the criteria for inclusion or exclusion. It was in this process that significant PSE was used.

Phase 3 was the assessment phase, which ran from August 2005 until July 2006. This phase was the period in which CoRWM finalised its assessment of the shortlist, and then agreed, finalised and drafted recommendations to government. These successive phases all included a very strong element of PSE throughout. This involved a 4-part process (entitled PSE1, PSE 2, PSE3 and PSE4). PSE 1 and 2 ran during the shortlisting phase, and PSE 3 and 4 ran during the final assessment phase. The main aims of these PSE programmes were as follows (derived from: Chilvers, Burgess, & Murlis, 2003; CoRWM, 2005b, 2006c; Collier, 2006):

Public and Stakeholder Engagement (PSE) 1: 4 November–5 January:

- Review the current radioactive waste inventory, the long list of options and the proposed screening criteria, and raise other relevant issues.
- Propose a shortlist of options.
- Propose option assessment criteria and the questions that these raise.

Public and Stakeholder Engagement (PSE) 2: April–5 June:

- Review the shortlist of options and the proposed assessment process.
- Comment on ethical issues relevant to assessing options.
- Raise issues on combining and implementing options.

Public and Stakeholder Engagement (PSE) 3: 5 October–6 February:

- Multi-Criteria Decision Analysis
- Assessment of inputs, weightings, outputs and option preferences.

Public and Stakeholder Engagement (PSE) 4: May–6 October:

- Consult on draft recommendations.
- Response from government.

CoRWM undertook two simultaneous and interrelated engagement processes, one to engage with the 'general public' and one with specific invited stakeholder representatives. In the Public and Stakeholder Engagement process, there were primarily three methods that were used (CoRWM, 2005a):

- discussions in public open meetings;
- discussions in citizen and stakeholder panels;
- responses to the website and consultation document.

CoRWM's decision-support process

As mentioned, the foundation of the decision-support process in Phase 3 was Multi-Criteria Decision Analysis (MCDA) complemented by something termed Holistic Analysis (HA). The MCDA involved a strong deliberative element so could more specifically be termed a participatory or PMCDA. In governmental decisions, a common tool is cost-effectiveness analysis (CEA), where the relative costs of alternative ways of providing similar kinds of output are compared in order to make a decision. In some cases, the alternative cost-benefit analysis (CBA) is used in which some important non-marketed outputs are explicitly valued in money terms. CEA and CBA are analytical ways of comparing different forms of input or output, in these cases by giving them monetary values. MCDA is slightly different in that it is concerned with techniques for comparing impacts in ways which do not involve giving all of them explicit monetary values, but rather in a policy context it involves a sequence of actions: identifying options for achieving the objectives, identifying the criteria to be used to compare the options, analysis of the options, making choices and providing feedback on the decision (Department for Communities and Local Government, 2009).

In CoRWM's case each of the options on the shortlist was 'scored' by a series of experts against a set of technical and ethical assessment criteria for each of CoRWM's waste streams (more on ethics below). The scores were then 'weighted' to reflect the relative importance of the different criteria to members, and to the input of stakeholders including publics. The results of this MCDA were that each option was ranked. At each stage workshops were held to assess the criteria and then also for a performance assessment of the criteria. Some 70 specialists from academia, science, consultancy and practitioner groups took part in the scaling and/or scoring workshops, with further expertise for each of the criteria. In short these can be summarised as *Safety, Social, Environment, Security, Economic, Burden on Future Generations, Flexibility, Implementability; Cost* and *Proximity/Need for Transport* (CoRWM, 2006a).

The MCDA approach works best where decision-makers can compare options that are directly comparable, and it is harder to apply MCDA to strategic issues where the options are not directly comparable i.e. have varying attributes, complexities and uncertainties, incomplete data, or where relative performance is derived from subjective assessment. In CoRWM's case, for example, they could not easily address what the main discriminator was between the long-term storage of radioactive waste and its disposal (i.e. long-term safety beyond the lifetime of the storage facility) (Collier, 2006). In short, technical criteria are relatively easy to compare using the MCDA approach, but other socio-economic and ethical criteria were not because they require other forms of judgement not adequately catered for in the approach.

Of particular interest in this regard was CoRWM's approach to incorporating ethical issues. In addition to the work in designing and running the PSE programme, CoRWM recognised that they lacked a full understanding of the ethical issues involved or how to approach them. During CoRWM's PSE1, the ethical concerns associated with RWM options were identified. Commonly the ethical issues are defined in relation to either environmental justice amongst people alive today (sometimes referred to as intragenerational justice), between human beings and the natural environment, and between people alive today and those alive in the future (intergenerational justice). These basic ethical concerns have been well established in the literature on RWM (Nuclear Energy Agency, 1995), and ethics more broadly are seen as an integral aspect of a socio-technical RWM approach (Shrader-Frechette, 1991; Hadjilambrinos, 1999; Cotton, 2008). The criteria used by CoRWM in the shortlisting options phase specifically incorporated ethical aspects from the start. A set of ethical questions was then proposed and developed for the second round of engagement (PSE2), which led into the subsequent option assessment Phase 3. CoRWM first underwent a process of gathering feedback from early PSE events involving roundtables, open meetings, citizens' panels and the national stakeholder forum, as well as a wide range of written and website responses (on CoRWM's website). Also, ethical discussions of the option assessment specialist panels took place on a range of topic areas (including the criteria of safety, transport, site security, environmental and socio-economic impacts, implementability etc.) and these were a key aspect of the MCDA process undertaken (Blowers, 2006).

So ethics formed part of the MCDA alongside the input of scientific and technical expertise. The MCDA stage addressed social and ethical issues directly and through weighting, and the implementation recommendations drew heavily on specialist ethical input (Collier, 2006). However, CoRWM's programme of specialist ethics and social science input was linked most directly to a stage termed the 'Holistic Analysis' (HA). The Holistic Analysis was designed to incorporate inputs from all the cross-cutting activities – PSE, scientific input, ethical input, and the benchmarking of criteria through specialist input. The aim was to use deliberative discussion forums as a means to explore the differences between shortlisted options. The HA broadly took account of combined technical knowledge, PSE input and CoRWM members' views on a range of issues such as storage lifetimes, the extent to which institutional control over a facility could be guaranteed into the future and the option to retrieve the waste from an underground facility (CoRWM, 2006b). In terms of ethical assessment specifically, in September 2005 CoRWM held a workshop, and this was to be the main vehicle for specialist input on ethical issues. It brought together members of CoRWM and various UK and international specialists in order to (cited in Collier, 2006, p. 39), see also (Blowers, 2006):

- Help [members] understand the importance of ethical considerations and how they may be taken into account.
- Inform and generate discussion on ethical issues to enable CoRWM, stakeholders and the public to think about the ethical aspects of the different options for managing radioactive waste and thereby:
- Provide an input into the PSE round associated with options assessment and to reflect on outputs from earlier rounds of PSE.
- Understand how ethics need to be integrated with scientific outputs in a process of holistic decision-making.

This workshop involved first developing a 'briefing pack' for CoRWM and participants in advance. The workshop itself took the format of a series of presentations and discussions on four main topics (Blowers, 2006):

1 In what ways is radioactive waste an ethical issue?
2 Inter-generational equity.
3 Intra-generational equity.
4 Ethics and environment.

After a process of deliberation, external participants were also asked at the end for their intuitive preference amongst the shortlisted options. Following the workshop, a report was made (Blowers, 2006) along with a video that was subsequently shown to the Citizens' Panels (Collier, 2006). This initial workshop was then followed by two option assessment 'ethics sessions'. At the October 2005 London plenary session, CoRWM members considered the pros and cons of the shortlisted options against a set of ethical tests based on the concepts that surfaced at the workshop. The December 2005 London plenary then considered the options against a set of environmental principles based in part upon the workshop outputs. As a result of the specialist input to the options assessment process and the feedback from the PSE programme, these events (and the feedback that followed) were a major contributor to the Holistic Analysis (Collier, 2006), but were also major inputs to the work on implementation of CoRWM's recommendations. From this range of ethical inputs into the process CoRWM concluded that, 'all in all, the ethical dimension of decision-making has played an integral role in the CoRWM process' (Blowers, 2006, p. 4), see also (Cotton, 2009). In essence there was strong confidence within the committee that the socio-technical and ethical nature of the problem was adequately addressed in the committee's deliberations and eventual recommendations.

The evaluation of CoRWM's decision-support process

Clearly there was a range and broad scope of deliberative, social and ethical input activities that sat alongside the scientific and technical input to the MCDA stage, concerns for subjective assessment addressed in the HA and opportunities for engagement intertwined with all aspects of each phase through the various stages of PSE. The independent contractor organisation Faulkland Associates was brought in from mid-2004 to provide an evaluation and overall assessment of the deliberative process quality, starting with the website and a trial of the Deliberative Mapping methodology mentioned in Chapter 6. In their summary evaluation, the lead author David Collier described CoRWM's engagement strategy as having five main strands (Collier, 2006):

- direct and ongoing engagement with stakeholders;
- structured consultations with stakeholders at national and 'nuclear communities level';
- structured consultation with the public from nuclear communities;
- structured engagement with a cross-section of the wider public;
- opportunities to comment for any organisation or individual.

The committee was clear in its commitment to transparency and inclusion, publicly recognising that this was the only politically viable course of action in avoiding further policy failure. On the face of it this was broadly achieved: public meetings were open, meetings from minutes archived in open access on the CoRWM website, and members of the committee were active and supportive of the engagement process in media coverage of the committee's work. The underlying principle was that participation from the public and other stakeholder groups should be *iterative* and *integrative* in nature (Chilvers et al., 2003). CoRWM's PSE programme was intended to be folded into the decision-making process (analytic-deliberative), rather than simply as piecemeal consultation or information provision after a decision was made. Transparency was also a key requirement. In some cases, this was as simple as holding all of the committee meetings open to the public. However, Wallis notes that the reality did not always meet the ideal. More significantly the Phase 3 MCDA, 'holistic' analysis and 'recommendations' sessions were public plenaries – essentially the process of conducting the decision-support process were held to direct public access and scrutiny. This was an experimental approach that carried considerable risk. There is a cliché in policy analysis that 'no-one likes to see the sausage being made', in other words the process of political deliberation and co-production of governance before a policy announcement is made is invariably a process of frustration, uncertainty and stakeholder conflict (see for example Isett & Miranda, 2015). Holding this in public can be potentially damaging to the credibility of that process and the people involved. However, it was clear that in this case the open scrutiny of CoRWM's deliberations nevertheless encouraged stakeholder support for the eventual recommendations.

To conclude, we can see that the CoRWM process was markedly different from all previous nuclear policy mechanisms in the UK. Indeed, it was arguably the most comprehensive deliberative dialogue experiment on a live environmental policy issue in UK history. The driving force of prominent social science and NGO voices on the committee were instrumental in ensuring the maintenance of the analytic–deliberative approach. However, this approach was subject to considerable scrutiny both during and after its conclusion.

Critiquing CoRWM

The process that CoRWM underwent was a novel experiment in analytic–deliberative decision-making on an unprecedented scale. Broadly speaking, the process design, activities undertaken and work ethic of the committee have been praised by outside commentators (Collier, 2006; Wallis, 2008), though it was not without critique. Collier notes that CoRWM acted more in the manner of a consultancy team rather than an oversight committee, tending to work directly on the delivery of outputs. The downside of this is that where the committee lacked expertise there was a tendency to look inwardly at their own resources within the diverse membership of the committee, and 'to frame knowledge needs as consultancy tasks, which may result in cost-effectiveness being emphasised above authority' (Collier, 2006, p. 7). There was also concern that the more the individual members prepared evidence, the less independent the committee appeared to be, thus damaging its legitimacy in the eyes of certain stakeholders. One area of particular concern was, as Wallis (2008) asserts, that CoRWM was in fact initially set up without expertise in the area of deliberative dialogue, and that's why Faulkland Associates were brought in to assist. There were in essence two risks to consider throughout. The first was that the process would not be suitably 'expert' in the sense that the wrong types of inputs in terms of information and expertise were utilised. The second was that the process would lack legitimacy, in the sense that it did not command public support for its eventual recommendations. Balancing these two elements was a key concern. CoRWM had to mobilise the necessary expertise to do its job, but could not be beholden to 'the experts'. The 'science on tap but not on top' adage was repeated by CoRWM members throughout. It had to be deliberative, but must balance that against the need for a robust technical assessment that matched subjective value considerations with technical criteria. The balancing of the analytic and the deliberative was a delicate and politically fraught task.

CoRWM was heavily criticised in the options assessment phase, in particular, for its *overuse* of PSE. Notable critics were the two former members of the committee Keith Baverstock and David Ball who resigned due to their perception of a lack of rigorous scientific expertise on the panel. They argued that the options assessment process had to inspire public confidence, but they described the process by which this was achieved as 'wayward', in the sense that CoRWM placed a great deal of emphasis upon gaining public confidence through engagement and consultation, but that this was done at the expense of recruiting and utilising the best scientific expertise and up to date research in the management of radioactive waste. They presented a sceptical approach to the value of PSE in steering the outcomes of the committee, arguing that too much engagement with non-specialists in the science (and indeed social science and ethics of RWM) would undermine public confidence. Thus, in the middle of the options assessment process they called for changes to the management structure and process of decision-making on the grounds of public safety, national security and environmental protection (Keith & Ball, 2005). As previously mentioned, it was broadly accepted by most parties in the UK's RWM options assessment process that inclusive and transparent decision-making structures are required in order to avoid wasting time and resources on technocratic planning and siting resulting in protracted conflict with an independently 'selected' host community (Atherton, 2001). So when the government set up the MRWS programme and later CoRWM they began from first principles, as Michael Meacher's' speech to Parliament at the start of MRWS stated: with 'a blank sheet of paper'.

In part this blank sheet was about considering the long list of potential options identified in an assessment of the technical literature on RWM options. However, it involved not only reassessing the technical criteria and potential solutions available, but also incorporating stakeholder and public values and viewpoints to be weighted across the full range of technical options from the start. Though many of CoRWM's immediate stakeholders accepted this argument, criticism persisted, and this criticism mainly focused upon CoRWM as a body that was too public engagement-focused. The House of Lords Science and Technology Committee report (SCST, 2004) echoed strong calls from within scientific and technical communities to start with a much narrower list of options and also to include a much stronger scientific presence on the committee itself. The report was described as an 'unequivocal condemnation' and 'the most scathing report' ever from a House of Lords Committee (Ball, 2005). In the option assessment process critics argued that 'esoteric' RWM options such as disposal in space or in ice sheets should be dismissed as impractical, unsafe or illegal and thus create a list that better reflected current technical best practice among RWMOs worldwide. CoRWM's RWM option assessment work was criticised principally on the basis that certain voices within the scientific and technical community were excluded from the process alongside specialists from the social sciences and humanities; covering such areas as deliberation, communication, risk perception, trust and ethics (Baverstock & Ball, 2005; Ball, 2006).

It also criticised the capacity of CoRWM to take on board and integrate science into the decision-making process – whether it was a sufficiently 'intelligent customer for technical input' – a problem described by Ball (2005) as one of *relativism*. Ball remarked that within CoRWM meetings members expressed views that 'the laws of science are as changeable as the laws of parliament' and, 'that no two scientists/engineers/geologists/etc. would give the same answer to any question', and repeated what Ball described as the overtly political slogan purloined from Churchill, that decision-making should be structured as 'science on tap not on top' (Ball, 2005, p. 26).

A prominent Royal Society report expressed similar concerns as the House of Lords Committee, suggesting that there were significant areas where citizen-stakeholder evaluations of risks contrasted with technical assessments. Of particular note was the strong public preference against the transportation of wastes from one region to another, contrasting with the low statistical incidence of transport-related incidents over several decades. Similarly, they note that there is unease with which public actors consider the intergenerational risks of radionuclide migration, whilst geological analysis purports a much lower risk (Royal Society, 2006). Thus the Royal Society report implicitly reiterates the epistemological conflict between statistical and cultural interpretations of risk and the relevance of these competing epistemologies in decision-making, as discussed in Chapter 4.

Some of the outside critique from former members, the Lords and the Royal Society concern whether or not the participation was doing the job that it set out to achieve. Integrating participatory–deliberative outcomes into the decision-making process in a satisfactory way is inherently challenging (Rowe & Frewer, 2000) primarily due to the difficulties of integrating science with participation. Prominent scientific authorities such as the Royal Society construe science as ostensibly objective and independent of value considerations. The integration of science with subjective values means that there is a perceived tension between rigour and political expediency – and this is presented in political discourse of RWM as something of a zero sum game. More participation means less scientific rigour. However, in CoRWM's defence, the 'technical criteria' and 'value-based criteria' were separated to some degree between the MADA process and the Holistic Analysis. The two were treated differently but both considered in the final outcome. It was really for this reason that CoRWM managed to resist these calls to reduce the range of options in its early phases or to change its decision criteria a priori to the MADA and HA, arguing that PSE strengthens the public legitimacy of these elements despite its lengthy and costly nature. Ensuring the legitimacy of the *process* was paramount – the move from long list to shortlist needed to have clarity and it had to be justified to government and to broader third-party stakeholder networks that were watching CoRWM's activities closely. CoRWM aimed to achieve this by sticking to the sequence outlined in its early planning phase rather than bypassing to fit a perceived scientific consensus on geological disposal. However, looking at CoRWM's work generally, we can see that what these critical responses to

CoRWM's work were calling for was better critical reflection on whether PSE approaches provide the best quality information on all aspects relevant to the option assessment process. In essence, opponents were challenging the notion that more and better PSE would automatically translate into better decisions (see Stirrat, 1997; Cooke & Kothari, 2001; Abelson, Forest, Eyles, Smith, Martin, & Gauvin, 2003) and it is important that these critiques are examined.

So far in this book I have presented a normative position, shared by many social scientists in the study of science and technology, that governments should reject technocratic approaches broadly in favour of participatory–deliberative ones. It is normative in the sense that the underlying assumption is that participatory–deliberative is a priori *fairer* than non-participatory rather than necessarily *better quality*. Underlying my argument is an egalitarian ethical position that concerns the meta-ethics of technology decisions. It is morally justified to expand the range of inputs (in terms of knowledge and voices involved) to a technical decision where risks are borne by the few on behalf of the many. As noted in the previous chapters, sustained critique in academic and policy circles has shifted public authorities in countries such as the UK from a public understanding of science to a public engagement model that involves bi-directional dialogue processes rather than one-way communication. And this is driven quite strongly by this underlying moral position. However, the problem of decision-making on radioactive waste management is not just based upon an (overly neat) divide between technocratic and participatory–deliberative approaches. The very nature of participation itself, its form, the motives of authorities that instigate participatory processes, and the monitoring of outcomes must be subject to independent scrutiny, and in that sense the ongoing evaluation of the PSE programme and the final recommendations to government was a welcome addition midway through the CoRWM decision process (see Collier, 2005, 2006). Such monitoring and evaluation was necessary due to the novel nature of the PSE methods employed. Information provision and consultation practices are commonplace in regional and national planning decisions, however, active participation, community involvement and shared decision-making responsibility are something of a 'new frontier' for policy-making (Organisation for Economic Co-operation and Development, 2001a, 2001b). One of the key factors for CoRWM's relative success was that there was sufficient support amongst the committee for such experimentation, and this too was supported by its allies and opponents within stakeholder networks and its government taskmasters.

One of the biggest risks from the outset of the CoRWM options assessment process was that it would be simply another form of persuasion rather than true *deliberation* with an outcome that benefits those that engage in the process. Previous MADA processes used by Nirex were criticised for exactly this reason (Stirling, 1996). It was important that CoRWM could demonstrate that their PSE strategy was not just public relations in disguise. To the sceptical mind it is necessary to examine the extent to which public support is being manipulated into a pre-chosen proposal by the supposed 'real' decision-makers, who may simply wish to use these participatory approaches as a smokescreen to hide the true decision-making process – a condition of the *post-political* where decisions reflect the interests of elites rather than bodies of engaged citizens despite the mechanics of talking and voting (see for example Swyngedouw, 2007). This commonly occurs in processes where the language of participation is used by decision-makers when participants actually have little or no decisional influence upon outcomes (the *deliberative speak* problem), where decision-makers adopt the rhetoric of inclusive dialogue without any of the accompanying devolved powers to participants (Hindmarsh & Matthews, 2008). Clearly from the evaluation of CoRWM this was not the case. CoRWM entered into the PSE programme in good faith, defending their analytic–deliberative approach against calls for its abandonment from prominent scientific authorities. It was, therefore, instrumental in trialling a more open and inclusive form of decision-making that had ramifications not just for the RWM decision, but for other areas of deliberative government policy-making at the time.

Methodologically, the critique of CoRWM is more complex. The novelty of the methodological approach combining MADA with HA raises concerns about how best to evaluate this as an analytic–deliberative process. As Fischhoff, Bostrom and Quadrel (1993) and Stern and Fineberg (1996) recognise, analytic–deliberative process success must involve good science, and the right science, good participation, and the right participants as well as integrating all of these elements in an 'accurate, balanced and informative synthesis'. It is the act of balancing these elements that is difficult. Getting the 'right publics' is a particularly difficult task. Top-down government appointed committee-led engagement programmes such as this can frequently prioritise the voices of those that express emotional detachment, political engagement, and social tolerance of policy outcomes over those that represent dissent, dissatisfaction or social opposition (see Tironi, 2015). In essence, the nature of the process is often designed in such a way as to maintain cooperative rather than antagonistic dialogue – often to the exclusion of important voices of opposition such as opposition groups, national NGOs and direct action campaigns that might disrupt proceedings. Cleaver (2001) discusses how participation-centred approaches to decision-making are based upon three tenets of faith. The first is that participation is an inherently *good thing* (especially for the participants). The second is that decision-making authorities commonly focus on 'getting the techniques right' as the principal means to ensure the success of PSE. The third is that considerations of power on the whole should be avoided as divisive or obstructive. There is commonly an assumption that getting people into the dialogue process is sufficient to ensure a fair and balanced decision process, the assessment of power dynamics within groups, information imbalances and representation that is fair across issues of age, gender and race is notoriously difficult. There are, therefore, a number of potential pitfalls involved in simply replacing technical with participatory–deliberative decision-making. Collins and Evans (2002) argue that the 'deliberative turn' has replaced the 'problem of legitimacy' (i.e. from reliance on expert opinion), with a 'problem of extension' whereby the involvement of many different voices in participatory procedures can be a hindrance to effective decision-making (see also Chilvers, 2008). Also, perhaps ironically, participatory methods in policy deliberation can have exclusionary effects, widening the gap between those that are able (and willing) to use these opportunities and those that are not (Mansbridge, 1980; Young, 2000). They may tend to bias the viewpoints of individuals that have the resources (i.e. enough free time) and the motivation to participate. Such critics argue it is those that are marginalised by policy decisions that have the greatest 'stake', and yet these groups often have the least access to participatory decision-making – due to self-perceived inadequate knowledge or lack of available resources. This is sometimes based upon a self-selection bias grounded in the capacity of individuals to act as deliberative citizens. Participants in technical deliberation in the UK are commonly older white males with tertiary education in the A/B social grade categories of profession. This is partially because of the time and other resource costs involved in participation being restrictive of other demographic groups, but also due to the implicit issues of power and cultural barriers to participation that exclude other ages, genders, races and classes from technological deliberation. Though CoRWM was open and transparent with free access to all 'publics', there are concerns that without actively adjusting their recruitment of participants from underrepresented groups, the decision-support input from deliberation is skewed and unrepresentative. This is a problem which affects many deliberative and inclusionary processes, and some such as Fishkin (1995) suggest that the only way around this is proper demographic sampling – to create a microcosm of broader society interests through statistical representativeness within a deliberative forum; though this did not occur in CoRWM's work.

More generally in the critique of CoRWM there are different evaluation criteria that could be applied. One commonly cited model for assessing the status of participatory processes is Arnstein's ladder of participation (1969). The ladder provides a useful evaluative yardstick against which to gauge the degree to which a PSE process is actually participatory in the sense of allowing citizen-stakeholder control within decisions. In the ladder model, *manipulation* and *information provision* represent the lowest levels of involvement whereby citizen-stakeholders are either lied to or simply told what the decision is (before or after the fact). The next rungs up are *consultation*, *partnership*, *delegated power* and then *citizen control*. The latter represents complete power to citizen-stakeholders. We might suggest that CoRWM's PSE model remained at the consultation rung of this ladder. Though PSE was integrated at all levels of the decision–support process, the outputs were still drafted by CoRWM itself: an expert committee (although the expertise was much broader than just nuclear industry-specific knowledge). There was no nuclear community representation on the panel (so no true partnership at this stage), and no opportunity for citizen drafting of recommendations (delegated power/citizen control). Although the participatory–deliberative model that CoRWM espoused did have considerable scope for involvement, and novelty in its application of deliberative methods, the structure of the committee as an advisory body meant that citizen power was limited by design.

Though the ladder model shows relatively little citizen control of the decision, CoRWM's process fairs better under other evaluative criteria. Renn and Webler's *fairness* and *competence* criteria (Renn & Webler, 1995) are also useful evaluative 'yardsticks' against which to measure process design. In this typology *fairness* is related access to decision-making forums and participation in a free and unbiased manner, without coercion or exclusion. *Competence* is measured in terms of the capacity of different voices to be involved in an informed and meaningful way. In this respect CoRWM's PSE process provided both fair access in the sense that all its meetings were public and there were opportunities to comment online and in person allowing input at all stages of the decision. It was also competent in the sense that both expertise from a range of technical backgrounds and lay knowledge was included (given the caveats mentioned about under-representation of certain demographic groups). We can see therefore that the success of the process varies when different criteria for evaluation are applied. However, thinking back to earlier chapters, in general one could confidently claim that the PSE programme had considerable success in achieving a postnormal scientific goal – it allowed a range of different actors the opportunity to comment upon and shape the direction of the decision process – expanding the realm of evaluation beyond narrow scientific peer review to broader stakeholder evaluation and critique, which is what the committee intended to do.

Though on the face of it we can claim the PSE programme was successful, another caveat to mention is that evaluating the detail of such processes is exceedingly difficult to do in parallel with running the dialogue process itself (Rowe & Frewer, 2004; Burgess & Clark, 2006) as Faulkand Associates did. In part this is because the roles of different actors involved commonly overlap. For example, the designer of the process may also be a facilitator of the dialogue, and possibly the evaluator of outcomes or the moderator of different stakeholder interests. The overlapping roles of designer, facilitator and evaluator, as Chilvers (2013) notes, make evaluation of such competencies ambiguous and difficult. The fact that Faulkland Associates both helped to design the participatory process and evaluate CoRWM's implementation of it, is a possible example of this overlapping competency and ambiguity of role. Moreover, evaluating both the outcomes, process and indeed the participants' own experiences of deliberation is challenging. This is primarily because the concepts of 'involvement', 'engagement' and 'participation' are not amenable to simplification and quantitative measurement; rather, they are multi-dimensional concepts, used by different actors to mean different things (Rowe & Frewer, 2004; Rowe, Horlick-Jones, Walls, & Pidgeon, 2005). Evaluating the usefulness or effectiveness of such processes remains difficult, also because terms like 'usefulness' are loaded with implicit normative values. Finding a benchmark to measure the 'usefulness' of PSE is therefore difficult to generate a priori without first examining the underlying values embedded in the evaluative framework. It then becomes difficult to declare whether any specific method is 'best' or indeed even the most appropriate one to the decision under consideration.

In answer to the problem of effective evaluation, Rowe and Frewer suggest that hybridity and complementarity between traditional methods (which might include opinion surveys, focus groups and established forms of social research method) with newer experimental deliberative methods, might overcome this problem (Rowe & Frewer, 2000). CoRWM's implementation of MCDA and the HA is one example of this – combining an established method of criteria assessment with a more subjective and deliberative approach that is innovative and bespoke to the decision context. Other aspects of evaluation are more process rather than outcomes-based – such as evaluating participant reflections upon what makes good deliberation (Webler, Tuler, & Krueger, 2001), and also attention to issues such as evaluating deliberative quality (see for example Graham & Witschge, 2003; Niemeyer & Dryzek, 2007); the efficacy of methods (Rauschmayer & Wittmer, 2006); experiences of comfort and satisfaction (Halvorsen, 2001) and how these then lead to longer term participant technical and social learning, pro-environmental behaviour change or engagement in other social and political issues affecting their communities of interest (Bull, Petts, & Evans, 2008; Muro & Jeffrey, 2008; Devine-Wright & Cotton, forthcoming). None of these latter elements were part of the formal evaluation of CoRWM's PSE programme and might make interesting follow-up projects now that the process is long finished – returning to participants to assess what changes might have occurred in their attitudes or understanding over the longer period.

Conclusions

Across many nuclear producing developed economies, the production of electricity has received the tacit support of governmental authorities after industry acceptance of responsibility to establish a final disposal route for industry-generated radioactive wastes. In the UK, however, the close ties between government-sponsored weapons programmes and commercial power generation interests led to a secretive and technocratic decision-making environment for RWM that has been continually mired in political controversy. The need for action in developing RWM solutions has increased with continued waste generation from reprocessing and decommissioning, but paradoxically, constant politicisation of the issue continued to delay progress in finding a solution, culminating in the failure of 1997's rock characterisation facility – a precursor step towards building a deep geological repository. With the failure of Nirex, government took on a greater and more active role in the RWM policy process than it had in previous iterations of siting procedures. This new role for central government came at the same time as a process of systemic change, specifically to the structure of planning processes occurring under Labour in the late 1990s and early 2000s, alongside an increasing desire for bi-directional public engagement on issues of science and technology. It is this combination of factors: industry failure, community involvement in planning and public engagement with science and technology, which led to the MRWS programme and the appointment of CoRWM as a mixed-interest body, with backgrounds beyond nuclear industry interests and the academic physical sciences and engineering.

CoRWM's extensive public and stakeholder engagement programme on options assessment presented new opportunities for the government and the devolved administrations. Looking back, we can see that CoRWM was an experiment in analytic–deliberative decision-making that has not been matched in UK public policy-making before or since. It was heavily influenced by academic thinking around participatory technology assessment, and the broader political shift within the Labour Party at the time towards inclusive dialogue as a mechanism to resolve policy disputes. The critiques of CoRWM's process concern both the nature of deliberative dialogue as a means to make a decision on technical matters, and upon the implementation and evaluation of a novel analytic–deliberative process. In the former, an array of scientific authorities criticised CoRWM as being too public focused and 'not scientific enough'. The geological disposal option had come about following decades of research. Across Europe and North America, deep geological disposal had both a scientific and political consensus, so why didn't the MRWS programme start from there? The answer is simply about different types of legitimacy in technology politics. Technical decisions must be socially robust, which means the source of decision-making must (among other factors) be trustworthy to all stakeholders involved. Going back to the blank sheet of paper option, where a long list was considered and then shortened through successive rounds of analysis, allowed a postnormal science of radioactive waste to emerge. The limited peer review of scientific experts from the House of Lords and the Royal Society (as two notable examples) was insufficient. RWM is a wicked problem where the underlying values at stake are ambiguous and ill-defined by science. CoRWM's insistence that the process of shortlisting and options assessment be adhered to, even in the face of scientific criticism from eminent scientific bodies, is testament to their commitment to this normative ideal. We can also observe, however, that CoRWM really was making up the process of deliberation as it was being implemented. This has some significant risks, as it is difficult to know in advance whether the right process is put into place, one that has the right science and the right publics as wells as one that is well facilitated and independent. Bringing in Faulkand Associates to provide advice and ongoing scrutiny was a vital step. It allowed CoRWM to be reflexive in its implementation of PSE and more skilfully blended the assessment of technical criteria through their workshop and external advice programme contributing to the MADA with the value considerations from expert ethics workshops and PSE contributing to the Holistic Assessment. What we see in the following chapter is that the eventual recommendation for long-term RWM was the same as it's always been – deep geological disposal, though with greater attention paid to the interim process of storage in advance of a final disposal route. However, this time the decision had greater political legitimacy because the process of deciding was far more fair and inclusive, in contrast to all other policy measures before it. What CoRWM did next, was to go beyond their initial remit and suggested a political process for implementing the geological disposal decision through a model of community volunteerism, partnership working and compensation to host communities. The so-called *Partnership* model is the primary issue under discussion in Chapter 8.

194 *Managing radioactive waste safely*

Note

1 The members at the final reporting stage were Professor Gordon MacKerron (Chair of the Committee who replaced the original chair who had taken up another appointment); Dr Wynne Davies (Deputy Chair), Mary Allan, Fred Barker, Professor Andrew Blowers OBE, Professor Brian D. Clark, Dr Mark Dutton, Colonel Fiona Walthall OBE, Professor Lynda Warren, Jenny Watson, Pete Wilkinson.

Bibliography

Abelson, J., Forest, P. G., Eyles, J., Smith, P., Martin, E., & Gauvin, F. P. (2003). Deliberations about deliberative methods: Issues in the design and evaluation of public participation processes. *Social Science and Medicine, 57*(2), 239–251.

Arnstein, S. R. (1969). A ladder of citizen participation. *Journal of the American Institute of Planners, 35*(4), 216–224.

Atherton, E. (2001). *Getting stakeholder issues into the management of radioactive waste.* Paper presented at the Values in Decision-Making on Risk (VALDOR), Stockholm.

Atherton, E., & Poole, M. (2001). The problem of the UK's radioactive waste: What have we learnt? *Interdisciplinary Science Reviews, 26*, 296–302.

Ball, D. J. (2005). Nuclear waste: Consult widely, decide wisely? *Chemical Engineer, 771*(September), 25–27.

Ball, D. J. (2006). Deliberating over Britain's nuclear waste. *Journal of Risk Research, 9*(1), 1–11.

Baverstock, K., & Ball, D. J. (2005). The UK committee on radioactive waste management. *Journal of Radiological Protection, 25*(3), 313.

Beveridge, G., & Curtis, C. (1998). *Radioactive waste disposal – where do we go from here?* Paper presented at the Nuclear Free Local Authorities Annual Conference, Caernarfon.

Blowers, A. (Ed.). (2006). *Ethics and decision making for radioactive waste.* London: Committee on Radioactive Waste Management.

Bull, R., Petts, J., & Evans, J. (2008). Social learning from public engagement: Dreaming the impossible? *Journal of Environmental Planning and Management, 51*(5), 701–716.

Burgess, J., & Clark, J. (2006). Evaluating public and stakeholder engagement strategies in environmental governance. In A. G. Peirez, S. G. Vas, & S. Tognetti (Eds.), *Interfaces between science and society.* London: Greenleaf Press.

Chilvers, J. (2008). Deliberating competence: Theoretical and practitioner perspectives on effective participatory appraisal practice. *Science, Technology & Human Values, 33*(2), 155–185.

Chilvers, J. (2013). Reflexive engagement? Actors, learning, and reflexivity in public dialogue on science and technology. *Science Communication, 35*(3), 283–310.

Chilvers, J., Burgess, J., & Murlis, J. (2003). *Managing radioactive waste safely – participatory methods workshop: Final report.* London: Committee on Radioactive Waste Management.

Cleaver, F. (2001). Institutions, agency and the limitations of participatory approaches to development. In B. Cook, & U Kothari (Eds.), *Participation: The new tyranny?* London: Zed Books.

Collier, D. (2005). *CoRWM PSE1 evaluation V4 (R04 C2022 R04-4).* Oxford: Faulkland Associates.

Collier, D. (2006). *CoRWM final evaluation statement (C2022 R08-3).* Oxford: Faulkland Associates.

Collins, H. M., & Evans, R. (2002). The third wave of science studies: Studies of expertise and experience. *Social Studies of Science, 32*(2), 235–296.

Cooke, B., & Kothari, U. (2001). *Participation: The new tyranny?* London: Zed Books.

CoRWM. (2004). Guiding principles. London: Committee on Radioactive Waste Management.

CoRWM. (2005a). *How should the UK manage radioactive waste? 2nd consultation document 4th April to 27th June 2005.* London: Committee on Radioactive Waste Management.

CoRWM. (2005b). Why we need to consult. Retrieved from www.corwm.org/content-413.

CoRWM. (2006a). *CoRWM Specialist workshops – Scoring, January 2006.* London: Committee on Radioactive Waste Management.

CoRWM. (2006b). *Managing our radioactive waste safely: CoRWM's recommendations to government.* London: Committee on Radioactive Waste Management.

CoRWM. (2006c). Programme of work. Retrieved from www.corwm.org.uk/content-591.

Cotton, M. (2008). Developing stakeholder and community decision-support tools for the consideration of ethics in UK radioactive waste management policy. (Unpublished thesis at the University of East Anglia, Norwich).

Cotton, M. (2009). Ethical assessment in radioactive waste management: A proposed reflective equilibrium-based deliberative approach. *Journal of Risk Research, 12*(5), 603–618.

Department for Communities and Local Government. (2009). *Multi-criteria analysis: A manual.* Wetherby: Department for Communities and Local Government.

Department for Environment Food and Rural Affairs (DEFRA). (2001). *Managing radioactive waste safely: Proposals for developing a policy for managing solid radioactive waste in the UK.* Retrieved from www.defra.gov.uk/environment/consult/radwaste/pdf/radwaste.pdf.

Devine-Wright, P., & Cotton, M. (forthcoming). Experiencing citizen deliberation over energy infrastructure siting: A mixed method evaluative study. In S. Bouzarovski, & M. J. Pasqualetti (Eds.), *The Routledge research companion to energy geographies.* Abingdon: Routledge.

Dietz, S. (2011). Strategic appraisal of environmental risks: A contrast between the UK's Stern Review on the economics of climate change and its Committee on Radioactive Waste Management. *Risk Analysis, 31*(1), 129–142.

Fischhoff, B., Bostrom, A., & Quadrel, M. J. (1993). Risk perception and communication. *Annual Review of Public Health, 14*, 183–203.

Fishkin, J. (1995). *The voice of the people.* New Haven: CT: Yale University Press.

Graham, T., & Witschge, T. (2003). In search of online deliberation: Towards a new method for examining the quality of online discussions. *Communications, 28*, 173–204.

Grimstone, M. (2004). *Ethical and environmental principles: A review of the influence of ethical and environmental considerations in the formulation and implementation of radioactive waste management policy* (670). London: Committee on Radioactive Waste Management.

Grove-White, R. (2000). 'Nuclear waste?' 'No thanks!'. Retrieved from www.nirex.co.uk/news/na01027.htm.

Hadjilambrinos, C. (1999). Toward a rational policy for the management of high-level radioactive waste: Integrating science and ethics. *Bulletin of Science, Technology & Society, 19*(3), 179–189.

Hajer, M. (1995). *The politics of environmental discourse: Ecological modernization and the policy process.* Oxford: Clarendon Press.

Halvorsen, K. E. (2001). Assessing public participation techniques for comfort, convenience, satisfaction, and deliberation. *Environmental Management, 28*(2), 179–186.

Hindmarsh, R., & Matthews, C. (2008). Deliberative speak at the turbine face: Community engagement, wind farms, and renewable energy transitions, in Australia. *Journal of Environmental Policy & Planning, 10*(3), 217–232.

House of Lords. (1999). *Management of nuclear waste* (third report). London: House of Lords.

House of Lords Select Committee on Science and Technology. (2001). *Managing radioactive waste: The government's consultation, 1st report, session 2001–2002 (HL Paper 36), introduction*. London: House of Lords.

House of Lords Select Committee on Science and Technology. (2004). *House of Lords Select Committee on Science and Technology report on 'radioactive waste management': The government's response*. London: House of Lords.

Isett, K. R., & Miranda, J. (2015). Watching sausage being made: Lessons learned from the co-production of governance in a behavioural health system. *Public Management Review, 17*(1), 35–56.

Keith, B., & Ball, D. J. (2005). The UK Committee on Radioactive Waste Management. *Journal of Radiological Protection, 25*(3), 313.

Kemp, R. (1992). *The politics of radioactive waste disposal*. Manchester: Manchester University Press.

Mansbridge, J. (1980). *Beyond adversary democracy*. New York: Basic Books.

Muro, M., & Jeffrey, P. (2008). A critical review of the theory and application of social learning in participatory natural resource management processes. *Journal of Environmental Planning and Management, 51*(3), 325–344. doi:10.1080/09640560801977190.

Niemeyer, S., & Dryzek, J. S. (2007, 7–12 May). *Intersubjective rationality: Using interpersonal consistency as a measure of deliberative quality*. Paper presented at the Advanced Empirical Study of Deliberation, Helsinki.

Nirex. (2002). *What is the Nirex phased disposal concept?* Harwell: Nirex.

Nirex. (2003). *Options for long-term management* London: Department for Environment Food and Rural Affairs.

Nirex. (2006). *A new way of thinking – Nirex's story: 1997–2005*. Harwell: Nirex.

Nuclear Energy Agency. (1995). *The environmental and ethical basis of geological disposal of long-lived radioactive wastes*. Vienna: Nuclear Energy Agency.

Organisation for Economic Co-operation and Development. (2001a). *Citizens as partners. Information, consultation and public partcipation in policy-making*. Paris: Organisation for Economic Co-operation and Development.

Organisation for Economic Co-operation and Development. (2001b). *Engaging citizens in policy-making. Information, consultation and public participation* (Policy Brief 10). Paris: Organisation for Economic Co-operation and Development.

Philberth, K. (1977). Disposal of radioactive waste in ice sheets. *Journal of Glaciology, 19*(81), 607–617.

Rauschmayer, F., & Wittmer, H. (2006). Evaluating deliberative and analytical methods for the resolution of environmental conflicts. *Land Use Policy, 23*(1), 108–122.

Renn, O., & Webler, T. (Eds.). (1995). *Fairness and competence in citizen participation, technology, risk and society* (Vol. 10). Dordrecht: Kluwer Academic Publishers.

Rowe, G., & Frewer, L. J. (2000). Public participation methods: A framework for evaluation. *Science, Technology & Human Values, 25*(1), 3–29.

Rowe, G., & Frewer, L. J. (2004). Evaluating public-participation exercises: A research agenda. *Science, Technology & Human Values, 29*, 512–556.

Rowe, G., Horlick-Jones, T., Walls, J., & Pidgeon, N. (2005). Difficulties in evaluating public engagement initiatives: Reflections on an evaluation of the UK GM Nation? Public debate about transgenic crops. *Public Understanding of Science, 14*, 331–352.

Royal Commission on Environmental Pollution. (1976). *Nuclear power and the environment* (6th Report). London: Royal Commission on Environmental Pollution.

Royal Society. (2002). *Developing UK policy for the management of radioactive wastes. Policy document 12/02.* London: The Society.

Royal Society. (2006). *The long-term management of radioactive waste: The work of the Committee on Radioactive Waste Management (CoRWM). Policy document 01/06.* London: The Society.

RWMAC. (2001). *Advice to ministers on the process for formulation of future policy for the long-term management of UK solid radioactive waste.* London: Radioactive Waste Management Advisory Committee.

Select Committee on Environment, F. a. R. A. (2002). *Third report. Radioactive waste: The government's consultation process.* Retrieved from www.publications.parliament.uk/pa/cm200102/cmselect/cmenvfru/407/40704.htm -note34.

Shrader-Frechette, K. (1991). Ethical dilemmas and radioactive waste: A survey of the issues. *Environmental Ethics, 13*(4), 327–343.

Stern, P. C., & Fineberg, H. V. (1996). *Understanding risk: Informing decisions in a democratic society.* Washington DC: National Academy Press.

Stirling, A. (1996). On the Nirex MADA [Multi-Attribute Decision Analysis]. Proof of evidence. In R. S. Haszeldine, & D. K. Smythe (Eds.), *Radioactive waste disposal at Sellafield, UK: Site selection, geological and engineering problems.* Glasgow: University of Glasgow.

Stirrat, R. (1997). The new orthodoxy and old truths: Participation, empowerment and other buzzwords. In S. Bastian, & N. Bastian (Eds.), *Assessing participation.* London: Routledge.

Swyngedouw, E. (2007). Impossible 'sustainability' and the postpolitical condition. In R. Krueger, & R. Gibbs (Eds.), *The sustainable development paradox: Urban political economy in the United States and Europe* (pp. 13–40). New York: The Guildford Press.

Tironi, M. (2015). Disastrous publics: Counter-enactments in participatory experiments. *Science, Technology & Human Values, 40*(4), 564–587. doi:10.1177/0162243914560649.

Wallis, M. K. (2008). Disposing of Britain's nuclear waste: The CoRWM process. *Energy & Environment, 19*(3/4), 515–557.

Webler, T., Tuler, S., & Krueger, R. (2001). What is a good public participation process? Five perspectives from the public. *Environmental Management, 27*(3), 435–450.

Western, R. (1996). Friends of the Earth and the Nirex Inquiry. Retrieved from www.foe.co.uk/archive/nirex/intro.html.

Western, R. (1998). The UK nuclear waste crisis. In F. Barker (Ed.), *Management of radioactive wastes: Issues for local Aathorities.* London: ICE Publishing.

Young, I. M. (2000). *Inclusion and democracy.* Oxford: Oxford University Press.

8 Partnership, volunteerism and ethical incrementalism

Introduction

To the then Labour Government in 2006, the Committee on Radioactive Waste Management's (CoRWM) process was deemed a political success. After the long period of scientific assessment and stakeholder dialogue concluded, Environment Secretary David Milliband (2006) stated that:

> CoRWM has set the standards for open and transparent advice that not only takes into account the best available expert input, but also the views of the public and stakeholders. We are committed to taking forward this important task to ensure the safe and secure management of our radioactive waste.

CoRWM's options assessment process concluded, and as per their Terms of Reference, final recommendations were delivered to government in a report on 31 July 2006. In the government's response to these recommendations they praised CoRWM, saying that: 'The open and transparent manner in which CoRWM has conducted its business has been ground breaking' (DEFRA, 2006, p. 3). This experiment in participatory–deliberative dialogue had delivered what government wanted, namely a set of recommendations that it could actively support. The previous failures of Nirex had created a political gulf between government and the nuclear industry, and perhaps more importantly, between government and the broader network of stakeholders in Cumbria – local government actors, environmental activist organisations at the local level and national ENGOs that campaigned against the RCF at Sellafield. Here the CoRWM process delivered a strategy that had socio-technical *legitimacy*, in the sense that both allied and adversarial stakeholder groups could support CoRWM's recommendations, there was no obvious flaw in its scientific assessment (because geological disposal was the 'industry best practice' model), and the two objectives of societal acceptance and technical feasibility were met. Thus, although a complete consensus amongst stakeholder groups was unnecessary from a policy perspective (nor was it achieved), the final report's recommendations were not actively opposed by any of the organisations either involved in or observing CoRWM.

The first of the 'headline' recommendations was that, in the long term, the disposal of radioactive waste deep underground (deep geological disposal) should be the final end-state for higher activity legacy wastes from previous and existing nuclear processes. The second recommendation was that greater attention should be paid to the interim storage of existing wastes on site at nuclear facilities. This was recognised as necessary given that the creation and operation of suitable facilities for disposal would likely take several decades, and that Sellafield with its high volumes of poorly stored legacy wastes presented an immediate environmental threat to the local environment. The third was that a new approach for *implementing* geological disposal should be factored into the site selection process. This approach should be based upon 'the willingness of local communities to participate, partnership and enhanced well-being' (CoRWM, 2006b, p. 3); based upon an equal partnership between government and potential host communities and upon a willingness to participate (a process referred to as volunteerism/voluntarism, see for example: Gunderson, 1999). It was the third recommendation that took CoRWM beyond its original remit, in that it was explicitly about siting rather than technological option appraisal. Fourth, CoRWM recommended that there should be the immediate creation of an oversight body to begin this process of implementation (CoRWM, 2006a, 2006b), echoing the Flowers report and RWMAC recommendations that independent oversight and delivery should be implemented in site selection; thus going beyond the role of CoRWM as a quasi-autonomous advisory group to government.

The move to implementation

Government accepted CoRWM's recommendations in 2006, stating that 'Government welcomes CoRWM's report and believes it provides a sound basis for moving forward. Most recommendations can be acted on immediately; others require us to undertake more work.' (DEFRA, 2006, p. 3). CoRWM's recommended *partnership* model (that was broadly accepted as the basis for the implementation stage decision-making) involved stakeholder and community representation and involvement throughout a multi-staged decision-making model. This voluntarist approach was to provide input and an element of community control over the technology strategy for RWM. This move to voluntarism is based, in part, upon the examination of international experiences of waste management practice in other nuclear power producing countries. Countries that have had (relative) successes in finding host communities have adopted one variation or another of a voluntarist model. Two notable examples in this regard are the Canadian experience of the Deep River LLW repository siting process in Ontario in 1995, which used a direct democracy and voluntarist siting process, which was heralded by proponents as a successful model to be copied by other nuclear power producing nations (Gunderson, 1999); and the combined mediation, voluntarist and social acceptance strategy demonstrated by the Swedish RWMO called SKB in 1992 (Elam, Lidberg, Soneryd, & Sundqvist,

2009). In both cases the voluntarist model contrasts with previous geology-led strategies, whereby concepts of local acceptance, and willingness to work in partnership with the RWMO became key criteria for siting success. Indeed as Darst and Dawson (2010) argue, it was the Swedish and Finnish models of voluntarist siting that paved the way to the partnership approach that CoRWM suggested and the government adopted.

Of concern was the development of an adequate PSE framework to assist in the voluntarist implementation strategy. A reconstituted CoRWM acted as an advisory body to this process. CoRWM was not the 'implementing' organisation with oversight over the process. That was left to ministerial oversight within DECC, based upon a partnership model with a volunteer community. One of CoRWM's political roles was to assess and comment upon the communications strategy. A working group with CoRWM, representatives from government departments, devolved administrations, NDA, regulators and the Nuclear Legacy Advisory Forum (NuLeAF) was set up to develop the PSE programme. A Geological Disposal Implementation Board (GDIB) developed a communications strategy including mail-outs, fact sheets and attendance at national stakeholder events to promote the implementation process using voluntary site selection. It was clear that through these oversight roles, the government was held to account in implementing its voluntarist approach and committing to the continuation of a PSE-focused decision-making process. Thus there was true policy evolution in site selection towards devolving the decision-making power to a partnership model; and avoiding the criticism of deliberative speak (Hindmarsh & Matthews, 2008) – i.e. simply using the language and terminology of participative decision-making in order to further a pre-made policy decision.

Voluntarism as egalitarian siting

The powers of community control, and the extent to which decisions become devolved to the local level are fundamentally ethical issues, specifically meta-ethical issues, in the sense that concern the process by which ethical decisions over site selection get made, and the voices that are heard within this decision process. Voluntarism is primarily based upon principles of *ethical egalitarianism* and *ethical autonomy* – they concern fairness in the opportunity for citizens to be involved without coercion in the decisions that affect them. It is important to reiterate the scales at which the UK government construe the problem of waste. It falls within a 'grand-scale' or megaproject mentality: a national problem requiring a locally embedded solution. Wastes are produced at numerous sites across the country, the electricity that was produced through nuclear power (and the defence of the country through nuclear weapons that in turn produce wastes) are, broadly speaking, beneficial to this wider national population. Risks are conversely concentrated and geographically situated in and around nuclear communities where existing sites hold these wastes. A national-level solution proposed by CoRWM involves safe interim storage (which benefits the local community in the short-to-medium term by reducing risks of radiation exposure), but the end goal is one (or perhaps more than one) disposal site(s). This means that the national problem/local solution model has inherent distributive environmental justice challenges. It is here that I assert a strongly normative position on this issue: government has a moral responsibility to make the process of risk/benefit distributions fairer between local and national scales. The voluntarist position is that communities must step forward ultimately to take on this additional risk burden on behalf of a broader society. This creates a problem of risk scaling. Specifically, it means a process of ever-diminishing geographic scales of risk: the spatial distribution of radiation and other environmental and health risks becomes ever more concentrated over time as the wastes are moved from their existing sites to become housed in one area. During the transit process for radioactive wastes, the risks are distributed along transport corridors, but once transported and housed within a repository, the locus of risk is concentrated to single location.

The CoRWM-proposed voluntarist model was aimed to reduce the coercive effect whereby central authorities impose the concentration of spatial scales of environmental risk. It is egalitarian in the sense that any community of citizens could enter into (first) discussion and (second) agreement with government to concentrate such risks. Within this, DECC identified three constituent bodies of interest in this community-focused decision process. The first is the *host community* (geographically defined as the owners of the land and the surrounding area, such as a town or village), the second is the *decision-making body* (the local authority, district council, county councils, metropolitan district councils, London Boroughs, unitary authority), and third, *wider community interests* (including neighbouring communities and broader stakeholder networks) (DEFRA, BERR, and the devolved administrations for Wales and Northern Ireland, 2008). Crucially, only the decision body has partnership decision-making control, this means that elected authorities at local and national levels of government enter into a decision together. However, the decision body can only take decisions once it has successfully canvassed the host community, and (to a lesser extent) the wider community interests.

As a point of *ethical egalitarianism*, the risks that are concentrated within the host community would be compensated for – distributive injustice would be alleviated by financial means, though there is a lack of clarity about the geographic extent to which these benefits are distributed beyond the host community. As an issue of *ethical autonomy*, the host community can be forced to accept the government's terms if the decision body voted against the community's interests. However, the legitimacy of the partnership agreement between local and national government is only valid if the local authority partner can prove that they had the full consent of the host community. It is in this way that the implementation model of partnership maintains the ethical autonomy of the host community, and provides a system for informed consent. The features of volunteerism, collaboration between local and national level decision-making bodies, a right for communities to withdraw and the ratification of local decisions by elected representatives shown in the implementation report, reveal a clear set of ethically informed principles for the approach taken in site selection. However, the range of partnership bodies that could be involved, the types of participatory–deliberative processes employed, the time scales for a right to withdraw, the manner of delivery and form of compensatory measures all required further detail and independent analysis. Many of these elements were negotiable terms once a volunteer community 'stepped forward', but nonetheless remain *discursive* or *meta-ethical* concerns. The question of who should have the right and responsibility to make the ethical decision over risk concentration had not been clearly resolved or ethically justified within policy from the outset.

Though government agreed in principle to what became known as the Three Ps model: *participation, partnership* and *packages* (Blowers, 2014); the issue of implementation and the structure for this proposed voluntarist partnership model required another political step. Specifically, the government needed guidance on how a 'society-led' process of site selection, where communities come forward to engage in talks about hosting a geological repository, could be integrated with the assessment of the physical geography of the volunteer sites. This rebalancing of the socio-technical aspect of waste siting towards the 'socio-' element caused some consternation amongst technical authorities; though it was widely recognised within radioactive waste policy networks that no other solution would be politically feasible, and amongst certain academics and environmental non-governmental organisations no other solution would be recognised as ethically legitimate. However, the role of geology in siting remained an issue of paramount importance if a voluntarist model was to be both politically successful and *passively* safe. This meant not only a balancing of technical elements of geophysical and engineered safety against political elements, but also a fundamental clash of moral principles between the egalitarian concept of procedural justice by which community-led commitments to the siting process are placed in primacy, and utilitarian commitments to reduce calculable risks to as low as reasonably practicable for the broader population of the regions affected.

Ethical incrementalism

To balance these two principles requires a combination of what Krütli, Flüeler, Stauffacher, Wiek and Scholz (2010) refer to as a *functional-dynamic* view of public involvement – that decision-making authorities must identify and develop distinct levels of participatory–deliberative engagement in such a way as to fit the corresponding technical and non-technical requirements of sequential decision-making process, and a broader meta-ethical consideration of *voice* (see Senecah, 2004): of who should be involved, at what level and how. Namely, the process had to be robust enough to negotiate a delicate balance of local and national scales of public interest. I argue that this is impossible to do if the decision process treats radioactive waste management facilities as inflexible technologies: that only by reducing the decision to a series of sequential, iterative steps can this balancing of the local and national scale of public interest be fulfilled.

It is here that I introduce the concept of *ethical incrementalism*. I argue that radioactive waste management organisations are bound by an obligation to balance fairness between local and national scales of benefits and risk, and moreover, to balance these between current generations and future generations given the long time frames for radioactive decay; and to ensure environmental protection for the biosphere, given that it does not have a political voice in decision-making. This is uncontroversial, in that similar principles have been adopted by national and international nuclear agencies including the Nuclear Energy Agency, and CoRWM itself (Nuclear Energy Agency, 1995; CoRWM, 2004). Rebalancing fairness between those affected and those making the decision has been a consistent challenge in radioactive waste disposal. However, I argue that a fair process is impossible to achieve if we continue to treat the problem of radioactive wastes as a grand-scale project. Grand-scale projects as mentioned in Chapter 2 require specialist infrastructure, have high decision stakes, commonly suffer unanticipated cost and time overruns, and are technologically inflexible (Genus, 2000). They suffer project inertia: once started there is no opportunity for the decision to be reversed, because the synoptic rationality of policy-makers means that they rarely examine the underlying premises of their decision (such as assuming a rational planning model where outcomes of policy are predictable, calculable and that policy-makers have access to information necessary in order to optimise the decision) (Collingridge, 1992). Moreover, alternative voices that might oppose the decision once it is running, may subsequently become marginalised, or outrightly ignored.

We see evidence of inflexible technology decisions leading up to the 1997 RCF proposal: from the non-decision-making pre-1976 when radioactive waste was treated as a minor or residual concern, to the Flowers report that revealed the extent of the intergenerational equity problem, the failures of Nirex to find sites for ILW or HLW in successive processes, and finally their failure in Sellafield based (in part) upon a lack of social acceptability for site selection within the surrounding nuclear community. Here, we see that the preference for the national scale of decision-making creates a centralised authority as an opponent of the local community. By centring the decision stakes upon a single repository site, the local community is inevitably taking on an unfair risk burden. If this is imposed by an outside authority, then the community rightly has moral grounds to reject the decision. Philosophers such as Shrader-Frechette (2002) assert that this rejection is justified due to a Principle of Prima Facie Political Equality (PPFPE). She argues that environmental decisions are unjust if communities do not have sufficient representation in the decision, do not have access to information about risks and burdens, are not adequately compensated, and do not have full autonomy (in the sense of fully informed decision-making capacity, unaffected by outside interference in a manner similar to that of medical patients) (see also Cotton, 2017).

My argument is that the PPFPE can never be achieved when decision stakes prioritise the national over the local. Radioactive waste management which continues with a settled normative position on geological disposal that prioritises a single site will continue to re-scale the decision to a national one, and will generate technological inflexibility that reduces the autonomy of local communities, and reduces the representation or 'Voice' (Senecah, 2004) of local actors. Ethical incrementalism is a normative principle that complements Shrader-Frechette's PPFPE. I take the premise of incrementalism to be about reducing the stakes to smaller, compartmentalised decisions rather than grand and irreversible decisions, for sequential and trial-and-error approaches, and for policy learning as a revolutionary rather than revolutionary perspective (as discussed in Chapter 2). I call it ethical incrementalism, because under these circumstances of grand and inflexible technology projects, a decision process that embeds sequential steps and multiple decision points will provide greater opportunity for *reversible* decisions. Reversibility of decisions is deeply important when we're discussing the management of risk burdens over thousands of years, when new technologies might feasibly reduce these risks in future, when unanticipated shocks to the system might require us to imagine a radically different response (for example the Fukushima disaster, see for example Molyneux-Hodgson & Hietala, 2015), and when communities are asked to be stewards taking on board these risk burdens on behalf of the broader society (Ahearne, 2000; Shrader-Frechette, 2000). It is ethical incrementalism rather than descriptive incrementalism, because it is the normative principle by which fairness for local communities in the face of national decisions can be achieved.

Ethical incrementalism in the Managing Radioactive Waste Safely programme

The CoRWM options assessment process was an example of ethical incrementalism in practice. Rather than simply a rerun of the decisions of the past, CoRWM looked at the range of different options that were possible to implement, moving through sequential processes of decision-making involving public and stakeholder engagement, assessing which were easy to exclude either on ethical or legal grounds, and then holistically choosing the right option based upon the evidence available to them, recognising the uncertainty and bias that might come into such a judgement (hence input into evaluating the underlying principles of their analysis, rather than a rational planning model where these are implicit). This is what other have called an analytic–deliberative process. What it allows is for the chosen option of interim storage followed by the geological disposal to be a *flexible* technology decision. It was possible at any stage of the option assessment process to reverse the decision, to exclude an option or bring one back into the discussion through an ongoing process of integrated dialogue and scientific assessment. It was a flexible technology decision because the underlying premise of the solution could be questioned, and the policy process did not 'lock-in' a specific solution from the start.

A dialogue-based and sequential system gave the MRWS programme not just the social acceptability needed to further the political process of finding a (largely) unopposed technology solution, but also the moral authority to proceed to the next step. When CoRWM recommended a partnership and voluntarist model for the implementation strategy for a geological disposal facility (GDF) they continued the underlying concept of sequential decision-making, reversibility, and hence were implicitly incrementalist. I suggest that it is an example of ethical incrementalism because the aim was always to balance the needs of a locally affected community, an unfairly burdened future society and the politically silent biosphere. The proposed implementation strategy continued this emphasis upon incrementalism through sequential decision stages: first, community participation in a discussion on the feasibility of RWM siting; and second, community participation on the decision to host a repository (and the right to withdraw at these two key decision stages) and, in principle, if ultimately they decide to host a repository then they were to receive a community benefits package in return.

The practicalities of this model were set out in an MRWS consultation document released in June 2007. It referred to the technical programme of a GDF, the process and criteria to be used to decide the siting of that facility (in particular the development of a voluntarism/partnership approach whereby communities are invited to express an interest in hosting an RWM facility without obligation, and then work together with government throughout the implementation process), and the assessment and evaluation of potential sites including the initial screening-out of areas unlikely to be suitable for geological disposal. The consultation closed in November 2007 and a White Paper was published in June 2008 (DEFRA et al., 2008). The White Paper set out the RWM framework and acted as a public call to invite communities to express an interest in the possibility of hosting a geological disposal facility. The document deals specifically with issues such as regulation, scrutiny and control of the geological disposal facility development, how the relevant planning processes might be addressed; the definition of 'community' for the purposes of site selection; how a partnership arrangement could support a voluntarism approach; the use of what were termed 'Engagement' and 'Community Benefits Packages' and the criteria for assessing and evaluating candidate sites and details of further consultation on the way in which these criteria should be applied (ibid.). The overall structure of this process is detailed in Figure 8.1. (Figure derived from DEFRA et al., 2008.)

The model has two distinct stages of decision-making, the first is the expression of interest stage and second is the decision to participate stage. The expression of interest stage is a very good example of *ethical incrementalism* in practice; this is because it provides an opportunity to explore a policy decision and its consequences for local community, whilst also being fully reversible. If after the engagement process the community lobbies the partnership organisation to remove consent for any further investigation of that site location, then the process can start again with a different volunteer. This is also true of the

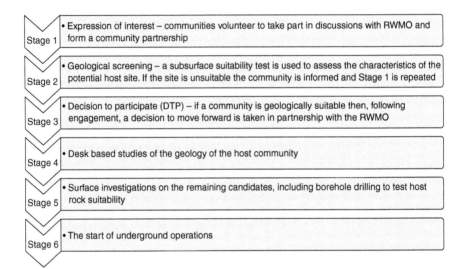

Figure 8.1 The stages of the voluntarist implementation process.
Source: author.

decision to participate stage, following geological site investigation the community still retains the power to remove its consent. This means that the flexibility of the technology decision is inevitably increased – a greater range of voices involved, the decision is not frontloaded in the sense that lock-in through decision-inertia occurs, and up to this stage all aspects of the decision are reversible.

The return to West Cumbria

The sequential decision stages were implicitly set out as an incremental process of siting. The stages were labelled as willingness to participate in an exploratory process for finding a site (termed the expression of interest stage, hereafter EOI). This is the first aspect of the voluntarist model in practice. There was to be no direct coercion from nuclear industry authorities or government to push specific local authorities to step forward. The model involves volunteer communities becoming subject to a desk-based evaluation of geological knowledge of the region to rule out areas that could not be suitable for a repository. If the community region passes the geological screening and is deemed suitable, the community partnership then, following an extensive internal public consultation process, internally takes the decision to participate (hereafter DTP). This meant further desk-based evaluation of suitable areas within the region, followed by surface and then underground investigations. At each stage communities are given the *right to withdraw* from the process up to a pre-defined point. (This is likely to be well before physical site development begins.) This is commonly referred to as a community veto in the academic literature and is seen as the balancing power for volunteer communities – that stepping forwards to accept the conversation with government does not tie the community to accepting the government's plan (see for example Gunderson, 1999; Hunhold, 2002).

The new, post-2006 implementation process shows some obvious similarities to previous siting processes – the technology under consideration was still deep geological disposal and, in practice, the community was the same. (West Cumbria was the only 'volunteer' for the EOI stage.) What differs this time is the incorporation of these distributive, procedural and recognition aspects more thoroughly within the process; providing institutional rebalancing to the elements of environmental injustice seen in the 1970s, 1980s and 1990s. Specifically as a distributive justice issue, there are two elements. The first concerns the legacy waste issue – one that dominates the overall RWM problem. At Sellafield the safe onsite storage of wastes is a top priority, within the MRWS process, this received greater recognition – that the current and shorter-term environmental safety of residents in Whitehaven and the other population centres surrounding Sellafield were of great importance, and so efforts have been made to reduce risks (based on a principle of reduction to as low as reasonably practicable – ALARP) not just the disposal of wastes as a long-term policy problem requiring a safe but ultimately political solution. Second, by adopting a voluntarist model, Sellafield was not assumed to be the de facto site under consideration and so risk distribution was not a predetermined outcome of an inflexible technology decision based upon technical criteria.

In the 1980s and 1990s Sellafield was judged by Nirex to be the best site because of the costs and risks associated with waste transportation. Yet, as discussed in previous chapters, this was largely a subjective judgement (the weighting of waste transport costs), and hence generated a technocratic policy solution that was democratically unjustified (see in particular Stirling, 1996). As the voluntarist siting followed a more transparent (and more environmentally just) options assessment process based upon evaluation of underlying public perceptions, ethical concerns and non-technical criteria, the risk distribution dimension had much greater flexibility, and stronger local democratic control. This latter factor reveals the procedural and recognition aspects of MRWS. Blowers (2016) suggests that Sellafield was inevitably going to step forward as the first volunteer. DEFRA's policy document clearly signposted the need for a community to volunteer that had existing interests and experience of the nuclear industry. Given that Sellafield hosts most of the existing radioactive wastes from the legacy of Britain's nuclear weapons programme and its reprocessing facilities, it came as a surprise to no one that it was the first to step forward. From the announcements of this voluntarist approach from government the first expressions of interest came forward from Copeland Borough Council, Allerdale Borough Council and Cumbria County Council – the upper tier local authority that also has responsibility for areas opposed to nuclear waste siting (specifically those in and around the Lake District National Park that remain concerned about the impact upon local tourism in the region).

All three of these councils planned to come forward with an expression of interest, and the positive sounds being made within government about the three Ps sweetened the deal. There was a tentatively positive attitude about the siting process this time around. The three councils joined together with multiple stakeholder interests to form a partnership. The councils negotiated a Memorandum of Understanding that bound them together, so that where decisions by one of the constituent decision-making bodies impacted one or more of the others, they would work to resolve any conflicts. Consensual agreement was needed between all three to proceed to the next stage in Cumbria. This involved working together to a common timetable, exploration of 'net support' across each of the communities that the authorities represent (and exhausting options to resolve outstanding issues where net support is not demonstrated), facilitating joint working, joint communication and a collective commitment to providing a credible decision to government with regards to moving forward in the MRWS process in Cumbria. Yet the most significant aspect of this political arrangement is that (Cumbria County Council, Copeland Borough Council, & Allerdale Borough Council, 2011):

> In the event that either a Borough Council (in respect of its area) or the County Council, in a Cabinet decision, or the Government, after considering the issues, continues to have genuine concerns and no longer wishes to participate, then the principles of partnership to which we have all been committed cannot be met and accordingly we would not proceed with the MRWS process in West Cumbria.

Moving to the decision to participate (stage 3 in Figure 8.1) required the agreement amongst the three parties. The partnership required consensus. It is important to note, however, that the West Cumbria Managing Radioactive Wastes Safety Partnership (WCMRWSP) was council-led (chaired by Councillor Elaine Woodburn of Copeland Council), though it also involved a broader range of stakeholder bodies within its 17-member roundtable. This includes the Lake District National Park Authority, local business interests, chamber of commerce, farmers' representatives, churches, voluntary organisations, trades unions and environmental/conservation organisations. Some of the national environmental non-governmental organisations did not take part due to continued misgivings about geological disposal, though they continued to take part in other ways: specifically, by engaging with local communities through their own networks, supporting local opposition movements and lobbying the councils.

The WCMRWSP was notable in the level and depth of engagement that took place within it. It ran a comprehensive public and stakeholder engagement programme within affected communities across the region, from schools to town hall meetings, workshops, leaflet campaigns, local media strategy and a range of phone and internet consultation approaches for canvassing input. This engagement included the one-way awareness raising activities, as well as two-way gathering feedback, maintaining a repository of evidence on the web, and cataloguing responses for further dissemination across the partnership. This was combined with technical assessment of geological data in the region, which too was deliberated upon with local stakeholders, to generate a comprehensive analytic–deliberative process for decision-making (for further discussion of analytic–deliberative processes in relation to RWM see: Chilvers, 2007). This level of engagement on a site-selection process was unprecedented. It was made possible only through the additional resources and capacity for engagement presented as part of the government's voluntarist model.

One of the important aspects of the engagement process was to assess the 'net support' for continued involvement in a GDF siting process in West Cumbria (proceeding to stage 4). In 2012 the Cumbria Brand Management Group commissioned the social research company Ipsos MORI to conduct a combined quantitative and qualitative study into what they referred to as 'baseline perceptions' of the Cumbrian/Lake District brand; the aim of which was to establish the impact that a decision to participate might have. The study used focus groups across both urban and rural areas of the UK, segmented according to frequency of visitation, and the frequency by which residents purchased produce from the region. They also did a small number of interviews with major retailers and distributors, importers of English products in overseas markets, with small independent retailers, and with Japanese and North American overseas residents who market tourism in Cumbria. They also used an online survey with senior executives from 200 businesses in the UK, and a nationally representative face-to-face survey (n = 2000). What they found was that Cumbria was perceived through the lens of *premium quality* branding, associating the brand with higher disposable income, being from higher social grades, being older and living in rural areas. All-in-all there was a positive attitude expressed towards the products produced in that region, and the sense that Cumbrian produce was traditionally crafted. This implies that it is imbued with the care and quality of associated hand crafted materials, including imagery that is nostalgic, evokes timelessness and a hence is a 'destination brand' – becoming part of the tourist experience itself. There was little distinction made between the Lake District and the broader Cumbrian region. What the qualitative work found was that Cumbria was identified as an area of geographic isolation, which accentuated the sense of tradition and authenticity: there was a perception that it was untouched by progress, and therefore was characterised as being pure and lacking in contamination. The positive associations concerned beauty, Cumbria's scenic quality, and as an expansive, open and untouched place (it must also be noted that it was perceived as rainy, windy, remote and congested in the summer) (summarised from Ipsos MORI, 2013).

These findings of the perceptions work were significant because they revealed Cumbria to be commonly identified as an unspoiled place, and that this is influential in maintaining the brand value of the region for future tourist activity and retail exports. By drawing attention to a deep geological disposal facility within the Cumbrian region, this raised concerns throughout the engagement process that the broader Cumbrian identity would be damaged due to stigmati-sation – that associations of dirt, pollution, and the active spoiling of a positive association with the area would occur, specifically because Cumbria and the Lake District were not distinguished by most people outside the region. This impact was then measured in terms of business confidence, the negative impacts on the perceptions of potential visitors and potential consumers of Lake Dis-trict/Cumbrian branded products. Their baseline research found that because of the GDF decision process, 17 per cent of businesses that use Cumbria and Lake District brands say publicity surrounding the possibility of hosting a GDF has had a very negative impact on sales. Moreover, 17 per cent reported a decrease in employment, a 43 per cent reduction in sales, 55 per cent reduction in profit margins, 45 per cent reduction in business confidence and 50 per cent reduction in visitor numbers (DC Research, 2013). Clearly concerns were raised that the negative economic impact of the GDF decision process was being felt in the region. What this reveals is that the information gathering process worked in synergy with the development of the broader 'uninvited' engagement (Wehling, 2012) with the issue of GDF decision-making. The real-time examination of socio-economic impacts to the region was fuelling social movements of opposi-tion that had formed an alliance with some local business interests in the Lake District and within Cumbria. All of this was of considerable concern, particu-larly to Cumbria County Council. At the county council level, issues affecting the broader Cumbrian region had very strong purchase, and these findings revealing the stark socio-economic impacts from just the *possibility* of a GDF were sobering.

Also of considerable concern within the partnership's analysis was the issue of hydrogeology. The hydro-geological debate about the suitability of the Bor-rowdale volcanic group and its surrounding areas resurfaced, having remained unresolved since Nirex's activities in the 1990s. As mentioned in Chapter 7, Stuart Haszeldine and David Smythe had written extensively in the RCF pro-posal inquiry about the risks posed by water intrusion through the fractured geology of the volcanic rocks of the surrounding region: questioning the suit-ability of West Cumbria to host a repository safely over the necessary time frames. Their work was instrumental in halting Nirex's RCF proposal in 1997, and they themselves had gone on record opposing deep geological disposal in this region. However, the sequential decision process, as outlined by govern-ment policy, required the British Geological Survey (BGS) to carry out a screening activity of the host geology in advance of the decision to participate. The scientific assessment was driven by the political process of voluntarism. The screening exercise was designed to eliminate any areas that were known to be unsuitable. The BGS presented a map that eliminated areas in the north and west of West Cumbria. It was at this point that the debates about geology became heated. Haszeldine and Smythe asserted that no areas in West Cumbria were safe, whilst the Nuclear Decommissioning Authority's Radioactive Waste Management Directorate (NDARWMD) argued that the BGS report showed areas that would be potentially suitable for further investigation. This assessment was supported by Jeremy Dearlove, the geologist hired by the partnership. It was at this point that the arguments became trans-scientific, concerning not just the evidence in front of the experts, but issues of opinion, the value of scientific consensus and what counts as good science. As Blowers (2016) suggests, the arguments and counter arguments between Smythe and Dearlove became increasingly personal. Dearlove suggested that Smythe's position was simply a personal opinion that did not stand in line with the broader assessments of the geological community. Smythe countered that Dearlove was trying to present him as a lone voice, when no such broader scientific consensus existed in opposition to his point of view. Blowers also notes that, although the partnership ultimately sided with Dearlove in deciding that there were at least some areas of West Cumbria that would be suitable geologically, it came down yet again to a decision between 'good geology' as the primary criterion for siting, versus voluntarism. Discussions concerned whether a less than optimal geological solution could be overcome using engineered barriers, thus making the decision about where to place the facility a primarily political one. Alternatively, if geology should come first, the optimal solution is conceived as that which provides the greatest safety from water intrusion through the outermost barrier (the rock itself). Yet again we see a conflict emerging about the fundamental values involved in how the decision is made, not just what evidence should be selected to make that decision. Science and politics were clearly entangled within this debate, and this was further obscured by the competing voices of experts engaged in a professional disagreement. These trans-scientific disputes were dictating the future directions of the policy process.

These two issues of economic impact and geological unsuitability remained controversial sticking points within the engagement process that the WCMRWSP oversaw. These issues were central to the mobilisation of the social movements of opposition, such as Save Our Lake District, encouraged by national ENGOs such as Friends of The Earth. Some local authorities, such as those representing tourism in the Lake District, lent their tacit support to this type of opposition. Some of the older campaign groups such as Cumbrians Opposed to a Radioactive Environment (CORE) gained renewed support. What differed this time, when compared with the pre-1997 RCF process, was that opposition had greater power to network and to influence the decision locally. New technologies of social media allowed rapid communication between distinctive local groups and thus coordination of action between them. This is one of the differences between twenty-first century collective action of siting opposition, and that seen in the 1970s, 1980s and 1990s. The rapidity of information sharing was greatly increased, those engaging had a much greater access to information about the proposals, the partnership, and what the stakes of the decision were. Knowledge is power in this scenario. Also, this time around, the opposition groups were engaging with a series of local authorities and other local stakeholders, rather than a more remote radioactive waste management organisation and a politically and geographically remote minister in charge. This fundamentally rebalanced the scales of engagement, both the partnership and those engaging with the partnership were closely embedded with one another, had access to the same information, and could all rapidly communicate with one another. In essence, the decision appeared to *feel* more local for many of the stakeholders involved because of time-space compression (Harvey, 1999) within communicative networks – literally the effort of communication and information-sharing across social networks was much reduced this time around, increasing its efficiency and empowering opposition movements in influencing the decision body.

Though social movements of opposition became emboldened by the findings of economic reports and scepticism about the geology of the region, the partnership held together. This was because there was considerable community buy-in to the process; the WCMRWSP was perceived as impartial and fair. However, the engagement process started to stir issues beyond the very narrow remit of DECC's voluntarist model. As Blowers (2016) reports, there was considerable lack of trust in the government to deliver what was promised. Much of this distrust probably stems from the memory of previous siting processes, particularly the 1997 RCF proposal. Issues such as future waste inventory from new nuclear build, the types and scale of wastes being produced, potential alternative radioactive waste management options, and more broadly about whether West Cumbria should simply reject the project altogether were raised. The engagement process was supposed to be defined around a specific topic – about whether to proceed to a mutual participation in further site investigation. But as with any narrowly bounded deliberative process there is the potential to open up dialogue to encompass a broader range of issues, perspectives and options – including those that are not under consideration for that particular decision (Stirling, 2004; Lehtonen, 2010). There was considerable concern amongst the various social movements of opposition that the decision was too *binary*. By framing the decision to participate as only geological disposal in West Cumbria or not, the decision lacked flexibility – it was perceived by many as pushing the members of the host community into a decision of either accepting or rejecting a megaproject with extensive socio-economic implications for their locality. This creates problems of bounded rationality, the people involved in making the decision are not evaluating all the possible eventualities from this decision – literally their capacity to make an informed choice was limited. This is the fundamental nature of megaproject decisions, as discussed in Chapter 2. The decision made by the councils under their memorandum of understanding, required net support from the host community and wider community interests (i.e. Cumbrian citizens who did not live in West Cumbria, and other business and policy stakeholders). But what the opposition groups insisted was that they didn't have enough information to meaningfully input to this decision. Moreover, public opinion was split. The Cumbria Association of local councils had canvassed opinion amongst town and parish councils on the decision to proceed. However, they found that only 8 out of 88 of these councils wanted to proceed, with 43 actively against. As representatives of the various Cumbrian communities at the lowest tier of government, this carried considerable weight. What we find, therefore, is that there was a lack of perceived *deliberative capacity* (Davies & Burgess, 2004) to engage in a decision of this size, and a lack of enthusiasm amongst locally representative elected authorities.

The outcome of the West Cumbrian Managing Radioactive Waste Safely Partnership

After considering the evidence from the geological assessment of the BGS, the socio-economic baseline data for the impact of a GDF, feedback from the host community and wider community interests through their PSE programme, the partnership delivered the final report that integrated all of this information in August 2012 (West Cumbria Managing Radioactive Waste Safely Partnership, 2012). This document became the primary decision-support tool for district and county council level deliberation on whether it was going to proceed to the next stage and enter the DTP process. The report is a substantial document, weighing in at 270 pages. It is important to stress that the report neither proposed a recommendation for the three constituent councils to follow, nor did it suggest an intended site, as these were outside the partnership's brief. The report documented the complex evidence-gathering process that the partnership undertook. It was shared with nearly 2400 people and organisations within Cumbria, and set the reference point for the councils' decision.

This model was a mirror to the CoRWM option assessment process. The partnership rather than taking the decision themselves, provided the assessment of the evidence base upon which elected authorities could make up their own minds. This is important because it provided a level of representative democratic legitimacy, which allowed Westminster to buy into the decision that was made. In terms of a broader political context at the time, in 2012 during the Coalition Government between the Conservatives and Liberal Democrats, the concept of the Big Society, was de rigueur. In 2011 the government legislated the Localism Act, the aim of which was to alter the powers of local government in England to facilitate the devolution of decision-making powers from central government control to individuals and communities. This is a partnership approach between local and national government in making this decision. The input from this broad network of local stakeholders was perhaps the zenith of this policy approach. But what it created was a degree of uncertainty within the council themselves. Blowers suggests that this represents a non-decision on behalf of the partnership, one that indicated uncertainty and a failure to bring its work to a purposive conclusion. This perceived uncertainty from the partnership led to the councils pausing their decision on voting. Issues such as unfavourable hydro-geology, the baseline economic surveys, the surveys of parish councils at the lobbying action and social movements of opposition were influential. And the councils recognised that there was a fundamental lack of trust at the heart of public perceptions of this process, government, and organisations like the nuclear decommissioning authority. There was concern that commitments would not be honoured, such as the commitment to provide community benefits. The councils therefore stalled progress, requesting more time to consider these issues in detail. This pause allowed the social movement of opposition to intensify their actions in West Cumbria, putting increasing pressure on Cumbria County Council to reject the decision.

The importance of Cumbria County Council cannot be overstated. The Memorandum of Understanding bound the three councils to share in a joint decision that respected the impacts across the two tiers of local government. It was this joint decision which ultimately led to the failure to proceed to the next stage. Within Cumbria County Council among the ten cabinet members, seven voted against. So even though the borough councils for Allerdale and Copeland voted in favour of progression to the next stage, Cumbria County Council in the next tier above, effectively vetoed the decision. Their joint decision-making through the Memorandum, bound the other two councils by the decision. As DECC announced it had: 'previously been agreed that parties at both Borough and County level needed to vote positively in order for the process to continue in west Cumbria' (DECC, 2013). The announcement was greeted with much enthusiasm from environmental campaigners; seeing this as a victory against the imposition of a GDF in West Cumbria.

We can see, in hindsight, that Cumbria County Council took a broader regional view – looking at impacts across the county as a whole. They recognised that although the development of the nuclear industry in Cumbria was an important aspect of its economy, and recognised that new nuclear build would play a part in that, they remained sceptical about the value of the GDF. It was clear that the county council felt the weight of the decision stakes. Even though the decision would have only progressed to participation in further site investigation, the baseline economic data and the study of changing regional economic development was showing that even this involvement in talk was having a negative impact. Cumbria, as indeed everywhere else in the north-west of England, was feeling the effects of economic austerity brought about by the 2008 financial crisis. The decision to withdraw at that time, in retrospect, seems prudent. The brand value of Cumbria, and its relationship to the Lake District specifically, was deeply important for continued socio-economic development across the region. Factoring in concerns over the region's hydrogeology, the reactions of protest organisations and a lack of a clear mandate based upon public perception studies of Cumbrian citizens, then on balance, we can see how Cumbria County Council saw the risks outweighing the benefits.

When the decision was announced, DECC recognised that the voluntary process had stalled. There was no pressure from the Department of Energy and Climate Change to continue despite the vote. The announcement by Edward Davey MP, Secretary for Energy and Climate Change, stated that (DECC, 2013):

> We respect the decision made today by Cumbria councillors. They have invested a great deal of time in this project and have provided valuable lessons on how to take forward this process in future. While their decision to withdraw is disappointing, Cumbria will continue to play a central role

in the energy and nuclear power sectors.... It is however absolutely vital that we get to grips with our national nuclear legacy. The issue has been kicked into the long-grass for far too long. We remain firmly committed to geological disposal as the right policy ... We also remain committed to the principles of voluntarism and a community-led approach. The fact that Copeland voted in favour of entering the search for a potential site for a GDF demonstrates that communities recognise the benefits associated with hosting such a facility.... We will now embark on a renewed drive to ensure that the case for hosting a GDF is drawn to the attention of other communities.

Meso-level decisions and the doughnut effect

Clearly, government had come to recognise the importance of upholding local democracy under the terms of the voluntarist agreement. This decision is a good example of an incrementalist policy process. DECC stated that it was going to take valuable lessons on how to take forward the process in future, a small trial-and-error development that is key to the nature of incrementalist policy-making. The setback of losing the vote in West Cumbria meant that DECC learned that they should better manage the different tiers of local government within the decision process. It became clear that a local host community might support the GDF proposal, but that when broader county-level interests (of neighbouring authorities) were considered, the risks outweighed the benefits. It is this meso-level scale of the decision which proved the sticking point.

It is unsurprising that neighbouring communities did not favour continuing to discuss anything related to a GDF. This is an issue that has been discussed before in relation to nuclear waste siting. Easterling and Kunreuther (1995) posit the notion of a *doughnut effect*. In contrast to what one might expect, citizens living directly closest to the GDF proposed location are in fact more likely to be accepting those that live further away. This counter-intuitive notion is a function of geographic variation in the expectation of risks and benefits. Those that are closest have the greatest political control, and also receive compensation in the form of benefits packages, job creation and regional economic development. They have a tangible stake in the outcome. Those in adjacent towns may perceive only the risks, the community stigmatisation that comes from hosting a nuclear facility, and the imbalance between the benefits felt within the host community and the surrounding region. This effect is clearly evidenced in the perception studies undertaken as part of the partnership's PSE programme. The brand value of Cumbria and its relationship to the Lake District remain important for multiple business sectors within the region. To those towns and villages in the Lake District, which were beyond the geographic 'zone' in which community benefits would be directed, the risks were felt most keenly. This is reflected in a lack of enthusiasm amongst town and parish councils across the county for a GDF. The voluntarist siting process is ill-equipped to deal with the concerns of these communities when county-level government is involved in making the decision. Here we see that the fundamental problem of scale, specifically the meso scale of the 'county', rather than the micro scale of the host community or the macro scale of the nation, became the weak link. How this scale was performed and represented within policy is important, as this was the factor that led to the failure of voluntarism in West Cumbria.

Conclusions

Clearly West Cumbria recognised its role in the development of the nuclear industry and was motivated by a range of underlying values. One of these is *stewardship* – that as the largest producer of wastes that community had a responsibility to engage in dialogue with the government on how best to handle it. Another was opportunity: with a declining industry presence, out-migration from the West Cumbrian region, and conditions of economic austerity, the promise of secured employment from waste management, and additional community benefits to the region were powerful motivating factors for Allerdale and Copeland Borough Councils. In many respects, they were right back to the same position as in 1996 – a Sellafield repository site. What was different this time was more recognition within the policy process for West Cumbrian identity as an energy producing (and waste producing) community, and greater power within the decision-making process. The WCMRWSP had full decision-making control on whether to proceed, and thus had more political leverage with nuclear industry and government authorities, such as the Nuclear Decommissioning Authority's Radioactive Waste Management Directorate (Nirex's successor) than in previous site selection processes. As the voluntarism aspect also included a package of direct funding for local engagement activities, the decision was more procedurally just, as it provided not only the opportunity to engage broadly on issues such as risk acceptability, community compensation and local environmental impacts (giving devolved powers to local authorities on the decision) but also the resources and capacity to engage (and thus meeting the requirements for *due process* in decision-making).

The voluntarist process was exemplary in many respects. The public and stakeholder engagement programmes were adequately resourced with input from central government, the impact upon regional economic development well thought through, with change tracked during the engagement process being a key feature. Issues surrounding Cumbria's hydrogeology, which had arisen in the 1990s, were discussed again. This time, however, the dissenting voices were given a platform to speak: they were not denounced and derided by a technocratic public authority. Though the processes of engagement and deliberation that the partnership undertook were laudable, in hindsight there are those that would argue it would have been preferable for the partnership to have made the decision itself. It was after all, the body that had the most comprehensive knowledge of the scientific, social, economic and perceptual issues involved. The 270-page final report was comprehensive and represented a fair depiction of the issues facing West Cumbria. This was not to be, however. Prevailing political forces, particularly the political philosophy of the Conservative Party within the Coalition Government, were influential. One of the policy agendas of David Cameron's government was the so-called 'bonfire of the quangos' – replacement of independent advisory organisations, select committees, and appointed bodies, with council or ministerial control.[1] This stands in opposition to the so-called deliberative turn discussed in previous chapters. There was both increased emphasis on devolving power to local government, and indeed to local communities under certain circumstances, but also maintaining representative democratic control on issues development. It is this notion of scale, not only in terms of the geographic area represented in the decision (micro-scale host community, meso-scale county and macro-scale nation), but also the scales of governance at which the decisions made, and how they are 'performed', is important. How the government responded to this scalar problem by reforming the policy process after the West Cumbrian decision, is an issue that is discussed in the final chapter.

Note

1 For example, in 2008 the planning for major infrastructure projects was overseen by the Infrastructure Planning Commission (IPC). This is an unelected body that's granted permits for development control for major projects. In 2011, however, the Localism Act, changed the governance structure – replacing the IPC with a major infrastructure unit within government. Decisions were then overseen by the minister in charge. The was a clear move towards replacing the decisions of unelected bodies with elected representatives.

Bibliography

Ahearne, J. F. (2000). Intergenerational issues regarding nuclear power, nuclear waste, and nuclear weapons. *Risk Analysis*, 20(6), 763–770.
Blowers, A. (2014). A geological disposal facility for nuclear waste – if not Sellafield, then where? *Town & Country Planning*(December), 545–553.
Blowers, A. (2016). *The legacy of nuclear power*. Abingdon: Earthscan from Routledge.
Chilvers, J. (2007). Toward analytic–deliberative forms of risk governance in the UK? Reflecting on learning in radioactive waste. *Journal of Risk Research*, 10(2), 197–222.
Collingridge, D. (1992). *The management of scale: Big organizations, big decisions, big mistakes*. Abingdon: Routledge.
CoRWM. (2004). *Guiding principles*. London: Committee on Radioactive Waste Management.
CoRWM. (2006a). *CoRWM publishes final recommendations for long term management of radioactive waste*. Retrieved from www.corwm.org.uk/content-1091
CoRWM. (2006b). *Managing our radioactive waste safely: CoRWM's recommendations to government*. London: Committee on Radioactive Waste Management.
Cotton, M. (2017) Fair fracking? Ethics and environmental justice in United Kingdom shale gas policy and planning. *Local Environment*, 22(2), 185–202.

Cumbria County Council, Copeland Borough Council, & Allerdale Borough Council. (2011). Memorandum of Understanding between Cumbria County Council, Copeland Borough Council and Allerdale Borough Council. Retrieved from www.westcumbriamrws. org.uk/documents/235-MoU_final_version_Dec_2011.pdf.

Darst, R., & Dawson, J. I. (2010). Waiting for the nuclear renaissance: Exploring the nexus of expansion and disposal in Europe. *Risk, Hazards & Crisis in Public Policy, 1*(4), 49–82.

Davies, G., & Burgess, J. (2004). Challenging the 'view from nowhere': Citizen reflections on specialist expertise in a deliberative process. *Health and Place, 10*(4), 349–361.

DC Research. (2013). *Baseline research for economic studies as part of brand management work for Cumbria and the Lake District.* Carlisle: DC Research: Economics and Regeneration, the Centre for Regional Economic Development (CRED), University of Cumbria and Red Research.

DECC. (2013). Energy Secretary responds to Cumbria nuclear waste vote [Press release].

DEFRA. (2006). *Response to the report and recommendations from the Committee on Radioactive Waste Management (CoRWM) by the UK Government and the devolved administrations.* London: Department for Environment Food and Rural Affairs.

DEFRA, BERR, and the devolved administrations for Wales and Northern Ireland. (2008). *Managing radioactive waste safely: A framework for implementing geological disposal.* London: Department for Environment Food and Rural Affairs, Department for Business, Enterprise and Regulatory Reform, and the Devolved Administrations for Wales and Northern Ireland.

Easterling, D., & Kunreuther, H. (1995). *The dilemma of siting a high-level nuclear waste repository.* Boston: Kluwer Academic Publishers.

Elam, M., Lidberg, M., Soneryd, L., & Sundqvist, G. (2009). *Demonstration and dialogue: Mediation in Swedish nuclear waste management.* Stockholm: Stockholm Centre for Organisational Research.

Genus, A. (2000). *Decisions, technology and organizations.* Aldershot: Gower.

Gunderson, W. C. (1999). Voluntarism and its limits: Canada's search for radioactive waste-siting candidates. *Canadian Public Administration, 42*(2), 193–214.

Harvey, D. (1999). Time-space compression and the postmodern condition. *Modernity: Critical Concepts, 4*, 98–118.

Hindmarsh, R., & Matthews, C. (2008). Deliberative speak at the turbine face: Community engagement, wind farms, and renewable energy transitions, in Australia. *Journal of Environmental Policy & Planning, 10*(3), 217–232.

Hunhold, C. (2002). Canada's low-level radioactive waste disposal problem: Voluntarism reconsidered. *Environmental Politics, 11*(2), 49–72.

Ipsos MORI. (2013). *Baseline perceptions of Cumbria, the Lake District and its brands. Research report on qualitative and quantitative work conducted by Ipsos MORI on behalf of the Cumbria Brand Management Group.* London: Ipsos MORI.

Krütli, P., Flüeler, T., Stauffacher, M., Wiek, A., & Scholz, R. W. (2010). Technical safety vs public involvement? A case study on the unrealized project for the disposal of nuclear waste at Wellenberg (Switzerland). *Journal of Integrative Environmental Sciences, 7*(3), 229–244. doi:10.1080/1943815X.2010.506879.

Lehtonen, M. (2010). Opening up or closing down radioactive waste management policy? Debates on reversibility and retrievability in Finland, France, and the United Kingdom. *Risk, Hazards & Crisis in Public Policy, 1*(4), 139–179.

Milliband, D. (2006, 25 October). Oral statement by David Miliband in response to the Committee on Radioactive Waste Management's report.

Molyneux-Hodgson, S., & Hietala, M. (2015). Socio-technical imaginations of nuclear waste disposal in UK and Finland. In R. Hindmarsh, & R. Priestley (Eds.), *The Fukushima effect: A new geopolitical terrain* (Vol. 29, pp. 141–161). New York: Routledge.

Nuclear Energy Agency. (1995). *The environmental and ethical basis of geological disposal of long-lived radioactive wastes.* Vienna: Nuclear Energy Agency.

Senecah, S. L. (2004). The trinity of voice: The role of practical theory in planning and evaluating the effectiveness of participatory processes. In S. P. Depoe, J. W. Delicath, & M.-F. A. Elsenbeer (Eds.), *Communication and public participation in environmental decision making* (pp. 13–34). Albany, NY: SUNY Press.

Shrader-Frechette, K. S. (2000). Duties to future generations, proxy consent, intra and intergenerational equity: The case of nuclear waste. *Risk Analysis, 20*(6), 771–777.

Shrader-Frechette, K. S. (2002). *Environmental justice: Creating equality, reclaiming democracy.* Oxford: Oxford University Press.

Stirling, A. (1996). On the Nirex MADA [Multi-Attribute Decision Analysis]. Proof of evidence. In R. S. Haszeldine, & D. K. Smythe (Eds.), *Radioactive waste disposal at Sellafield, UK: Site selection, geological and engineering problems.* Glasgow: University of Glasgow.

Stirling, A. (2004). Opening up or closing down? Analysis, participation and power in the social appraisal of technology. In M. Leach, I. Scoones, & B. Wynne (Eds.), *Science, citizenship and globalisation.* London: Zed.

Wehling, P. (2012). From invited to uninvited participation (and back?): Rethinking civil society engagement in technology assessment and development. *Poiesis & Praxis, 9*(1–2), 43–60.

West Cumbria Managing Radioactive Waste Safely Partnership. (2012) *The final report of the West Cumbria Managing Radioactive Waste Safely Partnership.* Whitehaven: Copeland Borough Council.

9   What next for nuclear waste?

Introduction

After Cumbria County Council voted to reject the decision to move towards participation in the next stage, this brought the Managing Radioactive Waste Safely Process to a close in West Cumbria. Although the Department of Energy and Climate Change remained optimistic that the voluntarism set out in the Managing Radioactive Waste Safely implementation programme (DEFRA, BERR, and the devolved administrations for Wales and Northern Ireland, 2008) would continue, no new volunteers have expressed any official interest at the time of writing. As a process of incremental policy learning DECC then had to re-evaluate its position. Then Secretary for Energy and Climate Change Ed Davey MP (2013) stated:

> My Department [of Energy and Climate Change] will embark on a renewed drive to ensure that the case for hosting a GDF is drawn to the attention of communities, and to encourage further local authorities to come forward over the coming years to join the process. At the same time, we will reflect on the experience of the process in West Cumbria, and will talk to the local authorities themselves and others who have been involved to see what lessons can be learned. No changes to our current approach on site selection will be introduced without further consultation.

Though DECC expressed optimism that a new community would come forward, none obliged. DECC intended to make changes to the process for implementation to overcome the difficulties they faced at the Cumbria County Council level, but was cautious about doing so without further stakeholder input. DECC issued a 'Call for Evidence' in May 2013, and then held a series of engagement events with citizens and nuclear community stakeholders in November and December 2013. The UK Government and Northern Ireland Executive also issued a joint consultation document in September 2013 looking at aspects of the siting process that could be revised or improved. The premise was that this would 'help communities to engage in it with more confidence, and ultimately to help deliver a GDF' (Department of

Energy and Climate Change, 2014, p. 9). Following the consultation period, DECC revised the 2008 Managing Radioactive Waste Safely Implementation strategy in a 2014 White Paper (ibid.). The new implementation framework for higher activity radioactive wastes again focused upon the siting of a mined geological disposal facility (GDF). What differed this time, was first, that national screening of geology now moved 'upfront' before a volunteer steps forward. Second, it was recognised that the GDF would house not just legacy wastes, but also wastes from new nuclear build. Third, the GDF was conceptualised as a 'major infrastructure project of national significance'. These three significant elements will be discussed in this final chapter.

Incremental policy learning

The White Paper set out the initial actions to be undertaken by the government, and by the new developer organisation Radioactive Waste Management Limited (RWM). RWM Ltd was formed primarily from the expertise within the (now defunct) Nuclear Decommissioning Authority Radioactive Waste Management Directorate. There was a growing tension within the radioactive waste policy community about the suitability of the Nuclear Decommissioning Authority as the body for implementing geological disposal. When the West Cumbrian process unravelled, there were growing calls for an implementation body to become a separate entity. The NDA has oversight over the contracting process for nuclear site clean-up and reactor decommissioning. The biggest budget item (funded by what was the Department of Energy and Climate Change, but since August 2016 is the Department of Business, Energy and Industrial Strategy) is the clean-up of Sellafield. Given that they are working with supplier organisations to provide this clean-up operation (and their progress has certainly been controversial),[1] there was always a potential conflict of interest. International Nuclear Services (INS, a wholly owned subsidiary of the NDA) manages the contracts on behalf of the NDA. This includes reprocessing activities at Sellafield, undertaken by Sellafield Ltd on behalf of the NDA. The products of decommissioning and clean-up are then packaged as wastes. There is therefore a (perceived) conflict of interest between waste production and waste management within the same organisation; particularly given that a lack of trust in the implementing organisation was one of the key factors that undermined public acceptance of the West Cumbrian decision to participate. Trust was undermined by recent failures of the NDA's contractors to keep clean-up costs under control (see Public Accounts Committee, 2014), but also the long shadow of Nirex is still a factor in industry–community engagement in West Cumbria and other nuclear communities (e.g. Bradwell, Elstow, Billingham after the four-site saga). However, RWM Ltd is perhaps simply a rebadging exercise. The core expertise within this industry involves considerable specialisation. Moreover, there is a general skills shortage within the British nuclear industry, so a totally 'new' RWMO with no link to previous GDF siting proposals is unlikely. The transfer of the implementation body to a new company with greater independence from the NDA was, however, an incremental step towards building trust within potential volunteer host communities.

Geological screening

Since the 2014 implementation White Paper, RWM spearheaded a geological screening exercise. This process of national geological screening presents the existing geological and hydro-geological information available on England, Wales and Northern Ireland up to a depth of about 1000 m. The screening covers aspects of the geologic environment that are pertinent to the GDF. This includes information about groundwater movement between the depth at which a GDF would be constructed and the surface environment (to give an idea of potential radionuclide migration to the human environment), and the modelling of future impacts such as ice cover (in the event of an ice age), or sea-level rise because of anthropogenic climate change. Other aspects including the distribution of natural resources (minerals, precious metals, fossil fuels or gemstones, for example) are pertinent to understanding potential future intrusions to a GDF – where future generations may dig or drill their way through the waste repository for extraction.

The aim of this was to 'provide the public with information about the geology of England, Wales and Northern Ireland. This will help communities decide in due course if they would be interested in hosting a GDF in their area' (RWM, 2016). The aim was to switch around the voluntarist and geological screening programmes. In West Cumbria, the community formed a partnership with local government and policy stakeholders, business interests and civil society groups including environmental non-governmental organisations, to express an interest in entering dialogue with government on hosting a GDF. Once this expression of interest had been put forward, the BGS began the screening of suitable geology. Now that process is reversed, with no voluntary community stepping forward in the interim, RWM is presenting a package of screening results for different locations. The aim is to be ready for when a community does step forward. The other factor is that the West Cumbrian deliberations on geology were extremely contentious. The actions of Professors Haszeldine and Smythe stood in direct conflict with those of Dearlove – the partnership's own independent geological expert. By providing the geological screening advice upfront, this has the potential to ameliorate such conflict in the future. To provide credibility of the geological evidence, the screening guidance was developed collaboratively with a community of geoscientists and broader stakeholder networks, including engineering expertise in GDF facility construction and maintenance. The draft guidance was also submitted to an independent review panel (IRP) established by the Geological Society. The aim of this was to check whether the screening guidance was scientifically sound, based upon the best available evidence, and whether it provided an adequate assessment of the long-term safety case for different locations for GDF siting across England, Wales and Northern Ireland. This movement of the draft screening guidance through sequential stages towards final approval is an example of postnormal science in action. Rather than limited technical peer review, the guidance was circulated and consulted upon within an extended peer community – different categories of risks and opportunities are identified through this process. By then using the guidance as a basis for further consultation with communities that may volunteer to host the GDF, the postnormal nature of the decision is anticipated by RWM. This is also indicative of changing scientific practices within radioactive waste policy communities – there is no sense that scientific expertise is privileged above social values, rather continuing the tradition started by CoRWM it is 'science on tap, not on top'. This change also helps to alleviate the problem identified within the West Cumbrian partnership's deliberations: that it was difficult for the community to assess whether voluntarism or geology should come first. The national screening programme will, therefore, assist potential new partnerships in making the decision to put in an expression of interest. In that sense, we can view the screening as a largely positive aspect of the new implementation programme following the 2014 White Paper.

New nuclear build

One of the most significant aspects of the 2014 White Paper was the explicit recognition that a GDF programme must account for new build nuclear power. Uranium, the source fuel for nearly all nuclear energy production, is a relatively common element that is often found in economically viable concentrations. Total quantities of uranium minerals resources are, as the World Nuclear Association puts it, greater than are commonly perceived and have been increasing (by at least one quarter since the early 2000s due to increased mineral exploration) (WNA, 2016). Within Europe, for nuclear electricity-generating Member States (15 out of the current 27 – or 14 out of 26 once The United Kingdom leaves the European Union following the 'Brexit' referendum vote), it is the energy source with the least price fluctuation and one of the lowest rates of CO_2 production (see for details the Uranium 'Redbook' OECD NEA and IAEA, 2014).

The capacity for nuclear power to meet long-term energy needs in the face of fossil fuel price shocks and concerns over the environmental damage from carbon dioxide has remained deeply attractive to many nations (even in the face of nuclear risks posed by accidents such as the 2011 Fukushima-Daichii disaster in Japan).[2] There has, until recently, been a slow decline of nuclear capacity across the nuclear power-generating countries of Europe and the USA in meeting a growing energy demand gap. In the UK, current power stations (including fossil fuel-based stations) have an estimated combined capacity of around 90 gigawatts (GWe) compared with a typical peak demand of around 60 GWe. However, since 2010, a total of 26 power stations (of 19 GWe of capacity) have closed, equating to a loss of 20 per cent of the UK's electricity generation capacity. By the end of 2030, a further 35 per cent (over 30GWe) of that 2010 capacity will close down (Central Intelligence Agency, 2012). This includes all but one of the UK's current nuclear power reactors. Peak demand is expected to rise significantly during this time period, as electricity is increasingly used to power transport (assuming a rise in electric vehicles) and heating. It is against this background that governments have become interested in the expansion of nuclear electricity generation in the twenty-first century – a phenomenon commonly described as a 'nuclear renaissance' (Nuttall, 2004; Darst & Dawson, 2010; Johnstone, 2010; Renzi, Cotton, Napolitano, & Barkemeyer, 2016). As the threat of anthropogenic climate change has continued to grow (and be acknowledged in global environmental policy), new nuclear build has been heralded by the industry and, in the UK by former Labour, and Conservative and Liberal Democrat Coalition, and current Conservative Governments, as a key transition technology in developing low carbon electricity systems to meet legally binding carbon dioxide reduction goals stemming from European commitments framed in domestic climate change legislation (namely the Climate Change Act 2008) (Bickerstaff, Lorenzoni, Pidgeon, Poortinga, & Simmons, 2008; Johnstone, 2010; Teräväinen, Lehtonen, & Martiskainen, 2011).

The UK's renewal of nuclear power began in earnest in November 2005 when then Prime Minister Tony Blair MP first announced an energy policy review to assess the viability of new build nuclear power. In 2006, a green paper was released, the principal conclusion of which was that: 'new nuclear power stations would make a significant contribution to meeting our energy policy goals' (Department of Trade and Industry, 2006). The principal motivation for this appeared to be a growing concern over the issue of anthropogenic climate change. Since 2007, the UK Government became something of a global leader in international climate change policy. Following on from European roadmaps for low carbon energy production, the UK interpreted their commitments to climate change through a programme of policy measures including the Climate Change Act 2008. The act sets legally binding carbon dioxide emission reduction targets, and there was a growing belief within government that this could only be achieved with the renewal of nuclear power, which in turn could only be achieved with government support. The other factor was the sense that new nuclear build could contribute to employment and prosperity in the UK, specifically by exporting to overseas markets whilst also respecting the imperative to counter the proliferation of nuclear materials for weapons purposes.

The key priority with regards to nuclear power was, as the 2010 Coalition Government saw it, to ensure the successful generation three programme of nuclear reactors to be built over the two decades up to 2030 (DECC, 2013). Part of this was to create a 'technology push' platform, of streamlining planning and design certification laws and offering economic incentives to support new build. However, it was recognised that under conditions of economic austerity, any new reactors must be wholly financed and built by the private sector with no direct public finance subsidy. From 2011 a deal was tabled with France's Electricité de France (EDF) Energy to build two Areva-designed European

Pressurised Reactor (EPRs) at Hinkley Point, Somerset, and two at Sizewell, Suffolk. EDF also proposed to work with a foreign investment partner, China General Nuclear Power Corporation (CGN), to deploy the Chinese Hualong HPR-1000 reactor at Bradwell, Essex. At the time of writing, Hinkley Point C Nuclear Plant (HPCNPP) has been granted development consent, and has come to the forefront of political debate over renewed nuclear power. The HPCNPP is a project that will construct a 3200MWe reactor adjacent to the existing site. First announced in 2010, and then granted a site licence in 2012, the project has a total financing cost of £24.5 billion, and has been controversial, principally due to the high 'strike price' that was promised: Government have guaranteed EDF a price of £92.50 per megawatt hour (Mwh), if Hinkley Point C is constructed, or £89.50 if EDF also develops another new reactor in Sizewell, Suffolk (reflecting the economy of scale from two reactors).

Within the government's nuclear energy strategy there was no specific mention of reprocessing spent nuclear fuel. THORP itself is due to close in 2018 once all existing reprocessing contracts have been fulfilled; and there are no new proposals for a replacement reprocessing facility. This brings the UK's reprocessing capabilities to a close. Within the new build policy there was, however, a need to plan for wastes arising from new nuclear build (in contrast to the early history of nuclear where the issue of waste was treated as a marginal or residual issue). Now a plan for decommissioning and waste management must be put in place before a new build reactor is granted planning permission, following similar models of nuclear policy in Sweden and Finland.

From a radioactive waste management perspective, the biggest concern amongst environmental organisations is the additional environmental impact of new build wastes, alongside the costs to the taxpayer associated with new waste streams. Estimates of the financial cost vary. The World Nuclear Association estimated that the disposal cost from UK nuclear power plants will cost operators a maximum of 71 p per MWh of power produced, less than 1 per cent of the cost of delivered electricity (World Nuclear News, 2011). In June 2016 former Energy Minister Andrea Leadsom declared that the estimated cost of decommissioning and long-term radioactive waste management for the new Hinkley Point C plant would come to £2 per MWh (contained within the £92.50 strike price).[3] In terms of volumes of wastes produced, the NDA models future waste arising from an EPR (the type seen at Hinkley Point C) at 600 m^3 of ILW (3200 m^3 of packaged wastes) and 4380 m^3 of LLW (6500 m^3 of packaged wastes), excluding wastes from decommissioning, interim spent fuel and waste stores (NDA, 2013, p. 19). We can compare this with the total volume of radioactive wastes from all estimated future arisings from all sources at 4,490,000 m^3 (unpackaged). Given the caveats discussed in previous chapters around trying to find an objective benchmark against which to scale the total volumes of radioactive wastes, we can at least see that for any given future nuclear reactor the contribution to addition waste stocks is relatively small. For many technical experts, the issue is a legacy problem; with the new generations of reactor designs, future waste arising can be minimised, and the decommissioning of the facilities pre-planned. This contrasts with the existing problem of trying to manage the Sellafield site.

Nevertheless, the significance of explicitly incorporating new nuclear build into governmental radioactive waste management strategy, is politically significant. When CoRWM was undergoing radioactive waste management options assessment, the issue of new nuclear build was excluded from the conversation. The chair of CoRWM, Prof. Gordon MacKerron, later expressed that this is perhaps naïve, given the movement within government towards the nuclear renaissance (Mackerron, 2010). Yet it was recognised that progress could only be achieved if radioactive wastes were treated as a legacy problem. Environmental activist organisations have long been concerned that finding a solution to radioactive waste disposal would open the floodgates to new nuclear build. From a strategic perspective, opposing or derailing policy dialogue on radioactive waste management is an effective means to stop nuclear industry expansion. It was therefore necessary for Nirex to provide some political distance between the waste problem and nuclear industry expansion. Nirex was originally set up by the nuclear industry, and when the 1997 RCF proposal failed, it needed to prove their credibility to a broad network of stakeholders including their opponents in ENGOs. Building trust in a renewed process under CoRWM, meant that radioactive wastes had to be framed as a legacy environmental problem managed on behalf of broader society and not as a boost to the ailing nuclear industry. It is difficult to tell at this stage what effect this change in policy will have. Clearly the new build policy has passed into the mainstream political agenda without widespread public opposition. There is no evidence of public outcry around new nuclear build despite the waste problem remaining unresolved. It remains to be seen if this issue is picked up in local-scale negotiations for future radioactive waste siting processes, however, and this is an incremental policy change that may further alienate communities from their participation given concerns that they may be writing a 'blank cheque' for the nuclear industry to continue to expand.

Nationally significant infrastructure projects

Since the late 1990s, there has been a long-standing political debate over how to reform planning systems for large scale infrastructure projects. Successive governments have pointed to the planning system itself to explain why there has been slow progress in getting major construction projects off the ground, citing the problem of excess time and cost involved in bringing applications to fruition. For example, if we take the development of onshore wind energy as a case study, research by the British Wind Energy Association showed that, in the period 1999–2005, the time taken to reach a final decision on wind energy applications steadily increased, taking an average of a year in England and longer in Wales, compared with 13 weeks for other types of major developments (Tomlinson, 2004). Moreover, studies of high-voltage overhead transmission lines (Cotton & Devine-Wright, 2010, 2013; Tobiasson, Beestermöller, &

Jamasb, 2015), the expansion of airports (Griggs & Howarth, 2004, 2013; Hayden, 2014) or nuclear reactors like Sizewell B (O'Riordan, Kemp, & Purdue, 1988) reveal a similar picture. Part of the problem is the decide–announce–defence strategy previously mentioned. In each of the cases cited here, the developer has applied for planning consent with very limited upfront community consultation. This has led to the development of social movements of opposition, in turn pressuring parliamentarians to resist the project. There is a familiar pattern of delays, cost overruns, planning inquiries and commonly project failure. As discussed in Chapter 2, the problem lies in the fundamental inflexibility of these technology projects: the specialised infrastructure, high capital cost, environmental impacts and high-stakes decision-making that makes them simultaneously desirable to central government, and deeply undesirable to affected communities. But rather than trying to increase the flexibility of major infrastructure project decisions, trade bodies and major developers such as transmission network operators, major energy producers and waste companies have often cited the *planning system itself* as the primary obstacle in the implementation of major infrastructures. From the lobbying of organisations like National Grid Plc. (see Cotton & Devine-Wright, 2010), the Former Labour Government raised concerns in Parliament that planning and development was moving at too slow a pace to meet sustainable development goals, such as meeting low carbon energy targets mandated by legally binding instruments such as the Climate Change Act 2008. The policy outcome was a series of planning reforms. The centrepiece of which was the concept of 'streamlining'.

Rather than recognise the inflexibility of technology proposals and approach decision-making in a more incremental way, the aim has been the opposite – to 'modernise' the system by increasing centralisation, giving more power to developers, and removing powers from local government to adapt, amend or block planning applications based upon an assessment of local needs and capacities, and environmental conditions. The current planning system for large-scale infrastructure projects began its life in a White Paper published by the former Labour Government on 21 May 2007. The core components of which were later adopted in the Planning Act 2008. At the heart of the Planning Act 2008 was the formulation of National Policy Statements (NPS) and a new oversight body to manage planning applications – the Infrastructure Planning Commission (IPC). These two instruments were designed to deal with what were referred to as Nationally Significant Infrastructure Projects (NSIPs). NSIPs are defined as major energy technology projects, airports, high-speed rail links or ports. Their national significance is primarily defined by their cost. The infrastructures designated in the National Policy Statements fall under the definition of megaprojects – the cost is commonly above the $1 billion threshold, their reach stretches beyond a locally affected community to broaden regional national infrastructure networks (Flyvbjerg, 2014), and so they have all the hallmark characteristics of inflexible technology.

The perceived failures of local planning authorities meant that Labour pushed to have an independent expert committee to oversee development consent for infrastructure projects. The IPC formally began operations in October 2009, receiving the green light from then Minister for Housing and Planning, John Healey MP, to begin receiving applications from developers as of March 2010. Former IPC chairman Sir Michael Pitt described the change as the long-overdue shake-up of the planning regime for major infrastructure, marking the separation of policy-making from infrastructure decision-making for the first time in UK planning history. The IPC promised to deliver an efficient and equitable planning process, alongside estimated taxpayer savings of £300 million annually, by bringing eight former consent regimes into one and reducing the time taken to make a decision from an average of 100 weeks previously, to less than a year (Pitt, 2010). Applications for development consent were decided by the IPC within a framework of National Policy Statements on each form of infrastructure (such as energy, airports etc.), which when completed, then underwent public consultation and parliamentary scrutiny. The government would then take account of the responses and the views of Parliament before designating the statement. If the relevant national policy statement or statements were in place, then the IPC subsequently made the decision on each application it received; if not, then the Secretary of State made the decision (Cotton, 2011a, 2011b).

The IPC process was heavily criticised by environmental organisations and conservation groups (see for example Friends of the Earth, 2008; Campaign to Protect Rural England, 2010) and in the popular press (Benjamin, 2007), as fundamentally challenging the legitimacy and democratic accountability of land-use decision-making. The IPC was an unelected body, and the planning process under the Planning Act 2008 didn't devolve power to local communities to influence changes to the local environment. The former Coalition Government under Prime Minister David Cameron also recognised this process as being undemocratic. Social scientists were concerned with whether land-use change is construed as primarily a technical activity or one which involves the making of political choices (Booth, 2009), that it fundamentally changed the nature of infrastructure governance in a way that empowered the market rather than the citizenry. To the Coalition Government, decision-making legitimacy was construed as providing ministerial oversight, in contrast to the deliberative turn that characterised New Labour's approach to local governance, where legitimacy was construed as direct citizen involvement rather than solely through elected representation. The Coalition Government remained enthusiastic about the streamlining agenda, however, and remain committed to giving more power to developers. There was a fundamental assumption that the neoliberal model of free market development would provide efficiency, despite evidence to the contrary (Bentley & Pugalis, 2013; Catney, MacGregor, Dobson, Hal, Royston, Robinson et al., 2014; Cotton, 2014). It's also important to note that in 2008–2009 the global financial crisis led to a change in government and growing conditions of austerity. This in turn led to a political rhetoric of infrastructure development as a means to ensure economic growth. The subsequent Localism Act 2011, was a further incremental step in this policy strategy. All the 'meat' of the Planning Act's reforms were retained, the significant change was the abolition of the IPC in favour of a major infrastructure unit within the Planning Inspectorate overseen by the Secretary of State.

The broader political context of this set of localist reforms was the so-called Big Society agenda. David Cameron wanted to grant local communities both greater power and more responsibilities. The term 'big society' was positioned against the concept of 'big government'; the Conservatives desired more community-level action to improve neighbourhoods, and a growing role for charities and other third sector organisations – taking responsibilities (and funding) away from local authorities. However, the big society quickly fell out of favour as a broader political strategy. It was criticised as another tool of austerity politics, where shortfalls in local government funding were expected to be made up by civil society organisations composed of self-motivated citizens, even though their citizens were not necessarily qualified to replace local government professionals. The Localism Act 2011 is also self-contradictory. On the one hand, it is a policy strategy aimed to empower local communities, but when it comes to major infrastructure planning it actually draws more powers to central government. It strips local authorities of their power to restrict certain kind of development that have been designated in National Policy Statements; restricts opportunities for local citizens to lobby local planning authorities to reject unwanted applications and removes the rights of local government to impose planning inquiries in the event of environmental controversy.

Radioactive waste as nationally significant infrastructure

When it comes to radioactive waste management in the post-West Cumbria decision, the Planning Act 2008 and Localism Act 2011 have become politically significant. The 2014 White Paper's most significant change in policy direction was a statement that ministers would prefer to work with public support, but reserved the right to take more aggressive action on planning if 'at some point in the future such an approach does not look likely to work' (Department of Energy and Climate Change, 2014). This provided the foreground of the policy decision to take a more direct approach to siting if a volunteer community would not step forward. From an ethical point of view this completely undermines the principle of voluntarism. One cannot volunteer if there is a threat of being forced to accept something. What this meant was that the government intended to fold the MRWS process into the existing nationally significant infrastructure planning framework.

On 25 March 2015, the draft Infrastructure Planning (Radioactive Waste Geological Disposal Facilities) Order 2015, late for the House on 12 January 2015, was approved (Ayes 277, Noes 33). The vote concerned a two-page statutory instrument to amend the Planning Act 2008 to include facilities for radioactive waste management. This includes the construction of one or more boreholes for scientific, construction or building work; or construction of a geological disposal facility. With this vote, the legal status of the MRWS programme changed. Disposal facilities are now considered as NSIPs and so the decision about their siting now lies in the hands of the Secretary of State for Business, Energy and Industrial Strategy, after receiving advice from the Planning Inspectorate. Jowitt, writing in the Guardian newspaper, notes that the move was barely noticed, that it was cast late in the day before Parliament was prorogued for the general election, stating that: 'Nuclear waste dumps can be imposed on local communities without their support under a new law rushed through in the final hours of Parliament' (Jowitt, 2015). This change in the law raises concerns that the voluntarist process will be abandoned in favour of a top-down solution. The former Conservative MP Zac Goldsmith criticised the move, due to a lack of public debate about this change in legislation. He states:

> Effectively it strips local authorities of the ability to stop waste being dumped in their communities ... If there had been a debate, there could have been a different outcome: most of the MPs who voted probably didn't know what they were voting for.
>
> (Cited in ibid.)

By moving RWM into the national infrastructure planning regime, it not only changes the way in which planning consent is delivered, it also changes the ways in which government authorities in local communities interact. Fundamental to this is the notion of the socio-technical imaginary – that complex social constructions surrounding technological developments, and their associated publics lead to very different policy outcomes (Jasanoff & Kim, 2009; Walker, Cass, Burningham, & Barnett, 2010). From previous work on high-voltage overhead transmission lines (Cotton & Devine-Wright, 2012), wind energy (Cotton, 2011a; Barnett, Burningham, Walker, & Cass, 2012) and energy-from-waste facilities (Cotton, 2014): a recurrent theme emerges. This is that under the Planning Act 2008, the centralisation of decision-making and the scaling of infrastructure decisions to the national level reshapes the ways in which public authorities imagine local community actors within planning processes. Specifically, they imagine local citizens as being insufficiently strategic in their thinking, concerned with local environmental impacts, house prices, local employment opportunities and place-protective action (i.e. they are, in effect, imagined as 'nimbies'; see Devine-Wright, 2013). If local actors become synonymous with protesters interested solely in local issues, then they are discursively constructed by centralised authorities as lacking the 'deliberative capacity' (Davies & Burgess, 2004; Dryzek, 2009) to engage on broader issues of regional or national significance. Their voices become delegitimised: they are no longer imagined as stakeholders that should be involved in decision processes, but simply local activists who should be mollified, or silenced. The UK's infrastructure planning regime pushes decision-making out of the hands of local communities towards developers and central government. As a socio-technical imaginary, the concept of a nationally significant infrastructure project means that all the important politics is 'performed' at the national scale. The process by which infrastructure is governed through National Policy Statements and where community involvement is only permitted at the local level, downstream of planning applications by specific developers, either creates or reinforces an *oppressive politics of scale*; and my concern (as indeed may be the implicit concern of many West Cumbrians) is that the government will wield this nation-scale socio-technical imaginary as a means to politically justify the abolition of voluntarism altogether.

The reformation of the radioactive waste management policy process through a national infrastructure planning lens has several fundamental challenges associated with it. A national-scale socio-technical imaginary invites a utilitarian solution: it frames the waste solution as being for the good of society, rather than exploring (from a more egalitarian perspective) what a solution means to an affected community before siting gets underway. This is problematic when we consider the messy and fractured historical and geographical relationships that nuclear communities have with the wastes that are produced. Bickerstaff (2012) and Wynne (1996) point to the history, economic and cultural geographies of West Cumbria as being intimately connected with the prevailing nuclear industry. The politics of radioactive waste is deeply enmeshed in the actors and events that have structured this past. This includes the actions of Nirex in the 1990s, but also the failures of the most recent voluntarist process. Local actors' historical knowledge, their sense of certain temporal and geographic distances (of future generations, past actions of RWMOs, of their relationship with Cumbrian tourism etc.), and differently imagined technologies and publics, create a complexity of engagement with radioactive wastes. This is similarly true in Bradwell, Elstow or Billingham (for example) where previous siting processes may sour relations with future RWMOs involved in implementing the new site selection process. A national scale process of decision-making ignores or glosses over this complexity. It pushes radioactive waste management back into the realm of centralisation, rational planning and technological inflexibility.

The voluntarist process in West Cumbria, with its long time frames of engagement, was in many respects a paragon of just process, and it was inherently incrementalist. An extended dialogue process with multiple stages of decision-making allowed trial and error to occur. The EoI stage allows policy learning amongst a variety of partisan political actors. This includes stakeholders within the local community, but also at the borough and county council-level representatives, scientific and technical specialists within the RWMO RWM Ltd, and ultimately for the Department of Business, Energy and Industrial Strategy, with which the decision ultimately rests. The GDF became what we might call a *boundary object* – in the sense that it was interpreted differently across different communities of practice (Star, 2010; Madsen & Noe, 2012). (The host community, for example, interpreted it differently to the geologists and environmental activist organisations, etc.) The conceptualisation of the GDF was plastic enough to adapt to the needs and constraints of all the different stakeholders employing the term, yet it was robust enough so that they could all come together in a dialogue process to familiarise themselves with the competing definitions and make meaningful political choices.

Dialogue allowed these different partisan actors to bargain and negotiate the science of West Cumbria's geology and hydrogeology, what compensation might mean to the community and how it might be distributed, about trust in the institutions involved and their long history in West Cumbria, about the brand value of Cumbria nationally and internationally and how a GDF would affect it, and how the different levels of local government should work together. Rather than assuming there's an optimal solution that could be decided in advance, by gathering all the available evidence and then assessing the criteria against which to measure success (as was done in the first exploration of West Cumbria in the 1980s and 1990s using multi-attribute decision analysis); this time there was no assumption that an optimal solution could be reached by weight of evidence alone. The process was incremental both in the way in which it was multi-staged (from expression of interest, through dialogue processes with the host community and other stakeholder actors, and then a decision to participate); but also in a sense that there was no assumption that a front-loaded megaproject was going to be built at the end of this process. The power of withdrawal from further negotiations lay in the hands of local government representatives – this allowed policy as trial and error – it allowed a change of policy direction to occur, avoiding lock-in. My concern is that as this process is refashioned as a national infrastructure project, this incrementalism *could* be abandoned in favour of a top-down rational planning model once again. From a purely strategic perspective this can only end in the same types of policy failure that we saw in the 1980s and 1990s, under Nirex's watch, and I would caution the Department of Business, Energy and Industrial Strategy against such a course of action.

Considering the role of scale

In Chapter 2, I outlined three elements necessary for achieving incremental technology decisions to combat the problems associated with inflexibility. To reiterate:

1   Consideration of the nature and role of expertise – how science, technology and engineering expertise engages with non-specialist lay expertise within a decision-making process.
2   The appropriateness of decision-making structures and processes, specifically how RWMOs have moved from decide–announce–defence strategies, whereby technical authorities make decisions based upon technical criteria and then communicate these to locally affected communities.
3   A consideration of the scale of the technology: its size, its cost, and the risk of project failure; and the scales of decision-making and the (often hierarchical) organisation of different decision-making authorities from the Department of Business, Energy and Industrial Strategy (DBEIS), and the

implementation organisation RWM Ltd down to host communities, their geographic relationship with one another and the different powers held by each.

I argue that decisions on radioactive waste management have become progressively incremental since the 1997 RCF proposal failure. However, the primary emphasis has been upon the reformation of points 1 and 2 in the above list. CoRWM went to great pains to detach scientific expertise from decision-making control. It focused upon both the role of scientific and technical expertise and how it could be integrated with lay expertise; and how a participatory–deliberative decision-support process could then integrate scientific and other value considerations in the appraisal of different radioactive waste management options. Latterly, the voluntarist process emphasised the structure of decision-making, specifically how communities could form effective partnerships to communicate their needs and aspirations with government over a GDF proposal. Both processes (CoRWM and the actions of the WCMRWSP) demonstrate a rebalancing of scientific and lay expertise, and an open, honest and indeed experimental approach to participatory–deliberative decision-support, becoming progressively more postnormal in their collective approaches to technological controversy. These factors in themselves are incremental policy changes. It is through a process of policy learning that opportunities for public participation became a mainstay of RWM, after decades of failed technocratic decisions. We can see, therefore, that the policy landscape had shifted in terms of process to provide greater flexibility. But what is lacking, is an appropriate understanding of scale, and why this is important to policy success.

There are two elements of scale that need to be discussed. The first is the scale of the technology itself and how that relates to *environmental justice*. Like all other countries considering the disposal of radioactive waste, the consensus has settled upon a national scale GDF. This means that all wastes produced within England and Wales will be transported and stored in the (eventual) facility. This means that any community deciding to host a GDF will be required to accept wastes from outside the community. The difficulty here is in the geographical relationship between isolated, economically marginalised and peripheral communities (such as West Cumbria), and with metropolitan centres which have benefited more greatly from nuclear electricity production. This is significant because there may be insider/outsider political conflict. In work that I've done with colleagues on other energy-related technologies such as energy from waste, electricity transmission systems and shale gas extraction (Cotton & Devine-Wright, 2013; Cotton, 2014; Cotton, Rattle, & Van Alstine, 2014), one of the most important discursive constructions of these technologies is through a lens of geographic (sometimes called intragenerational) environmental injustice. This concerns the unfair distribution of risks and benefits: specifically, a sense that rural communities are expected to bear the burden of energy production (in this case by accepting radioactive wastes), whereas urban centres feel only the benefits. Moreover, decisions about energy resource extraction, electricity production and transmission are made by decision-makers within urban environments (whether in Westminster or the headquarters of transnational energy companies), but the practices of extraction, production and waste management nearly always occur in rural locations. This relates distributive environmental justice – that risks, costs and negative externalities are concentrated in specific (rural) locations, with procedural environmental justice – the decision-making processes favour urban people, and urban identities over rural ones. In short they become rural energy sacrifice zones to power urban centres by virtue of urban elites making the decisions that affect the rural periphery (Fox, 1999; Lerner, 2010; Hernández, 2015).

We see these debates around environmental injustice, rural versus urban identities, and the concept of rural sacrifice zones being played out in the deliberations in West Cumbria. One of the critical issues discussed in the WCMRWSP deliberative process was the sense of ownership of the waste problem and the responsibility that came with it. This is an issue of problem framing. Communities around Sellafield are likely to be more amenable to accepting waste management facilities specifically for the wastes produced at Sellafield itself, rather than taking all wastes in from across the country. There is perhaps a simple risk-benefit logic to this. The legacy wastes at Sellafield are not safe in their current form. Housing these wastes in a GDF would ultimately improve community safety. They are likely to be less willing, however, to accept wastes from other communities. It may stimulate perceptions that accepting more waste (than they currently have) would increase the risk to the community, making it not only any less safe, but also less desirable due to the stigmatisation that would occur. There is a persistent fear that Sellafield will become the nation's nuclear waste dust bin – and so concepts of the nation scale play out in the local community deliberations about fairness, environmental justice and responsibility. Accepting that Sellafield needs a safe long-term radioactive waste management solution is an expression of stewardship ethics: of a community taking responsibility for the legacy problem that it has created over time. Accepting wastes from other communities becomes a concern of conflicting ethical principles: between egalitarian ethics and utilitarian ethics. The nation scale GDF invokes utilitarian ethics of minimising risks to the aggregate populations, versus an egalitarian ethics that suggests that accepting wastes on behalf of society is a *supererogatory* act (it is above and beyond 'the call of duty'). Asking a single rural community to take on this burden scales the problem in such a way that the perceived risk of health and environmental impacts, socio-economic decline and stigmatisation become too great to bear – particularly now that new build nuclear wastes are likely to be housed in the same facility. It is then rational, therefore, for the communities around Sellafield to reject such a proposal.

I return to the work of Cox in illustrating this problem. To reiterate, Cox (1998b) defines two types of scalar relationships. The first is a *space of engagement* whereby scale is an emergent property through networks of social interaction. The second is a *space of dependence* – a broadly fixed, geographically situated arena within which individuals become embedded in political, socio-economic and environmental interests. Spaces of engagement are sets of relations that extend into and beyond spaces of dependence as a means to construct relations: networks of association, exchange, and politics that are relational and contingent upon the particular networks and associations in any given instance (see also Jones, 1998). These scales are *performed* in the sense that different actors will use concepts of scale to their advantage within political negotiations. Different categories of scale are frequently defined within policy and then reified within planning practice; enacting a type of political separation between the predefined scalar boundaries. Social actors then try to challenge or reinterpret these scales in order to further their own strategic agendas (Johnstone, 2014). This is termed 'jumping scales' – and we saw this playing out in the deliberations amongst the WCMRWSP: protest in direct action campaigns aimed at re-scaling local decisions (on where a GDF is sited) to national and indeed global levels of environmental impact and decision-making (for example refocusing debate on the polluting nature of nuclear power, the alternative waste management options available or local on-site waste solutions to each of the respective power stations, for example); and a breakdown between the borough council-level of Copeland that was supportive of further exploration of GDF feasibility versus the county council level (the next level up), which is concerned more with broader socio-economic development of the Cumbrian region. The lesson for the government is that the meso (or regional) scale of decision-making required greater attention. The decision-making process should have been incrementally reframed to better alleviate the concerns of Cumbria as a whole. But in the White Paper, government re-scaled the problem to the national scale, and is considering ways in which Cumbria County Council could be bypassed by re-scaling the partnership agreement to the borough council level. This demonstrates the performativity of scale for different political actors. Government has tried to simultaneously perform both a 'more national' and 'more local' scale at the same time. Realising that in West Cumbria the county council level was the political scale at which the policy 'failed', government has incrementally changed the policy through the White Paper, which has the potential to exclude or diminish the powers of this scale of local government. In terms of Cox's (1998a, 1998b) work, this means that the government is trying to *compress* the scale at which a decision can be made (to the borough council level), whilst simultaneously arguing the national importance of the GDF as a megaproject (see also Swyngedouw, 2004; Johnstone, 2014). I argue that this will simply encounter further resistance because local community activists including local politicians, business groups and national ENGOs will act to re-scale the problem to a regional (meso scale) one: emphasising the environmental effects beyond the host community, the broader effects upon tourism and regional brand identity, and (implicitly) highlighting the so-called doughnut effect: that it is the surrounding communities rather than the host community which suffer the impacts most severely because they are not cushioned by job creation or compensation packages. From a decision-scaling perspective, therefore, it behooves the government to ameliorate the impacts at

the regional scale, rather just the host community scale. It is necessary for government policy on radioactive waste management specifically, and major infrastructure planning more generally, to join the respective geographic and
governance scales of the regional or meso level to allow public actors significant
voice in the strategic development of regional and national infrastructure planning. If they fail to do this, then patterns of procedural injustice will be repeated
and reinforced with each new siting process, leading to further cycles of distrust,
public opposition and project failure.

Policy recommendations – down-scaling radioactive waste

Throughout this book, I have argued that radioactive waste disposal facilities
are examples of megaprojects which are fundamentally inflexible. If we look at
policy evolution over time we see a series of incremental changes have improved
the flexibility of policy considerably. In the 1950s, radioactive waste management was treated as a minor or residual concern. Technological optimism and
Cold War secrecy allowed the continuation of an inflexible technology programme – the desire for a nuclear weapons programme meant that the government created a 'technology push' strategy in West Cumbria. Sellafield was a
military site producing military technologies. Civilian nuclear energy production was a secondary function. Given Sellafield's commercial success, this
encouraged a broader national nuclear solution to the post-war energy supply
problem in the 1960s and 1970s. It was during this period that we saw sustained
nuclear expansion, though the Flowers report highlighted the intergenerational
injustice posed by radioactive wastes, which meant that the problem could no
longer be ignored. Nirex's actions in the 1980s and 1990s to find sites for both
high-level waste and intermediate level waste were, therefore, an incremental
policy change. Nirex was set up by the nuclear industry. In its early incarnation,
it represented industry interests – so finding a quick solution became the goal,
thus allowing the industry to continue to expand. Their first site selection processes were, therefore, almost entirely rational/centralised/technocratic/oppres-
sive: trying to find optimal geology for a GDF and then imposing that decision
on the communities selected on geological criteria (or other factors such as
proximity to transportation networks or favourable political conditions –
leading to the four-sites saga discussed in Chapter 3). When this failed, the
incremental policy learning was to improve community participation to get
better buy-in to the decision. Site selection was still highly technocratic, but
there was some consultation going on (Nirex's The Way Forward programme)
and community perspectives did form part of the multi-attribute decision analysis that took place. When in 1997 RCF proposal failed, a more significant
change in policy occurred, though this too was incremental – this step change
towards greater participatory–deliberative decision support was based upon a
type of trial-and-error policy learning. It was a change that came about from
policy failure, rather than being rationally decided in advance. Scientific and
technical expertise changed from being the primary driver of policy, to being a

resource used in making societal choices. The CoRWM process used analytic–deliberative methods to arrive at the decision to employ interim storage and then geological disposal. This was based upon the best evidence of the time, and reflected a consensus within international radioactive waste management policy communities. The recommendation was, however, legitimate in a postnormal scientific sense because it had been appraised in a broader peer community of social scientists, ethicists, and non-specialist citizen-stakeholders. The voluntarist model of site selection too was an incremental policy change. The success of the participatory approach used by CoRWM encouraged government to continue with a 'bottom-up' model that rescaled the decision to the host community level. When this failed at the county council level the re-scaling of the decision to the national scale was another incremental policy step – though I have argued it was a step in the wrong direction.

At all points of this policy development process, there has been an assumption that a GDF megaproject can be implemented somewhere in England, Wales or Northern Ireland. (Scotland remains exempt, as higher activity waste policy is a devolved issue.) I challenge that assumption. The scale of the technological decision means that no individual decision-maker can understand the myriad complexities and impacts across multiple geographic and temporal scales. These include (but are not limited to) the impact of a GDF on tourism, on the socio-cultural character of the community and how it is perceived, of the safety of the technology solution over very long time frames, of how radiological risks can be communicated to future generations in such a way that stewardship of the waste can be maintained, of the injustices between the host communities and their neighbours, and between rural communities and their urban counterparts. The problem is one of bounded rationality and synoptic rationality. Even if we were to increase opportunities for public participation, essentially gold-plating the deliberative nature of the decision-making, these problems will still be encountered. Decision-makers either at the borough council level, the county council level, or in central government cannot make a rational decision in advance that incorporates these different factors and optimises a solution whereby a GDF will be both ethically legitimate, and publicly acceptable. As an incrementalist, I argue that we need to de-scale both the technology and the decision stakes in order to achieve a socially acceptable solution. This means that we must think through alternative strategies to the status quo incorporating both alternative technologies and alternative decision scales to those currently offered in the 2014 White Paper.

Deep borehole disposal – an incremental solution

De-scaling radioactive waste disposal does not mean abandoning deep geology as a solution altogether. In Scotland, the higher activity waste policy has abandoned geological disposal in favour of above-ground long-term storage whilst an alternative technological solution is found. Their work on the strategic environmental assessment of geological disposal led the Scottish Parliament to make this decision. They therefore stand alone amongst advanced economies with nuclear power capabilities in their forgoing geological disposal. In England and Wales long-term storage is part of the solution, whilst political progress on the GDF is sought. However, my recommendation is that we consider an alternative solution to the very high activity wastes to make progress towards the long-term safe management of these radiotoxic materials. My *imperfect* solution to this problem is disposal of higher activity wastes (spent fuel, vitrified high level waste and plutonium) in deep boreholes.

The deep borehole disposal concept

Deep geological disposal in a mined repository emplaces high-level and inter-mediate level wastes at depths of 500 m to 1000 m. Deep borehole disposal is a concept of disposing higher activity radioactive materials (with small volumes) in extremely deep boreholes as deep as 5 km beneath the surface. This relies primarily on the thickness of the natural geological barrier to safely isolate the waste from the biosphere over the very long time periods in which the wastes remain active (Brady, Arnold, Freeze, Swift, Bauer, Kanney et al., 2009b). In the 1950s, the concept of deep borehole disposal was considered by a number of RWMOs, but was ultimately rejected as it was believed to be beyond existing drilling capabilities. It was considered too expensive and too dangerous as result. However, recent improvements in drilling and associated technologies and advances in the sealing methods for deep boreholes have prompted the re-examination of this option. As Beswick, Gibb and Travis (2014) argue, there has been minimal investment into this method in recent decades, but it poten-tially offers a safer, more cost-effective, secure and environmentally sound solu-tion to the long-term management of high-level radioactive wastes than mined repositories. This technology is already being trialled in the USA, where the Department of Energy has followed the recommendations of a presidential Blue Ribbon Commission into alternative radioactive waste disposal options. The DoE has initiated a programme led by Sandia National Laboratories, to investi-gate deep borehole disposal with the objective of taking it to a full-scale demon-stration (though not yet with actual radioactive waste – it is still at the proof of concept stage for the borehole drilling) (Brady, Arnold, Freeze, Swift, Bauer, Kanney et al., 2009a). It is also being considered in Sweden as an alternative to their repository concept for spent fuel. The ENGO Miljöorganisationernas kär-navfallsgranskning (MKG – or the Swedish NGO Office for Nuclear Waste Review), states that (cited in Ozharovsky, 2016):

> new drilling technologies have appeared relatively recently, the very deep borehole drilling method has been developed, to a depth of five kilometres, where the radioactive waste can be completely isolated from the biosphere … Intensive research is being done in the United States into whether such boreholes may be suitable … at the present time and with present knowledge, the […] method appears to be a superior solution … and should therefore be investigated further.

The deep borehole disposal method involves sinking a large-diameter cased boreholes at depths of between 4 km and 6 km into the granite at the base of the continental crust, and then deploying packages of high level radioactive waste into the lower reaches of the hole before sealing it above, or at the top of, the disposal zone and backfilling the rest of the borehole. This method offers a number of potential advantages. The first is greater isolation and safety due to the depth at which the wastes become emplaced. Wastes at this depth are out of physical and chemical contact with the near-surface circulating groundwater, as these very rarely extend below 1 or 2 km depth (Bucher & Stober, 2000). The second is of greater political significance, as Beswick et. al (2014) argue:

> At a few tens of millions of dollars per borehole, a [Deep Borehole Disposal] DBD programme is likely to be significantly more cost effective than a mined repository, estimates for which range from hundreds of millions to tens of billions of dollars. Furthermore, the nature of a mined repository requires that high 'up-front' costs are incurred before any waste is emplaced and substantial operating costs follow, possibly for hundreds of years. By contrast, DBD is effectively a 'pay as you go' scheme that allows a small disposal programme to be expanded as required or a large one to be terminated at any point (and for whatever reason) without any significant further cost.

It is this factor that makes deep borehole disposal politically suitable from an incrementalist perspective. The first is the reduction in the financial cost. The megaproject with its $1 billion plus price tag encourages inflexible decision-making from a centralised authority. Whereas this smaller 'project scale' (Flyvbjerg, 2014) intervention, is more suitable for a decentralised, and local authority-led decision model. It is the pay-as-you-go approach – and is fundamentally incremental.

Conclusions

By proposing a small number of boreholes in a first phase disposal programme, this will demonstrate three things. The first is the demonstration of safe technology. One of the difficulties with a mined GDF is that there is no demonstration of a safety case upon which a local community can base its risk management decisions. As Ewing (2014) argues:

> We should benefit from the sobering reality of how difficult it is to anticipate future failures even over a few decades. We should be humbled by the realisation that for a geologic repository we are analysing the performance, success vs failure, over spatial and temporal scales that stretch over tens of kilometres and out to hundreds of thousands of years.

Simply put, the decision stakes are so high it is rational for local community to reject a GDF on precautionary grounds. However, the deep borehole disposal option allows a smaller-scale intervention for high-level waste disposal that can be actively monitored (albeit over a short period of time) and provides a demonstrable safety case with empirical (rather than modelled) data. It is the *demonstration* of success which is the important aspect from a political perspective. Public perceptions of the risk involved in high-level radioactive waste management are interpreted through an understanding of risk histories, familiar and demonstrated technologies (Wynne, 2006; Parkhill, Pidgeon, Henwood, Simmons, & Venables, 2010), and temporal and geographic distances. The deep borehole disposal option increases the geographic physical (and hence psychological) distance of the risk from the community (simply put, it is further away the deeper it goes). It also makes the technologies of radioactive waste management socio-culturally visible – a physical demonstration model which can be implemented quickly (time frames of five years rather than 100 years) encourages community engagement with the technology in a manner that is *tangible* rather than abstract and statistical. It is in that sense, psychologically *closer*. These are all ways in which deep borehole disposal provides a more flexible technological strategy. It allows trial-and-error policy-making because a small number of boreholes can be implemented, their socio-economic and cultural impacts upon a local site community monitored, deliberated and learned from, and adjustments through small steps and policy learning can be taken. It also means that the complexities of the entire national radioactive waste management challenge do not have to be resolved all at once – wastes can be disposed of locally within specific municipalities where the wastes already exist. Due to the depth at which the boreholes are constructed, it reduces the need for geological screening. At the base of the earth's crust there is a negligible chance of water intrusion causing radionuclide migration back up to the surface. This reduces the requirement proving a safety case based upon the host geology of a specific location. In essence, this disposal strategy has a certain 'placelessness' – and many of the scientific controversies surrounding the suitability of host geology that occurred in the West Cumbrian deliberations would be ameliorated. From a political perspective, deep borehole disposal removes the nation-scale/ local-scale conflict because of this placelessness. It would allow nuclear communities to dispose of some of their most active wastes locally. I call this *municipal radioactive waste management* – a local solution to a local waste problem. This is an element that could be described in terms of ethical incrementalism. By allowing a community to dispose of its own wastes, it improves opportunities for voluntarism and the social control of the technology at the local/regional level. It reduces the need to think of the problem in national terms, because the wastes do not all need to be relocated to a single national site. It also, therefore, reduces many of the problems associated with environmental injustice between the host community and other nuclear communities that produce wastes, between rural and urban populations and between host communities and their immediate neighbours. It would allow a radioactive waste management programme to be framed in terms of local stewardship ethics rather than through a conflict between principles of utilitarian and egalitarian ethics, and I argue this is an essential component in providing broader community support for a radioactive waste disposal solution.

The final caveat to this argument is that deep borehole disposal is only suitable for higher activity wastes – for spent fuel and other small volume wastes such as plutonium. This means that for the much larger volumes of intermediate level wastes a different disposal solution is still required. However, there are two options in this regard. The first is that you combine deep borehole disposal with above ground or near surface shallow disposal of intermediate level wastes. The above-ground solution is favoured in Scotland, and in principle I agree with the perspective expressed in Scottish higher activity waste policy. The deep borehole disposal solution justifies this choice, in the sense that since the 1970s, geological disposal in mined repository has been favoured as the scientific consensus or best practice method; yet this belies a potentially cheaper, more incremental, and potentially safer solution for higher activity wastes given the recent advances in drilling technologies and borehole construction/backfilling. In short, a technological solution which is preferable on safety and political grounds has emerged in the interim period between the failure of the last GDF solution and the implementation of the next one. Given the very long lead times for construction of a GDF it behooves RWMOs to explore deep borehole disposal in the interim. The second option is that you explore both deep borehole disposal for higher activity wastes and a GDF for intermediate level wastes in parallel. The argument here is that if a borehole solution can be demonstrated to be effective, this will facilitate public trust in the implementing RWMO. By demonstrating safe disposal, it becomes easier politically, to build rapport with the communities where the boreholes are constructed, and thus encourage voluntarism for a GDF. This is because the decision is more incremental. The community takes a small step with a deep borehole, learns from that experience, and then if this is successful on environmental, safety and socio-economic grounds, any GDF becomes less of a 'large leap into the unknown' for that community. By creating the additional decision steps, by descaling both the technology and the decision frame, we create an ethically incremental radioactive waste disposal solution that is more likely to be supported in the communities affected.

Notes

1 Nuclear clean-up is the largest budget item of the former Department of Energy and Climate Change, (and now the Department of Business, Energy and Industrial Strategy). Yet the management of the Sellafield clean-up operation is escalating. According to a 2014 report by the Public Accounts Committee (PAC), the estimated cost of cleaning up the Sellafield nuclear reprocessing site (Thermal Oxide Reprocessing Plant – THORP) had risen from £67.5 billion in 2013 to £70 billion in 2014 (Public Accounts Committee, 2014). This led to MPs calling for the NDA to terminate its contract with the private consortium – Nuclear Management Partners if performance did not improve.

2 At the time of writing there are 60 new reactors under construction, with China, India, Russia and the United Arab Emirates the largest players (IAEA, 2016).
3 It is also notable that the source of these costs is difficult to pin down.

Bibliography

Barnett, J., Burningham, K., Walker, G., & Cass, N. (2012). Imagined publics and engagement around renewable energy technologies in the UK. *Public Understanding of Science, 21*(1), 36–50. doi:10.1177/0963662510365663.

Benjamin, A. (2007, 6 November). Critics dismiss planning bill as 'developers' charter', *The Guardian*.

Bentley, G., & Pugalis, L. (2013). New directions in economic development: Localist policy discourses and the Localism Act. *Local Economy, 28*(3), 257–274.

Beswick, A. J., Gibb, F. G. F., & Travis, K. P. (2014). Deep borehole disposal of nuclear waste: Engineering challenges. *Proceedings of the Institution of Civil Engineers: Energy, 167*(2), 47–66.

Bickerstaff, K. (2012). 'Because we've got history here': Nuclear waste, cooperative siting, and the relational geography of a complex issue. *Environment and Planning A, 44*(11), 2611–2628.

Bickerstaff, K., Lorenzoni, I., Pidgeon, N. F., Poortinga, W., & Simmons, P. (2008). Reframing nuclear power in the UK energy debate: Nuclear power, climate change mitigation and radioactive waste. *Public Understanding of Science, 17*(2), 145–169.

Booth, P. (2009). Managing land-use change. *Land Use Policy, 26*(1), 154–159.

Brady, P. V., Arnold, B. W., Freeze, G. A., Swift, P. N., Bauer, S. J., Kanney, J. L., et al. (2009a). Deep borehole disposal of high-level radioactive waste. Albuquerque: Sandia National Laboratories.

Brady, P. V., Arnold, B. W., Freeze, G. A., Swift, P. N., Bauer, S. J., Kanney, J. L., et al. (2009b). Deep borehole disposal of high-level radioactive waste. *Sandia Report SAND2009-4401, Sandia National Laboratories, Albuquerque, New Mexico.*

Bucher, K., & Stober, I. (2000). The composition of groundwater in the continental crystalline crust. In K. Bucher, & I. Stober (Eds.), *Hydrogeology of crystalline rock*. Dordrecht: Kluwer.

Campaign to Protect Rural England. (2010). The Infrastructure Planning Commission (IPC), from www.planninghelp.org.uk/planning-system/planning-for-major-infrastructure-projects/major-infrastructure-the-infrastructure-planning-commission.

Catney, P., MacGregor, S., Dobson, A., Hall, S. M., Royston, S., Robinson, Z., et al. (2014). Big society, little justice? Community renewable energy and the politics of localism. *Local Environment, 19*(7), 715–730.

Central Intelligence Agency. (2012). *World fact book country comparison: Electricity – consumption*. Washington DC: Central Intelligence Agency Office of Public Affairs.

Cotton, M. (2011a). Public engagement and community opposition to wind energy in the UK. In M. Tortoro (Ed.), *Sustainable systems and energy management at the regional level: Comparative approaches*. Hershay, PA: IGI Publishing.

Cotton, M. (2011b). Public participation in UK infrastructure planning: Democracy, technology and environmental justice. In M. Cotton, & B. H. Motta (Eds.), *Engaging with environmental justice: Governance, education and citizenship*. Oxford: Inter-Disciplinary Press.

Cotton, M. (2014). Environmental justice challenges in United Kingdom infrastructure planning: Lessons from a Welsh incinerator project. *Environmental Justice, 7*(2), 39–44.

Cotton, M., & Devine-Wright, P. (2010). NIMBYism and community consultation in electricity transmission network planning. In P. Devine-Wright (Ed.), *Renewable energy and the public: From NIMBY to participation* (pp. 115–130). London: Routledge.

Cotton, M., & Devine-Wright, P. (2012). Making electricity networks 'visible': Industry actor representations of 'publics' and public engagement in infrastructure planning. *Public Understanding of Science, 21*(1), 17–35.

Cotton, M., & Devine-Wright, P. (2013). Putting pylons into place: A UK case study of public beliefs about the impacts of high voltage overhead transmission lines. *Journal of Environmental Planning and Management, 56*(8), 1225–1245.

Cotton, M., Rattle, I., & Van Alstine, J. (2014). Shale gas policy in the United Kingdom: An argumentative discourse analysis. *Energy Policy, 73,* 427–438.

Cox, K. R. (1998a). Representation and power in the politics of scale. *Political Geography, 17*(1), 41–44.

Cox, K. R. (1998b). Spaces of dependence, spaces of engagement and the politics of scale, or: Looking for local politics. *Political Geography, 17*(1), 1–23.

Darst, R., & Dawson, J. I. (2010). Waiting for the nuclear renaissance: Exploring the nexus of expansion and disposal in Europe. *Risk, Hazards & Crisis in Public Policy, 1*(4), 49–82.

Davies, G., & Burgess, J. (2004). Challenging the 'view from nowhere': Citizen reflections on specialist expertise in a deliberative process. *Health and Place, 10*(4), 349–361.

DECC. (2013). *Long-term nuclear energy strategy.* London: Department of Energy and Climate Change.

DEFRA, BERR, and the devolved administrations for Wales and Northern Ireland. (2008). *Managing radioactive waste safely: A framework for implementing geological disposal.* London: Department for Environment Food and Rural Affairs, Department for Business, Enterprise and Regulatory Reform and the devolved administrations for Wales and Northern Ireland.

Department of Energy and Climate Change, & The Rt Hon Edward Davey. (2013). Written ministerial statement by Edward Davey on the management of radioactive waste. London: Department of Energy and Climate Change.

Department of Energy and Climate Change. (2014). *Implementing geological disposal: A framework for the long-term management of higher activity radioactive waste.* London: Department of Energy and Climate Change.

Department of Trade and Industry. (2006). *Our energy challenge – securing clean, affordable energy for the long-term – energy review consultation document.* London: HMSO.

Devine-Wright, P. (2013). Explaining 'NIMBY' objections to a power line: The role of personal, place attachment and project-related factors. *Environment and Behavior, 45*(6), 761–781.

Dryzek, J. S. (2009). Democratization as deliberative capacity building. *Comparative Political Studies, 42*(11), 1379–1402. doi: 10.1177/0010414009332129.

Ewing, R. C. (2014). *Projecting risk into the future: Failure of a geologic repository and the sinking of the Titanic.* MRS Proceedings, vol. 1665, Cambridge, Cambridge University Press, 15–21.

Flyvbjerg, B. (2014). What you should know about megaprojects and why: An overview. *Project Management Journal, 45*(2), 6–19.

Fox, J. (1999). Mountaintop removal in West Virginia An environmental sacrifice zone. *Organization & Environment, 12*(2), 163–183.

Friends of the Earth. (2008). *Question and answer on the Planning Bill.* London: Friends of the Earth.

244 *What next for nuclear waste?*

Griggs, S., & Howarth, D. (2004). A transformative political campaign? The new rhetoric of protest against airport expansion in the UK. *Journal of Political Ideologies*, 9(2), 181–201.

Griggs, S., & Howarth, D. (2013). 'Between a rock and a hard place': The coalition, the Davies Commission and the wicked issue of airport expansion. *The Political Quarterly*, 84(4), 515–526.

Hayden, A. (2014). Stopping Heathrow Airport expansion (for now): Lessons from a victory for the politics of sufficiency. *Journal of Environmental Policy & Planning*, 16(4), 539–558.

Hernández, D. (2015). Sacrifice along the energy continuum: A call for energy justice. *Environmental Justice*, 8(4), 151–156.

IAEA. (2016). The Power Reactor Information System (PRIS). Retrieved 6 July 2016.

Jasanoff, S., & Kim, S. H. (2009). Containing the atom: Sociotechnical imaginaries and nuclear power in the United States and South Korea. *Minerva*, 47(2), 119–146.

Johnstone, P. (2010). The nuclear power renaissance in the UK: Democratic deficiencies within the 'consensus' on sustainability. *Human Geography*, 3(2), 91–104.

Johnstone, P. (2014). Planning reform, rescaling, and the construction of the postpolitical: The case of The Planning Act 2008 and nuclear power consultation in the UK. *Environment and Planning C: Government and Policy*, 32(4), 697–713.

Jones, K. T. (1998). Scale as epistemology. *Political Geography*, 17(1), 25–28. doi: http://dx.doi.org/10.1016/S0962-6298(97)00049-8.

Jowitt, J. (2015, 15 October). Law changed so nuclear waste dumps can be forced on local communities. *Guardian*. Retrieved from www.theguardian.com/environment/2015/apr/05/law-changed-so-nuclear-waste-dumps-can-be-forced-on-local-communities.

Lerner, S. (2010). *Sacrifice zones: The front lines of toxic chemical exposure in the United States*. Cambridge, MA: MIT Press.

Mackerron, G. (2010). Personal communication at the *Participation, Power and Sustainable Energy Futures* seminar, Sussex University, October 2010.

Madsen, M. L., & Noe, E. (2012). Communities of practice in participatory approaches to environmental regulation. Prerequisites for implementation of environmental knowledge in agricultural context. *Environmental Science & Policy*, 18(0), 25–33. doi: http://dx.doi.org/10.1016/j.envsci.2011.12.008.

NDA. (2013). 2013 UK radioactive waste inventory: Scenario for future radioactive waste and material arising. Harwell: Nuclear Decommissioning Authority and Department of Energy and Climate Change.

Nuttall, W. J. (2004). *Nuclear renaissance: Technologies and policies for the future of nuclear power*. Florida: CRC Press.

OECD NEA, & IAEA. (2014). *Uranium 2014: Resources, production and demand*. Vienna: OECD Nuclear Energy Agency and the International Atomic Energy Agency.

O'Riordan, T., Kemp, R., & Purdue, M. (1988). *Sizewell B: An anatomy of the inquiry*. Basingstoke: Macmillan.

Ozharovsky, A. (2016). *When haste makes risky waste: Public involvement in radioactive and nuclear waste management in Sweden and Finland*. Retrieved from http://bellona.org/news/nuclear-issues/radioactive-waste-and-spent-nuclear-fuel/2016-08-21710.

Parkhill, K. A., Pidgeon, N. F., Henwood, K. L., Simmons, P., & Venables, D. (2010). From the familiar to the extraordinary: Local residents' perceptions of risk when living with nuclear power in the UK. *Transactions of the Institute of British Geographers*, 35(1), 39–58.

Pitt, M. (2010). Introducing the Infrastructure Planning Commission. *Proceedings of The Institute of Civil Engineers*, 163(2), 54–54. doi: 10.1680/cien.2010.163.2.54.

Public Accounts Committee. (2014). Public Accounts Committee – forty-third report. *Progress at Sellafield*. London: Proceedings of the Public Accounts Committee.

Renzi, B. G., Cotton, M., Napolitano, G., & Barkemeyer, R. (2016). Rebirth, devastation and sickness: Analyzing the role of metaphor in media discourses of nuclear power. . *Environmental Communication*. doi:10.1080/17524032.2016.1157506.

RWM. (2016). *Working collaboratively to manage radioactive waste*. Harwell: Radioactive Waste Management.

Star, S. L. (2010). This is not a boundary object: Reflections on the origin of a concept. *Science, Technology & Human Values*, 35(5), 601–617.

Swyngedouw, E. (2004). Globalisation or 'glocalisation'? Networks, territories and rescaling. *Cambridge Review of International Affairs*, 17(1), 25–48.

Teräväinen, T., Lehtonen, M., & Martiskainen, M. (2011). Climate change, energy security, and risk – debating nuclear new build in Finland, France and the UK. *Energy Policy*, 39(6), 3434–3442. doi:http://dx.doi.org/10.1016/j.enpol.2011.03.041.

Tobiasson, W., Beestermöller, C., & Jamasb, T. (2015). *Public engagement in electricity network development: A case study of the Beauly–Denny Project in Scotland*. Cambridge: Faculty of Economics Working Paper, University of Cambridge.

Tomlinson, C. (2004). *Wind energy & planning: An overview*. London: British Wind Energy Association.

Walker, G., Cass, N., Burningham, K., & Barnett, J. (2010). Renewable energy and sociotechnical change: Imagined subjectivities of 'the public' and their implications. *Environment and Planning A*, 42(4), 931–947.

WNA. (2016). *Uranium supply*. Retrieved 8 September 2016, from www.world-nuclear.org/information-library/nuclear-fuel-cycle/uranium-resources/supply-of-uranium.aspx.

World Nuclear News. (2011). *Waste costs for UK new build*. Retrieved 11 August 2016, from www.world-nuclear-news.org/WR_Waste_costs_for_UK_new_build_0912111.html.

Wynne, B. (1996). May the sheep safely graze? A reflexive view of the expert–lay knowledge divide. In S. Lash, B. Szerszynski, & B. Wynne (Eds.), *Risk, Environment and Modernity*. London: Sage Publications.

Wynne, B. (2006). Public engagement as a means of restoring public trust in science – hitting the notes, but missing the music? *Public Health Genomics*, 9(3), 211–220.

Index

waste encapsulation 18
Waste Isolation Pilot Plant (WIPP) 11–15, 17
waste volumes 25–6, 35, 111
West Cumbrian Managing Radioactive Waste Safely Partnership (WCMRWSP) 208, 211–12, 216, 233–5; *see also* Allerdale Borough Council; Cumbria County Council,

Copeland Borough Council; Managing Radioactive Waste Safely (MRWS); partnership approach; voluntarism
Windscale 23–34, 60–1, 63, 66, 68, 69, 76; inquiry 68–9, 86; pile fire 63–4
World Health Organisation 114
worldview 39–40, 42, 45; *see also* discourse

Yucca Mountain 11–15, 37–8, 123, 148

For Product Safety Concerns and Information please contact our EU
representative GPSR@taylorandfrancis.com
Taylor & Francis Verlag GmbH, Kaufingerstraße 24, 80331 München, Germany

www.ingramcontent.com/pod-product-compliance
Ingram Content Group UK Ltd.
Pitfield, Milton Keynes, MK11 3LW, UK
UKHW021616240425
457818UK00018B/594